Behind the Legend
THE MANY WORLDS OF
CHARLES TODD

Charles Todd with travel trunk, c.1871

Behind the Legend
THE MANY WORLDS OF
CHARLES TODD

DENIS CRYLE

Australian Scholarly

© Denis Cryle 2017, 2019

Second edition 2019
First published 2017 by
Australian Scholarly Publishing Pty Ltd
7 Lt Lothian St Nth, North Melbourne, Victoria 3051

tel 03 9329 6963 / *fax* 03 9329 5452
aspic@ozemail.com.au / www.scholarly.info

ISBN: 978-1-925588-09-5

ALL RIGHTS RESERVED

Front cover: Charles Todd in his library, c.1900. GSP: SLSA B3785
Cover design by Wayne Saunders

To the scholars whose research and writing contributed significantly to this biography: George W. Symes, Kevin Livingston, John Jenkin

Contents

Preface to the Second Edition .... *ix*
List of Illustrations .... *x*
Acknowledgements .... *xi*
Maps .... *xii*
List of Abbreviations .... *xiv*

Introduction
Charles Todd and the Making of a Modern Nation 1

Part I
'From small things': Apprenticeship and Promotion (1826–70)
1: Greenwich: The Makings of an Astronomer.............................. 15
2: Cambridge: Status and Respectability 29
3: The Opportunity of a Lifetime: London to Adelaide 45
4: Superintendent of Electric Telegraphs 56

Part II
'Out of adversity': Enterprise and Acclaim (1870–86)
5: The 'Great Work' and its Aftermath (1870–73) 77
6: Postmaster General in the 1870s:
   The Robbery and Commission of Inquiry 103
7: Observing the Transits of Venus (1874 and 1882):
   The Trials of a Colonial Astronomer 114
8: Mapping the Climate, Settling the Land 130
9: Renewal and Recognition:
   The European Tour of 1885–86.. 145

Part III
Contested Ascendancy: The Illustrious Civil Servant (1887–1910)
10: 'The heat and burden of the day':
    Todd's Cable Diplomacy Before Federation........................ 169
11: 'Time Lord':
    Todd's Elusive Pursuit of Standard Time in the 1890s 187

12: Weather Wars: Todd and Clement Wragge 204
13: Deputy Postmaster General:
    Negotiating the Federal Bureaucracy 222
14: 'An astronomer at heart': The Final Decades 243

Notes *259*
Select Bibliography *304*
Index *308*
About the Author *313*

Preface to the Second Edition

This second edition of *Behind the Legend* offers readers a number of improvements on the first. Not only is Todd's great Overland Telegraph Line adventure better documented in map form than previously, but the text has been revised throughout, and the referencing, both archival and secondary, made more explicit.

A good biography is always to some extent a collaborative endeavour, and I am grateful to the Todd family, to South Australian scholars and to reviewers for their close reading and careful feedback on the text over the last eighteen months, not least because it confirms that the narrative is of importance and interest to them.

The biography has cast valuable light on members of Todd's young family, some of whom emigrated and settled in South Australia, becoming, in turn, part of his own story. Further family details have since come to light and been included in the narrative where space permits.

That not everything about Todd's remarkable life and work has been encompassed in this volume is scarcely surprising, given the unusual range of his activities and interests. But it is hoped that this overdue biography will continue to act as a point of reference for future scholars and specialists committed, as I have been, to recognising a seminal figure of undoubted national importance.

Denis Cryle
December 2018

List of Illustrations

1. Map of the Northern section of the Overland Telegraph Route showing telegraph stations and other relevant sites, Symes and Ward, 1980–81, p. 67; Taylor, 1981, p. 181
2. Map of the Southern and Central sections of the Overland Telegraph Route showing telegraph stations and other relevant sites, Symes and Ward, 1980–81, p. 67; Taylor, 1981, p. 181
3. Charles Todd with travel trunk, c.1871. GSP: SLSA B6793
4. Portrait of Sir George Biddell Airy, 1877. NLA: PIC/4061
5. Portrait of Charles Todd as a young man, c.1845. GSP: SLSA B69996/11
6. South Front of the Cambridge Observatory, undated. CU: IoA
7. Glass plate of Charles and Alice, c.1855. GSP: SLSA B69996/9
8. Sir Richard Graves MacDonnell, 1860. SLSA: B11112
9. Charles Todd and the Overland Team, 1872. SLSA: B69996/15
10. Charles Todd with Order of St Michael and St George medal, 1880. GSP: SLSA B69996/19
11. Refracting telescope by T. Cooke and Sons of York, 1871. CU: IoA
12. Todd weather map showing moist conditions along the OT Line. Benoy: BoM
13. Fanny Todd, c.1865. GSP: SLSA B 69996/27
14. Todd Family group at the Adelaide Observatory for Lizzie's 1897 visit. GSP: SLSA B69996/70
15. Clement Wragge, c.1901. SLQ: JOL 161210
16. Todd Synoptic Chart showing weather movement WA to SA, 1883. Benoy: BoM 18830803c
17. Adelaide Conference delegates, May 1905. SLSA: PRG/280/1/29/267

Acknowledgements

At the outset, I wish to thank members of the Todd family for their generosity and encouragement, especially Stephen Gillam-Smith, who assisted with the illustrations and family details, Lady Adrian and Barry and Ola Todd, all of whom went to considerable trouble to provide me with valuable source material.

For the research undertaken on Todd's early years in the United Kingdom, I am indebted to the Islington Local History Centre, the Greenwich Heritage Centre, Geraldine Charles, archivist at the National Maritime Museum, as well as to staff of the Caird Library of Royal Museums Greenwich.

My thanks to the Cambridge University Library for making available archival and manuscript material on Todd; to Chris Jakes and the Cambridgeshire Collection of the Cambridge Central Library; to Mark Hurn at the Cambridge Institute of Astronomy, as well as to the Cambridgeshire Archives.

For the bulk of the records relating to Todd's life, I am especially grateful to the friendly efficiency of the State Library of South Australia, the South Australian State and Australian Archives, along with the University of Adelaide archival collections.

Thanks also to Christina Hunt and the library staff of Central Queensland University, to the University of Queensland and Fryer Libraries, and to the State Library of Queensland and John Oxley Library. Other Australian institutions which provided support and materials were the State Library of Victoria and Latrobe Collection, the National Library, the Australian Dictionary of Biography archive at the Australian National University, and the State Library of New South Wales and Mitchell Library.

To academic colleagues across Australia who made available records and manuscript sources, as well as providing valuable encouragement, I take the opportunity to thank and acknowledge Ann Moyal, Donald Lamberton, Kevin Livingston, John Jenkin, Elizabeth Morrison, Richard Yeo, Steve Mullins, Mac Benoy, Tony Rogers, Bob O'Sullivan and Ray Boyle.

Nor should I forget to acknowledge my Alexander Technique teachers for their patience in improving my study and writing performance. Finally, a personal thank you to my family: Max for his scientific mind, and especially to my wife Aileen who took the trouble to proof read and discuss editorial changes to the manuscript drafts.

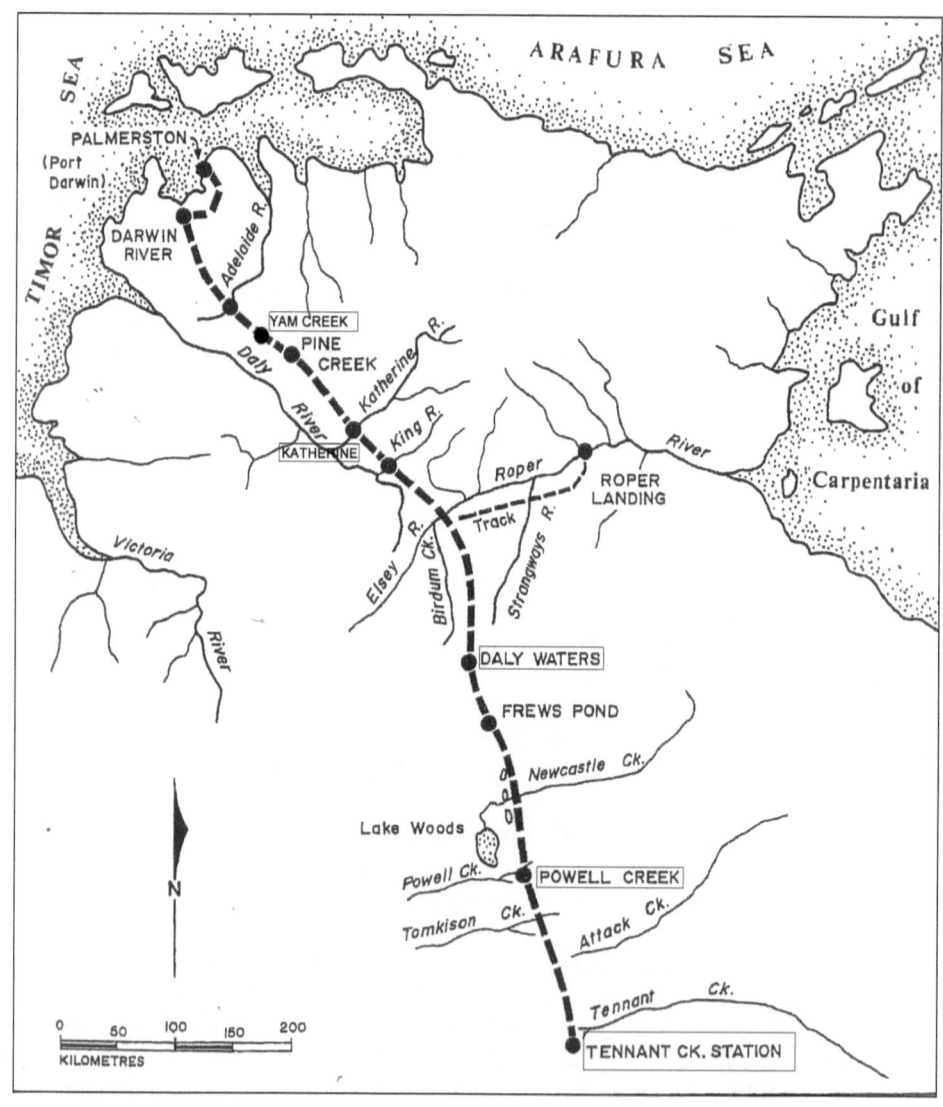

1. Northern section of the Overland Telegraph Route (Symes and Ward, 1980–81; Taylor, 1981)

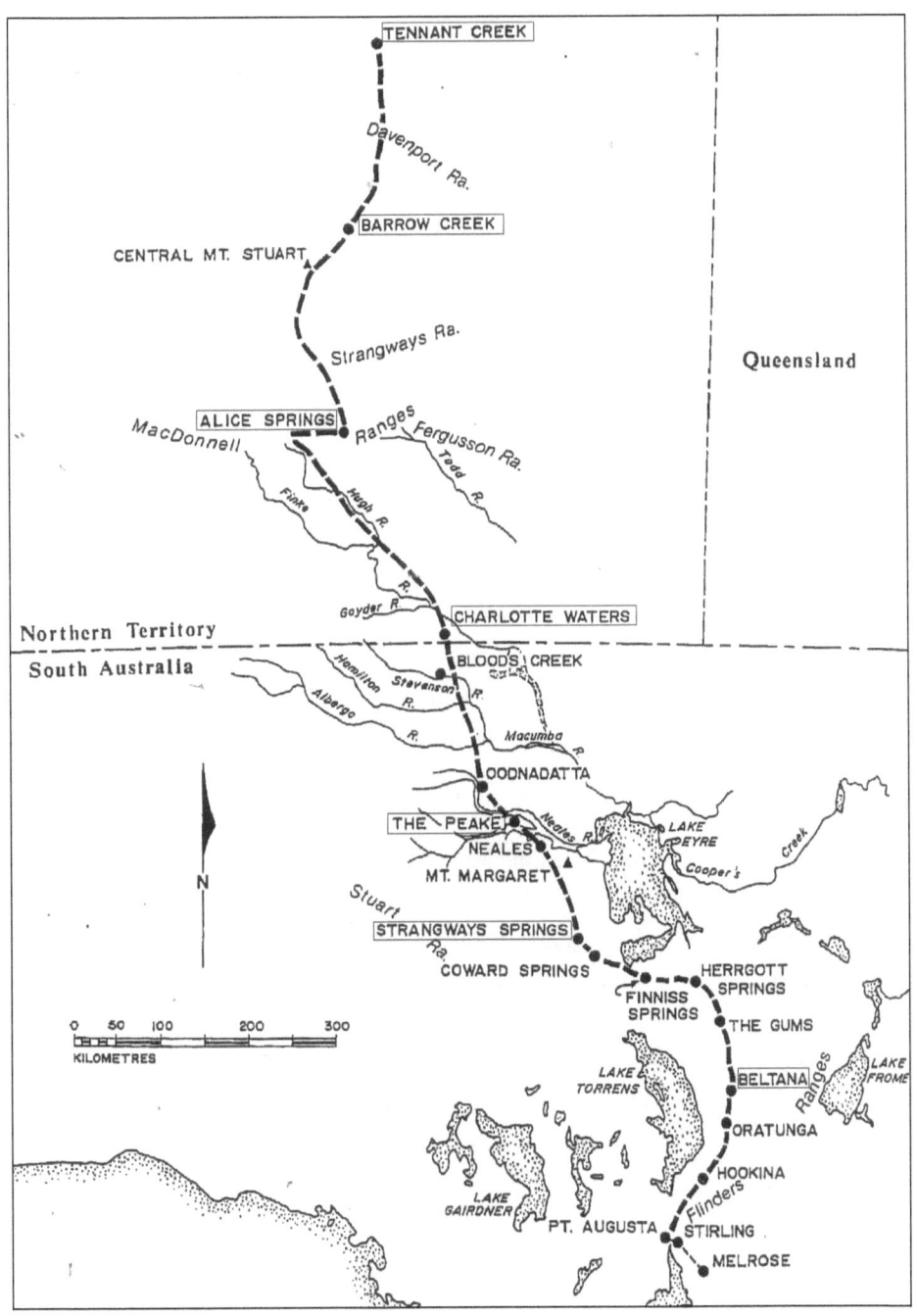

2. Southern and Central sections of the Overland Telegraph Route (Symes and Ward, 1980–81; Taylor, 1981)

List of Abbreviations

ASSA	Astronomical Society of South Australia
AA	Australian Archives
AAAS	Australian Association for the Advancement of Science
ADB	*Australian Dictionary of Biography*
BAAS	British Association for the Advancement of Science
BAT	British Australian Telegraph Company
CUA	Cambridge University Archives
CUP	Cambridge University Press
EE	Eastern Extension Telegraph Company
GSP	Gillam-Smith Papers
IoA	Institute of Astronomy
MNRAS	*Monthly Notices of the Royal Astronomical Society*
MUP	Melbourne University Press
NAA	National Archives of Australia
NLA	National Library of Australia
NMM	National Maritime Museum
QV&P	*Queensland Votes and Proceedings*
RGSSA	Royal Geographical Society of South Australia
SASA	South Australian State Archives
SAPD	*Southern Australian Parliamentary Debates*
SAPP	*Southern Australian Parliamentary Papers*
SLSA	State Library of South Australia
SLV	State Library of Victoria

Introduction

Charles Todd and the Making of a Modern Nation

Charles Todd (1826–1910), born into a humble London family, achieved rapid fame within his lifetime. With the successful completion of an Overland Telegraph Line across the Australian continent in 1872, he was mythologised within a short space of years and 'well on the way to becoming a legend' by age 46.[1] As major beneficiaries of incoming telegraph news, colonial newspapers played a decisive role in shaping the legend of 'Telegraph' Todd. Despite Todd's insistence after the event that his officers and men be given equal credit for what he considered a national project,[2] the colonial press persisted, not without reason, in singling out Todd for special recognition. By the time of his widely reported 1873 address refuting 'naysayers' of the ambitious project, metropolitan papers throughout Australia extolled the epic construction of the international cable link as 'a model of human perseverance and exertion'.[3] In reality Todd enjoyed a relationship with the press which was more complex, ranging across diverse topics including meteorology and astronomy as well as telegraphy. But only after his successful trip to Europe in the 1880s was there growing recognition of his other achievements. Beyond relevant government and professional bodies in Britain and Australasia, however, his earlier romantic association with the Overland Telegraph Line constituted his claim to fame in the eyes of the colonial public, and his eventual knighthood at age 67 was generally viewed as belated recognition for his 'great telegraphic work'.[4]

How did Todd, still a prominent public figure in later years, view this entrenched historical verdict? Honoured as he was, he was no less gratified by the recognition which Cambridge University and the Royal Society of London accorded his scientific labours in astronomy and meteorology. By the turn-of-the-century, he considered his reputation as Telegraph Todd 'far too eulogistic'.[5] At the time of his retirement in 1905, aged 79, he continued to insist that the overland saga 'did not need retelling' and that 'he did not like the personal element which such a story involved'.[6] By then Todd rightly anticipated that the same narrative would dominate public acknowledgements thereafter, while the real romance – his marriage and colonial life with Alice Gillam Bell (1836–98), daughter of a self-made Cambridge family, who emigrated to South Australia with him in 1855 – would remain obscure. At the time of his death in 1910, the London *Times* upheld such expectations when it reminded British readers of 'the adventurous progress of the engineers through Central Australia' and concurred that 'the knighthood conferred by Queen Victoria was well earned'.[7] From a biographical perspective this has proved unfortunate. For in the course of his own lifetime, Todd enjoyed wider recognition not solely as 'Telegraph Todd' but as a 'splendid civil servant of many parts'.[8] In 1891, there was widespread commemoration of his 50th year as a civil servant, and of his 60th a decade later. Nor was it simply a matter of longevity but one of productivity, for he had indeed enjoyed a notable career. Despite this, the mythologised view of Todd as outback hero would predominate for another century to the detriment of the complex but no less remarkable life which this biography sets out to document.

Commemorating the Line:
Todd's changing twentieth century profile

Over the next century, as successive Overland Telegraph commemorations marked his historic reputation, Todd's personal profile nevertheless continued to evolve. Between the wars, when the Australian pioneer legend held sway, Todd's outback telegraph was seen as following in John McDouall Stuart's tracks rather than as pioneering in its own right. At the time of the 80th Overland Telegraph anniversary, Frank Clune, a prolific popular writer, first took up the serious challenge of writing a full-length account of the Line's construction. But his was not biography, for the general belief persisted that its construction as a nation-building project had been 'the combined endeavours of many men' rather than the work of prominent individuals. In alleging, contrary to the historical evidence, that Todd had 'not personally taken part in the construction of the line in the North,' Clune echoed early critics like Charles Patterson who claimed that he (Todd) had taken 'the main credit' for its completion to the detriment of those who went on to explore the outback in its aftermath.[9] Consequently Clune's popular account, researched over several years, did little to encourage a closer biographical study of Todd. The same writer was inclined to dismiss Todd's technological contribution, referring only in passing to his early years of 'stargazing' and describing his life-long interest in electrical engineering as a 'hobby'.[10] Mid-century commemoration of the Overland Telegraph did not therefore imply wholehearted celebration of Todd's personal endeavours. Indeed, the collective ethos and revisionist interpretation underpinning the pioneering legend proved detrimental to a serious understanding of Todd's involvement as a major long-term actor.

Clune's popular interpretation was not however the only one to emerge in the course of the 1952 commemorations. Lorna Todd's series of newspaper articles devoted to her father constituted a useful corrective to the prevailing school of thought. Todd's youngest daughter Lorna, who lived with him at the Observatory in his later years, had foregone the opportunity to write the biography of her father. Only in her mid-70s did she make a belated contribution in the newspaper series, entitled 'Telegraph Todd and the Overland Line,' which appeared in the Adelaide *Chronicle* during December 1952.[11] This series and her subsequent contributions in the form of newspaper pieces and monographs were undoubtedly stimulated by her unsuccessful opposition to the ongoing demolition of the Adelaide Observatory, where she had grown up.[12] As the youngest in a family of six children, Lorna had not been born at the time of Todd's great telegraphic achievement, but her anecdotes about her parents' early experiences of Cambridge and colonial life were not all fabrication, as she enjoyed access to her father's papers for at least a decade after his death. Her narrative of the overland telegraph was less orthodox since her writings were more concerned with Todd's moral qualities, notably his sense of 'buoyancy and vision – against the almost unbelievable opposition he encountered' than with recounting details of his expedition.[13] In publishing her account of their family life for the first time, Lorna exhibited the same keen sense of social observation and wry humour which characterised her father's earlier letters to Alice from the Northern Territory. Importantly in a second series of five articles in 1953, she recounted the lives of Todd women, absent from previous accounts, asserting that life at the observatory was 'not all work'[14] and confirming that both her father and mother, with their adult children, continued to be active in Adelaide society in later life.

A decade after Lorna's death, the centenary celebrations of the Overland Telegraph Line excited renewed press interest with most major Australian papers publishing supplements replaying the events of 1870–72. The centenary of 1972 also stimulated interest in Todd's telegraphy on the part of such bodies as the Institute of Engineers and Australia Post. In the latter's abbreviated and well-illustrated account, Todd and his men were heavily profiled while Alice, 'whose name lives on in the heart of Australia, the Alice Springs,' also received a mention.[15] In keeping with pioneering views, she was depicted as the epitome of colonial womanhood, left to her own resources when her husband was away building telegraphs. Their correspondence at a critical time, when Charles was sent to save the expedition in the Northern Territory, was a seminal document for biographical purposes but received little serious attention from researchers. It was in the context of centenary commemorations that Major General G.W. Symes, who had documented central Australian exploration and contributed to the 1972 centennial symposium,[16] began compiling a Todd biography. Of the many biographical entries which had appeared in dictionaries and encyclopaedias on Todd to that time, Syme's entry of 1976 for the *Australian Dictionary of Biography* was the most authoritative.[17] Determined to correct exaggerated claims surrounding the Overland Telegraph Line, including a lingering misconception that Todd possessed the unlikely middle name of Heavitree, he adhered closely to Todd's official reports, while conceding that:

> The man himself remains a shadowy figure because a well-rounded biography of him has not yet been written.[18]

Before suffering a severe stroke in late 1980, Symes managed to document Todd's life up to the period of his overland telegraph achievement. After many years of assembling material, most of it relating to Telegraph Todd, he struggled however to shape it into narrative form or connect the various threads of Todd's complex career, leaving some four decades of Todd's later life untouched. But his preliminary investigation of his subject's early years, his detailed knowledge of Todd's movements and decisions in the field, combined with his archival research into Todd's business dealings, bequeathed historians a valuable legacy comprising several definitive episodes.

Symes' sustained contribution influenced subsequent writers in their treatment of Todd and the overland telegraph. Peter Taylor, who published a detailed account of the Overland Telegraph Line's construction in 1980,[19] drew heavily on Symes' research for his introductory chapter on

Charles and Alice in what was otherwise a conventional account. While Symes focused on Todd's specific challenges in the field, Taylor provided a valuable overview of the same three-year event as a complex series of dramatic episodes comprising multiple actors across a range of locations. Taylor's detailed study threw further light on Telegraph Todd by showing that his role as its overall co-ordinator demanded not merely great stamina and flexibility but also high levels of communication across a range of interested groups. More sustained scrutiny of Charles' and Alice's lives would be undertaken by one of their British descendants, Alice Thomson in 1999. Thomson's search for her Australian ancestors differed markedly in style and approach from Symes' material to which she had access. Compiled hurriedly without written sources or a bibliography, it was in her own words 'by no means a definitive biography,'[20] in its over reliance on contemporary interviews and family anecdotes.

Despite their different approaches to the topic, Taylor's and Thomson's books raised a common biographical conundrum concerning Todd's central role in the building of the Line. Mindful of the authoritative assessment of W.H. Bragg, Todd's son-in-law, that 'he [Todd] had no commanding personality,'[21] Taylor conceded at the outset of his account that, while Todd was 'a good administrator ... he had none of the charisma one expects of a great leader'.[22] If Taylor was inclined to depict Todd as an anti-hero forced into action by drastic circumstances, Thomson was more precise in her view that Todd was 'no Amazon explorer' like Francis Younghusband or Scott of the Antarctic.[23] Herein lay Todd's biographical challenge and attraction. For contrary to Symes' not unreasonable assumption that he would continue in the same administrative tradition, Todd chose in fact not to emulate his Victorian superiors – autocrats like George Biddell Airy at Greenwich or Governor Richard MacDonnell in Adelaide – preferring more liberal management techniques in order to gain the loyalty of his workforce. In so doing, he injected a number of distinctive personal traits into his administrative style, among them 'kindly courtesy and good humour,'[24] while offering greater opportunities for women and younger workers in his departments. Todd's unorthodox management style, anathema to his contemporary critics, goes some way towards explaining the reluctance of earlier historians and biographers to proceed with a more detailed study of his life and personality. Only more recently has he received recognition as a modern manager rather than a Victorian autocrat.

Todd's 'Coming of Age':
the rebirth of Australian telecommunications

In her monumental study *Clear across Australia*, Ann Moyal brought a stimulating yet critical perspective to bear on the Overland Telegraph Line, declaring it 'the most significant feat of engineering in 19th-century Australia'.[25] She began by qualifying popular aspects of the overland telegraph legend, by giving credit for the initial concept to Governor MacDonnell while proclaiming Todd's Victorian counterpart, Samuel McGowan, the real 'father of Australian telegraphy' on the grounds that he was 'more experienced and better informed'. She was nevertheless firm in the conviction that it was upon Todd's powers of organisation and determination that the whole superstructure of this very complex enterprise would depend, extolling him for the genesis and execution of a modern 'management plan'.[26] Anticipating the national mood of the Bicentenary, Moyal also asked questions about the project's impact on the indigenous inhabitants for the first time. Despite Todd's specific instructions to his parties not to interfere with their camps and burial grounds, Aborigines would increasingly be forced to compete with construction parties on uneven terms for 'vital waterholes'.[27] Moyal's strong grasp of historical personalities and the strategic political environment inspired a number of writers to re-examine Todd's achievement. That he had come of age as a national figure was clear in the following decade, when the *Australian* newspaper declared him the inspiration for its 1997 Communicator of the Year award.[28] Don Lamberton, delivering the 2000 Telstra oration on Todd, at a time when the status of public servants had considerably diminished, called for 'a big thick Life, rich in detail,' concurring with Moyal's assessment of Todd as 'a skilled networker, a good people person and good strategist … Above all he was a great manager'.[29]

The Bicentennial commemorations of 1988 stimulated greater heritage awareness and the prospect of gathering into a single collection a range of Todd's personal items scattered across different institutions in South Australia and Northern Territory. As an avid collector of astronomical and telegraphic instruments, Todd would have approved such a plan. But when the Adelaide telecommunications museum at Electra House[30] was dismantled by Telecom in the early 1990s, history seem destined to repeat itself at Todd's expense. Ironically at the time of Telecom's decision, Todd's national profile was increasing and telecommunications was attracting unprecedented attention from government bodies and historians alike. Telecom itself helped to stimulate this upsurge by funding several national communication projects, including Moyal's work and Kevin Livingston's *Wired Nation Continent*.[31] As the centenary of federation approached, Livingston, a telecommunications historian based in eastern Australia, took up the challenge of a Todd biography two decades after Symes. Unlike most of his predecessors however Livingston was less interested in Todd's overland telegraph phase than in his later years as administrator of the Line. His 1996 study confirmed that telegraphy continued to play an important role in Todd's career, especially during the regular postal and telegraph conferences in which he figured prominently prior to federation. Accordingly, he concluded his entry for the *Oxford Dictionary of Biography* with the observation that Todd was 'the key technical figure in Australia'[32] at a time when its colonies were increasingly divided over their geopolitical loyalties to competing international cable routes.

Livingston concurred with previous assessments of Todd as 'a splendid civil servant' without confining his attention to his hard-won success of 1870–72. Todd's administrative ability, which ranged over three departments until age 80, promised, along with the theme of affective and family ties, to become an important organising principle for the purposes of biography, ranging as it did over his initial years in Britain and prominent mid-career in South Australia to the federal bureaucracy by the end of his career. Precedents for extended biographies of colonial civil servants are rare, in contrast with those of explorers and politicians.[33] This, in spite of recent assertions by Sheldrick and Jenkin, that South Australian departmental heads such as Goyder and Todd enjoyed more prominent public careers than most of their political counterparts.[34]

With the upsurge of research into telecommunications history and policy, which accompanied Telecom's merger with the Overseas Telecommunications Commission in 1992 and the partial privatisation of Telstra in 1997, Todd assumed still greater importance nationally and internationally, not simply for the Overland Telegraph Line, but as a veteran policy player and influential negotiator with the Eastern Extension Telegraph Company (EE) on behalf of the Australian and New Zealand colonies. In an era when questions of privatisation, competition policy and monopoly had moved centre stage, telecommunications historians grew more critical of Todd's co-operation with private enterprise,[35] influenced as he was by his early British experience with private telegraph and railway companies. Livingston, who had by now begun gathering official and archival material on Todd, embraced this 'eastern Australian' perspective, describing his subject in a biographical essay of 1997 as 'a powerful technocrat' in federating Australia.[36] Like Moyal and Lamberton, Livingston remained convinced that Todd was well worthy of a biography and, in the same essay, asked relevant questions about his capacity to withstand public and political pressure. While accepting Symes' and Ward's caveat that, as a veteran civil servant, Todd 'knew when to accede to his superiors,'[37] he advanced a bold new interpretation of Todd's civil service career as one of transformation from the better-known Telegraph Todd of mid-career to a still more senior position of exercising 'power behind the throne,' a role of which only the most formidable civil servants have been capable. Such questions could be best answered by further archival research in the United Kingdom and Australia. But Livingston's premature death in late 1998 meant that he was never allowed to explore his contradictory views. For on the one hand, he had shown in his national study that Todd's contribution to Australian communications policy had been exceptional, at the same time as he voiced criticism of his staunchly held pro-South Australian and pro-EE positions.

Todd, scientist and collaborator

At a time when the centenary of federation inspired greater recognition of Telegraph Todd, historians were also returning to the neglected aspects of Todd's science in his capacity as South Australian observer. In 1993, Edwards, following Symes' biographical example, compiled a succinct account of Todd's contributions as astronomer and timekeeper, focusing on the last decades of the 19th century when his 'systematic astronomical work'[38] at the Adelaide Observatory began. In the wider field of colonial astronomy, Orchiston's series of articles confirmed the late 19th century as an eventful one for colonial astronomy.[39] Orchiston was particularly interested in amateur astronomers like John Tebbutt and their participation in local societies, but made only passing mention of Todd's longstanding presidency of the South Australian Astronomical Society,[40] leaving Haynes et al to document the contribution of government observers. Their history, while including extensive coverage of Todd's collaborators like Charles Russell, devoted a mere three pages to Todd himself, on the grounds that 'his first professional priorities were not astronomical'.[41] These new astronomical histories, while well researched and informative, provided biographical snapshots rather than in-depth portraits of their subjects. In keeping with the collaborative traditions of scientific research and publication, their primary focus was on key scientific events of the period – the transit of Venus observations and the Carte du Ciel star mapping project – rather than the extended lives of individuals. Consequently, both Todd and his protracted collaborations with other colonial observers throughout the late 19th century were largely unacknowledged.

An important exception which laid the basis for a more sustained understanding of Todd the scientist was Jenkin's deeply researched 2008 biography of William Henry and William Lawrence Bragg, Todd's son-in-law and grandson respectively. Both these future Nobel Prize winners were South Australian-based in their earlier careers and members of the Todd family circle. As a South Australian graduate and distinguished career scientist, Jenkin combined his life studies of these two prominent achievers with sustained attention to their institutional affiliations in South Australia and the United Kingdom. In view of the weight of his eminent subjects and the book's extended timeframe, it may have been tempting to pass over Todd, as the ageing patriarch of their family circle. But such is not the case. Jenkin shares both W.H. Bragg's admiration for Todd's administrative ability and W.L. Bragg's nostalgic affection for his longstanding observatory routines.[42] In so doing, he draws together a number of the significant biographical themes of the current biography. Not only does Jenkin pay attention to Todd the civil servant and to his close family ties but to the overarching importance of scientific training and collaboration, the latter as relevant to Todd as it is to his younger family members. After welcoming W.H. Bragg into his social circle on his arrival in Adelaide, Todd acts as both mentor and collaborator to his introverted son-in-law, sharing his interests in seismology and wireless experimentation.[43] Jenkin's perceptive profile of Todd at various points of his study, before the Bragg family depart for the United Kingdom, encourages closer investigation of Todd's longstanding belief in early Australian science and scientists as well as his capacity to prepare his own circle and staff for distinguished careers.

As a generous commentator on colonial science, Todd was careful to recognise the work of his colleagues, including that of his critics, when he addressed national and international forums on such subjects as telegraphy or meteorology. Yet despite his wide-ranging participation in colonial conferences, he was to face the prospect of prolonged dislocation at the end of his career when the Commonwealth proceeded to centralise science, a scenario with serious personal as well as professional implications. In their study of colonial meteorological conferences, Home and Livingston demonstrate how Todd persisted in promoting co-operation in the form of a joint weather service for national purposes. Yet Todd continues to occupy a diminished national profile in the recent literature on federation and science in striking contrast with his elevated telecommunications role. As 'the only survivor from the previous era,' he was left to put the unpopular case for continuing state involvement in science in 1905 under threat of a decline which, according to Livingston and Home, was 'by no means inevitable'.[44] Conversely the brash and intemperate career of meteorological centralists like Clement Wragge has been elevated at the expense of Todd's diligence over many decades which included his years in the federal civil service.[45] The politics of science under an early Commonwealth dominated by the eastern states has not given Todd's work due consideration. Yet his illustrious civil service and scientific career in many fields mark him as a great Australian, comparable in stature with 'federation fathers' such as Kingston and Forrest, with whom he worked closely. For Todd was responsible for much of the physical infrastructure of intercolonial communications, so essential for nationhood, and had been a long and distinguished policy contributor across an unusual range of fields.

Tempting as it is to treat Todd's scientific contributions in geographical isolation, it is important to recognise that he used the intercolonial telegraph as well as an extensive correspondence to collaborate with scientific colleagues in eastern Australia well before the overland telegraph link was in place, a practice which he subsequently extended to Western Australia. In this respect the activities ascribed to Telegraph Todd have been too linear and focused on a single network since telegraphy underpinned his other scientific interests in meteorology, astronomy and surveying.[46] Recent historians have done much to revive Todd's reputation in meteorology, most notably Mac Benoy who, after uncovering and scanning Todd's numerous weather maps, compared his meteorological reach favourably with advances in North America.[47] Within Australia, Todd and his South Australian predecessors' preservation of continuous rainfall records has received contemporary recognition in the rapidly emerging field of climate studies.[48] Far from being parochial, Todd's interest in long-term climate patterns was driven as much by international events as by local weather recording.[49] By the time of the Overland Telegraph's 140th anniversary in 2012, Todd's telegraphy had become but one of many facets of his complex career under examination from a range of speakers, on topics extending from astronomy and meteorology to surveying, postal administration and electrical engineering.[50] For Todd, as Benoy insists, was a unique phenomenon of his time – a polymath – but remains a more elusive biographical subject than ever on that account.

The present project: themes, narrative and structure

It is an historical irony that Todd's extraordinary industry over a long and eventful career have made him such a daunting subject for intending biographers, ranging as they must over a vast and dispersed archive. One significant challenge lies in structuring and acknowledging his many and varied achievements. For his unconventional career carried a range of competing responsibilities within his departmental duties. Having identified the major themes of the substantial secondary literature, the task of the biographer is to explore these through time and organise them as a life narrative.

The current biography is divided into three broadly chronological parts within which individual chapters focus on particular interests and shorter time periods. Part I (1841–55) outlines Todd's early years in the British civil service, a critical period neglected by previous scholars while paying attention to his family and social background, a topic largely absent from Todd's own official writings, though not from his correspondence. Part II (1855–86) deals with better known aspects of his mid-career: 'Telegraph Todd' and the epic building of the Overland Telegraph Line, incorporating neglected issues such as race relations and Todd's close contact with Alice and his extended Adelaide family at this period. No less importantly, Part II situates the 'great work' in the context of Todd's other substantial commitments of the mid-late 1870s: the re-organisation of his Post and Telegraph department in the course of a Commission of Inquiry, the challenge of establishing the Adelaide Observatory and preparing for the transits of Venus, not to mention the ongoing expansion of his telegraphic projects and meteorological work, prior to his belated trip to Europe and overseas recognition.

If Todd's many worlds are in competition and at the risk of collision in Part II, Part III (1887–1910) further explores the variable success of Todd's interventions and unusual influence as cable diplomat and timelord, before his difficult transition from the colonial to the federal civil service in the last decade of his career. In documenting his final neglected years, Part Three returns to themes discussed in Part One and to longer life cycles, notably his science and family ties. Preoccupied with meteorology at the turn of the century, Todd was nevertheless unwilling to abandon his first love, astronomy, in the face of declining funding and public indifference. Less visible as the nocturnal component of his career, astronomy was to remain an important unifying principle across the different phases of his life.

Part I

'From small things': Apprenticeship and Promotion (1826–70)

1

Greenwich: The Makings of an Astronomer

On the morning of 6 December 1841, Charles Todd, a blue-eyed, dark haired youth of 15, was preparing himself for a short but important journey. No longer a pupil of the Roan School in central Greenwich, he had been recently summoned, with others from his class, to the Royal Observatory to begin his working life.[1] Punctuality and neat appearance would be essential; his sisters, Mary and Elizabeth, took some trouble on that occasion over their quietly spoken but intelligent brother. To his mother Mary, an invalid, Charles was equally attached and conscious of the need to earn a living.[2] For the Todd family was not wealthy and recent misfortune had compounded their material situation.

Before breakfast, Charles parents, devout Dissenters for whom education and self-improvement were paramount, prayed for their son's success. In offering earnest morning prayers on that chilly December day, Charles' father, Griffith Todd, was well aware of the family's predicament. 1841 had proved a particularly difficult year in his bid for commercial success as a grocer and tea merchant. Only a few weeks earlier, his commercial premises in Church Street had been flooded when an unprecedented high tide on the Thames swept over large tracts of Greenwich and Deptford. According to one account, 'a vast number of craft broke loose' and several lives were lost when unprecedented flooding and gale force winds destroyed large quantities of flour and goods stored in cellars and basements.[3] A second source confirmed extensive flooding at that period in the commercial premises at Greenwich, where several hundred people had been involved in bailing out floodwaters from riverside shops, most notably in Church Street, where the Todds had their grocery business.[4] It was a major setback to Griffith's and Mary's chances of prosperity after a decade of hard work in their new location. At such moments even the faithful were prone to doubt and foreboding. But there was no question, for the time being at least, of returning upstream to Islington. Griffith's stubborn determination, backed by Mary's devotion and support, would lead him to rebuild and carry on. Persistence in adversity became a Todd trait, one which would continue with their children.

A decade earlier, Griffith had taken the bold decision to move Mary and his young family of five across the river from Islington,[5] where the Nonconformist Todds had been well established, to expand his grocery premises at Greenwich in the hope of a better situation. Not an educated person, Griffith also held out hopes that his young family would benefit by attending the various educational establishments for which Greenwich was renowned – including its naval institutions and private academies for the education of young women. Among the most notable of these was the Royal Observatory, established in 1675. Now, Charles his second son had, through his mathematical performance at school, gained the opportunity to enter the Royal Observatory. There was no question in the mind of his parents that Charles would spend his life working at a counter as they were obliged to do. Like his elder brother, Griffith, he must also earn a living to support the family at such a critical time. The time for amusing his family by 'playing the parson' as he was wont to do when a child, was now past.[6] Their prayers for Charles that day were at once a blessing and an obligation.

With the family's exhortations ringing in his ears, Charles set out across the Greenwich Park that chilly morning with a mixture of excitement and trepidation. He had long been curious about the Observatory situated above the town with its fine view of the Thames and London. Born in Islington in 1826,[7] Charles had nevertheless spent his youth in Greenwich and, from an early age, watched the ritual of the time ball being dropped from the Observatory tower each day at 1 o'clock, or listened for the sound of the cannon alerting Thames shipping on foggy days. He had seen carriages with important uniformed visitors ascending Croom's Hill and learnt of the formidable George Airy for whom he would now be working. For Charles and his fellows, young and impressionable, Airy was an imposing figure who ran the Observatory with the unquestioned authority of the ship's captain. Mistakes would not be lightly forgiven, while insolence or laziness would result in certain dismissal. As he ascended the pathways towards the Observatory, Charles recalled his impressions as a Roan pupil, of Sunday services held at St Alfege Church,[8] where he had caught sight of Airy's short but imposing figure worshipping there with his beautiful wife, Ricarda and their family.[9] Mindful of his father's advice to please his stern employer and prove useful, Todd assembled with other newcomers at the Observatory entrance. He was pleased to recognise fellow Roan School pupils; others from the local Hospital School were unknown to him; a small army of recruits recommended to Airy by local headmasters for a pressing scientific task.

After identifying themselves, they were taken upstairs into the great octagon room, a veritable temple to science in which fear gave way to fascination. For the elevated star room, as it was also known, housed important telescopes and astronomical instruments, including 17th century clocks with four foot pendulums devised by the best clockmakers of the

Portrait of Sir George Biddell Airy, 1877

day. Here they were instructed to sit on stools at large tables and prepared to set about their work under the supervision of one of Airy's assistants. Their tasks were mathematical, for they were being employed as human computers, calculating machines, in keeping with Airy's grand plan to reorder the Observatory and advance British astronomical science.

Where had Charles honed his youthful mathematical skills, so important for his future advancement? No doubt Airy, as a trustee of the Roan School, played his part in ensuring that applied mathematics, along with reading and writing, held a place in its elementary curriculum. In the case of the neighbouring Hospital School where standards were not as high,[10] many upper school pupils went on to join the navy. In the 1840s only two masters supervised six hundred boys, half of whom were deemed illiterate. At the Roan charitable school which Charles and his brothers attended, behind St Alfege in Roan Street,[11] the same expectation prevailed that many boys would go to sea. At around two hundred in 1838, its numbers were smaller than those of the Hospital School, although standards there were not much better[12] and irregular attendance was still a concern in a decade when the average length of school attendance was between one to two years.[13] At more established Greenwich educational institutions, naval pupils benefited from instruction in surveying and navigational techniques. But at large and less well-equipped charity institutions, such as the Hospital and Roan schools, expanding numbers forced the authorities to implement a monitorial system, under which upper school pupils were expected to instruct their juniors. In all likelihood, Charles served in this capacity in the Roan upper school, before his selection to the Observatory.

In addition to his early schooling, Charles' youthful aptitude for mathematics may have been stimulated by his father's commercial activity. Lorna Todd, in her youthful Adelaide years, came to greatly admire her father's dexterity at mathematics, recalling that 'he could add three columns at once, for I was told that so often as I tearfully laboured over my pounds shillings and pence sums'.[14] When Griffith Todd discontinued shop work and returned to London in later life, he set up as an accountant[15] following in the footsteps of his own father, George Todd, who had made his living as a stockbroker in London.[16] In addition to school instruction, mathematical education was also available through private tuition and public lectures. Outside schools and academies, arithmetic was encouraged as a form of rational entertainment during the early 19th century. By the 1830s, newspaper columns catered to young readers interested in arithmetic,[17] and classes in mathematics were being offered at mechanics institutes where self-improving Dissenters like the Todds were active participants.

Seated at the high table of the Octagon Room by 8 am that December morning, Charles and the other recruits were confronted with large books of early observations, sets of mathematical tables and forms which Airy had designed and numbered in sequence.[18] These forms had been standardised as part of the Observatory's regular observations for the *Nautical Almanac*. To all but trained staff, their complexity and abstruse astronomical terms still posed significant challenges. Like those seated around him, Charles was gripped with occasional bouts of 'computer fear' at not being able to understand the symbols placed in front of him, or knowing how to fill in the spaces correctly, using sets of tables supplied for the movements of the various planets. One of Airy's assistants, Hugh Breen, was on hand to direct their efforts, though not all beginners were as comfortable as Edwin Dunkin, who stated, albeit after the event, that the skeleton forms were so well laid out that 'any intelligent careful computer could hardly go astray'.[19] In the case of individual planets like Venus or Mars, the books of ancient observations supplied raw figures such as the geocentric longitude and latitude. But other variables, like the earth's heliocentric longitude and radius vector, still had to be deduced, before consulting logarithmic formulae in Lindenau's tables with which to compute the heliocentric place of the planet in question.[20] After a tentative start, Charles had begun to fare better, though he remained nervous about making mistakes. Existing reduction forms suggest that the work of young computers, embellished with rough calculations in the manner of modern exams, was scrutinised and signed off by assistants, with ticks or crosses liberally applied.[21] After four to five hours of concentrated work, under examination conditions, Charles began to flag, recalling that 'the first day seemed the longest day of my life. I thought it must be nearly 4 o'clock when I heard the 1 o'clock time ball drop'.[22] It was as if his first day would never end. When it eventually terminated at around 4 pm in the winter evening, he felt, despite nervous fatigue, a sense of exhilaration at passing a severe test and earning his first wage: 6d per day, if casual, or three pounds ten shillings per month.[23]

In some respects, Charles had been fortunate starting in December. For during the winter months, computers worked only eight hours, albeit with few breaks, because of the failing light. But during the longer summer evenings, they were expected to work twelve-hour days, with only an hour break.[24] On more than one occasion, Todd recalled that first day at the Observatory, remarking that 'Sir George Airy who was said to have no bowels was determined to get as much work as possible out of everyone under him and to make them do their duty'.[25] A decade after Airy's death in 1892, he was more generous about the impact of his long computing vigils, recalling that 'the more difficult the problem was to solve, the greater pleasure I had in solving it'.[26] Charles' initial time at the Observatory was largely devoted to reducing the 'ancient observations' which Airy had inherited from his predecessors and which he still considered 'not so forward as I would wish'.[27] For Charles and his fellow workers, such computing tasks proved a steep learning curve in their early months. By 1842, the situation began to improve and operations shifted to an enlarged computing room where newcomers swelled their numbers to fourteen. Their protracted labour became a source of pride to Airy who proudly displayed thirty sheets of the reductions of the planetary observations from 1750 to 1832 to his Board of Visitors.[28] Conscious of the burden on his permanent staff, in terms of observation, reduction and supervision, Airy decided to relegate some of their more routine tasks to his computers, to save time and money.

This decision in turn relieved his responsible junior workers from the monotony of their unending mathematical reductions. Charles, who was among this group, recalled how in early 1843:

> I used to take the readings. In times of disturbances, we used to sit opposite the instruments continually noting the movements. Every minute or oftener we had to recall the ups and downs of the magnetic and meteorological instruments.[29]

An added attraction when assisting in the new magnetic and meteorological department was being allowed time outside to check the readings of instruments located in the Observatory grounds, albeit under the watchful eye of Airy, who was quick to reprimand his juniors and deducted their pay for boyish outbursts or distractions. Even away from their stools, there was to be little relaxation in the pace of work. In addition to daily checks of the external rain gauges and self-registering thermometers, both in the air and on the Thames, two hourly observations were undertaken of all the principal instruments.[30] Despite the intensity of this monitoring regime, Charles' involvement within two years of entering the Royal Observatory was a positive sign, for he was being given additional responsibilities.

While assisting with regular observations, Charles made himself known to several of Airy's assistants, not only Hugh Breen who supervised the reductions, but also James Glaisher, whom Airy had chosen to run the new magnetic and meteorological department. A dynamic figure, he pursued an independent public career while working at the Observatory and was to be the most distinguished of Airy's assistants. Largely self-taught, Glaisher was an atmospheric physicist who conducted pioneering research on radiation and the humidity of the air.[31] Recognising his talents after employing him at Cambridge, Airy, after his appointment as Astronomer Royal, had brought him across from the Cambridge Observatory to Greenwich, where he remained until his retirement in 1874.[32] His successful example inspired bright newcomers in the computing workforce.

At the time when Charles had begun magnetic observations in 1843, Glaisher was looking to hire new assistants from the junior staff. One of these coveted positions went to Charles' colleague, Edward Dunkin, who entered the Observatory three years before him in 1838. According to his biographer, Dunkin, like Charles, was a 'highly intelligent youth from a lower middle-class background whose parents could not afford to send him to university'.[33] While Edward's brother was still employed in 'less advanced calculations,' he himself advanced more quickly and became the envy of his peers, securing promotion as a permanent junior assistant. Charles, who continued to seek Glaisher's patronage over the next decade, was among those who envied Edward his promotion, one which was to launch him on a long and exemplary career as a loyal assistant to Airy and respected member of the astronomical community. He and Charles would continue their friendly rivalry in the scientific world over future generations, Dunkin, as stolid civil servant and representative of the scientific establishment,[34] and Todd as a more adventurous colleague inspired by Glaisher's example.

Unlike the Dunkins or the Breens, a second family group with whom he worked, Charles was forced to develop greater independence from the outset; for he lacked the close companionship or strong paternal support available to these families. Charles' younger brother, Henry, who would eventually follow him to the Observatory, was seven years younger, and did not enter the computer workforce for another decade, unlike the closely-knit Breens with whom Todd was to work at both the Greenwich and Cambridge observatories.[35] The Breen family who lived in Park Street Greenwich were fortunate in gaining entry to the observatory through the services of their father. Hugh Breen, an educated science teacher from Armagh Ireland, facilitated the entry of no fewer than three of his sons into the Observatory in his capacity as supervisor of Airy's reductions. The second son, James, with whom Charles would also work subsequently at Cambridge, was, like Edwin Dunkin, one of a small group of very able computers to secure permanent work at Greenwich. Hard-working, the Breen boys enjoyed the further advantage of collaborating and publishing scientific papers with their father and with one another, thereby increasing their chances of promotion and job security. But the health risks of their strenuous and irregular work remained considerable. The first son, also named Hugh, started on the same project as Charles in 1839, but had to revert to occasional night duties on account of his frail constitution.[36] His tenuous situation and the plight of John Breen, the third son, were in some respects more representative of the experience of the computer workforce. John started as a computer at age 14, but despite a promising start, success eluded him. The need to care for his widowed mother eventually forced John Breen to seek a mercantile position in London.[37] Charles himself knew that, without sustained exceptional performance and good fortune, neither he nor his fellow computers could hope to remain in post after turning 21.

To compensate for their occupational confinement, young computers like Charles relied on regular physical exercise, taken on long summer evenings and on Sundays between family devotion and church attendance. Walking to nearby Blackheath or along the Thames were popular boyhood pastimes, along with fishing and boating amidst the bustle of the incoming London ferries. For Greenwich was a popular down river attraction for Londoners seeking a day out. During the great three-day feasts of Easter and Whitsunday, thousands of Londoners descended on Greenwich by boat and rail to spend leisure time in the Greenwich Park and at amusement fairs at Blackheath.[38] For the London labouring classes, with whom Charles and his family mixed freely at such times, astronomy was more a matter of entertainment rather than observation: a 'penny a peep' show, to be viewed by night with a pocket telescope on Greenwich Park.[39] For the more dedicated local amateurs, an old ship's spyglass might be purchased, at the considerable sum of ten shillings. For others, the dramatic and unexpected appearance of celestial phenomena like meteors and comets was still a subject of ominous speculation. In March 1843, when Charles was employed at the Observatory, the approach of a comet inspired dread in sections of the British populace, including some Greenwich believers, as a portent of 'Armageddon'.[40] In 1880, while observing a similar phenomenon, Todd recalled the 1843 visitor, and identified the causes of the superstition attached to it, explaining how both the comets of 1843 and 1880 'rushed with enormous velocity into close proximity to the sun ... almost grazing the sun's surface' at their closest point of orbit (perihelion).[41] Unlike his fearful contemporaries, young Charles had soon learnt at the Observatory that comets were in fact 'members of our solar system' travelling 'in elliptical orbits around the Sun' and 'not supernatural signs at all!'[42]

In matters of religion, the Todd family, while devoutly Nonconformist, were open to such insights and exhibited a broad pattern of church affiliation during their Greenwich years. Griffith and Mary had a number of their children baptised in the Anglican church of St Alfege[43] in an age when it was not uncommon for Sunday congregations to attend different churches and hear sermons by visiting or resident clergy. Charles himself, having attended St Alfege regularly as a pupil of the Roan school, was sensitive to the social standing of Anglicanism and would remain so during his later years in Adelaide. While joining the ranks of the moderate Congregational denomination, he preferred to send his own sons to the Anglican St Peter's College in Adelaide, rather than to its Methodist rival, Prince Alfred College.[44] In embracing Christianity and astronomy, Todd would generally refrain from pronouncing publicly on matters of controversy between science and religion. Nor did he write much on the subject. When he occasionally did so, he was usually attempting to dispel the ancient yet lingering superstition that the appearance of comets brought portents of doom. Speaking at the Stowe Congregational Church where he worshipped regularly in later his life, Todd addressed his audience with the following question: 'many phenomena of the universe are interpreted as menacing ... Yet might they not equally be regarded as an omen of good?'[45] In retrospect, Todd's ability to combine science and Nonconformity owed more to what has been called 'old dissent,' founded upon 18th century notions of enlightenment and compatible with scientific empiricism, than to its more evangelical 19th century expressions.[46]

While Greenwich had become a thriving transport and communications hub by the early 19th century, its imperial legacy also exercised a romantic appeal on its impressionable youth, commemorated through its buildings and monuments to past military heroes such as General James Wolfe at Québec and Lord Nelson at Trafalgar. Even before the Naval College was relocated there in 1873, the presence of numerous Trafalgar veterans, residing in close proximity at the Greenwich Hospital[47] during Charles' childhood, provided the young Todds with tales of adventure and exploits, at a time when Britain's influence was expanding and its commercial supremacy at sea was now undisputed. Inspired by their energetic environment, the young Todds were inspired by Victorian optimism, with its characteristic blend of modernity and tradition. As Todd later acknowledged, he was a child of the Victorian empire, still able at the turn of the century to recall 'the Queen's first visit on November 9, 1837 to be at the Lord Mayor's banquet' and 'the report of the Tower Gun fired on November 9, 1841 when the present King was born'.[48]

By the time he was working as a computer, Charles was aware of the significant part that the Observatory played in the wider British world.

The experience of Charles' elder brother, Griffith, who left Greenwich to join the merchant navy in India at age 18, could nevertheless be a sobering one. In April 1844, the year after he volunteered, Griffith wrote a homesick letter to his family from Calcutta to inquire whether the £25 which his parents had lent him for his passage had been safely returned to them. He was, he confided, still in debt for his marine outfits, 'not so comfortable out here as I would like' and suffering 'very bad health' in the old pilot brig to which he had first been assigned.[49] Griffith's tone towards his family was dutiful, yet affectionate towards his ailing mother, his young sister Elizabeth and little Henry. Above all he was missing Charles, only 18 months younger than himself, and wished 'he was here with me,' adding 'I hope that if he leaves the observatory that he will have as good a situation'. The sadness which tinged Griffith's letter would recur, for although he worked his way up through the service, becoming a junior in 1846 and a second mate by 1848[50] his Indian career was blighted by personal tragedy. Griffith outlived no fewer than three wives there, before he himself died in 1857, leaving three orphaned children,[51] whom Charles undertook to assist after they emigrated as young adults to Australia.

If Charles had ever felt the urge to join his older brother on his Indian adventure, he soon recognised that his abilities were more intellectual than physical. While drawn to the sea, he became more interested in the science of navigation and the technology of underwater cables than in a career with the merchant service or the British navy. When he did eventually set sail for South Australia a decade later, Charles confessed to his family:

> Before I experienced a sea voyage, I imagined it would afford many incidents to write about ... But such at least with us has not been the case. Day has succeeded day, and week by week with but little variety.[52]

All of which did not prevent him at the outset from busying himself with the instruments on board, explaining to his family that 'I frequently took observations, but as I always made the same position as the captain and had to trouble him for his quadrant, and afterwards to compare my watch with his chronometer, I discontinued, being satisfied that their results agreed'. While Griffith was drawn to the physical activity of boating and the sea, Charles was more navigator than sailor, as his letter which included detailed navigational and meteorological observations, would later confirm. The inclusion of these records was primarily for Henry's benefit, for his young brother had, by then, opted to follow in Charles' footsteps rather than Griffith's and start work as a mathematical computer.

By the time Charles had received news of Griffith from Calcutta in 1844, he was no longer restricted to computing, but had begun working with telescopes at the Observatory as well as with the meteorological instruments. For one of the essential tasks of the Royal Observatory pursued by Airy, was that of astronomical timekeeping. This was far removed from innocent stargazing in which young Charles could indulge on Greenwich Hill when returning home. In order to maintain the *Nautical Almanac*, the authoritative guide for British mariners, the Greenwich Observatory was committed to undertaking regular observations of selected 'clock stars', at a range of positions, over a three-year period.[53] Its published observations allowed British vessels to establish their own positions at sea, using a combination of their sextant readings and chronometer times. Tracking 'clock stars', so named for their visibility and proximity to the celestial pole, were not the only astronomical observations undertaken by newcomers like Charles. According to Airy, 'the sun, moon and planets' were also observed 'at every practicable opportunity through all hours of the night'.[54] Airy's resolution imposed a strict regime of observation on his workforce, one which, in the opinion of Edwin Dunkin, 'tested the endurance of young observers to the limit'.[55] Dunkin, who shared one of the mural circle instruments with Todd and others, recalled 24 hour long observation sessions, starting at 3 am in the morning and concluding at 3 am on the next. On one such evening, Charles fell ill and had to return home. Although he had taken the precaution of finding a replacement before departing, he was roundly reprimanded the following day by Airy who insisted that 'a good astronomer, Mr Todd, dies at his post'.[56]

Of the planets under constant observation, Airy gave precedence to the moon, and retained a lifelong interest in lunar theory even in retirement. In 1844, the Astronomer Royal went so far as to state that 'but for the demands of accurate lunar determinations as aids to navigation, the erection of a national observatory would never have been thought of'.[57] Well before his great transit circle telescope had been perfected in 1850, Airy had begun working on another instrument – the altazimuth – combining altitude and azimuth, the angular distance along the horizon. Airy designed it specifically for observing the moon, not only at the meridian but 'through entire portions of her orbit', since 'one fourth of the moon's course is absolutely lost' and 'one half is very imperfectly observed'. As a mark of his paternal favour, Airy gave Dunkin charge of the newly installed altazimuth instrument during 1846, while young Hugh Breen was employed in the astronomical department as an additional assistant for the same purpose.[58] With some eight thousand lunar observations now rescued from oblivion by Airy's toiling computers, Todd knew that the great projects of reduction upon which he and his fellow computers had embarked were drawing to a close. By late 1846, with Breen's departure to the Cambridge Observatory, Todd was still not considered for a more secure position within Airy's personal establishment.

A youthful and unique portrait of Charles painted at this period hints at his uncertain future. Well-dressed in a suit and cravat in keeping with the 'gentlemanly demeanour' valued by Observatory assistants,[59] his is an alert rather than commanding presence, in contrast with that of his elder brother Griffith who appears more mature and robust in a similar painting. As a family practice, these individual paintings commissioned in the age before photography, became more commonplace and say much about the social aspirations of Todd's parents for their offspring. Yet, despite his undoubted progress, Charles is not yet dignified in his portrait with the instruments of an astronomer, unlike his elder sister Mary, an accomplished pianist, who holds a sheet of music in her hand. In later life, Charles valued his early portrait sufficiently to have it sent to Australia from Cambridge, perhaps in memory of those hopeful yet uncertain Greenwich years.[60]

If Charles worked hard under Airy's strict direction, he also set out to impress Glaisher and appeared to enjoy his work in the magnetic and meteorological department. The appearance of a brilliant aurora australis at the end of Todd's life brought back memories of an earlier experience in 1846 at the Greenwich Observatory, when 'a magnificent disturbance' produced by a solar flare 'affected the instruments of the observatory for a couple of days'.[61] With Glaisher intent on viewing the magnetic storm outdoors, Charles was left inside to monitor the phenomenon 'as I had charge of the observations and had to examine the instruments every three minutes ... On that occasion the magnets at the Cape of Good Hope and Hobart and several other far distant places were disturbed'. As Superintendent of Electric Telegraphs, he would encounter the same phenomenon in South Australia, most notably in 1859 when it assumed the proportions of a global phenomenon. In that year, when a solar storm of unprecedented intensity played havoc with telegraph equipment, Todd's scientific training helped him to recognise what came to be known as the 'Carrington Event,' named after one of his former British colleagues, Richard Carrington.[62]

Compounding the uncertainty of Charles' long-term prospects was the furore which erupted around Airy and the Greenwich Observatory during late 1846 over its failure to locate the mysterious planet Neptune.[63] Instead, a French astronomer, Le Verrier, laid claim to this discovery after

Portrait of Charles Todd as a young man, c.1845

Airy had failed to act on the advice of a young visitor and Cambridge mathematician, John Couch Adams who had already calculated the position of the unknown planet. Within Cambridge University and more widely in the British press, Airy was roundly condemned not only for disregarding the work of a promising young British talent, but also for allegedly assisting the French in making their successful discovery. Todd makes no mention of this controversy which raged for more than a year, nor did Airy make much of it in his 1847 report. But there can be little doubt that Todd's subsequent horror of public controversy dates from this extraordinary outburst of scientific infighting, during which many of Airy's colleagues, disillusioned with the inflexible operations of his 'celestial factory,' rounded on him and 'bloodied his nose'.[64]

In contrast with Airy's reputation, Charles was by this period aware of Glaisher's rising star as the magnetic and meteorological department continued to expand at Greenwich. With the compilation of regular meteorological reports for official publication, Glaisher's work was commanding increased influence, not only within the United Kingdom but also abroad. After a magnetic and meteorological conference, convened at Cambridge in 1845 reported favorably on the progress of weather work, the British Association for the Advancement of Science (BAAS) recommended in September 1846 that 'the magnetic observatory at Greenwich be permanently continued upon the most extensive and efficient scale' and that branches be established at existing overseas observatories in South Africa, India and Australia.[65] Its resolution constituted a glowing endorsement which not even the powerful Airy could reverse. For ambitious newcomers like Charles, the recognition of meteorology gave fresh hope of professional advancement. It was not the first time that the wider British world beckoned. If his brother Griffith could leave England to pursue a career in India, why could not Charles also find scientific employment in a far-flung British establishment?

By the time of the BAAS announcement however, time was running out. At twenty years of age, Charles could expect to leave the Royal Observatory by the following year, unless a more permanent position arose. Since he would then be expected to fend for himself at 21, the meagre earnings of part-time computing would scarcely suffice, forcing him to abandon science altogether. James Breen's departure for the Cambridge Observatory did not improve the situation and Todd duly left the Royal Observatory in late January 1847. It would be almost another year before he learnt that a junior assistant, a 'Mr Morgan' working with Breen at Cambridge, had discontinued his post there.[66] Without delay, Charles seized the unexpected opportunity and lodged an application for the position, asking Glaisher to support it. It proved a shrewd choice for Glaisher had previously been Airy's assistant at Cambridge and had personal experience of the duties expected there. Moreover Glaisher, at several points in Charles' early career, saw his scientific potential in a way that Airy did not. Writing directly to Professor James Challis, then in charge of the Cambridge Observatory, Glaisher confided in January 1848 that 'Mr Todd will assist you very well. I found him to be most useful to me and I was sorry when he had to leave the Observatory'.[67] As a further mark of his support, Charles also took Glaisher's testimonial with him to Cambridge, describing him as 'a faithful and useful assistant' with 'the necessary qualities for a good observer as well as for a good and quick computer. He is also neat in his work and therefore I introduce him with some confidence'.[68] It was not a scholarship to the great university or its colleges, but for young Charles Todd it was a vital stepping-stone to professional success and future independence.

2

Cambridge: Status and Respectability

It was not a long journey to Cambridge. Prior to his appointment on 7 February 1848,[1] Charles was able to travel by train from central London to Cambridge in only two hours, a considerable saving in time, instead of the long road trip by coach. At a personal level, the speed of rail travel helped mitigate Charles' initial sense of isolation from his family in London. At Greenwich, he had seen how the railway brought Londoners down river in increasing numbers. The extension of the south-east railway had however sparked protracted controversy within Greenwich, where the mooted construction of a tunnel under the Park, in close proximity to the Royal Observatory and its sensitive instruments, met with powerful opposition and forced the railway company to reroute its line by 1846.[2]

Of special interest to scientists like Charles was the potential of an allied development, the electric telegraph. A recent British invention, it developed alongside the expanding rail system and was integrated within it for the purposes of timetabling and signalling. By the time Charles undertook his northern journey, eastern counties' railway engineers had constructed telegraph lines along the length of the route from London towards Norwich. Whether Charles, as an interested passenger, yet grasped the significance of this new technology, so critical for his own career, is doubtful. But further trips between Greenwich and Cambridge stations, where the telegraph offices were located, served to arouse his youthful interest in its undoubted potential. On his first journey north, Charles took time to peruse rural Cambridgeshire,[3] much of it now drained for agriculture and increasingly prosperous. Its tranquillity and slower rhythms differed markedly from the bustle of the Greenwich docks and streets to which he was accustomed. Once he reached Cambridge station, Charles was made aware that his journey was not yet over. Local opposition to the coming of the railway to Cambridge had ensured that it merely skirted the town at its southern end rather than penetrating into its centre. Unlike Greenwich folk, the Cambridge authorities feared that weekend trains from the metropolis would bring an influx of Londoners and that disorder and immorality would result among the local student population.[4] Charles would soon learn that the railway was also disrupting established river traffic along the local River Cam to London.

After travelling through the medieval streets of the township and glimpsing the colleges and spires of its great university, Todd continued north by cab across the Cam, passing Castle Hill, the ancient site of Roman settlement, before turning north west along Madingley Road. Here on a rise in the countryside, he reached the entrance of the secluded observatory where he was to spend the next six years living and working at close quarters with a former Greenwich associate, James Breen, under the direction of Professor James Challis. As Charles ascended the leafy driveway, he caught sight of the impressive complex, an elegant two-storey stone edifice, built in the style of a Greek Doric temple and ornamented with the symbol of Osiris, the Egyptian god of the afterlife.[5] Professor and Mrs Challis' quarters were located at the southern end of the building, while Breen and Charles would share apartments in the northern wing. Charles was no longer viewed as a boy computer; he had, within a short space of years, entered the ranks of the astronomical fraternity.

At £70, Todd's annual salary as junior assistant was not substantially greater than his recent Greenwich earnings of £66 a year.[6] But according to one Cambridge science historian, the 'comings and goings' of observatory staff were in part motivated by the financial advantages offered at Cambridge.[7] Not only was their accommodation provided but assistants received a supplementary 'allowance for candles,' an expensive and much used commodity by nocturnal astronomers. In addition Charles, by dint of sustained industry, would be able to secure pay rises to guarantee him financial independence. By early March when the observatory syndicate formally approved his annual salary as junior assistant,[8] Charles was already proving his worth. In his capacity as junior assistant, he was expected to take meridian observations, alternating with James Breen on the transit and mural circle instruments during 1848.[9] But he soon showed his capacity to engage in other work, especially the magnetic and meteorological observations which he had practised under James Glaisher at Greenwich.

South Front of the Cambridge Observatory, undated

On 22 February 1848, Charles wrote a long letter to Glaisher describing an aurora which he and Breen observed that morning at Cambridge. After describing its changing colour, intensity and position in considerable detail, he went on to explain that Challis 'was out at the time, so that I was entirely alone and was obliged to leave at times to take transit observations'. He added, as if to confirm the confidence Glaisher had shown in him, that 'Mr Challis was very pleased with the report that I gave him of it, indeed [the aurora] was almost as brilliant as the one last October'. He signed the letter with an elaborate flourish, a mark of new-found confidence. Auroras and 'solar halos' were attracting considerable attention at both the Greenwich and Cambridge Observatories.[10] Later that year, Challis published a detailed report in the *Cambridge Chronicle* concerning an aurora borealis postulating that 'its central part is not a fixed point but oscillates in a capricious manner… the perturbations of the three observatory magnets used to record it were very remarkable'.[11] Though Todd did not receive a mention on this occasion, he was nevertheless gaining a degree of recognition for himself. For when the *Chronicle* published its weather report in April of that year, 'Charles Todd' was identified as its sole author. Such a public acknowledgement would have been unthinkable under Airy.[12]

An immediate difference from Greenwich was the manner in which

Challis ran his observatory. An Anglican clergyman, he was politely spoken and of a more kindly disposition than the unforgiving Airy. In his annual reports Challis wrote in complimentary terms about his assistants' work, taking the trouble to identify them by name and commending their 'zeal and energy' on more than one occasion.[13] Indeed the hard-working Challis expected his assistants to exercise initiative, for he took his teaching duties at Trinity College seriously and did not exercise the strict surveillance which pervaded the Greenwich workplace. Charles' early months at Cambridge were full of promise. At the same time as he was winning the respect of colleagues, he made his first attempt to enter polite Cambridge society. Knowing that he would not enjoy access to college life within the university, Charles had secured the name of a prominent Nonconformist family, the Bells, who resided in the township.

One Sunday in early 1848, relieved of his observatory duties, he set out along Madingley Road towards the township. It was a considerable distance of several miles and could become difficult in wet conditions, but he was not usually alone. Walking was a popular form of exercise at Cambridge, preferred to riding, and he routinely passed many Cambridge men from the colleges taking their 'constitutionals'[14] in the direction of neighbouring villages. Charles' destination on this occasion was Free School Lane, an established street in central Cambridge bounded on one side by the Corpus Christi College. He had taken the trouble to make a formal appointment on this occasion. For the Bells, while Nonconformist and unconnected with the university, were well-to-do and their house at number three was a substantial three-storey building. Charles was about to enter a different social world.

According to family sources, it proved 'a fairly formal visit' during which Charles was reputed to be 'on his best behaviour as young men were in those days in the presence of ladies'.[15] Invited back by Mrs Bell in subsequent weeks, Charles was conversing with his host who had offered him cake and sherry white wine, when a 'strangely un-Victorian' episode ensued. Mrs Bell, who had a number of daughters, had broached the subject of marriage with Charles, now approaching 22. At this turn in the conversation, Charles politely demurred that 'no one would want to marry such an uninteresting fellow,' whereupon a voice in the room exclaimed 'I will marry you Mr Todd!' Turning to his respondent, Charles noticed the Bell's blue-eyed daughter Alice, sitting reading a book on a hearthrug before the fireplace. Before he could manage a reply, Mrs Bell intervened and sent her young daughter back to the nursery in disgrace. The 'Alice incident' has been retold subsequently as a defining moment in their initially awkward friendship. Certainly, Alice never lost her capacity for candour mingled with kindness. It would take several years for their friendship to blossom, for Alice to reach maturity and for Charles to regain his youthful confidence in Cambridge society after isolation in the observatory and Airy's stern legacy.

In keeping with most Nonconformist circles, the subjects of conversation in the Bell household ranged across business, chapel and town affairs. Edward senior, who emanated from London had entered the local corn and seed trade after marrying Charlotte Clark in 1818, then a resident of nearby Fulbourn.[16] He began in partnership with Henry Marshall[17] and struggled in the early years to establish himself. Charlotte assisted the family materially by making fashionable straw bonnets, an item then much in demand. From her mother Charlotte, Alice would inherit a love of fashion as well as her religious devotion. For it was Charlotte who worshipped at the local St Andrews Street Baptist Church[18] before her marriage and who brought up her family in strict accordance with its teachings. Despite the dominant Anglican faith within Cambridge, the Baptists, representing the town interest, were the most active of the Nonconformist denominations. In many respects Charlotte's example was reminiscent of Charles' own mother, Mary. But Charlotte's early marriage concealed a secret which Charles would only belatedly learn.

At the time of the 1841 census, the large Bell family resided at Peas Hill, Edward's business premises in the town centre. Edward,[19] then 47, was listed in the same census as a seedsman and Charlotte at forty years as a bonnet maker, with no fewer than ten children of whom Alice, then four and half years, was the third youngest. A famous silhouette of the Bells, commissioned at Christmas of the following year,[20] shows Alice and her many siblings standing adjacent their seated parents with her mother holding young Henry Bell, their last child born only a few months earlier. Later presented to the Australian outback town of Alice Springs, it tells only part of their story. Motherhood proved to be not only daunting for Charlotte, but heartbreaking for the entire family. In the years before Charles' arrival at Cambridge, the Bells lost no fewer than five of their children to illness and outbreaks of disease. Not only did baby Henry succumb in a matter of months but an elder brother, William passed away in the same year, aged 20; Charles Bell in the following year aged 5, Eliza at the same tender age in 1845 and James two years later, aged 19.[21] One tragedy followed the next and, although the family were relatively prosperous in their new premises at Free School Lane by the time Charles made their acquaintance, Alice had grown up in a household haunted by death, one in which religion became the main solace for family grieving. She would grow up knowing little of the university nearby nor indeed about the financial dealings of her father and elder brother, Edward. Confined to home and chapel in her early years, Alice learnt to sing and play the piano, or read and sit at her fine inlaid sewing table, fulfilling her parents' ambition that she would survive into adulthood and grow up a lady. Under the weight of family circumstances, Charles may well have admired her innocence and spirit but his hopes of forming an attachment, if they yet existed, must have been at best tenuous.

A report commissioned by the Board of Health in 1849 on the state of Cambridge's sewerage, drainage and water supply highlighted the potentially deadly conditions which prevailed within the town. With an increase in Cambridge's inner city population had come the risk of serious disease, particularly cholera but also smallpox and malaria,[22] for the Cam which flowed through the city carried a lethal combination of dead animals, decomposing matter and effluent which could not be easily isolated from the town's water supply. Consequently few of its residents, the Bells among them, could hope to escape the ongoing impact of water-born contagion, as cholera revisited the township in new and more deadly strains during the mid-19th century.[23] One respectable resident wrote at the time of 'the sad mortality among my acquaintances – It makes me grateful to God for the continuation of my own life'.[24] So alarming was the health report that, when a major fire destroyed part of the town centre in the same year, the town corporation elected not to rebuild parts of the inner city.

At Cambridge, Charles' time for socialising, however pleasurable, was limited by his observatory duties and irregular hours. The Observatory's first assistant James Breen, regarded by Airy as 'a rough genius,'[25] maintained a vigorous work ethic worthy of the Royal Astronomer himself. At times, Challis undertook observations with one or other of his assistants, reporting in 1848 to the observatory syndicate that:

> Pressure of work with the Northumberland telescope in observing planets and comets compelled me after February 1848 to restrict the meridian observations of moving bodies to the newly discovered planets. Of these, Flora, Metis, Astraea and Neptune were observed in 1848.[26]

In addition to the sensational Neptune discovery, the late 1840s saw an upsurge in the sighting and naming of minor planets, many of them located by amateur European astronomers, beginning with Hencke's discovery of the asteroid, Astraea, in 1845. Consequently, Charles, who had been largely confined to observing the transits and zenith distances of clock stars since arriving at Cambridge, was now able to expand his knowledge to planets and stars. Even after Charles' arrival, Challis remained overworked and in arrears with reductions and printing. Meticulous and painstaking, Challis insisted on undertaking the time-consuming tasks of checking the final proofs of complex observation charts himself, leaving him at times to regret not only the time spent in meridian observations, but also the expense and time involved in their publication.[27]

Challis, unlike Airy, was of a more nervous disposition.[28] Unkind anecdotes circulated about his dependence on pragmatic Mrs Challis when a burglar entered the isolated observatory late at night. Yet history has almost certainly been unkind to Challis over his unfortunate role in the Neptune affair. Dismissed as the astronomer who had failed to find the new planet, Challis had done more than Airy to locate it. It was he who had recommended John Couch Adams, a young Cambridge student and protégé, to Airy with the mathematical solution and subsequently searched during August 1846 in a bid to locate it at Airy's belated request. After the announcement of Le Verrier's triumphant discovery at the Paris Observatory, Challis was left to humbly explain these difficult circumstances to the Cambridge University Senate,[29] including the fact that he had actually sighted it on several occasions but lacked the vital star map available to his continental rivals. After the event, British honours over Neptune went to John Couch Adams.[30] By the time Charles arrived, Adams, who was curator at the observatory, was being feted in the university and in the press.[31] Of humble disposition, Adams, now recognised as the co-discoverer, befriended Charles who took the opportunity to view the new planet for himself. Along with Challis, the mild-mannered Adams was a very different role model to the forceful Airy.

One of Charles' important new responsibilities at Cambridge was the care and maintenance of the great Northumberland telescope, still in use today. A giant 12-inch refractor, with a focal length of 20 feet,[32] it weighed two and a half tons and was a gift from the Duke of Northumberland, subsequently high steward of the University. Airy, then serving as director of the Cambridge Observatory, was sensitive to the instrument's value and the importance of its donor. Consequently he expended considerable time and effort in improving its performance, purchasing an expensive eyepiece, adjusting the complex mountings and housing it in an equatorial dome before relinquishing it to the incoming Challis. Charles soon recognised the challenges associated with manoeuvring and operating such a massive telescope, one which was capable of tracking comets across the northern sky with as many as 295 available positions to the observer.[33] A further challenge with which Airy and his successors had to contend was to construct a clock of sufficient power to manoeuvre such a telescope. In order to achieve this, Challis ordered and added ten sets of additional weights to complement those attached to one of the supporting poles. This counterpoint mechanism, weighing over 750 pounds, was located in a well inside the dome. In the event that the clock stopped, Challis or his assistants had to descend into the well with a lantern at night to restart it.[34] A further hazard when tracking with the Northumberland arose when rotating the dome using long levers and a ratchet mechanism moving on cannonballs. For if any of the other levers not in use had not been properly fastened, they could swing around and strike the observer a severe blow to the face. It must have taken Charles as incoming assistant considerable time to master 'old Northumberland' and put its unique capacities to best use. Regarded as the pride of the observatory, it was often the main object of attention when visiting dignitaries called.

Challis and his small staff were not always forewarned of such evening visits, which occasionally occurred without notice. In late 1847, Challis and his wife had been forced to leave a banquet in town and return to the observatory after no less a personage than Prince Albert 'invited himself to the observatory at very short notice' in order to 'see all the objects of interest that could be viewed through the large telescope'.[35] Once Adams had been recognised in 1848 for his role in locating Neptune, there was a steady flow of visitors, increasing demands on Challis' precious time. Not surprisingly, his expectations on Charles as second assistant rose accordingly. Challis ran the Cambridge Observatory as a distinguished teaching and research facility at which staff had to demonstrate 'the construction and use of instruments at the observatory during the day' while 'direct[ing] observations and reductions by students at night'.[36] Consequently Charles was expected to instruct as well as observe and to demonstrate the necessary social skills which would later serve him so well in elevated colonial circles. Because of the vagaries of the weather, the capacity to instruct was an essential staff skill. In September 1849, when the Duke of Northumberland's sister Lady Elgin, accompanied by Lady Augusta paid a visit, one member of the party recorded that 'it rained cats and dogs and of course we saw nothing but the instruments'. Challis who was on hand for the occasion improvised 'an excellent lecture on the Northumberland telescope and answered an infinitude of astronomical questions with which Lady Elgin had come charged'.[37]

Clearly Charles would face a considerable challenge when having to host such visits. Unlike Greenwich where he had been mostly confined to working in silence on a stool, Charles was now able to develop social and teaching skills in the presence of visitors of wide ranging backgrounds. That he soon became comfortable in his new role is confirmed by the account of Josiah Chater, a Cambridge resident who visited the observatory with his brother in October 1848. Chater remembered being 'introduced to Mr Todd, a very nice young man and very clever [who] showed us the instruments three of which we had a peep through'.[38] It must have been a visit of considerable duration. Not only did Charles show them the stars and the moon but they accessed the Northumberland telescope and observed 'the planet latest discovered called Neptune, about as big as a star of sixth magnitude'. Charles himself warmed to his visitors who thanked him for 'a very great deal of useful information' and left highly gratified by their 'evening's entertainment'.

Under Challis' supervision, Charles was also mixing with other young British astronomers, destined to make their mark in Victorian science. Apart from the quietly spoken Adams who later nominated Charles for an honorary degree at Cambridge, the observatory attracted such talents as Richard Carrington who, according to Challis, observed with the transit and mural circle in the autumn of 1849. Carrington, the same age as Charles, was a Cambridge graduate and wealthy amateur who subsequently gained practical experience at Cambridge and Durham Observatories before winning distinction in the 1850s for establishing that the sun was 'indeed a magnetic body'.[39] As part of the ongoing exchange of staff between Greenwich and Cambridge, Breen's younger brother, John, arrived to observe 'for the sake of practice,'[40] while Charles' younger brother, Henry, also visited to observe and assist his elder brother with reductions. It would prove a valuable opportunity for Henry as well as Charles, for it was here that Henry first met his future employer in J.C. Adams.

Just how many relatives and friends visited Charles at the Cambridge Observatory is difficult to determine. By way of confirming his new-found status with newcomers, Charles indulged his life-long taste for expensive imported teas, possibly sent to Cambridge from his father. The Todds at Greenwich were by now more comfortably situated away the bustle of Church Street at Ashburnham Grove. Nor did London visitors have to return to town for overnight accommodation, for Charles could offer them quarters adjacent to his own at the observatory. One relative to avail himself of this hospitality was his cousin Richard Todd, who spent a fortnight with Charles and was 'greatly delighted by getting a view of some of the heavenly bodies through the large instrument'.[41] Charles, at his informative best, showed Richard the moon through the Northumberland telescope, using a magnification of three hundred, which he explained was 'the most definite'. Impressed by the power of the Northumberland and the panorama before him, Richard described it lyrically as 'a grand sight which I shall never forget... The surface of the moon appeared to be far more rugged than that of the earth and as the dark part of the moon came into the field, I could see the tops of the mountains lit up by the rising sun and looking like islands of light in a sea of darkness'. Richard's record of his experience is a timely reminder that scientists like Charles were not the only ones to wax lyrical over the heavens. For Richard, a staunch Baptist and future missionary to Australia, the moon, sun and planetary system were the work of divine creation.

Despite the stern morality of the Victorian age, the mid-19th century was a romantic period in which the British royal couple of Victoria and Albert were idealised by the public. For young Alice and Charles, models such Princess Charlotte and Prince Leopold, whose portrait hung in Charles' family home, may well have remained influential.[42] Earlier in the century, Princess Charlotte of Great Britain had controversially broken off her arranged engagement to marry the dashing Leopold. While the progress of courtship was 'somewhat slower'[43] in this instance, Charles now older and more independent was undoubtedly drawn to young Alice: her skin, hair and dress, replete with petticoats, bonnet and crinoline, in keeping with the femininity of her social position. He also knew that any long-term friendship would be accompanied by material and professional expectations on the part of Alice's family who were destined within a generation to move to a manor house at nearby Chesterton. While Charles was enjoying salary increases at the observatory, firstly in February 1850 when his annual wage rose to £80 and again in 1853 to £90,[44] his chances of further promotion and a higher salary were by no means guaranteed.

The prominence of death in Alice's youth may well have heightened her early romantic attraction for Charles, while a new and unexpected family loss drew them more closely together. One Sunday in mid-September 1851, Charles attended the St Andrews Street Baptist Church only to learn of the death of Alice's older sister, Charlotte Diana, earlier that morning.[45] For Alice and her remaining siblings it was a further call to devotion and prayer. That Charles was close to young Charlotte at that time is confirmed by a surviving bible in his possession which he had given her six months earlier as 'her sincere friend'.[46] Had Charles, in view of Alice's age, befriended Charlotte, some four years older at the behest of the Bells? For when Charles visited the family on the occasion of the

1851 census, Charlotte Diana was the only Bell daughter present with her parents on that evening.[47] If so, her loss may have marked the beginning of a new courtship pattern sanctioned by the Bells involving Alice, who was now 15 years old. In keeping with Victorian expectations, gifts were an important preliminary to engagement and there is subsequent evidence of such attention to Alice on Charles' part. For Charles and Alice's daughter, Lorna later wrote:

> I have found when turning out old books several leather bound volumes of a religious nature sent to placate Mrs Bell. The inscriptions begin 'To Alice Gillam Bell, from her friend Charles Todd,' later 'From her admirer Charles Todd' finally 'From her devoted admirer Charles Todd'.[48]

Apart from material considerations of wealth, the issue of religion was a major consideration for the Bells in any eventual match. The co-existence of religion and science was becoming uneasy in Cambridge by the middle of the 19th century as claims by geological scholars threatened accepted wisdom about the age of the Earth. Around the same period in 1853 William Whewell, the autocratic master of Trinity College, published his pamphlet *Of the plurality of worlds* in which he reversed his previous position and argued in keeping with religious tradition that life existed solely on the Earth.[49] Todd, a believer like most scientists of his day, chose like his colleague James Breen not to engage in such speculation. Within the city of Cambridge the churches were divided over the writings of the university. At the St Andrews Street Baptist Church, William Robinson who revitalised the congregation after his appointment in November 1850 had already entered the fight in defence of the bible and the view of Genesis that the Earth had been created in six days.[50] As presiding minister at Charles and Alice's marriage several years later, Robinson was not however entirely sceptical of the work of science. Despite their differences Charles found a measure of accommodation in his exhortation that Christians should nevertheless 'prize the labours of scientists, while rejoicing that God's purposes have a beginning and an end'.[51]

Although Charles' friendship with the Bell family was now well established, he spent most of his time in the company of James Breen, Challis' first assistant at the observatory. Their association strengthened in early 1851 after Challis suffered a breakdown which he subsequently attributed to overwork at the observatory. In his report of that year, he nevertheless expressed confidence in the 'zeal and ability of his assistants' who were left to undertake most of the observations and reductions. For the latter task, they could rely on the part-time services of their younger siblings, though this proved to be only a temporary expedient; for however much they desired regular work, neither John Breen nor Henry Todd gained secure employment at Cambridge in the short term, leaving their elder brothers to undertake most of the reductions themselves.

Following Breen's example, Charles sustained an intense schedule of observations in Challis' absence. In addition to observing recently discovered minor planets like Parthenope and Eunomia,[52] they enjoyed considerable success in tracking Faye's comet, rarely seen in the northern hemisphere. Three decades later in 1880, when Charles was studying a bright southern comet of comparable orbit, he recalled how:

> We were fortunate enough to observe Faye's comet in 1850 and 1851 at Cambridge on November 28, 1850 and followed it up till the month of March following. It was excessively faint even through the 12 inch Northumberland telescope, and was I think seen only at two other observatories.[53]

For the purpose of tracking comets, the powerful Northumberland telescope was a valuable asset which Breen and Charles put to effective use. Breen, who was collaborating on scientific papers with his older brother Hugh at Greenwich and with Challis, demonstrated his considerable knowledge of comets in *The Planetary Worlds*, his popular astronomical work published in 1854.[54] Charles, despite his vigorous involvement as his co-observer, did not yet commit to writing papers or books, as Dunkin was also doing at Greenwich under Airy's patronage. In addition to refining his social and teaching skills, Charles preferred to spend his time experimenting with new techniques and exploring their applications to astronomy.

One such innovation which attracted him was photography, a relatively new invention for astronomical observation. With Challis back at the helm, Cambridge Observatory had been asked by the British Association for the Advancement of Science to map part of the moon's surface. A laborious project, begun by Breen, it involved drawing different parts of its surface before connecting them and reducing them to scale.[55] The project had not advanced far by 1853–54, when Todd saw an opportunity to begin experimenting with photographs of the moon for mapping purposes. Todd in all probability had visited the Great London Exhibition of 1851 at which the Americans, William Bond and J.A. Whipple,[56] displayed two daguerreotypes they had taken of the moon. While at Cambridge, Charles took what he later claimed to have been the first photo of its kind in Britain during 1853–54.⁵⁷ Neither Breen nor Challis were satisfied with the photographic result,⁵⁸ but it was testimony to Charles' willingness to experiment as opportunities arose.

Around the same period, Todd became actively involved in a new and more immediate experiment. During 1852–53, Airy, after a protracted stand-off with the Southern and Eastern Railway Company, entered into more co-operative arrangements with its telegraph engineer Charles Vincent Walker. With Walker's assistance, Airy connected the Royal Observatory to the railway's telegraph network and linked his astronomical clocks to those in the city in order to distribute standard time 'along all the principal railway lines diverging from London'.⁵⁹ In late 1852, as Airy began negotiating with the Admiralty about the possibility of erecting time balls driven by the telegraph current, he entered into a lengthy correspondence with Challis about using the telegraph to more accurately determine the longitude of his Cambridge Observatory. Such a measurement was fundamental for triangulation and shared astronomical calculations between observatories.

Knowing that the Cambridge Observatory like most other European observatories was not yet connected to the telegraph grid, Airy approached the Electric Telegraph Company to organise a connection between Greenwich and the Cambridge railway station. Convinced by Airy that telegraphic communication between observatories 'would soon be looked upon as indispensable,'⁶⁰ Challis was supportive despite the fact that any exchange would have to be organised from the Cambridge railway station rather than from the security of the Madingley Road complex. By May 1853, they came to the conclusion that the determination could best be achieved by using two observers, one at each institution, to send and record telegraphic signals before changing locations and repeating the signaling exercise on the following evening. There is anecdotal evidence to suggest that Challis was not comfortable with the new technology of electricity. The main reason for Todd's direct involvement appears to have been the fact that the experiment coincided with the meeting of the board of visitors at the observatory, where Challis, Adams and Breen would be required. Accordingly on 4 May, Challis announced that 'Mr Todd will be the Cambridge observer ... who can be accommodated he tells me at his father's Greenwich house', while the visiting observer from Greenwich would have 'board and breakfast at Mr Todd's apartment here'.⁶¹ For this important assignment, Airy chose his trusted assistant Edwin Dunkin.

It would prove to be an important episode in the history of telegraphy and astronomical measurement. But how well prepared was Todd and how much had he learned about the new phenomenon of galvanism as it was then known? He had in his personal possession a copy of Airy's well-received Ipswich lectures of 1850, but these dealt solely with matters of astronomy. One possible source of inspiration was the Greater London Exhibition of 1851 at Crystal Palace which featured a series of important exhibits on electric telegraphy, among them samples of Charles Walker's cable used between Dover and Folkstone in 1849, and more pertinently an exhibit of the five-needle telegraphic apparatus of Cooke and Wheatstone used by the Electric Telegraph Company on its western railway line.[62] Apart from this special event two years earlier, Charles would have to rely almost solely on his knowledge of operations at the Cambridge railway station. On the other hand, Dunkin, whom Airy confidently introduced to Challis as a 'well educated and well-mannered man,"[63] had been working at first hand with Airy and had observed his recent experiments with the telegraph. Undoubtedly Charles' earlier rivalry with Dunkin, now Airy's sixth assistant and commanding a higher salary than Breen as senior assistant, was rekindled by this new arrangement.[64] Certainly Charles would be at a disadvantage in the first phase of their joint observations. He would have to transport one of the observatory chronometers some distance to the station and undertake signalling there in a very public and much noisier environment than the Greenwich Observatory. The Electric Telegraph Company shared some of these concerns, sending its own official to monitor proceedings at the station in the event of mishaps. Todd had clearly undertaken careful preparations with local railway officials in the preceding weeks. Before travelling to Cambridge station on Tuesday evening 17 May, he first observed and recorded the times of the series of Greenwich clock stars, the usual preparation when several observers were involved. Once at the station he duly sent Dunkin 151 signals in 29 batches between 11 pm and 12 midnight that evening.[65] He then travelled to Greenwich the following day to repeat the exercise on the evening 18 May at the Royal Observatory.

Airy who was monitoring Todd's endeavours at Greenwich reported favourably on the first night's work, writing to Challis that 'your signals were very vigorous and good,' although Dunkin complained that he had insufficient time between signals to observe and record them.[66] On the second night allowance was made for the fact that observers were alternating their signals every 15 minutes, and short spaces of 15–20 seconds were introduced between batches, this time with Dunkin at Cambridge and Todd at the Royal Observatory. Keen to see his family, Charles left the Royal Observatory after completing his observation of the 12 clock stars required. He was due to return by train the next morning to Cambridge where Dunkin, who had been granted a holiday by Airy, was spending his leisure time with John Couch Adams. No doubt Dunkin, whose main task was to compare his own data with that of Todd before returning to Greenwich, also found time to inform Charles of observatory gossip and more importantly about the recent telegraph experiments there. For Airy as supervisor, the visit was also an information gathering exercise, since both Adams and Dunkin would be in a position to update him on the Cambridge Observatory and Todd's performance. In this respect his terse remark to Challis after the event was suggestive when he wrote: 'Mr Todd escaped yesterday without my having the opportunity of seeing him'.[67] On the verge of expanding his electric telegraph network from Greenwich to the southern coast, the Astronomer Royal was on the lookout for able recruits to his proposed galvanic department. Not one to forget his early charges, Airy was already looking to bring Todd back to Greenwich, but for the moment he would bide his time.

Several months elapsed before Airy recalled Todd to Greenwich to participate in further galvanic experiments with the telegraph. When the Astronomer Royal moved, he did so quickly and decisively, alerting Todd in April 1854 to an expected vacancy in the Observatory at the end of that month, with ongoing 'charge of the galvanic and chemical apparatus of the Astronomical Observatory'.[68] At £130 per annum the new salary was more attractive than Todd's Cambridge stipend and more importantly, would place him on a firmer footing as Airy's assistant at the Royal Observatory. Once he had consented, Charles would have little time to farewell Alice and the Bells, prepare his effects and take the train back to London. It proved an awkward moment in his relationship with Alice; yet, in an age when engagements were often protracted, Charles undoubtedly saw promotion as improving his marriage prospects and confided as much to Alice. A further complication arose concerning Henry, Charles' younger brother, still working with him as an assistant computer and living in his observatory apartments. Once Charles accepted the Greenwich position, Challis would no longer countenance this arrangement, forcing Henry to accompany his elder brother to Greenwich in the hope of finding fresh employment there.

After Charles announced his decision, a disappointed Challis confided to Airy that 'he is a very deserving young man and is well worthy of a better situation than his present one'.[69] The loss of such 'a valuable assistant' was further acknowledged by the local Board of Visitors.[70] In the same vein, the letter which his colleague Breen sent him after the event confirmed that Charles' astronomical contribution had been significant; he reported that 'very little has been done since you left ... We are still engaged on the 49th Meridian work which you had left almost completed if you remember'.[71] At the time of his departure at age 28, Charles had his talent acknowledged and his ambition recognised. His hopes for a period of leave to spend time with his family at Greenwich were to be disappointed. Challis would not release him until 27 April, while Airy demanded he arrive at the Royal Observatory before the end of the month to 'learn the arrangement of the galvanic wires which are somewhat complicated and require much study,'[72] relenting only to allow him 'one or two days of holiday if you desire it'.[73]

3

The Opportunity of a Lifetime: London to Adelaide (1854–55)

Todd's new appointment to the Royal Observatory was different from any of his previous assignments. He was no longer confined to long hours of observation, but spent his time away from the Royal Observatory assisting Airy's new collaborators, the Electric Telegraph Company and the South-East Railway Company in their joint time distribution projects. The Observatory had already been connected by electric current to the southeast railway line and to time balls erected in the London Strand and at the central post office. But problems with these ambitious long-distance experiments persisted, sometimes intractably, before a regular time service was established.

Todd knew upon his arrival at Greenwich that his decision to return had been the correct one. As Dunkin had intimated, the Observatory had been undergoing a steady transformation during Charles' years at Cambridge. In 1851 Airy had installed his remarkable transit circle, quickly recognised as a model of accurate astronomical timekeeping.[1] By wiring the transit circle and his new Shepherd's clock to the Observatory's own telegraph lines, Airy had begun his ambitious time distribution projects in earnest. When he arrived to start work in May 1854, Charles could hardly have ignored the new master clock mounted at the Observatory gate for the public to see. He soon discovered three more sympathetic clocks installed in the chronometer room, computers' room and Airy's dwelling house on site.[2] These were in turn connected to the large Chester battery room in the basement where some 72 platinum batteries equipped with Smee cells drove time signals the length of the burgeoning telegraph system.[3] Charles' difficult task, as Airy would constantly remind him by letter and in person, was to maintain this galvanic system both within and outside the Observatory. With Henderson now overseas and Dunkin still employed on longitude determinations, Charles was now to all intents and purposes Airy's guiding hand. His departmental associate was William Ellis, well known to Todd since 1841 when they started work together at Greenwich as computers.[4] Like Charles, Ellis had also recently returned from a university observatory at Durham, but without much experience in galvanic practice. Yet Todd, more than his Greenwich associates, understood that he was at the forefront of an exciting technological development and on the brink of a remarkable career in the 'galvanic magic' of the new telegraphy.

By 1854 Airy was looking to expand the time service and reassure the Admiralty that the Observatory's time signals were entirely reliable. As Charles soon discovered, this was far from the case. At its experimental London sites on the Strand, at Lothbury station and London Bridge, Greenwich time signals were not infrequently 'irregular,' 'weak for several days' or simply non-existent. Sent to investigate, Todd sought to remedy ongoing problems of battery power by cleaning contact springs and oxidised connections, before reporting back to Airy that the faulty apparatus were often 'very dirty' or 'exhausted'.[5] Without adequate power, the magnets would not activate the spring to drop the time ball. By now he had learned that while standard Smee batteries were suitable for operating the observatory clocks, telegraph batteries used for sending the time signals to the sites in London were more complex [6] and required ongoing trials, using a greater variety of types to reduce oxidation and prolong battery life.

Despite the frustration and time involved in tracing faults from both ends of the wires, Charles enjoyed meeting and discussing such problems with the new generation of engineers, most of them enthusiastic if at times frustrated by the unpredictability of their new science. A conscientious worker, Todd found himself on more than one occasion caught in a crossfire of different opinions between his ETC contacts and Airy at Greenwich. In the course of his duties he met William Preece, then an electrical engineer with the ETC and rising star of the post office in later years.[7] It marked the beginning of a long professional and family friendship which would endure for half a century. With Preece's colleague, Latimer Clark, who was destined to play a major role in British underwater telegraphy in coming decades, he also enjoyed good relations and would continue a correspondence during his Australian years.[8] During 1854 failures were still relatively common. Preece, for example, reported to Airy in November 1854 that 'the 1 and 2 o'clock currents failed again today' while Latimer Clark complained in the same month that 'our Strand ball frequently fails at one but drops at two,'[9] before Airy himself noted tersely a few days later that 'the current to London failed totally yesterday'.[10] With the London *Times* newspaper following these experiments closely and large crowds gathering at 1 pm to watch the spectacle of the time ball drop, there was much at stake. So much in fact that, by early 1855, Latimer Clark announced the temporary suspension of further time ball drops for fear of 'further unfavourable publicity'.[11]

After considerable outlays in time and money the electric drop of the time ball at the ETC's office in the Strand was discontinued.[12] Todd, in view of Airy's ongoing concern about the accuracy of the London Bridge clock and time ball, continued to monitor them in early 1855,[13] though most of his energies were now being directed to time distribution along the south-east railway line. In comparison with his sustained astronomical training, Todd's telegraph experience during 1854–55, however intense, was still relatively brief. He was fortunate to find a valuable mentor during early 1855 in Charles V Walker, the South-East Railway Company's acclaimed telegraph engineer who had done so much to launch the time signals project and establish railway telegraphy in Britain. By the time Charles began work with the galvanic department at Greenwich, Walker was already a prominent figure among British electrical engineers with a series of successes to his credit, including significant battery improvement, the insulation of telegraph wires with gutta percha (rubber) and the first message by submarine telegraph.[14] After founding the London Electrical Society and editing the *Electrical Magazine* in the 1840s, Walker had by 1850 published an important work on the electric telegraph which sold several thousand copies.[15] In 1854 when Todd began working under Airy's direction, Walker was invited to lecture at the Royal Institution in preparation for his successful election to the Royal Society two years later.[16] Charles was therefore associated with Walker at the high point of his career. Walker, 14 years older than Todd, was both painstaking and accommodating in his dealings with the Observatory and its employees. Along with the ETC's engineers, Airy acknowledged him as a key figure and promoter of the ambitious time distribution projects.[17]

Fortuitous circumstances played a part in Todd's working relationship with Walker whose railway office was strategically located midway between London and Dover at Tunbridge station. It was from Tunbridge, today's Tonbridge, connected by wire to through stations and branch lines, that Walker conducted the business of the South-East Railway's telegraph operations, 'befriending and assisting all stations' including Todd's operations from Greenwich.[18] At Walker's suggestion, Airy had first contemplated sending galvanic currents from the Observatory to drop a time ball at Dover on the southern coast. With the support of the Admiralty, Airy ordered and installed an electric clock and time ball in the old navy yard at the Channel port of Deal north of Dover.[19] First activated by Walker in May 1854 around the time Charles returned from Cambridge, the Deal time ball was not yet fully operational and, for most of 1854, gave Todd considerable trouble. In addition to his London duties, Todd had ongoing responsibility for maintaining the zinc and graphite batteries for Deal signals at the Observatory and for liaising with local workers there in the event of repairs. When the current failed and the time ball refused to drop, Todd *en route* to Deal by train – a distance of some eighty miles – would stop at Tunbridge to confer with the knowledgeable Walker.

In late 1854, electrical problems with the Deal time ball became the subject of regular reporting to Airy. Todd's routine was to set out by morning train from Greenwich, change at Ashford and stay as long as was required at the Royal Hotel in Deal. Finding no one on his initial visit, with the necessary technical information, he proceeded in his own words to 'trace the course of the wires' and make himself 'thoroughly conversant with the circuits and the ball apparatus'.[20] After replenishing the batteries and repairing a fault in the release apparatus, Charles demonstrated the system to local employees the following day and dropped the ball by current before returning to Greenwich armed with a detailed drawing of the Deal circuits with which to make adjustments to the Observatory batteries. A few weeks later, on learning that Greenwich had not received a return signal from Deal, he took an express train to Deal, arriving on the evening of 30 January 1855 with a chronometer which he used to detect a fault in the semaphore clock. With coastal winds blowing 'half a gale from the north-east,'[21] it was not a pleasant trip, and he did not like depending too much on railway officials. In communication with Airy, Todd disputed Walker's own opinion that the fault had arisen 'from a want of battery-power at Greenwich,' and argued on this occasion that the source of the problem existed at Tunbridge, Airy, promising more battery power from the Observatory, could only retort: 'make all *perfectly* right at Deal and let Mr Walker demonstrate. And then make all *perfectly* right at Ashford'.[22] Having given Todd his terse instructions, Airy was watching Charles' performance with unusual interest. For the Deal time ball was not the only thing which now hung in the balance. Unbeknown to Charles, Airy had set him a test as severe as any in his early career and one upon which his future career would now depend.

For several months the Astronomer Royal had been in correspondence with the Colonial Office about a position which had arisen in the colony of South Australia for a superintendent of electric telegraphs 'with desirable experience in astronomical and meteorological observation'.[23] Initially Airy identified Todd's predecessor J.C. Henderson as the person 'of conduct and spirit able to undertake a new enterprise in a new country'.[24] So convinced was Airy that Henderson was the right person for the South Australian position that he undertook to write to him, then in Canada to give him priority. When Henderson politely declined on the grounds that there might not be permanent work in South Australia once the proposed telegraph line between Adelaide and Port Adelaide was built,[25] Airy's dilemma intensified. He next considered Todd, describing his proficiency as 'almost equal to Henderson's' but he still doubted 'whether he [Todd] has the boldness and independence of character which may be required in an Australian establishment and whether he would be willing to leave England'.[26] When Sir George Grey replied impatiently that such a person could still fill the position satisfactorily, Airy, always a stern judge of moral character, decided to make the time ball difficulty at Deal the decisive test of Todd's capacity for the overseas position.

It would indeed prove a test of the sternest order. Todd, while unaware of Airy's intentions, stated as much on 1 February when he declared that 'the arrangement of the galvanic connection between Greenwich and Deal bids fair to be a troublesome matter'.[27] The onset of harsh coastal weather now conspired against any positive result. With snow falling across England until the end of May, Glaisher at Greenwich would later recall how 'the cold set in on the 10 January and continued with little intermission until 26 June'.[28] Airy too, in his official report of 1855, acknowledged the difficult state of affairs at Deal where 'the severity of the weather had frozen the sulphuric acid of the batteries to the state of jelly'.[29] Exposed to the full force of the winter gales over several days, Charles, in defiance of Airy's predictions, exhibited remarkably clear thinking in such trying circumstances. Not for the last time did he demonstrate the combination of physical and mental resourcefulness which would serve him so well in Australia. On 3 February he improvised by pouring seawater onto the frozen plates and, by 5 February, was ready to drop the time ball, reporting back to Airy that 'everything here is now in perfect order'.[30] By 6 February after Walker had attended to the connection at Tunbridge, Airy reported favorably to Todd that his return signal from Deal to Greenwich was now 'very strong and much stronger than formerly,' before recommending he return to Tunbridge to familiarise himself with details of the 'various mechanisms there'.[31]

Airy reacted to Todd's success with a mixture of satisfaction and embarrassment. In correspondence with the Colonial Office he declared that Mr Todd 'has dispatched this business so well as to raise himself greatly in my estimation'.[32] He lost no time in sending a letter of offer to Todd at Tunbridge where he would break the return trip to consult with Walker about the recent situation. After organising a successful time ball drop on 7 February, Todd duly left Deal by train. Continuing bad weather made for significant delays along the line. By the time he reached Tunbridge, he was exhausted and carrying a severe cold after prolonged exposure to the wild weather.[33] Consequently he was in a state of some emotion when Walker, whom he would later describe as a friend, produced Airy's letter and he was able to scan its contents. Until then he had gleaned no knowledge of the protracted Colonial Office inquiry. Todd was deeply grateful. But when Airy, impatient to resolve the matter, pressed him to reply 'as immediately as possible,' he responded the following day that he was keen to consult 'a valued friend at Cambridge' before accepting, and requested two days leave of absence to travel there immediately.[34] Contrary to one biographer's supposition that he must have accepted the offer immediately before consulting Alice,[35] Charles did in fact make a hasty journey in person to put the proposal to Alice. With the prospect of a handsome annual salary of 400 pounds, he was confident that his offer of marriage would now receive a favourable hearing from both Alice and her parents. But would a small colony on the other side of the world prove an attractive location for such a young bride? He may still have harboured misgivings as he arrived once more at Cambridge station.

1855 proved to be a most exciting year in Charles' life, although in the second week of February his future still lay in the balance. Had Alice decided not to accompany him to South Australia, he might well have declined Airy's offer and remained at the Greenwich Observatory. With less than 48 hours to consider Charles' proposal, Alice gave the decisive answer 'I will go with you Mr Todd,'[36] and with it, an acceptance of marriage. Whereupon Charles telegraphed Airy at Greenwich announcing that he was 'quite decided' to accept his offer. When asked in later life what had given him most pride in the course of his long career, he recalled 'the day of my marriage to the daughter of Edward Bell of Cambridge who bravely consented to share my lot in a new and strange land'.[37] The rapid turn of events in February 1855 confirmed that their relationship had indeed been close during Charles' later years at Cambridge. Since his return to Greenwich in the previous year, Charles had enjoyed little free time with

Alice. No letters between them have survived this period, though Charles may have been tempted to use the telegraph to communicate with Alice while travelling and working along the south-eastern railway line. Yet the new electric medium, exciting as it was, proved to be expensive and less suited to the intimacy of their friendship. For her part, Alice would remain an unrepentant letter writer throughout their long years together and, in all likelihood, this was their main form of communication during the hectic 1854–55 period, albeit subject to the maternal scrutiny of Mrs Bell.

With their future decided, Charles would have to postpone their reunion once more in order to meet the pressing demands of his new position. As superintendent of electric telegraphs he was expected to select his own equipment and workers before travelling overseas. On the vital question of recruitment, he resolved the matter expeditiously by recruiting a single assistant, Edward Charles Cracknell, a young married man with 'considerable experience in the management of philosophical instruments'.[38] Cracknell, who would work closely with Todd on telegraphic matters over many decades, was in all probability known to Airy as an instrument maker after arriving in London in 1848. Todd soon put Cracknell to work checking and testing the equipment which began arriving in the coming months. Confident, on the basis of discussions with Airy, that additional staff could be trained after his arrival in Adelaide, he nevertheless took the precaution of contacting the noted South Australian explorer, Charles Sturt, on a range of issues, not least the suitability of local conditions and climate for telegraphic construction. Sturt, as South Australia's former Surveyor General, had first-hand experience of the harsh continental climate during his exploration of its inland river systems.[39] He gave Todd cautionary advice about the practical difficulties he could expect to encounter. In response to Todd's specific questions about the availability of timber and the frequency of storms, Sturt was reassuring but alerted Todd to the ever present threat posed by white ants to telegraph poles in South Australia. To offset such problems, Todd resolved to carry double insulators and to treat poles with cyanide before erecting his lines.[40]

In the flurry of correspondence over equipment, Charles was equally anxious to ascertain the state of astronomy in South Australia for the purpose of ordering the necessary instruments. On this point, Sturt was less encouraging, for although the Adelaide survey department possessed an astronomical clock, Todd would still have to procure a transit instrument for timekeeping purposes. Airy, when offering assistance, was quick to remind Todd that 'astronomy is not your prime business'.[41] From the outset the Astronomer Royal envisaged only 'a small instrument' was required, to be housed in an inexpensive building in Adelaide with little in the way personal assistance. Even though Charles was more ambitious about the prospect of a colonial observatory, his initial astronomical and meteorological equipment remained scanty when compared to the tons of telegraph equipment he was about to procure: 'insulators, galvanised iron bands, zinc and copper plate, cable wire, gutta percha insulation, electric magnets and needles, lightning conductors clocks' and other instruments.[42] Conscious of the wedding date scheduled for early April in Cambridge, Charles worked tirelessly from the family home at Greenwich to ensure that his equipment would be in good working order and available on time for shipment within the next three months. In dealing with a bewildering array of intermediaries and departments, not to mention Airy, Walker and Latimer Clark who provided valuable input, Charles was able, only ten days before the wedding date, to write to the South Australian agent general in London. He appended a detailed list of equipment and estimates worth some £1770, explaining how he 'had bestowed a great deal of consideration and time to the matter with the kind of telegraph I have selected and the quantity of stores I consider it necessary for me to take out'.[43] It was testimony to his organisational capacity and ability to access the necessary advice, although it would be another three months before everything finally fell into place.

With his official preparations now in train, Charles travelled to Cambridge for the wedding which the Bells had undertaken to organise. Before leaving the family home at Greenwich, he received a letter of congratulations from his former Cambridge associate, James Breen, who offered to mentor young Henry Todd should he seek re-employment there, adding of Charles himself that 'you will have to rough [it] a little at first' in Australia.[44] Charles' and Alice's wedding at the St Andrews Street Baptist Church on 5 April[45] was in all probability a simple ceremony at a time when elaborate Victorian weddings were confined to the social elite. Both Breen and Henry would have attended the reception, though Charles would not see Breen again, struck down prematurely at forty by tuberculosis.[46] Strangely no photo of the wedding couple has survived, leading their daughter Lorna to speculate as to whether her 17-year-old mother 'wore white or a dove coloured Pelerine and bonnet' for the occasion.[47] A formal photo taken of the young couple shortly after the wedding however evokes the historic moment – Charles bespectacled in cravat and long coat, sitting with Alice, her hair long and parted, wearing a formal gown trimmed with lace, and her wedding ring visible as she holds up a decorative chain.

Apart from the Cambridge newspaper notice, no detailed account remains of the union, except a brief extract of Charles' speech at the reception, in which he asserted that he was 'going to Australia in the hope of being instrumental in bringing England and Australia into telegraphic communication'.[48] It was a bold statement, consistent with his letter to Sturt in the previous month and worthy of the ambition of his 'big thinking' mentors, C.V. Walker and Latimer Clark. With his brother already in India Charles was not simply thinking about the Adelaide enterprise. At Greenwich in the previous year, he had seen British forces embarking for the Crimea and recognised the strategic importance of telegraphy in the Far East. His role in its relentless extension would indeed come and, once in South Australia, he rarely missed an opportunity to publicise its potential. After the excitement of the wedding, Charles lodged with the Bells at Cambridge attending to personal effects with the same detail that characterised his telegraphic preparation. Among these items were 'toothbrushes for self and Alice for the voyage' and 'hair-pins for Caroline,'[49] Alice's trusted older servant who would now accompany them to Australia. It was socially accepted at the time for women to travel together on long sea voyages. Consequently Charles and Alice were accommodated in separate commodious cabins at the stern of the vessel. There was a further reason for such an arrangement. By the time the party boarded the *Irene* with the Cracknell family in late July, Alice was in the early months of pregnancy, a state which may have been recognised by her mother Charlotte. Charles too was made aware of her condition at the outset of the voyage, for Alice experienced bouts of sickness for the first month, unlike Charles who, after the rough Channel departure, seemed relatively unaffected. Excited by the prospect of fatherhood, he reassured the Bells of her good health in his long October letter, recalling the recent marriages of his sisters and enquiring of their young children. Alice, aided by Caroline had made her own preparations for the voyage, taking her sewing and piano which she played on board for the Sunday service as well as at singing concerts, making her in Charles' words 'a favourite with all'.[50] Caroline, though overawed by their lengthy sea voyage, gave Alice good service both on board and throughout their early Adelaide years together.

A unique personal document of more than five thousand words, Todd's account of the five-month voyage on board the *Irene* provides clear confirmation of the young couple's intention to participate actively in Adelaide society. Conscious of his new official status, Charles took a prominent role on board, befriending Captain Bruce with whom he compared navigational instruments, leading the Sunday church services and other official events, while befriending the passengers, some of them returning to Adelaide with information about conditions in the new

Glass plate of Charles and Alice, c.1855

colony. 'Let [no] one suppose he is going to study at sea,' he began, in his family letter, 'especially when he has pleasant fellow passengers ... I did however study [and] generally practised with the telegraph instruments for two hours a day,' adding that 'Mr Cracknell, I fear, will never make a good reader; in other respects I think he will be very useful and I am very pleased with him'. Limited by the conditions at sea, Todd nevertheless demonstrated his capacity for scientific observation, in keeping with the terms of his appointment. On deck, he was still able to view and identify planets – 'Venus before sunset, Jupiter at sunset'. Having first provided his readers with a succinct account of the calculation of the latitude and longitude at sea, he was in September increasingly interested, in the sight of the southern stars, 'the Magellan's clouds and Southern Cross, conspicuous along with the planet Mercury, which I had never seen in England with the naked eye'.

In further anticipation of his Adelaide duties, he was recording daily variations in the range of temperature on board in a log, attached at the end of his letter, largely for Henry's benefit. As the *Irene* entered the Southern Ocean however they began to experience 'bad cold weather,' in direct contrast to the warnings of passengers about the imminent 'heat, fleas and hot winds' they would encounter in the colony. By early November after reaching the South Australian coastline, prediction became reality when the *Irene* was becalmed off Kangaroo Island and exposed to hot, northern summer winds. On reaching Cape Jervis and Port Adelaide, Charles accompanied by Alice, who was now some five months pregnant, journeyed along the Port Road, stopping three miles from Adelaide to lodge with friends of Mrs Bell, the Halls at Woodville. Despite periods of tedium, Charles and Alice had by then shared moments of humour – trying to dine in swelling seas – of drama – they had almost been demasted on the high seas, and of tragedy – when the Cracknell's infant died on board; all of which left Charles, in his final address of thanks to their captain, 'very grateful to our heavenly Father for having brought us on our way in safety'. Upon arrival, he concluded his long account to his family with the optimistic assurance that 'I have been well received by the Governor and Heads and am, I can assure you, quite an aristocrat here'.

4

Superintendent of Electric Telegraphs

Upon their arrival in Adelaide, the young couple made a more humble start than Charles had his family believe. After their temporary accommodation with the Halls, Charles and Alice settled into unpretentious premises in Sturt Street where their first child, Charlotte Elizabeth (Lizzie) would be born in mid-March 1856.[1] As her pregnancy advanced, Alice continued to rely on Caroline for domestic support, recruiting Irish immigrant girls into service only as their family grew. From the outset, living costs in Adelaide were high while basic commodities like water had to be purchased on a daily basis from a delivery cart.[2] Alice's robust health and sense of adventure proved more than equal to the physical demands of her colonial routine but their early summers in Adelaide tested the young couple, Charles in the field and Alice on her walks to and from the shops in Hindley Street. Todd's comparative meteorological records confirmed the 1850s as a period of soaring temperatures,[3] at a time when his young family had not yet adopted the local practice of escaping to the coast for extended periods during intense Adelaide summers.

For Charles, there were also professional challenges. For while immigrant labour was relatively plentiful at that time, the departure of skilled workers to the Victorian diggings threatened to upset Charles' plan to recruit and train his workers locally. In the weeks after their arrival, Todd and Cracknell spent most of their time landing, checking and transporting telegraph equipment from the Port to their first Adelaide office at Neale's Exchange. While doing so they were perplexed to discover that a makeshift telegraph line already existed between the busy Port and the city. Upon making enquiries, Todd learned that a local entrepreneur, James MacGeorge, had proceeded with its construction despite government advice of Todd's imminent arrival. In the interim, the Adelaide business community rallied behind their 'local man 'and his cheaper alternative.[4] Such sentiment was not unusual; for at that time, domestic telegraphs in Britain were still controlled by private companies like the Electric Telegraph Company with which Todd had dealt, rather than administered by the British government which nationalised them a decade later.

At a time when local infrastructure was a priority in South Australia, Todd was caught up in the divisive politics of colonial development. Within weeks of his arrival, the Superintendent of Electric Telegraphs was summoned by the Colonial Secretary to a personal audience with Sir Richard MacDonnell, the colony's formidable new Governor. If Todd's department had been placed under the administration of the Commissioner of Public Works, there could be little doubt who his real supervisor would be. A tough military officer with a reputation for severity,[5] MacDonnell was an intimidating figure who was not inclined to foster democracy in the new colony or deal kindly with its colonial officials. As it transpired, MacDonnell was still keen for Todd to proceed with his brief to construct a line to the Port, while insisting that he be furnished with a simple statement of the comparative expenses and advantages of the proposed new government line over MacGeorge's existing one.[6] As Airy had intimated before his departure from England, Todd was now expected to put aside his other scientific duties – astronomical and meteorological observation – in order to focus on the relentless building of telegraphs. Under Airy he had passed his first test for the South Australian position in early 1854. Two years later, he was confronted with a fresh challenge at the time when he had yet to erect a telegraph line.

While relatively short, the line between the Port and Adelaide was essential for business in the colony. After furnishing MacDonnell with the relevant details, Todd began the task in early 1856 along the low-lying route, albeit at increased cost in view of the need for a submarine cable at the Port and for underground lines in Adelaide streets.[7] The chief difficulty of the Port line, completed in February, was its lack of profitability in the first year of operation in competition with MacGeorge's more established enterprise. With only meagre profits to be had, Todd would later allude to his fledgling Port venture as 'the day of small things'. Within a short time,

Sir Richard Graves MacDonnell, 1860

he passed his colonial test by building telegraph lines beyond Adelaide to Gawler, with plans for further extensions to Kapunda, Mt Barker and Strathalbyn. While doing so, he began to address the everpresent risk of termite destruction to which Sturt had alerted him by importing jarrah hardwood poles from Western Australia. Along the routes, there was ongoing negotiation with local government boards and residents, anxious about the impact of new telegraph routes on much-needed tree cover, a situation compounded in country districts by the need to clear well back from the lines as a precaution against fire. As he proceeded, Todd reduced the expense of construction, at the same time increasing profitability from £366 in 1856 to £1800 by 1857. As revenue from the Port line increased and MacGeorge's enterprise faltered, Todd recalled that 'we were passing beyond the small things and our infant enterprise had become an established success'.[8] When his Port rival eventually succumbed, Todd tactfully offered to purchase MacGeorge's plant for £60 on behalf of the government and took down his competitor's unsightly wire comprising 'old brown insulators' supported by 'rough and barked gum saplings,' though not before he recruited some of MacGeorge's competent workers to his own telegraph department.[9]

MacDonnell was sufficiently impressed with Todd's work and his handling of the difficult Port situation to accede to a more ambitious request from his Superintendent of Electric Telegraphs: a visit to Melbourne with a view to establishing direct telegraphic communication between the South Australian and Victorian capitals. It promised to be a diplomatic mission of some importance. That the Governor had decided to send Todd in defiance of his Councillors,[10] who believed that Todd's responsibilities were paramount, placed he and Cracknell as Acting Superintendent under renewed pressure. After travelling to Melbourne by steamer in July 1856, Todd met with the Victorian Colonial Secretary and Commissioner for Trade and Customs who introduced him to his Victorian counterpart, Samuel McGowan. McGowan, a Canadian pupil of Samuel Morse,[11] shared Todd's ambition and was planning to link not only Melbourne and Adelaide, but also Sydney and Hobart by telegraph. In the early years of what became a close professional friendship, Todd deferred to McGowan as more knowledgeable, on the basis of his Canadian experience and construction of several lines in Victoria joining Melbourne and the goldfields. One mark of Todd's respect was his willingness to adopt the Morse transmission system which McGowan had introduced to Victoria. In the interests of their joint telegraphic venture, Todd decided, after conferring with McGowan, to employ the American system in preference to his own Henley magnetic instrument on the grounds of its simplicity, cheapness and superiority over long distances.[12] He would still use Grove batteries as in the United Kingdom, while adopting an improved version of Morse's double action instrument for larger centres like Adelaide.

Todd demonstrated a willingness to accept advice from professionals in Melbourne in the same way as he had entered into discussions with telegraph and railway engineers in Britain. As well as McGowan, an early acquaintance with considerable knowledge of telegraphy was the mercurial Joseph Oppenheimer, destined in time to become a close collaborator and family friend. Based in Melbourne in the late 1850s, Oppenheimer was employed by Meyer and Company, suppliers of wire and insulators to the Victorian government.[13] While there, he extended the firm's activities to neighbouring colonies including Tasmania and South Australia. Todd, reporting back to MacDonnell in late July, wrote positively of his first weeks in Melbourne, after the Victorian government instructed McGowan to confer with him on the construction of an inter-colonial line. In the same letter, he was also pleased to report that, after frequent urging of Meyer and Company, 'Mr Oppenheimer and Mr Jackson were planning to visit Adelaide,' assuring MacDonnell that, 'the latter's experience here will be most useful in carrying out our waterworks in Adelaide'.[14]

In Todd's absence from South Australia, Cracknell bore responsibility for the recently constructed Port line to Adelaide. By August he was growing nervous about the prospect of negative publicity during his superior's prolonged absence. Short-staffed and unable to supply Adelaide newspapers with timely information when a night steamer arrived unexpectedly, Cracknell was forced to defend his department from complaints by the Adelaide press about delays during August and September. Exonerated by the Governor on this occasion, he was nevertheless disconcerted by MacDonnell's subsequent visit to inspect his sensitive Henley magnetic equipment at short notice in the company of the recently arrived Oppenheimer. In correspondence with Todd, Cracknell recounted the details of an unfortunate incident during which 'a small particle of dust [had] settled on the point of the switches' disturbing the 'operations of the needle,' adding wryly that 'it had worked well enough all the morning previous but His Excellency must have frightened it as it was all right soon after he left'.[15] On this occasion, Cracknell was saved further embarrassment by Oppenheimer who calmed the situation by observing that the government's Port line was 'the best constructed he had seen for some time'. It constituted a salutary moment for Todd; for when Oppenheimer returned to England a few years later, he maintained a long professional correspondence with his South Australia's Superintendent of Electric Telegraphs, most of which was based upon their shared commitment to improving telegraphy.

Todd spent August in Melbourne working through the details of the joint agreement on the Adelaide–Melbourne line. This involved technical issues and equipment but also financial projections and negotiations over the shared costs of construction. For this reason he kept in regular touch with MacDonnell who supported the initiative in South Australia's Legislative Council. Although Todd made little headway with MacDonnell's request that Victoria pay for part of the line beyond its borders, he knew that the South Australian telegraph line would assist both the Murray River trade and agricultural interests in the south-east of the colony, allowing them to tap the large Melbourne market more effectively. The joint agreement with McGowan, finalised by the end of the month, was essentially a business document which addressed questions of public charges and privacy, as well as a joint resolution that 'proceeds derived from inter-colonial messages should be equally divided' between the two colonies.[16] Todd, still a relatively junior player in the eyes of Victorian authorities, had made significant progress on behalf of South Australia. No less importantly, he had established good working ties with McGowan in preparation for their combined construction phase.

From the outset of his Melbourne visit, Todd planned to return overland from the Victorian border in order to find a viable overland route to Adelaide. Such a journey, comprising hundreds of miles of mostly unsurveyed country, required careful preparation and consultation. By now Todd was riding regularly in the course of his duties; but he was hardly a colonial bushman and his proposed overland journey from Portland on the south-west Victorian coast, the designated connecting point with the Adelaide line, was the first real test of his stamina in the field. On this occasion he relied in part on the exploration experience of South Australia's Commissioner of Police, Peter Warburton, who provided him with a trooper to accompany him through harsh terrain. Unlike much of the Victorian route for which McGowan was responsible, much of the South Australian route still lacked either survey information or an established road system to guide him. Consequently Todd was obliged to investigate not one but multiple routes as he proceeded, covering some 800 miles (1,300 km), more than double the actual distance from the border to Adelaide.

On 2 September, he left Portland for Mount Gambier, 'carefully examining the nature of the country and timber on my way'.[17] The availability of suitable timber for poles along the route was critical if the onerous task of transporting timber was to be reduced. At first the coastal route proved the driest but lack of timber and the limestone soils, which made sinking poles difficult, forced him inland. By late September he reached Guichen Bay where the party remained for several days 'rendered necessary by the tired condition of our horses and the indisposition of our trooper'. Upon resuming the journey on 22 September, Todd inspected country as far as Pelican Point, camping out after finding a suitable way with 'but little clearing and mostly good ground'. Following the ridges to avoid swampy terrain, he then approached the coast and the Coorong Lagoon, describing it as 'extremely picturesque' and 'the soil, sandy, free apparently from rock and requiring no clearing'. After three weeks of travel, he reached the Murray Lakes, having unsuccessfully tried to cross Lake Albert by boat before detouring to Wellington, Goolwa and Strathalbyn where he deemed the dense high scrub blocking his way along the ridges as 'too narrow to erect a line of telegraph'. Armed with a survey of Goolwa, showing the islands and channels at the Murray's mouth, Todd crossed to Hindmarsh Island and proceeded by tramway from Port Elliot to Adelaide.[18] At the time he much preferred the Willunga route to Mt

Barker and Strathalbyn as 'by far the better and easier for the construction of the line'. In the course of one month, Todd and his escort had ridden rough and hard, forcing him, as he confided to McGowan in late October, 'to [compose] my weary bones as well as circumstances will permit'. In a sympathetic response, McGowan informed Todd of his own schedule and plans for another 'pilgrimage' to the Ovens diggings, Portland and Mt Gambier. Gifted with a buoyant temperament like Todd, McGowan remained enthusiastic about ongoing projects in Tasmania and New South Wales, but apprehensive about the impact of the weather on his local construction schedule with 'continued heavy rains retarding progress seriously'.[19] When Todd furnished MacDonnell with a report of his journey and construction estimate of £20,000 in the same month, he urged his own government to begin construction during the summer months in order to avoid similar setbacks. For the South Australian route was longer and its challenges, especially the shifting and sandy channels draining from the Murray Lakes into the sea, would prove formidable.[20]

Having arranged for their respective lines to meet at the border, the Victorian and South Australian construction parties set about their work during 1856–57, with McGowan expecting to complete the Victorian route in early 1858. As colonial rivalries came into play, Todd grew sensitive to comparisons with the more experienced McGowan and to persistent criticism of the inevitable delays. On the question of costs, he was confident that 'returns will be very large' and that 'the line will quickly pay for itself'.[21] In mid-1857, he predicted that the South Australian section from Adelaide would be open as far as Goolwa at the end of that year, after which he planned to lay a submarine cable across Lake Alexandrina to rejoin the wire above ground to Mt Gambier. Deprived of the services of Cracknell who departed South Australia in late 1856 to take up the senior position of Superintendent of Electric Telegraphs in New South Wales, Todd delegated sections of the work and inspected construction as it proceeded, albeit more slowly than he had hoped. The difficulties which arose clearing the bush and transporting poles were, he argued, more severe on the South Australian side than in Victoria; transporting poles up the Goolwa channel proved particularly arduous while 'the erection of a line across the flats had not been unattended with danger; some bullocks had been lost and, in one case, the driver, bullocks and dray narrowly escaped destruction'.[22]

The most challenging part was still to come. The heavy submarine cable which arrived at Port Adelaide in November 1857 had to be transported overland on five drays along the difficult Strathalbyn route to Goolwa, where it was further delayed by a shortage of barges. Meanwhile McGowan was making more rapid progress across the border in opening the Ballarat and Sandhurst lines. The Victorian section was now scheduled to open in early February. Todd still hoped to complete the South Australian section by April, but further complications arose. In addition to ongoing construction delays, Todd faced a series of personal challenges in January during and after the laying of cables under Lake Alexandrina and the adjacent Goolwa and Holmes channels. 'The cable gave us a great deal of trouble,' he later recalled, 'the installation of the line seriously affected by its proximity to the sea'.[23] With official and public expectations running high, Todd worked under renewed pressure to open the line by early 1858. His superior, the Commissioner of Public Works sought to placate MacDonnell and the government over the delay, while Todd wrote to the Adelaide papers, stating it was due to causes 'over which I have no control'[24] and explaining that his exhaustive testing of the underwater sections had shown some of the cable to be defective. Citing McGowan, Todd attributed this 'curious phenomenon' to chemical changes which had occurred during its storage and transport under hot conditions.[25] Eventually the South Australian line was fully opened in late July by MacDonnell, who took the opportunity to deflect criticism of Todd and to praise his 'indefatigable and skilful exertions [of which] he could not speak too highly'.[26]

No sooner was the inter-colonial line in place than the Australian colonies began to grapple with a more ambitious proposal to link the continent to the expanding international telegraph system. As early as May 1858, British civil engineer Lionel Gisborne had written to the Secretary of State for the Colonies proposing an international link from Java to Moreton Bay, using a series of underwater cables.[27] At a time when neither the Red Sea nor Indian cables were yet in place, Todd was asked by MacDonnell, on the basis of Gisborne's letter, to report on the viability of the project and to outline the conditions under which South Australia would be willing to contribute a subsidy to support Gisborne's venture.

Todd, under pressure of clerical work after the completion of the inter-colonial line to Melbourne, penned a detailed report in early December 1858 on the feasibility of Gisborne's scheme. He was still inclined to disregard such proposals until a cable from England to India had been successfully completed – fully a decade away. Of the three schemes under review, he preferred Gisborne's which proposed landing a cable on the north Australian coast. Unlike MacDonnell, however, he thought the scheme 'so important' that the co-operation of all the colonies would be required.[28] In discussions with the Governor, Todd expressed sufficient reservations to sway MacDonnell against outright support for Gisborne's plan. MacDonnell enclosed Todd's report in his reply to Stanley and described the ambitious scheme as premature, specifically because Gisborne had failed to fix a point on the north Australian coast where his cable might be landed.[29] With debate over the international link still in its infancy, MacDonnell reiterated South Australia's preference for a northern overland route a year later, 'though I am not aware that anyone previous to myself has called attention to the latter route and though at first it has few advocates'.[30]

In hindsight, questions have been asked about which of these two notable South Australians should be given credit for first canvassing an overland telegraph route across the centre of the continent. Contemporary historians are quick to agree that MacDonnell, a tireless promoter of land exploration, was its first official advocate.[31] But Todd's input, as MacDonnell acknowledged at the time, was fundamental. In his later years, Todd remained sensitive to allegations that he had merely followed the Governor's lead. Recalling his own interest in an overland scheme, he stated on several occasions that it predated Stuart's successful continental crossing of the 1860s and had been stimulated by A.C. Gregory's expedition across the northern continent into Queensland in 1855–56. Todd also claimed to have first fixed a point of entry at Cambridge Gulf, Gregory's point of departure on the far north coast of Western Australia.[32] Prior to 1859, however, documentation for this speculative claim is inconclusive based on the dates given by Todd.

Complicating the issue of historical authorship is the fact that Todd's report for MacDonnell was never published. However much Todd's retrospective claim as the originator of the idea has been challenged, his input was essential from the beginning and cannot be lightly dismissed. One early biographer, G.W. Symes, believed the question of recognition to be a matter of opinion, describing MacDonnell and Todd as a 'remarkable combination'.[33] Todd certainly acknowledged MacDonnell's official role in his retrospective accounts. The strategic issue which both Todd and MacDonnell had grasped, was not simply the final destination of the cable but its point of arrival on the north coast. Less is known, however, about the influence on Todd of Benjamin Babbage, an explorer and scientist with whom he was on good terms in his early Adelaide years and who played a subsequent role in directing Todd to the journals of John McDouall Stuart.

Within a short space of years, Todd had reached a critical point in his early South Australian career under MacDonnell's powerful patronage. It was certainly at MacDonnell's request that Todd in July 1859 produced a seminal report on the international cable link. With Babbage and Warburton engaged in exploration north of Port Augusta, and Stuart's increasing forays into the interior,[34] Todd was growing more hopeful of an overland solution. His 1859 report, after canvassing four different routes, speculated that an overland route across the continent might yet prove 'the easiest and cheapest mode of joining the Australian capitals'.[35] With the reproduction of his detailed report in the *Sydney Morning Herald*[36] of August 1859, Todd established himself as a colonial authority on proposed international routes. Along with his grasp of the detail and necessary resources, he was arguably the superior strategist in his initial reluctance to commit South Australia alone to what was regarded as an improbable route 'until it [be shown] to traverse country available to settlement'.

At this early stage, Todd, with good reason, viewed any such ambitious project as a collective one, in keeping with Gisborne's view that the large subsidy required would need not one but several colonies to commit to it. Mindful of MacDonnell's forthright views, Todd was also influenced by McGowan and Victoria's position, one which he considered fundamental in any future decision. McGowan, unlike Todd, preferred the sea route proposed from India to King George Sound on the Western Australian coast to Gisborne's own plan for an underwater cable from Java to the Gulf of Carpentaria and Moreton Bay. While keeping the Western Australian option alive, Todd continued to monitor the progress of continental exploration closely and canvass the possibility of an overland route, not least because it 'would not be more than half the distance, while the cost would be only one fourth' of the other schemes under discussion.[37] In view of the fact that Gisborne was proposing to use cables similar to his own ill-fated line under Lake Alexandrina, Todd continue to harbour serious doubts about the likelihood of its success. Shortly afterwards, when the dramatic failure of the exorbitant Atlantic cable venture cast a shadow over Gisborne's hopes, Todd became still more convinced that English investors placed too much emphasis on underwater cables rather than committing to 'long land lines through unsettled country'.[38] A further decade of speculation would elapse before either Todd's predictions or his personal resolve could be fully tested.

During the late 1850s, Todd's substantial responsibilities as Superintendent of Electric Telegraphs, including supervision in the field and negotiations with McGowan, necessitated extended periods of absence from his young family. During his stay in Melbourne, Alice was expecting their second child, Charles Edward, born in April 1858,[39] at a time when his father was still grappling with unexpected difficulties completing the intercolonial line. By now, Charles and Alice were living in more commodious North Adelaide premises, with their own garden and orchard. Writing to her elder sister, Sarah Squires, Alice regretted the 'dear quiet life of old Cambridge,'[40] but enjoyed sitting and reading in her garden and working in the orchard. While Caroline assumed responsibility for young Elizabeth, Alice had been free to go out and visit. The arrival of a second child required greater involvement on her part. In later life, she and Charles were still closest to their elder children; Charles to Lizzie who was talking and reading at a young age; Alice to Charles Edward, in part due to a scare in the pregnancy when she fell from a tree while picking almonds in the garden.[41] Despite Lorna's later remarks about her mother's difficult early situation, Alice's isolation in early Adelaide was in part self-imposed. In keeping with her strict Cambridge upbringing, she was critical of Adelaide society for being 'stuck up ... They think of nothing but dress and going out and giving parties,' confiding to her elder sister that 'I much prefer being at home than going to the grand affairs at Government House'.[42] Her views were not exceptional in South Australia, at a time when the Nonconformists – Methodists, Congregationalist and Baptists – enjoyed numerical superiority and greater influence than in other Australian colonies. Conscious of her improved colonial status, Alice acknowledged that Governor MacDonnell's invitation was 'a great compliment paid to us,' devoid of the discrimination with which the Bells had grown up at Cambridge. She was equally gratified that the colony made vaccination available to her young children, a service unavailable to her own brothers and sisters while growing up in England. In an age of sabbatarianism, Sundays were especially important for Alice as days of rest and worship. As she explained to Sarah:

> Every Sunday morning we get up early and I help Caroline as much as possible ... We all get off to chapel by 10 o'clock ... Caroline enjoys going to a chapel near us as the Ministers are good plain men and she seems to understand everything they say.

Conscious of Charles' official position, Alice attended Government House functions with him, including the Queen's Birthday levee, while reserving the right to criticise the extravagance of Government House society. She could do so, comfortable in the knowledge that many local Nonconformist merchants were equally sceptical of Anglican pretention and the Government House set.[43] The proliferation of churches and Sunday schools in Adelaide during the late 1850s was also to her liking. Within a short time after their arrival, she and Charles aligned themselves with the

Congregationalists, preferring the community-spirited example set by its Reverend Thomas Stow to the 'excessively godly' leadership of the Baptists under David McLaren.[44] As in Cambridge the example set by individual ministers proved decisive in attracting a following. Recruited by George Fife Angas and supported by the London City Mission, Stow proved to be an outstanding preacher and unifying force among the Protestant sects of early South Australia. After establishing a temporary place of worship in Wakefield Street, he campaigned on behalf of the Nonconformists against state aid to established denominations until his resignation due to ill health in September 1856.[45] With Alice committed to charitable work, Charles also became involved in Congregational affairs, serving on a committee to fund and build a new church in North Adelaide. Once an Observatory building became available on the West Terrace Parkland in 1860, the Todds worshipped in the city centre, becoming lifelong members of the historic Wakefield Street Church.

Like Stow and his fellow Congregationalists, who at first worshipped in humble premises, Charles had been forced to suspend his scientific ambitions, pending the provision of suitable premises and equipment. At a number of points, his reports of the 1850s voice growing frustration with his role as Superintendent of Electric Telegraphs to the exclusion of his scientific responsibilities. In January 1858 when Todd first secured funding for meteorological instruments, he regretted that 'my time is too broken' and acknowledged that 'my meteorological observations during the past year possess but little value owing to my frequent absence from home'.[46] On the subject of astronomy however, he continued to report that 'no steps have as yet been taken towards establishing an astronomical observatory for which the large sum of £1200 would be required to provide, not simply a building, but the necessary instruments and electrical connections to Melbourne and Sydney establishments'.[47] Charles' ambition for an Adelaide Observatory had been in part sustained by his visits to Melbourne and encounters with fellow scientists, most notably with Robert Ellery and the distinguished German meteorologist, Georg Neumayer. In later life, when he and Ellery were 'the best of friends,' Todd wrote of their first Melbourne meeting in 1856, that 'you were already doing good useful work' at the Williamstown Observatory, albeit in humble timber premises next to the telegraph office.[48] Ellery was eventually rescued from this unsatisfactory location when the Victorian government belatedly accepted Neumayer's suggestion to remove its operations to an isolated hill above the Botanic Gardens, pending the construction of an observatory there.[49] If Ellery supported Todd's endeavours to the point of lending his South Australian colleague a transit instrument from the former Williamstown site, Todd also found inspiration in Neumayer's charismatic example and personality.[50] Amply endowed with magnetic and meteorological equipment by his Bavarian patron, King Maximilian, Neumayer proceeded to travel extensively throughout Victoria, establishing several hundred magnetic stations in preparation for his comprehensive Victorian study.[51] Before returning to Europe in 1864, Neumayer wrote to Todd recommending that he endeavor to convene an intercolonial meteorological conference in the interests of science, for he recognised in Todd a kindred spirit, capable of pursuing his own unfulfilled colonial ambition.[52]

Upon his return to South Australia, Todd astutely lobbied government in the wake of his successful telegraph projects. At the opening of the intercolonial line to Melbourne, he took the opportunity to address none other than Governor MacDonnell and the Commissioner of Works on the benefits of astronomical science:

> He stood before them not merely as connected with the operation of the electric telegraph, but as the humble representative of another science which is destined to accomplish wonders in the world to which they owed their presence in the colony – the science of astronomy.[53]

Despite the frustrating delay in constructing an Adelaide Observatory, Charles continued to pursue and publicise his astronomical observations. Using Ellery's table of directions, he identified a 'splendid comet,' and provided newspaper readers with information about its antecedents.[54] The *Advertiser* carried a series of reports on the 'long expected comet of 1556' and expressed its gratitude to Todd for his 'valuable astronomical communication'.[55] In his detailed letter to the same paper, Todd recalled his own Cambridge observations of 1850–51 with James Breen, concluding that their observations had been 'of great use to Le Verrier in prov[ing] most conclusively that it was not identical with the celebrated comet of Lexell'. Despite his limited time, Todd continued his press commentaries on a range of astronomical phenomena, most notably comets, conveying information from the Melbourne and Sydney Observatories to the public. In view of his meagre resources during the early Adelaide years, Todd sustained his astronomical endeavours as science educator and practitioner by collaborating with both professionals and amateurs, enjoying early success in recruiting observers outside Adelaide.

By contrast with his telegraph duties, Todd's scientific endeavours proceeded at a snail's pace. In his 1861 report, he conceded that 'no steps have yet been taken towards the erection of the astronomical Observatory'.[56]

Despite the relentless demands on his time, there was no doubting his determination or ambition in urging the building of an observatory, 'conscious that such an establishment as a national one, would require constant attention and a closer application to purely scientific pursuits than I could possibly give'.[57] Before Todd left London, Airy had warned him to moderate his expectations of any such establishment in South Australia. Yet when called upon, the Astronomer Royal acknowledged Todd's determination by providing him with information about appropriate instrumentation and the design of his building. With £350 placed on the parliamentary estimates, Todd had written to Airy in 1858 about the purchase of instruments for his much-awaited Observatory. Two years later, after work on the West Terrace site was completed, he again asked the Astronomer Royal for advice on the building plans, while warning against the likelihood of my 'undertaking much observation work'.[58] Airy replied in the following month advising him on the best position to place an anemometer on the three-storey tower, and recommending 'the smallest transit circle and the largest equatorial' as the 'best for you'.[59] Six months on, Todd was still hesitant about prospects, confiding that:

> My time is so much occupied in the management of the Telegraph Department and involves so many journeys that I feel it would be wrong to undertake other duties so important as the equipping of the observatory at the present moment.[60]

He still hoped to erect a time ball for shipping at the Port and link electric clocks at the Post Office, Telegraph Office and railway terminus. But for the time being he was confined to limited transit observations and occasional observations with the equatorial, his only astronomical observations for that year being 'observations of the Great Comet of 1861 and the transit of Mercury in November,'[61] a phenomenon which he described in the *Advertiser* as 'not of so rare occurrence as a transit of Venus' though 'nevertheless extremely interesting'.[62]

Situated at some distance from the city centre, in a suitable orientation on the West Parklands, the Observatory building was removed from the glare of street lighting and separate from the prestigious institutions which would grace North Terrace. Yet its substantial four acre grounds (1.6 ha) were well suited to the needs of a growing family which now included their second son Hedley, born in mid-1860.[63] A visionary concept, the Adelaide Parklands were nevertheless seen at the time as general purpose space for a range of groups and activities, including arriving immigrants, displaced Aborigines and grazing animals not to mention stone quarries and rubbish tips.[64] The West Parklands site designated for the Observatory previously housed a reception centre and a hospital for newly arrived immigrants.[65] It would take another decade before the management of the Parklands improved and the Observatory took on a dignified appearance. With the appointment of governesses for the children and ground staff, the West Parklands location was fertile territory for Alice's philanthropic work among the poor and destitute of the west Adelaide streets. A far cry from the pretensions of North Adelaide, the small Observatory complex was increasingly the magnet for newly arriving family members during the 1860s, among them Charles' niece, Frances (Fanny) the eldest of Griffith George's children. Family ties drew members of the closely knit Todd and Bell families together across the world. During 1861–62, Alice herself undertook the long return journey on the *Irene* with daughter Elizabeth to visit her parents in Cambridge. To Charles' delight, they returned with Frances, orphaned after the death of her parents in India.[66] Then aged 12, she lived with the Adelaide family, becoming their housekeeper by the end of the decade and befriending the Todd children, who now included two more daughters, Maude and Gwendoline. Both Maude and her older brother Hedley, after his recovery from a serious childhood illness,[67] thrived in the outdoors of their Observatory home, learning to ride and drive from a relatively early age.[68]

In the early 1860s, Todd, unwilling to abandon the idea of an overland route, monitored reports of inland exploration closely in the press. In November 1861, he wrote despondently to Airy of the 'melancholy fate' of the Burke and Wills expedition,[69] while awaiting 'with no ordinary anxiety the result of Mr Stuart's present journey'.[70] Todd continued to pin his hopes on Stuart's northern forays but with the departure of Governor MacDonnell in 1861, he was left to make his case unaided. In early 1863 however, encouraged by the bid of incoming Governor, Dominic Daly to annex the Northern Territory, Todd delivered a detailed address to the Adelaide Philosophical Society on colonial telegraphy in the presence of the new Governor. In his impressive exposition, Todd again floated the option of an overland line to the north coast, 'but only on its being shown a route could be found which would be available for occupation'.[71] While optimistic that Gisborne might yet adopt his own longstanding project, Todd still faced considerable local scepticism. One member of Stuart's exploration party who was present at the meeting, F.G. Waterhouse, contradicted the speaker on the vital questions of available inland timber and the practicality of sinking poles into the hard granite of the MacDonnell Ranges. In the ensuing discussion, Todd defended his claim on the basis of his experience along the Adelaide–Melbourne line, most notably concerning the unsuitability of soils and the prospect of damage to the line by the Aborigines. For Waterhouse and other South Australians, such an inland route could never compete in commercial terms with a land line from Moreton Bay in Queensland. Summing up the inconclusive Philosophical Society debate, the Chief Secretary warned that rapid pastoral expansion into the Plains of Promise of north west Queensland would ensure that the northern colony developed its own overland connection to the Gulf of Carpentaria, unless South Australia established a successful settlement on the north Australian coast. In the face of these serious reservations, Todd, encouraged by South Australia's successful annexation of the Northern Territory in late 1863, was undeterred. In official reports, he maintained his claim that 'no insuperable obstacle stood in the way of the overland route'.[72]

If Todd, unlike McGowan in Victoria, was optimistic about the prospects of an inland telegraph route, he was less sanguine about the uncertain state of underwater cable technology. After a series of expensive failures, neither the British government nor British cable companies were prepared to invest in high-risk expensive ventures in the early 1860s. Only with the belated success of the Atlantic cable in 1866 did their reluctance give way to qualified optimism. In late November of that year, Todd, writing to Oppenheimer in England, expressed renewed confidence that:

> The success attending the Atlantic Cable Expedition this year is very gratifying and, should both cables continue to work well, we should have entered on a new era of ocean telegraphy and Australia will soon be voltaicly united to the Mother Country.[73]

Although South Australia's early attempts at northern settlement proceeded tentatively, news of Goyder's survey expedition to the Northern Territory[74] encouraged Todd in the hope that 'should the nascent colony go ahead, telegraphic communication will soon follow'.[75]

With an upsurge of international cable proposals to construct connections from India to King George Sound (Western Australia) and from Java to the north Australian coast, Todd continued, in his widely disseminated reports, to report on the financial and strategic merits of each proposal, while recommending that the colonies co-operate in this 'great work'.[76] While Gisborne's renewed efforts were no more successful than previously, the British Indian Telegraph Cable Company (later the Eastern Telegraph Company) was now poised to enter Asia, floating a new company for this purpose, the British Australian Telegraph Company

(BAT) in order to connect Singapore to the Australian mainland. In spite of his own hopes for South Australia, Todd's commentaries maintained a national perspective in recommending that, whatever the outcome, colonial governments retain control over their land connections and fix charges collectively by joint conference, leaving overseas companies to bear the risk of underwater construction. Todd recognised that the stakes were high and that the outcome was destined to shape colonial telecommunications for the rest of the century.[77] As the focus of colonial interest shifted from Western Australia to a connection from Java on the grounds of reduced cost, Queensland, supported by Todd's former deputy Charles Cracknell in New South Wales, came out in support of a different proposal by the Eastern Asia Telegraph Company to land an underwater cable line on the Queensland coast in the Gulf Carpentaria, albeit subject to financial support from the Dutch and Indian colonial governments.[78]

By early 1869, Captain Sherard Osborn, with backing from the British Indian Telegraph Company, was offering to replicate Queensland's scheme, independent of Dutch support and with the more flexible option of landing its cable in either the Northern Territory or Queensland. The British Indian Telegraph Company, led by future cable king John Pender and other influential Manchester merchants, was in the throes of laying a series of cables between England and India, with ambitions of further eastern expansion.[79] In correspondence with Osborn during 1869–70 Todd canvassed both the west coast and eastern seaboard options before mooting a transcontinental line from Port Augusta in the lead up to Osborn's Australian visit of April 1870.[80] With the real likelihood that an international link would soon proceed, business considerations weighed more heavily in negotiations. Not only did Osborn and the newly-formed BAT, with whom he was affiliated, choose to deal with individual colonies to the exclusion of others, they sought to shut out future international competitors by insisting on exclusive rights to colonial subsidies for a ten-year period. Instead of forming a common front, as Todd had hoped, individual colonies, including South Australia, proved vulnerable in their negotiations to the BAT's relentless policy of divide and rule.

Todd's conduct during Osborn's historic visit became the subject of a protracted controversy. On his arrival in Adelaide, Osborn was referred by Governor Fergusson to the Chief Secretary, H.B.T. Strangways, a forceful but unpopular Liberal politician who subsequently took most of the personal credit for snatching success from Queensland on behalf of South Australia in a race for the BAT contract. According to his later version of events,[81] Strangways sent Osborn to Todd as the local authority on telegraphic construction; but upon receiving little satisfaction, Osborn duly returned to the Chief Secretary for advice. Strangways would further imply that Todd had been tardy in supplying him with the urgent report he requested, with which to assure the BAT of his government's intention to proceed. Had Todd, a keen political strategist, really prevaricated as Strangways later claimed? Strangways' account of the episode, written in the early 20th century before Todd's death, dismissed him as a young civil servant who 'always discharged his official duties efficiently [but] never took any unnecessary responsibility on himself'. Theirs was an unlikely political alliance, given Todd's friendship with Governor Fergusson and the prospect of a fresh election in mid-1870.[82] In his own version of events, Todd asserted that, before Strangways sent Osborn to him, he himself had visited Governor Fergusson to recommend proceeding with the project; after which, 'anxious it be done either by the Governor or by the Commandant,' he afterwards consulted with Strangways himself and had 'a keen remembrance of the pleasure you stated in an undertaking I had so long cherished'.[83]

That Todd had indeed taken decisive steps was abundantly clear from his report of 18 April to the Treasurer.[84] On the basis of several interviews with Osborn, Todd enumerated the advantages of working with 'an experienced and powerful company' and recommended that legislation be introduced to raise a loan for the construction of an overland line. Well aware that under the influence of Queensland, the BAT might choose to bypass Port Darwin and land a cable at Burketown in the Gulf, Todd was keen for the South Australian government to construct a line to Port Darwin to connect to the incoming BAT cable. He did not automatically exclude Queensland on that account. Instead, he canvassed a number of options in his report, including the land line which the BAT had proposed from Port Darwin to connect to Queensland. With commendable objectivity, he mooted the possibility of inviting Queensland to connect with South Australia's cable at the Roper River to 'remove all cause for jealousy,' and the benefit of sharing cable revenue, predicting that the BAT would support 'two independent routes' rather than a single line as less prone to interruption. Was it this conciliatory tone which Strangways mistook for indecision, as MacDonnell had done previously? Replete with statistics and the costing of £80 per mile for the two possible routes to either Port Darwin or the Roper River, it was undoubtedly a timely document, if optimistic in estimating overall construction at £120,000. Even at this late stage of events, Todd still considered the enterprise to be a collective undertaking, a view supported by South Australia's Treasurer John Hart and others in the parliament on financial grounds.[85] Strangways' dismissive account of Todd was contradicted in the parliamentary debate over the Bill, during which several members acknowledged Todd's input, including 'very valuable information on the subject'.[86]

When a second Strangways administration introduced a Port Darwin Telegraph Bill in May 1870, Hart's preference for the construction of a line jointly funded with Victoria was overridden in favour of legislation empowering South Australia to proceed alone. The majority of parliamentarians enthusiastically endorsed Strangways' Bill and were prepared to repudiate Queensland's prior claim to the international cable, comfortable in the belief that 'they would not be going in the face of Mr Todd but following his recommendations'. Todd had in fact canvassed several options in his report to the Treasurer but, after discussions with Osborn, he recognised that neither Queensland nor the BAT might countenance a land connection with South Australia at the Roper River.[87] If a new Hart Ministry continue to harbour doubts about the prospect of a 'white elephant,'[88] a few members led by Ebenezer Ward roundly condemned the overland project as 'the maddest scheme ever introduced'.[89] Although Strangways' colonial career would end prematurely, Ward, a liberal newspaper proprietor and future Todd departmental Minister for Agriculture and Education, would prove a tireless parliamentary controversialist. In later years he would re-emerge as one of Todd's most vindictive critics.

Even after the Bill was passed, confusion persisted. Was Osborn acting on behalf of his own company, the Telegraph Maintenance and Construction Company or for the BAT, the Pender Company with which it was affiliated? It was a dilemma which neither Strangways nor Todd could resolve. Only South Australia's resolute Agent General in London, Francis Dutton, who shrewdly bought BAT shares to attend its meetings, could unravel this enigma. Not until mid-August of 1870 however, was he able to confirm that the company had indeed declined Queensland's last-minute request to carry its cable around the coast to Burketown.[90] In September, the BAT was still insisting that South Australia introduce further legislation before it would proceed, repudiating Todd's statement that its proposed completion date of 31 December 1871 was 'a moral notice not a legal one'. Reviving the Queensland option, the BAT now insisted that, should South Australia breach its contract and fail to meet this deadline – little more than a year away – it would be 'empowered to construct alternative lines by land line from Port [Darwin] to another point on the coast'.[91]

Part II

'Out of adversity': Enterprise and Acclaim (1870–86)

5

The 'Great Work' and its Aftermath (1870–73)

As events continued to unfold rapidly, Todd had, in the space of a few months, moved centre stage. He was no longer simply a local source of advice, but recognised as the planner and potential architect of the entire overland telegraph scheme. Overawed by the scale of the task, he later confided how he had spent 'sleepless nights' and 'anxious hours' grappling with the enormous logistical difficulties it presented.

> It was my life's ambition; what I had eagerly looked forward to, but now that its weight rested upon me, I must confess it at times seemed too heavy to bear.[1]

His capacity to launch such an initiative was confirmed by the important decision to divide the line's construction into three sections, 500–600 miles in extent, with each allotted to five or six parties covering some 100 miles (160 km)[2] in order to progress the whole work simultaneously. Yet, he still lacked co-ordinating authority, after the South Australian government placed both the southern and northern sections in the hands of private contractors, leaving Todd to supervise the long central section. It was hardly a case of Todd 'running his own show'. Political hubris, of the kind exhibited by Strangways and his fellow politicians, was alive and well throughout the project, not to mention competition from fellow managers and workers in the field. In deciding to accompany his workers, Todd would operate outside his usual Adelaide environment, and would be dealing with hardened bushmen, not all of whom were from South Australia or used to taking orders. Todd knew that the long labour of construction which the telegraph project entailed would leave his larger parties, totalling some 500–600 workers in all, more vulnerable than Stuart's expeditions, with the attendant risks of limited water supplies and scurvy. Accused of being 'too soft' on his workers at the time of his appointment as Postmaster General,[3] Todd would prove an inspiring leader, capable of dealing with difficult individuals, while evincing an everpresent concern for the welfare of his workers.

As overseer for the central section, Todd consulted with Benjamin Babbage about Stuart's surveyed route and was soon made aware that it diverged considerably to the east, and if replicated, would increase the length of his own task by over one hundred miles.[4] The alternative was to proceed to the west of Stuart's route and find a way through the towering granite cliffs of the MacDonnell Ranges which threatened to block the advance of his own parties. In early July 1870, he directed John Ross to proceed north to Beltana, where a small surveying party would be provisioned 'to determine the best route for the line of electric telegraph with a view to cut Stuart's tracks north of the Centre'.[5] Time was critical, since Todd planned for his own construction parties to reach the start of the central section by late September.

In other respects, Todd's detailed instructions adhered closely to Stuart's in cautioning his construction parties of 15–20 persons to 'advance only after water sources had been identified'.[6] He also cited Stuart on the value of 'digging in the beds of circles' when looking for water, adding that 'mound springs may sometimes be discovered by a fringe of rushes or reeds upon an apparent sandhill'. The existence of such springs, later to be recognised as 'natural outlets for the waters of the great Australian Artesian Basin,'[7] proved essential for central Australian explorers such as Stuart and those who emulated him. Benjamin Babbage, who had identified such sites in the late 1850s during survey work around Lake Torrens, confirmed their value in discussing Stuart's journals with his friend. The extent of these water sources, upon which the Aborigines also depended, would not only dictate the expedition's progress, but also the location and establishment of telegraph stations which Todd planned to construct along the route, notably at Strangways and Peake stations, for 'although the water quality was poor – rain water having to be collected for the batteries – it [would be] suitable for the horses and camels,' keys for the line maintenance.[8]

In planning the entire line, Todd also realised that Stuart had diverged to the east of a direct Port Darwin route, before reaching the northern coast near the Roper River in the Gulf of Carpentaria. George W Goyder, South Australia's well respected Surveyor General, was one who had successfully surveyed the Northern Territory coast in the vicinity of Port Darwin. Only Goyder and his band of experienced surveyors from the arduous 1868–69 northern expedition possessed the requisite field experience to follow Stuart's charts and, where required, take new surveys along the way. Despite rivalry between the survey and telegraph departments, Todd enjoyed good relations with Goyder, an administrator of great energy and good will like himself, who generously offered Todd the use of experienced surveyors, many of whom would serve with distinction as overseers of Todd's overland parties. For all the talk of an empty continent, Todd was sufficiently familiar with Stuart's journals to recognise the prospect of Aboriginal resistance. Stuart avoided confrontation and restricted the size of his parties for greater mobility, unlike Burke and Wills who had moved more slowly, burdened down by stock and equipment. After consultations with Goyder, Todd adopted his colleague's policy of non-fraternisation towards the Aborigines[9] and incorporated it into the long list of regulations he was preparing for overseers of the telegraph construction parties. To avoid open confrontation, loss of life and time, Todd's instructions made it clear there was to be no communication with Aboriginal women, the 'property of natives was not to be touched' and 'no one is to visit the natives without special permission'.[10] For the purpose of self-protection, each worker was issued with a pistol and with instructions on how to use it, although Alfred Giles, who accompanied the expedition, recalled that they were 'old-fashioned' with 'flimsy cartridges,' so that there was 'always uncertainty about whether they would go off'.[11]

Once he had dispatched Ross and McLachlan to explore northern gaps in Stuart's route, Todd prepared, in late August, to send off the northern construction party on the steamer *Omeo*, and could be seen on the wharves busily engaged 'to the last minute' in its preparations.[12] In a characteristically optimistic farewell address, Todd again stressed the 'national importance of the project' and his own 'feelings of confidence' in the superior preparation and equipment taken on board. In spite of the fact that the northern section had been contracted by private tender, with Adelaide surveyor, William McMinn appointed as government overseer, Todd continued to stamp his personal authority on the project. A week later, he was recruiting and briefing parties for the central section which were also due to leave Adelaide and travel inland 500 miles (800 km) north from Port Augusta to Mt Margaret and the Peake to begin poleing. In order to supervise the central section, Todd decided at the outset to absent himself from Adelaide, leaving his deputy, W.J. Cunningham, in charge of the Post Office, while he travelled up the southern section, by now in the start-up phase. Alfred Giles, who joined the venture, remembered that 'we first had to attend at Mr Todd's office to sign-on and were informed that our wages were to be one pound a week and food'.[13]

Giles who, like Edward Bagot, was heavily involved in the project from the outset, later wrote of the preparations at Port Augusta, as the southern terminus, during July–August 1870, that 'the magnitude of the work would scarcely be estimated by the present generation'.[14] With the arrival of the southern and central construction parties, it was transformed into a giant depot for thousands of sheep and hundreds of bullocks, horses and camels, in preparation for an epic endeavour akin to the great wagon trains of the American West.[15] Bullocks were deemed critical in the outback for heavy work, although camels, introduced into South Australia on Thomas Elder's northern runs, were also made available to the expedition.[16] Their value to the expedition was soon to be demonstrated by their Afghan drivers, who used them to transport poles and wire up the line.[17] Drawn not only from Afghanistan but from the Indian Subcontinent and Middle East, the cameleers would continue to play a vital role as outback carriers for the rest of the century. Todd had contemplated using camels as early as 1863, and his field diaries confirm the involvement of the Afghans in the preparatory stage. In early November 1870, he and Babbage took the opportunity to familiarise themselves with their Muslim religion and customs, visiting their camp at Beltana, 145 miles (230 km) to the north of Port Augusta, and meeting with their spiritual head, Hadji Mullah Meharbarn, 'a fine intelligent man' as Todd described him.[18] Eager to adhere to the tight timeframe of the project, and in the continuing hope of expanding the colonial horse trade from India via Port Darwin, the expedition would still rely heavily on bullocks and horses, though the latter were frightened by camels and more inclined to drain valuable outback waterholes in their extreme thirst.

Todd's diaries of the trip north from Port Augusta provide a detailed account of the conditions and of his complex responsibilities in the field. He had delegated his portfolio responsibilities in Adelaide, but the South Australian government continued to consult him in his absence. Knowing that it was essential to publicise the project, Todd sent back regular reports to Adelaide, declaring that 'everything so far has gone well'.[19] In the field, he was preoccupied with provisioning the parties and organising the movement of telegraph materials, a task shared between the camels and bullocks, the latter capable of travelling no more than fifty miles per week.[20] His own party, comprising 25 workers with teams of horses and bullocks travelled slowly, accompanied by a 'great number of auxiliary contract teams bearing rations and materials weighing many hundreds of tonnes'.[21] Despite the monotony of the landscape, he enjoyed the outdoors, describing the south-east breezes as 'bracing' and the atmosphere as 'wonderfully transparent'.[22] Each morning, Todd, Babbage or Giles took their bearings using a sextant or theodolite, in order to align their movement with Stuart's previous charts. A constant concern of Todd and the surveyors accompanying him was the availability of timber along the route for use as telegraph poles. It would afford a variable and, at times, meagre supply, 'plentiful at Mount Eyre' but 'not so plentiful nor nearly so fine at Greenwell Creek' the following day.[23] For the purposes of the central section, Todd's parties could not rely on locally available timber, and would have to wait for most of their supplies to arrive before proceeding. After reaching the Peake with Todd on 10 November, William Whitfield Mills wrote that 'several men became unwell' and recounted how 'at the Sunday church service of 23 October, the Bible reading could not proceed because the flies were 'almost blinding'.[24]

Todd stayed at the Peake depot, the designated end of Bagot's section, for most of November, returning south to Strangways Springs (see Map 2) to hear of Ross' inconclusive forays to the north, after which he sent one of the overseers who had fallen ill back to Port Augusta.[25] For the purposes of his central section Todd delegated authority to a hand-picked team of surveyors, among them A.T. Woods a Goyder recruit, who was eventually responsible for finding the critical route through the MacDonnell Ranges. By December, Todd had moved south to Mount Margaret and Beltana, in order to organize the northwood movement of building materials and supplies for the different section parties. The first of the six sub-sections had already begun work north from the Peake in January 1870. But the most northern of Todd's parties, under W. Harvey, was not scheduled to begin poleing until late May 1871, little more than six months before the date of the South Australian contract deadline.[26] Todd's instructions to his overseers were suitably strict and precise concerning each of their tasks assigned to the six teams, from cutting timber to digging and raising the telegraph poles.[27] It was exacting work in harsh conditions with limited tools. Todd left nothing to chance, even illustrating his precise instructions and warning his overseers against 'any departure from the specifications which may lessen the stability or insulation of the line'.[28] Once these were issued, Todd returned from Beltana to Port Augusta, stopping along the way to inspect the southern section and confer with E.M. Bagot, the southern contractor who had begun poleing in early October. On his return to Adelaide, Todd remained confident about the outcome, affirming that 'there seems every prospect of the work being completed within the specified time'[29] and that 'my plans have prospered beyond my expectations' in a summary report for the English mail.[30]

In reality, progress was being made primarily in the southern section rather than in the centre, where his parties were still searching for a gap through the MacDonnell Ranges. On the basis of Woods' regular reports of late 1870–early 1871, Todd became 'seriously dismayed'[31] at the lack of success in finding a path through the Ranges. Only on 11 March 1871, did one of his surveyors, William Whitfield Mills, discover a passage 'about thirty miles east of Stuart's track with numerous waterholes and springs, the principal of which is the Alice Spring which I had the honour of naming after Mrs Todd'.[32] To Mills, rather than Ross, also went the distinction of naming the nearby Todd River (Map 2), which, though usually a dry creek bed, had now begun to flow after the summer rains.[33] Although he was no longer in the field, Todd recognised these finds as auspicious as well as personally satisfying, in so far as they confirmed a passage through the Ranges for his central section and the discovery of much needed permanent water. On the northern section, by contrast, early progress in constructing the line under the supervision of Darwent and Dalwood had been hampered by the onset of monsoonal rains. Their parties only managed to clear a further hundred miles of track to the south of Port Darwin before a series of strikes and the departure of some forty workers led William McMinn, the young government overseer, to take an unprecedented decision. In early May 1871, McMinn abruptly cancelled the northern contract of Darwent and Dalwood on the grounds of 'mismanagement' and their 'inability to do the job'.[34] Kept at arms length by the political ministry of the day, Todd deplored McMinn's decision after he learned of the news. For, when Darwent and Dalwood's parties abandoned their work and prepared to return angrily to Adelaide, it lost the expedition much needed time and labour.

Todd knew that, after protracted negotiations in May between the BAT and the South Australian government, a formal contract, had been finalised under which the financial penalties for failing to meet the looming January 1872 deadline were considerable. In the event of breach of contract, the terms of agreement specified that South Australia would be expected to service the 6% per annum interest on the massive underwater cable loan. Moreover, the company was empowered under article 12 of the same agreement to extend its underwater cable beyond Port Darwin to Queensland in the event that South Australia failed to complete the task.[35] It imposed a policy of brinkmanship, with 'all the elements of high drama' throughout 1871, as the BAT 'contrived to get one colony against the other ... to ensure an outcome which would be most favourable to itself'.[36] Political broadsides erupted during the same month, when Queensland's Superintendent of Telegraphs, William Cracknell, brother of Todd's former associate, cast doubt over South Australia's chances of success, asserting that 'there seems little prospect of the work being completed for many months' and concluding that 'the Port Darwin line will not be completed by the time specified and when completed cannot be depended upon for regular communication'.[37] Todd was sufficiently incensed by Cracknell's prediction to issue a public rebuttal which was printed in the press throughout the colonies, while South Australian Chief Secretary, William Milne, undertook to write to his counterparts in the eastern colonies insisting that 'there seems every probability of communication being established at the end of the present year.' He went on to elaborate South Australia's substantial progress in 'erecting 700 miles of line' and transporting 'large quantities of material' besides cattle and sheep into 'the very heart of Australia'.[38] As public champion of the 'great work,' Todd's optimism was undiminished. But upon learning of McMinn's precipitous decision in July, he sensed in private that Queensland, which was rapidly progressing its own telegraph line up the eastern coast as far as Cardwell by early 1870, remained a serious competitor. Should the South Australian project founder, Queensland was poised to extend its inland route as far as Normanton in the Gulf to join with the underwater cable.[39]

After belatedly learning of McMinn's action in July, Todd acted quickly, instructing his central parties to continue poleing beyond their designated limit into the abandoned northern section. He also dispatched additional rations to his crews and, at emergency cabinet meetings of the government, argued that the Roper River (Map 1), which enjoyed access to the hinterland south of the Katherine, should be made the base for a rescue expedition, instead of Port Darwin.[40] Todd had reliable information that the Roper was navigable and that a depot upstream would save much needed time and labour in provisioning construction parties inland. His recommendation was overruled by Chief Secretary Hart and responsibility for the northern section entrusted to a railway engineer, Robert C. Patterson. Todd's frustration over the decision led him later to observe, not without bitterness, that 'the whole of Mr Patterson's expedition was sent to Port Darwin and to this may be attributed nearly all his disasters'.[41] Patterson, charged by the South Australian government to lead the second relief fleet, was a tough-minded and experienced engineer, but he was, from the outset, frustrated and pessimistic about the outcome of his assignment.

Independent and proud by nature, he listened to and concurred with Todd's argument to adopt the Roper as the expedition's preferred base of operations. The Hart government's intransigence now precluded this, while it also deemed Patterson's stock – some 500 bullocks and 170 horses – sufficient for him to complete Darwent and Dalwood's abandoned work. Upon his arrival in the north in mid-September, Patterson confirmed the seriousness of the situation at Port Darwin, with 'work at a standstill'.[42]

Patterson, who designated himself Master of the Northern Expedition in official correspondence, was soon at odds not only with the government resident at Port Darwin, Boyle Travers Finniss over the conduct of the expedition,[43] but also with J.A.G. Little, Todd's senior departmental officer who had been appointed to head the Port Darwin telegraph office. Like Todd, Little found Patterson to be determined, but stubborn and single-minded. During one such incident, Patterson persisted in sending a construction party further south, despite Little's objection that 'we would have no way of keeping them in supplies'. After which Little noted tersely in his diary that 'no argument of mine would move him'.[44] Complicating Patterson's and Little's testy relationship was the presence of Todd's nephew, Griffith George Todd. A young cadet who had accompanied Little to Port Darwin, Griffith was put to work on the wharves and in the telegraph room. In volunteering for Port Darwin, he was following in the footsteps of his deceased father, also Griffith George, who had volunteered for the Bengal Marine service of the East India Company in the 1840s.[45] Writing to his brother Charles in Adelaide from Port Darwin, Griffith described the outdoor conditions as 'very rough ... tallying cargo as it comes ashore from the *Bengal* ... We commence at 6 am and work until 6 pm with two hours interval between 12 and 2 – when it is too hot to work'.[46]

Little, his supervisor, was experiencing increasing difficulty in rallying his workers as the tropical summer advanced. When the *Gulnare*, sent from Adelaide to Port Darwin with men and materials for the Roper River, ran aground in October, Little described it as 'disheartening' and a 'crushing blow for Patterson'.[47] The arrival of the cable ship, the *Investigator*, at Port Darwin in late October to bring the underwater cable ashore, briefly revived hopes of reinforcement, until its Captain Halpin set too high a price on making the relief trip to Adelaide. Gloom again descended upon the expedition, compounded by the conviction that failure to complete the land line would jeopardise the cable agreement. Little was despondent at the thought of such 'a fine steamer lying idle, when there is every prospect that our men are starving, probably dying and the whole expedition failing'.[48] Furious with the government, Patterson affirmed, in his reports to Todd, that 'success was never possible with Port Darwin as the base of operations' and strongly recommended that 'the expedition could only be saved by strong reinforcements of stock and plant from Adelaide to be sent to the Roper'.[49] Back in Adelaide, Todd grew increasingly frustrated with the tactics of the Hart ministry. Conscious of the looming January deadline, he used Patterson's reports in cabinet meetings to exert pressure on the Ministry over its refusal to countenance the Roper as the alternative site of operations. The commercial interests and government members dictated that Port Darwin would remain the major northern port. Only in December 1871, after Little confirmed the gravity of the northern situation, did the Hart Ministry overturn its original decision and summon Todd to head a new relief expedition. It was a humiliating backdown, one which Todd savoured more than he could publicly admit, though he did not 'look forward to any recognition by the Hart government'[50] and publicly castigated it after the event for incurring additional expense of £30,000–£40,000 in delaying the Roper option.[51]

With the onset of the wet season and his remaining bullock teams decimated by pleuro-pneumonia and exhaustion,[52] Patterson further lamented to Todd that 'the horses cannot stand the climate and they are too light for the work'.[53] Unwell, medicated and 'not relishing getting up at all,'[54] Patterson fully expected to be replaced and informed Todd that he was 'only too happy to be relieved of his post ... The invincible force of circumstances having been against me from the beginning'.[55] Patterson was also becoming apprehensive about the capacity of his parties to receive supplies or defend themselves. One of Ralph Milner's party, contracted to drive sheep up the line, had been killed at Attack Creek (Map 1), and the same party set upon at Newcastle Waters by a large group of blacks, 'being compelled to fire' and 'only getting through the country by a miracle'.[56] In early November, Burton's northern party had also been ambushed and forced back to the Katherine when trying to reach the Roper River overland.[57] As he prepared the *Bengal* to depart Port Darwin for the Roper, Patterson was aware that the Roper was very different territory from Port Darwin, where the Larakita (Larrakeeyah) were generally friendly, albeit under siege from their hostile neighbours, the Woolner (Djerimanga).[58] In correspondence with Todd, he confessed his apprehension to Todd at the prospect of renewed attacks on ration parties approaching the Roper landing, estimating the number of natives involved in one such instance at 'from 100 to 200'.[59]

The task now looked more formidable than ever. But Todd, optimistic by nature, remained a cool strategist with a clear overview of the entire project. For he knew, in spite of Patterson's depressing dispatches, that steady progress was being made by parties elsewhere. Since mid-November, section B of the South Australian leg had been completed and, by the end of the following month, poles in sections C and D of the central section were also up and ready. At his instructions, Todd's own teams, having completed the central section, were advancing into section E further north, as the wet began to descend. Had the Darwent and Dalwood fiasco been avoided, he mused, the line might well have been ready by January and onerous financial penalties avoided. Although Todd would have preferred to wait out the wet season before proceeding north, the government's insistence forced him to prepare for a prompt departure. With a mixture of elation and apprehension, Todd said his farewell to family and friends. Yet amid Todd's moment of triumph at the Ministry's expense, there was a sombre reminder of what might follow. Before embarking from Adelaide on the *Omeo* in early January 1872, he learnt of the tragic death of Kraajen, a telegraph operator attached to one of his central parties. Unable to locate water along the track north of Charlotte Waters, Kraajen had gone ahead of his advance party only to perish of thirst 'at the foot of a telegraph pole'.[60] The real prospect of losing whole construction teams over the coming months, isolated in the wet and deprived of provisions, was a deeply troubling one both for Todd and for Patterson who was anxiously awaiting assistance at the mouth of the flooding Roper River.

On the long journey up the east coast in the *Omeo*,[61] while restless and unable to sleep, Todd retained his sense of humour, describing to Alice how passing vessels called on a nearby island to deposit and pick up letters in a 'cave called a post office, the only one without a postmaster…fully exposed to the sea which beats in'.[62] In spite of the expedition's predicament, his long letters from the north were full of such banter, designed to lift the spirits of his anxious family. More serious matters were soon at hand, for no sooner did Todd reach Maria Island in late January than he was confronted by Patterson, who, emboldened by pride and despair, believed Todd had come north to rob him of his authority and the chance of gaining personal credit for the construction project. Further aggravating relations between them was the fact that Patterson had seen Todd's private telegrams to Little, in which he dismissed Patterson's November report as 'unnecessarily alarming'.[63] Their rivalry might have ended there, for Patterson was prepared to tender his resignation on the spot. Despite provocation, Todd wisely decided not to sack Patterson and risk a repeat of the Darwent and Dalwood fiasco of the previous year. Instead, as he later explained to Alice:

> He [Patterson] is naturally despondent, disgusted with his position and the work and has no confidence in the line ... Yet I believe he means well and would do nothing dishonourable. He doesn't seem to realise the extent to which his own feelings influenced his activities and the spirit of his party. My plan (I tell you in confidence) was to keep him away from the working parties as much as possible.[64]

It was an astute example of how to 'manage in a hard place'.[65] But Todd would still need to assert his authority during the difficult months which they were forced to spend together.

Decisive measures were needed immediately, if the expedition was to be salvaged. Conscious that 'unless we got inside and succeeded in landing the horses, the reinforcements would be useless,'[66] Todd negotiated with his sea captains about entering the mouth of the Roper River in order to reinforce the river landing upstream. To placate the reluctant skipper of the *Omeo*, he assumed written responsibility on behalf the South Australian government in the event of a mishap. The relief party then took the decisive step of crossing the river mouth at high tide, with the steamer *Young Australian* towing the *Bengal* behind it. The *Omeo*, was able to proceed 40 miles (64 km) upstream before landing the horses at the depot, a total distance of 85 miles (136 km) from the river mouth (Map 1). In his dispatch of mid-February, Todd recalled 'the hearty cheers which greeted our arrival and the relieved looks of those who had been penned up for so long'.[67] For Todd personally, it was indeed a moment of triumph over those who, in his words, 'so strenuously opposed the Roper being used'.[68] That evening, both he and Patterson addressed the parties and drank to the success of their mission in a show of unity designed to reinvigorate morale; whereupon Little noted, 'all seem to be contented and willing for work'.[69] Yet, if Patterson was heartened by this success, he remained deeply resentful of Todd's presence, and would later proclaim the decision to cross the bar as his own,[70] though Little who had reached the Roper from Port Darwin in early January, confirmed that the decision had indeed been the Postmaster General's.[71] Their time for premature rejoicing was short-lived, as the monsoon soon returned with renewed force, making sleep difficult and dumping twenty inches of rain in February, after the heavy downpours of December and January – a total of 60–70 inches in three months.[72] Despite his meteorological training, Todd was baffled and tested by the intensity of the summer weather. Aware of Alice's continuing fears for his health, Charles sought to reassure her, taking precautions in the trying climate and explaining that 'I am well except in the morning when I retch violently and have severe trembling fits – till I take some brandy and water – and after that before breakfast sometimes have to take a glass of sherry and quinine before I can recover'.[73]

While ascending the Roper River, Todd was aware of 'two or three distinct tribes [which were] all speaking different languages,' for he was passing from the coastal territory of the Mara and Alawa tribes into those of the Wilingura and Jungman who dwelt further inland. He was also aware that they might be regarded as intruders since 'they themselves are very ceremonious when they wish to pass through the territories of another tribe and go through a number of preliminary courtesies – if so they of course cannot understand our want of politeness'.[74] Impressed by the physique of the coastal blacks, Todd described them as 'fine muscular fellows considerably over 6 feet high,'[75] led by their chief Bungawa. The protracted ascent against the Roper's rising waters gave Todd ample time to observe the local tribes who were 'very numerous and were much excited at seeing such strange monsters as the steamers must have appeared'.[76] While he considered the coastal blacks to be friendly, Todd took the precaution of 'not accompanying them to their encampment,' nor would he allow fraternisation in the Roper camp itself.

Notwithstanding the adoption of Goyder's policy,[77] smaller parties of whites working away from the landing were more vulnerable. In one incident, a group of four men who had been sent to cut wood near the mouth of the Roper, complained to Todd that they had been 'surrounded by the blacks, robbed' and 'had their boat cut adrift,' forcing them to return seventy miles on foot. But when Todd descended the river to inspect the scene, he began to doubt their version of events, for he found 'the camp intact and their swags untouched'.[78] The inland Aborigines who accompanied Todd downstream were adamant that the coastal Mara should be pursued and shot but Todd thought otherwise, and waited on their chief Bungawa for his version of the incident. After a brief but tense exchange with Bungawa, Todd concluded that his people had not stolen the boat and that 'they would not have come to us again the second day' if they had taken the axes and the swags.[79] The incident revealed Todd's coolness and fairness under pressure. After concluding that the woodsmen had failed to fasten their boat securely, he wrote to Alice that 'I did not feel myself justified in detaining or punishing the blacks now in my power,' though in other letters, he remained convinced of the need to 'demonstrate our power' when it was overtly challenged.

After his initial elation, Charles was afflicted with the same emotions as his parties, as they waited for the waters to subside, anxious for the safety of those stranded inland and fearing 'many deaths, the parties being so inadequately provisioned'.[80] While sharing the discomfort and lack of sleep with others in the camp, Todd relived Patterson's earlier frustrations when the *Tararua*, dispatched to assist them, missed the mouth of the Roper River.[81] To relieve the monotony of waiting, Todd, accompanied by Patterson and Little, descended the Roper and explored the northern coastline, eventually meeting up with the wayward vessel at Maria Island in early March. At times the monsoon abated and, on one such evening, Charles wrote that 'on looking to the north I jumped for joy to see the seven stars of the Great Bear, a sight I had not seen for over 16 years'.[82] It awoke many memories of places and friends, not least his fateful speech at the Cambridge wedding, when he had vowed to extend the British telegraph network abroad. Determined to keep himself busy, Charles was, by now, homesick like most of his officers. He wrote fondly to Alice and his children to acknowledge 'your kind letter, also Fannie's, Lizzie's and Charles' whom I need not say much pleased me after my long absence'.[83] He had not yet met up with his nephew Griffith, still at Darwin manning the telegraph station for Little, but had received a 'very nice letter from him' which confirmed his intention to turn his nephews, Griffith and William, into 'first-class operators'.[84] Along with family letters, shared photos, by this time commercially available, helped to bridge the gap with loved ones in Adelaide. While Alice spent time with 'little Gwennie,' teaching her to recognise her father's portrait in the Observatory, Charles himself acknowledged, 'I do so like the photos and feel quite homesick,' reassuring Alice that the children's portraits have been 'well looked at' here.[85]

In the Roper camp, Todd continued his evening schedule of report writing, and was heartened to receive an encouraging message from the incoming Chief Secretary, Henry Ayers, 'wishing me good speed and associating my name with the great work in the most graceful terms'.[86] Charles was also devouring newspapers, including London broadsheets dispatched to him from the Observatory, complaining to Alice at one point that 'the file of Adelaide papers is very meagre and incomplete … they would be most interesting here'.[87] At the Roper camp, Captain Sweet, skipper of the ill-fated *Gulnare*, was proving his worth as a photographer, after taking 'a splendid photo of the *Omeo*, *Young Australian* and *Bengal* at the Roper landing'.[88] Charles, convinced that 'this is a unique event in our lives,' was keen to have his own photograph taken 'in regular bush rig' to mark the occasion.[89] Keen to promote co-operation and a team ethos, he decided on several group photos,[90] one of which was to become the iconic image of the expedition. Featuring Todd, opposite Patterson, flanked by Little and Mitchell, in front of a wagon it accentuated Todd's short stature, at 5'4' (162 cm) in the company of his taller officers. But it also marked him as a leader, imbuing him with the air of calm authority for which he became renowned after the event. Although Charles considered it a very good picture of himself, his family's reaction was somewhat mixed. Lizzie, his outspoken eldest, did not think 'the photo of you in your bush clothes very flattering,'[91] when compared with her father's more fashionable portrait, taken with his trunk before the northern voyage. Alice, maintaining household economies in his absence, complained about the high cost of Sweet's work, considering the same portrait overpriced at three shillings and four pence each.[92] Yet Sweet's photograph did indeed capture 'a unique one in history,' and would be reproduced many times both in and outside Australia thereafter.

Alice hoped that Charles would return to Adelaide by ship in late March 1872, but there was still much to be done before the stranded inland parties could be relieved and the interrupted poleing progressed to completion. Patterson was preparing to set out along Elsey Creek which linked the Roper camp to the line when Richard Knuckey unexpectedly burst into the camp with news of the situation inland. As one of Todd's surveyors for the now completed central section, Knuckey, following Todd's instructions,

Charles Todd and the Overland Team, 1872.
L to R: J.A.G. Little, Robert Patterson, Charles Todd, A.J. Mitchell

had continued to move up the line, despite flooding which threatened to reduce the northern landscape to a vast inland sea. Though short of supplies, Knuckey succeeded in locating several of the stranded northern parties and sent Burton's beleaguered men near Daly Waters much-needed sheep. After which, he and his party tracked up the boggy Elsie Creek (Map 1) and arrived at the Roper landing around Easter with 'only a few mouthfuls of flour left'.[93] It was one of many heroic acts performed at that time by land and sea and one which, according to Little, 'took everyone by surprise ... caus[ing] extreme satisfaction'[94] while giving the leadership a much-needed boost in morale. Todd, who lauded Knuckey to Alice as 'one of the most energetic officers we have,'[95] much preferred the new arrival to the sullen Patterson. His leadership qualities and bush craft were soon called upon by Todd in running telegrams by pony express across the gap between the northern and southern sections of the line. Unlike his rivalry with Patterson, Todd's long association with Knuckey would continue for several decades, after the latter's appointment as Inspector of Telegraphs. It was to Knuckey to whom Todd would delegate responsibility a few years later for the construction of the hazardous South Australian telegraph leg across the Great Australian Bight to Perth.

Armed with Knuckey's fresh information, Todd proceeded to draw up a plan for the completion of the line in the coming dry months. With Patterson keen to supply his stranded northern parties overland, Todd instructed Knuckey to return south, in order to establish a pony express service capable of carrying telegrams across the closing gap. Todd himself, accompanied by Little, would return to Port Darwin and attend to the line abandoned by Darwent and Dalwood's parties as far south as the Katherine. In April 1872, as the monsoon abated and construction parties began to resume work, Todd also learned of the exploits of his nephew Griffith, whose attempts to restore communication between Port Darwin and Katherine had been undertaken at considerable personal risk.[96] As he reported to Alice:

> He's [Griffith] looking well – but he has a bad hand. I am rather anxious about him. Everyone speaks well of him and he's very attentive.[97]

Charles had further reason to be proud of his nephew, for it was upon Griffith Todd's on-the-spot advice that Little began to introduce iron poles on the northern section rather than wooden ones, a task which Todd himself, lacking horse transport, was forced to delegate to Little.

As work resumed on the northern section, Todd's return from Port Darwin to the Roper in late May should have been personally satisfying.

But, despite Todd's carefully worded reports exonerating Patterson from charges of mismanagement or insubordination, their personal rivalry resurfaced sharply during their final weeks together on the Roper. Todd was now planning a long return journey overland to inspect the line in person southwards from Daly Waters, with the intention of establishing station sites along the way. After his return from Port Darwin, he was seeking to complete the line as quickly as practicable, although Patterson had other ideas, maintaining that the work would not be ready before September or even October.[98] Even before they had set out on their tour of inspection together, a confrontation loomed after the teams in Patterson's section were issued with dual sets of instructions. When Patterson again threatened resignation, Todd demurred, explaining that his recent intervention had merely been a suggestion. In private, Todd complained to Alice that 'Patterson is awfully lazy and hardly ever speaks to the men,' yet still believed he had made the right decision in not dismissing him, since 'many would have said I got rid of him through personal feelings and for my own self-glorification'.[99]

Although they were no longer confined together in the camp, the journey together proved a tense affair, not least because Todd was now inspecting parts of the line for which Patterson was responsible. Notwithstanding, Alfred Giles, who encountered them together on the track as he was carrying rations south from the Roper, reported that Todd maintained his usual cheerful demeanour. When advised that the country they were about to travel over would be without water, he joked 'But I carry my Wells with me!' turning to a party member of that name.[100] If his leadership style demanded he avoid personal quarrels in public, Todd was nonetheless fastidious about construction matters, ordering that twenty poles be erected per mile at South Tomkinson for greater stability rather than the usual ten per mile, to the consternation of the men there.[101] Neither Todd's private correspondence nor Patterson's tortured journal suggest that their working relationship improved with time or ended well.[102] Still predicting 'certain ruin' unless his views were heeded, Patterson still believed that Todd had taken 'too sanguine a view' of their situation, recently compounded by bad news in the previous month that the underwater cable to Port Darwin had been interrupted. Todd, in keeping with his administrative outlook, may have considered it a further setback, but it also freed South Australia from the financial penalties which would have been imposed under the BAT contract. For his part, he was 'glad to be free of Patterson' when they finally parted company in mid-July. While Patterson returned north to complete his section of the line, Todd continued south to inspect the central and southern sections.

Throughout 1871–72, when Charles Todd was absent in the north, Alice and the children maintained their busy schedule of parties, visits, schooling and church functions. The spacious grounds of the Observatory and surrounding parkland afforded the Todd children ample scope for exploration and play, offering them all of the physical and outdoor attractions enjoyed by other colonial youth. With the Observatory's instrument rooms out of bounds in their father's absence, Charles and Hedley occupied their time driving horse carts, erecting flagpoles, trapping birds and scouring the grounds.[103] For their part, Lizzie and Maude were becoming socially active, attending parties and enjoying sleepovers with a widening circle of Adelaide friends. Reading was also a popular pastime. At 16 Lizzie, was now reading a different book every week.[104] Punctual and informative in letters to her father, Lizzie kept him informed about his niece, Frances ('Fanny') Todd, whom Charles had given away six months before[105] in marriage to the son of a family friend, Charles Willoughby Davies. Subsequently, Fanny and Charles Willoughby would raise a sizeable family[106] on Mattawarrungala station, east of Hawker, where she settled with Davies after their marriage. Both Charles and his daughters remained in close touch with the Davies and, after Lizzie informed him of the death of Fanny's first child, Charles, on his return trip to Adelaide, took the opportunity to visit the Davies in the north-west of the colony.

Other young family members like Fanny after arriving from England also found initial employment in the large Todd household. William Bell Squires, a nephew of Alice's and the most recent arrival, helped out around the Observatory in Charles' absence, attending to the horses and carriages as well as taking meteorological observation in the grounds under Alice's supervision. Like Charles' own nephews, Griffith and Charles, orphaned after the death of their father in India, William would subsequently find employment in the colonial civil service. Along with the responsibility for this widening family network, Alice kept watch on the family finances, while maintaining her active social and charity work around the city. During regular walks to shop in the city, Alice familiarised herself with women and their families in the neighbourhood, and helped to raise subscriptions for widows, inviting the frail and elderly into her home, practices which she continued in Charles' absence.[107] The recent arrival of Charlotte Bell, Alice's wealthy and imposing mother, had brought changes to the Todd household; she was reputed by Lorna to have been shocked by the carefree lifestyle of the children and exerted pressure on their parents for them to be given formal instruction and a religious education, such as she had given Alice in Cambridge.[108] Alice, devoted daughter though she was, did not succumb to maternal pressure, taking pleasure in her children's physical activities and good health, in contrast with her memory of the illnesses which had afflicted her own brothers and sisters in childhood Cambridge.[109] Education, along with good health remained a parental priority. In a letter from the Roper to his sons, Charles was insistent that they 'persevere,' since:

> Many boys no older than you have to go out into the world and earn their living – but you and Hedley will, I hope – should my life be spared – have several more years at school ... Do all you can to secure the first-class education such as I wish to give you.[110]

Parenthood had inspired Charles to renewed thinking about education. Even on the Line, he discussed it with his officers, in a time when compulsory Education Acts were being introduced across the colonies. In keeping with his own social background and experience, he was keen for South Australia to incorporate industrial and domestic training into its school curriculum and would later play an active role in supporting such initiatives in the interests of social advancement and class mobility.[111]

By mid-1872 however, the family's hopes for Charles' prompt return to Adelaide were dwindling. Letters to their father from the Todd children became less regular, while Charles' own long letters from the Roper virtually ceased after he began his long journey south. Alice continued to carry the weight of their correspondence, still conscious of the fate that might befall them without Charles. Under the influence of Reverend Symes, the new evangelical pastor at the Stow Congregational Church, Alice was becoming more detached from Adelaide society. She 'did not care for large parties' and 'would not have gone to the Milne's but for Lizzie'.[112] She discouraged Observatory visitors on Sundays in favour of hymn singing and Bible studies with the children. All the while, Alice continued to write regularly to Charles throughout late 1872, 'mounting the map of the Overland Telegraph from the office between the hall door and the dining room door' of the Observatory so that 'I may constantly watch where you are'.[113]

As his inspection party moved slowly down the line. Charles' time was now taken up with supervising the construction of station buildings and the installation of telegraph equipment, to ensure prompt transmission, once Patterson's men had completed poleing and strung the wire. The inland telegraph stations needed to be self-sufficient, housing their own supplies, horses and equipment in the event of breakages along the Line. After he left Patterson and travelled south in July 1872, Todd was moving through country previously traversed by Stuart. His exploration party had been pushed back at Attack Creek a decade earlier by the local Warramunga tribe.[114] Todd decided not to locate a telegraph station at Attack Creek, notwithstanding its permanent water supply. Instead he decided to erect a wooden building at Tennant Creek further south, to connect with the more substantial stone structures being established at Barrow Creek and Alice Springs (see Map 2). As a precaution against future hostilities, the stations constructed under Todd's supervision were designed not only to house substantial cable equipment, but also to protect the telegraph operators, who had, in many cases, volunteered to remain there after the construction phase. One Alice Springs occupant would later describe them as 'miniature forts,'[115] with loopholes for rifles in case of attack. It was one thing to pass through tribal territories without acknowledgement, as Todd himself well knew; it was another to compete with local tribes for scarce resources like water. This scenario gave rise to a deadly confrontation at nearby Barrow Creek station[116] 18 months later, where surprise raids by the local Kaititja people[117] claimed the lives of two telegraph staff, including the stationmaster, J.L. Stapleton. On that occasion, Todd became personally involved, rushing Stapleton's wife to the central telegraph office in Adelaide to hear the final morse code message of goodbye from her dying husband. Throughout such episodes,[118] Todd's prime concern would lie with the safety of his men and the welfare of their families. After arrest warrants were issued for six Kaititja Aborigines,[119] a small relief party took more than a month to reach the beleaguered station which in the meantime came under renewed attack. A few days later, a party of linesmen returning to the station were also caught up in the confrontation which, according to the police, resulted in the deaths of three local tribespeople, none of whom were on their warrant list.[120] When alluding to the Barrow Creek episode a decade later, Todd reported tersely that 'the perpetrators of the attack were never caught'.[121] For he realised that, without adequate protection, remote telegraph workers would remain vulnerable.

Under such circumstances, it is difficult to assess the extent to which Todd was afterwards prepared to abandon his policy of restraint at the Roper towards the Aborigines in favour of harsher measures.[122] Always concerned for the physical safety of his staff, Todd had achieved remarkable results in restricting construction casualties during 1870–72 to no more than half a dozen. Indeed, he had taken great care in his instructions to overseers to avoid conflict with the Aborigines. Nevertheless, linesmen travelling between stations to check the state of the wire remained more vulnerable to attack around creeks or when resting from the midday heat. By the mid-1870s, Todd would complain in a letter to George Airy about the ambush of his outback staff, confirming the dispatch of a police party 'to arrest the murderers,' before concluding that 'these are the difficulties we have to contend [with] in pioneering lines through the wilds of Australia'.[123] While the grim tone of his letter may have been an attempt to impress Airy, it marked a significant departure from the previous letters which Todd had sent to Alice from the Roper a few years earlier. His unofficial correspondence suggests that his attitude would harden over time towards Aboriginal obstruction occurring periodically along the Line.

Certainly Todd, when returning overland with his small inspection party in late 1872, was vigilant on their behalf. They reached Barrow Creek almost three months after Todd had left the Roper, and a month after he and Patterson had gone their separate ways. Patterson still had important work to do in the north section in preparation for joining the wire between the central and northern sections.[124] A few days before this was due to occur at Frews Ponds in late August, Todd, pushed south and, on 22 August 1872, camped at Central Mount Stuart (Map 2). Climbed and named by Stuart a decade earlier, it was located at the heart of the Australian continent. Having chosen this landmark to announce the culmination of his mission, Todd tapped into the wire using a pocket relay, and alerted the South Australian government that the Line would be operational by 1 pm that day. In addressing the Chief Secretary, Todd, despite the temporary failure of the underwater cable, proclaimed the completion of the much sought-after link to 'the mother country and the whole of the civilised and commercial world,' crediting the colony of South Australia with the feat, 'notwithstanding the delays and mishaps which have occurred'. In his prepared statement, Todd acknowledged Stuart and 'the conspicuous features of central Australia bearing his name,' while expressing his own satisfaction at 'seeing the successful completion of the scheme I officially advanced some 14 years ago'.[125]

Designed to capture the imagination of both the government and the public, his message provided skilful publicity for both the project and its organiser. That evening, he received formal messages of congratulations from Governor Fergusson and the Mayor of Adelaide, as well as compliments from the acting government resident at Port Darwin.

Messages continued to flow late in the evening until 3 am, when cold and exhaustion descended and the wire fell silent. Next day, news of the expedition's success galvanised the city of Adelaide into a state of excitement. To celebrate the event, flags were raised at the post office and other government sites. In the same issue as it published Todd's news and the ensuing correspondence, the Adelaide *Advertiser* rehearsed the 'long ordeal' begun in 1870, before concluding that 'by far the wisest thing done was to send Mr Todd to the scene of action, whereupon the progress made in the work was most encouraging and satisfactory'. There was no doubt that Todd had become the hero of the hour and of the colony itself. Yet, even at the height of his achievement, he was thinking of Adelaide and of home, where, as Alice confirmed:

> The congratulations by persons calling and by letters have been overwhelming – the first to call was the Private Secretary John A. Ferguson, early on Friday morning and he was so pleasant, then later in the day numberless friends and all were so hearty – I felt quite overpowered.[126]

Their spirits uplifted by the historic evening, Todd's party continued south, entering territory which would retain longstanding associations for Charles and Alice – the site of Alice Springs, the local telegraph station (Map 2). It was from here that Alice learnt at first hand of the project's success, replying excitedly to Charles on 5 September:

> I was so pleased to have a nice chat with you yesterday at Alice Springs ... All say I shall not be able to see you at all for the first day; the public are going to have you all to themselves.[127]

Upon his arrival at Alice Springs, Charles saw little water in the dry bed of the Todd River which flowed only sporadically after summer rains. If Alice appeared unaffected by the compliment paid to her in the naming of the spring and the telegraph station nearby, Charles recognised the potential of the site as the central link of his overland network, and set about organising the construction of a substantial stone station, 'some 7 to 8 rooms in extent' with the capacity for 'large quantities of rations and stores'.[128] It would be more than half a century however before the local settlement took the permanent name of Alice Springs or came to assume national familiarity as 'the Alice'.[129]

After leaving Alice Springs, Charles moved steadily southwards. He maintained regular telegraphic communication with Alice as he proceeded. On 9 September, she acknowledged his message from

Strangways Springs, with a simple statement: 'I am so thankful you are nearing home'.[130] Ten days later, she was equally glad to learn that he had previously passed through Charlotte Waters (Map 2). Their new system of communication was not without its difficulties. Accustomed as she was to letter writing, Alice felt awkward in the presence of telegraph operators during their intimate chats,[131] and was unnerved by the abrupt arrival of a birthday telegram from Charles during a church service![132] She was frank when Charles indicated his intention to visit their niece Fanny at Mattawarrungala, *en route* to Adelaide, observing that while 'Fanny will be pleased to have you, you must not stay more than one night'.[133] In lighter moments, Alice looked forward to having 'that bright happy chap' return to the Observatory, but waxed indignant at Charles for daring to '[ask] Mr Cunningham how I looked ... I do not get any thicker'.[134] When Charles jokingly declared his attachment to his hammock, she bandied affectionately:

> I am perfectly satisfied with my beautiful bed. I have such a beautiful home and soon shall have my own dear husband.[135]

As the day of his return drew close, Alice confessed to becoming 'ill with excitement'.[136] She took care to preserve Charles' letters from the north, so that 'you could compile an account from them I should think, couldn't you?'[137] Solicitous of her husband's growing reputation, Alice was equally keen to maintain her privacy, ordering Charles at one point to 'take care to burn my letters, I don't want them flying all over the Bush'.[138] Charles did not accede to her wish but kept them secure *en route* to Adelaide. 'Sun-browned, and weather-stained but cheerful,'[139] he boarded a train with a small party which included Knuckey and Bagot, escaping public notice along most of the line, until they reached Riverton, some forty miles north of the capital. Here, he and his party were greeted with flag waving and cheering. Alice had alerted him that, for the time being, 'you are to be allowed to come home quietly'.[140] Fearful lest she become 'too excited,' she sent Charlie and Hedley to meet him in the wagonette, while 'I shall stay home with my three daughters and think each minute an hour'.[141]

The celebration banquet, held on the evening of 15 November after a processional march from north Adelaide by the construction teams, was a grand affair, convened in the Adelaide town hall. Six hundred people, including the leading dignitaries of the city and colony, attended in honour of the overland telegraph construction parties which were seated at tables the length of the hall, their wives accommodated in the gallery. Todd himself took pride of place at the head table between Governor Fergusson and the Chief Secretary, Henry Ayers. Ayers was the first to rise and speak, crediting Todd with the grand conception 'which had occupied his mind more or less for the last 15 years'. After a series of congratulatory speeches, Todd rose and responded on behalf of the construction parties. Describing the project as a 'labour of love,' Todd was at pains to praise those 'upon whom the heat and burden of the day' had fallen.

Yet the Adelaide banquet was not without surprises for Todd. In the first instance, Robert Patterson's absence from the reception would prove an omen of difficult events to follow. The second surprise, a more pleasant one, was Ayers' unexpected announcement that Todd had been awarded a Companion of the Order of St Michael and St George (CMG). So too had Francis Dutton, South Australia's industrious Agent General for his labours in supplying the expedition with much-needed European materials at short notice. For the same reason, Henry Ayers, a veteran of South Australia's factional politics and advocate of settling the north, was elevated to a knighthood as leader of South Australia's presiding administration. If some, regarded Ayers' knighthood as opportunistic,[142] Todd bore him no resentment,[143] preferring instead to forge an alliance with the influential Ayers, as one of the political powerbrokers of the colony. Subsequently, Todd would turn to him for confidential advice, when succeeding administrations baulked at the ongoing expense required to maintain the great telegraphic project.

At the London banquet of celebration, held on the same day as the Adelaide event, John Pender, director of the British Australian Telegraph company which had laid the underwater cable to Port Darwin, acknowledged Todd as the man of the hour, but gave greatest credit to South Australia's departing governor, James Fergusson, who like McDonnell before him, had been a strong supporter of the overland project. South Australia's Agent General, Francis Dutton, who had played a key role in negotiations behind the scenes, made much of Todd's role, both as planner and organiser in a situation 'attendant with great fatigue and some danger'.[144] A third banquet, held in Sydney to coincide with the Adelaide and London events, was a more subdued affair from which colonial unity was conspicuously absent. Instead, local feeling continued to run in favour of Queensland. John Robertson, New South Wales' Premier, endorsing Queensland's position, asserted that 'the line that was at first contemplated by way of Queensland would ultimately be our means of communication'.[145] Nor was he averse to repeating long-held prejudices in eastern Australia against a transcontinental line, on the grounds that the harshness of its isolated location would ultimately ensure its failure.[146]

Charles Todd wearing his Order of St Michael and St George medal, 1880

In spite of calls for colonial unity within London circles, inter-colonial relations soured abruptly in following weeks, when press allegations surfaced that the Line had not been adequately constructed. In Brisbane, where South Australian parties returning from the Northern Territory docked *en route* to Adelaide, the disgruntled Patterson's outspokenness in the presence of Brisbane journalists helped fuel damaging rumours about the impending failure of the new Line. Claiming Patterson as its source, the Brisbane *Telegraph* published a scathing article on the prospects of the Overland Telegraph Line and, in anticipation of its imminent failure, called immediately for a second cable from Java to Normanton. For 'we learn,' it asserted, that 'the makeshift line at present in use is so badly built that there is no possibility of relying upon it for any lengthened period'.[147] Such a damning prediction, sourced to a senior member of South Australia's own construction teams, cut short the mood of congratulation shared by Todd and his officers. Most, including Todd, were deeply distressed by the rumours which followed Patterson and his returning parties to Adelaide.

An optimist by nature, Todd had assumed, after completing the 'great work,' that unanimity would be restored. But he misread Patterson and the depths of resentment which he continued to harbour towards both himself and the South Australian government. By the first week of December, news of the Brisbane allegations reached the Adelaide press, prompting questions in the South Australian parliament concerning the Line's condition. If Todd, recalling the fears which Alice had shared with him a few months earlier,[148] doubted Patterson's veracity in denying the press statements attributed to him, he still sought to exonerate Patterson from the charge of discrediting their achievement. In a report to the Chief Secretary, Todd sought to reassure him, after consulting Patterson, that 'there is no foundation for the statements that have been made'.[149] He remained, nevertheless, deeply offended by claims about the Line's imminent collapse. Recognising that the allegations threatened to 'prejudice me in the estimation of the public,' he was even 'willing to resign should further enquiry find otherwise'.

To appease parliament, Todd penned a more detailed report over the Christmas period, after receiving fresh reports on all sections of the Line. As previously, his own comments on Patterson's section remained positive in stating that, 'with the exception of about 35 miles of line south of the Elsey, and a few miles north, where the poles are small, a better line could not have been erected'.[150] Yet, despite his efforts, the feud between Patterson and the government continued to escalate, as his allegations against Todd became more pointed and personal with claims that Todd had not only accepted 'the credit of the press and public... quickly and without demur,' but, more seriously, had contrived to 'keep the full facts about the condition of the line from the government' and 'had not the generosity to say one word in my defence throughout their entire correspondence'.[151] By now, Todd's patience was running low, although he continued to argue that Patterson should receive the bonus of £500 which the government had initially awarded him.

Todd knew the meaning of bad publicity and had no desire to unnecessarily protract nor inflame their dispute. In private correspondence with the Chief Secretary, he still felt obliged to repudiate as 'wholly unfounded' Patterson's claims, in particular 'his statement that I was opposed to going up the Roper with the *Omeo*,'[152] as well as his attempt to take credit for 'the taking of the steamer *Omeo* a hundred miles up an almost unexplored river and to which the whole success of the expedition was due'.[153] In his rejoinder, Todd dismissed as 'entirely wrong' the claim that he had concealed from the government the threat posed by white ants to wooden telegraph poles and that he had exaggerated expenditure on the

Line by a figure of almost £100,000. Aware of the ongoing risk posed by white ants in the Northern Territory, Todd insisted that re-poleing was a maintenance issue, rather than one of crisis proportions and directed his northern parties to renew their labours. By April 1873, he dispatched work parties under Knuckey to return to the Roper and replace the existing wooden poles with a thousand iron poles recently imported from the United Kingdom.[154] Once Todd had fully documented the state of the overland line and disproved these allegations, morale improved both within the government and his own workforce. Even more protracted arguments about the excessive cost of the Line subsided after South Australian wheat farmers successfully used the international telegraph link to London for the first time to dispose of their recent harvest on the British market.[155]

Given the ongoing politics which surrounded its construction, Todd's discretion and reluctance to take personal credit for the overland telegraph line were understandable. Another decade would pass before Todd set down a more extensive account of his 'great work' in telegraphy. He did however prepare and deliver a lecture on the subject to the local Philosophical Society in July 1873,[156] prefacing his own achievements with an overview of British telegraphic development. Todd set out to repudiate longstanding critics of the overland scheme, reminding his audience that 'the whole history of telegraphs is but a long series of triumphs over difficulties'. Difficulties there had certainly been. But in regarding it as 'the great work' of his career, Todd promoted it as a collective endeavour rather than the work of one individual, as the press and public preferred to describe it. In hindsight, it had been an unprecedented and exhilarating three years, some of it spent away from the Observatory and his growing family. The strain of it would not be easily overcome, even in a relatively young man of 46 years. To Dutton, he confided in its aftermath how 'he was wearied to death at the end of a long working day'.[157] As Todd's 1873 lecture circulated in the colonial press, the *Empire* recommended it to Sydney readers as 'a model of human perseverance and exertion,' describing Todd as 'the leader in this great work'. [158] Illustrated newspapers also began lionising Todd's achievement, reproducing not only sketches of the Roper and of the iconic group photo taken there, but also an individual portrait of Todd proudly wearing his CMG award. Increasingly the spotlight shifted to Todd himself, his scientific training and administrative expertise, in keeping with established biographical tradition.[159] For Todd, history would have to wait. Other tasks were now beckoning, not only in colonial telegraphy, but also in postal administration and science.

6

Postmaster General in the 1870s: The Robbery and Commission of Inquiry

While Todd's prominent role in constructing the overland telegraph had dispelled lingering doubts about his ability to manage such a complex department, his protracted absence from Adelaide prevented him from gaining a better understanding of the postal side of his portfolio. After his triumphant return to Adelaide, he was secure in his position but still lacked time to overhaul the regulations and improve working conditions in his new department. Given the ongoing sensitivities[1] over the amalgamation of the postal and telegraph services after his appointment as Postmaster General in 1870, it was not surprising that postal officials, many of whom had worked for Todd's predecessor, James Lewis, considered that their new departmental head had neglected his postal responsibilities in favour of the great overland telegraph project. Moreover, the amalgamation process had stalled in his absence, with departmental responsibilities shared between Henry Hurst in the post office and William Cunningham in the telegraph office. Although Todd had been on friendly terms with Lewis,[2] he was now cast in the role of usurper and their relations became more strained, compounding the difficulty in mastering his enlarged responsibilities. A critical example was Lewis' reluctance, during Todd's absence in the Northern Territory, to provide oversight of the new Post Office building, completed and opened in May 1872 while Todd was absent.

Erected at a cost of over £50,000, and boasting a tower higher than that of the Adelaide town hall, the new Post Office headquarters drew praise from British visitors like Trollope[3] for the fineness of its architecture and the grandeur of its central hall.[4] But it would soon prove inadequate for the postal workers employed there, some of whom had become disenchanted after Lewis' reassignment to the customs department, leaving his acting successor, Hurst, in an untenable situation. Upon his return to Adelaide, Todd was frustrated to learn that his plans to incorporate the telegraph offices in an adjacent space had been set aside.[5] Now his telegraph staff had to be accommodated within the new building, with the education department offices upstairs and extensive postal services on the ground floor, situated in cramped offices adjacent to the large central public hall. Another of Todd's ongoing concerns, never corrected in the original design, were the cumbersome fittings for the busy post office rooms, which further reduced the already limited space and created serious congestion when the voluminous inland mails were being sorted and dispatched.[6] Such confined spaces made proper supervision difficult, while the long hours of work, often involving casuals, threatened to compromise security, especially at night. It was not long after an exhausted Todd resumed the reins as Postmaster General in early 1874 that a serious crisis developed which gave him little respite.

The flashpoint occurred on 29 April 1874 with the dramatic news that a robbery had been committed at the central Post Office in King William Street. One of the clerks arriving for work before 6 am sounded the alarm after discovering that many letters had disappeared from pigeonholes and registered letters in the inland safe had also been taken.[7] He promptly alerted the Post Office Secretary Henry Hurst, who had inspected the offices before retiring around 11.15 pm on the previous evening. Realising the gravity of the situation, Hurst contacted the police and sent a message to Todd by 8 am. That morning, Todd was still at the Observatory, but lost no time getting to the Post Office to find Hurst, in the company of a police constable, undertaking a preliminary investigation of the crime scene and questioning employees. On the basis of his immediate inquiries, Hurst provided Todd as Postmaster General with a brief report outlining the facts which had come to light in those first confusing hours. There were, he noted, few clues for the police to go by, since 'there does not appear to have been any forcible entrance affected' and 'none of the windows or doors have been disturbed'.[8] Hurst believed that the robbery had taken place between 11.30 pm on the previous night and 4.45 am on the morning of 29 April, and that 'the thief had hidden himself on the premises, especially as the door at the bottom of the stairs, leading from the inland office to the cellar was open; and also the door from the cellar to the yard'.[9] It appeared likely that the theft was the work of insiders, a line of inquiry which brought Hurst's own evidence under intense scrutiny in the months to follow.

Some time elapsed before the full extent of the robbery was revealed. The stolen bank remittances, including notes destined for the Moonta mines,[10] were worth over £1700, a large sum of money at that time. Nor were the lost remittances confined to a few individuals. For, in addition to servicing the business community, the Post Office also acted as a repository for public savings and conducted a brisk trade in money orders. As departmental head, Todd was acutely aware that the security breach at the Adelaide GPO 'very naturally created a feeling of uneasiness in the public mind'.[11] Adelaide newspapers, unsure as to whether it had been the work of one or several persons, described the theft as a daring and serious robbery. In parliament, the Blyth government promised that 'no action would be spared' to find the perpetrators and increased its reward for information about the incident from £100 to £200.[12] Progress in solving the mystery was hampered by the fact that none of the stolen banknotes reappeared in local circulation.[13] On the basis of Hurst's and Todd's initial investigation, the *Register* was prepared to concede that 'there seems to be no evidence of neglect on the part of the officials in the establishment; they appear to have carried out in every particular the arrangements which have always been in force'.[14]

From the outset, Todd was convinced that the robbery was not the work of postal staff. Yet the closer he and the police examined the situation, the more vulnerable the security of the building and its offices began to look. Hurst presumed that the safe from which most of the valuables had disappeared had not been properly locked on the previous evening. But the clerk responsible vouched for its security. Todd then asked Hurst whether a duplicate copy of the safe key existed and if so where? He was preparing to check with Lewis, his departmental predecessor, when Hurst produced the second key from a locked drawer, along with other items, which Lewis had handed over to him before his departure as Postmaster General. On examining the duplicate key for the safe, the police inspector with them noticed that it appeared shiny and much newer than the post office original.[15] Had the second key been copied, and, if so, had this occurred before Todd's appointment as Postmaster General? An alternative explanation was that the second key had simply worn down because of the safe's difficult lock and been replaced. But the circumstantial evidence did little to relieve pressure on Hurst or his hapless clerks.

The *Advertiser* in particular was less well disposed to Todd and his workforce after a previous well publicised security lapse. Its concern over the GPO incident was compounded by the recent loss of a letter bag from a country office *en route* to Adelaide. Delays in tracking its disappearance at the GPO gave the police insufficient time to follow up the theft, with the result that 'the mail boy responsible… is supposed to have escaped to one of the other colonies'.[16] Had something similar occurred in the case of the Adelaide heist? Even after an official investigation failed to uncover new leads, the *Advertiser* considered the GPO robbery in particular to have been inadequately explained. At Mount Gambier, the *Border Watch* appended to its report the announcement that 'Mr Todd proposes to have a night watchman for the protection of the Post Office and also double locks' but that 'nothing positive has yet been discovered relative to the robbery'.[17]

In 1874, as the South Australian government reviewed the terms of its European mail subsidy,[18] grievances harboured by Adelaide merchants over the mail service and their declining share of the river trade in competition with New South Wales, took a political turn. In the wake of the robberies, the Adelaide business community called for the de-amalgamation of posts and telegraphs, issuing a string of subsequent complaints against Todd's department,[19] and lobbying for a commission of inquiry into the workings of the Post and Telegraphs department. The Chamber's views were widely publicised including its resolution that 'in consequence of recent robberies and irregularities in the post office, public confidence in it is destroyed and it is desirable that steps should be taken for the better administration of the Department'.[20] When the Commission was announced in August, the Chamber of Commerce was sufficiently influential to have its director, William Longbottom, appointed as a member of the Commission. Although the business lobby was careful not to assign personal blame to Todd after the robbery, its campaign to reduce the Postmaster General's responsibilities was calculated to appeal to politicians when it stated that 'the management of both Post Office and Telegraph offices is too much for him (Mr Todd);' and 'it is suggested that the Post Office should be under a Minister of the Crown'.[21]

The appointment of an inquiry also gave Todd's critics within the civil service, including his departmental predecessor James Lewis, the opportunity to revisit earlier grievances over his appointment. Yet, along with criticism of Todd in some quarters, there was also good will and recognition of his services, both inside and outside parliament. The Commission, chaired by South Australia's well respected Sheriff, William Boothby, chose to tread more cautiously than the Chamber of Commerce under the circumstances. For, as the *Advertiser* conceded:

> It was unquestionably very unfortunate for testing the value of the amalgamation of the Post Office and Telegraph departments, that the energies of the head of the department should, at the time of beginning the experiment, have been necessarily and solely devoted to the work required to make the telegraph line a success.[22]

The same editorial pointed out that Todd had pre-empted the work of the Commission in several respects, most notably in redrafting regulations and addressing issues of staffing and security well *before* the embarrassing robberies had taken place. When the Commission began taking evidence in late August, it soon emerged that Todd had been redrafting staffing regulations for the postal department both before and after his great overland telegraph undertaking, in keeping with the spirit of amalgamation.[23] In absence from Adelaide, his draft instructions had not yet been codified, while his requests for increased expenditure on staffing had either been struck off the financial estimates by Cabinet or were still awaiting consideration.[24]

The scope of the Commission was sufficiently broad to inquire into the workings of Todd's department as well as the robberies. Moreover Todd acknowledged that such a serious and unresolved matter had 'cast a general gloom over the department, placing every officer in the General Post Office in a most unenviable position'.[25] By the time the Commission began taking evidence, some four months after the felonies, Todd no longer believed that the culprits could be caught or brought to justice, confiding to his Victorian counterpart, that 'there was still no clue' as to the identity of the robbers.[26] His brief note of late July 1874 to Turner, Victoria's Deputy Postmaster General, gives a valuable insight not only into the careful preparation which Todd undertook before giving evidence to the Commission, but into his attitude to the crisis and to the perceived benefits which might rebound to his department. For some time, he had been awaiting copies of both the Victorian and New South Wales postal regulations in order to compare them with those of his own department. Having not yet received a copy from Turner in Victoria, Todd sent him a reminder in late July, explaining that:

> There is a strong feeling against the Department in consequence of which I hope the enquiry will set right ... I shall avail myself of the present pressures.[27]

Todd's last phrase was a telling one; for amid the seriousness of parliamentary and public concern, there was also a quiet confidence that the opportunity had come to set right many of the workplace frustrations which Todd and his staff had endured since his 1870 appointment as head of the amalgamated Post and Telegraph services.

Armed with timely documentation and almost four years of practical experience, Todd set out to turn what could have become an inquisitorial exercise into a positive outcome. Amid everpresent concerns with security, he was looking to raise other departmental concerns at the Commission, confiding to Turner that 'we have never had in the colony an efficient or proper system of official inspection'.[28] To that point in time, Todd shared this role with his two deputies at a time when new post offices were being opened with increasing frequency across the colony. Scheduling trips around their other arduous duties was becoming increasingly difficult for all three senior officers. With copies of the recent New South Wales and Victorian regulations, received only weeks before the Commission sat, he was now better placed to embark on a mission to reform his sprawling department and combat the imputations of inefficiency levelled against it. In his professional determination to update South Australia's Postal Act, Todd planned to pre-empt the Commission and emerge from the ordeal with his reputation enhanced.

It did not take long for the Commission to appreciate the depth of Todd's knowledge of his department and the inadequacy of the existing postal regulations. At his first appearance before it in early September, he coolly offered 'to assist you in every way in asking [the witnesses] questions'.[29] After declining the suggestion that he be co-opted onto the Commission in a non-voting capacity,[30] the Commissioners nevertheless conceded the Postmaster General the right to comment on evidence given by other senior officers, including former Postmaster Lewis. In November, Todd chose to exercise this option when disputing both the views of witnesses and of Commissioners concerning the effectiveness of departmental inspections and tracking of missing country mails.[31] On the other hand, the Commission was inclined to agree to the amendments he proposed to the existing Post Office Act of 1866 and to his suggestion that letters be registered as a means of protecting the public from pecuniary loss.

A fundamental question raised by the events of 1874 was their lasting impact on Todd's own position and duties. In formalising his staffing profiles, Todd was determined to relieve himself of some of the administrative detail which dogged most senior postal officials. In seeking to do so, he pointedly rejected the evidence of his predecessor, Lewis, asserting that:

> Of course, it is quite impossible for me to devote my services so exclusively to the post office as he [Lewis] did. And, as a matter of fact, I do not think it is the duty of the Postmaster-General to do as he did, because I think the Postmaster-General may be much more profitably occupied than in assisting to sort and dispatch the mails.[32]

During his second appearance before the Commission in late 1874, Todd provided valuable insights into the demands of his position and the changes that he was looking to effect. He put a forceful case to the Commission for delegating some of his responsibilities in declaring:

> I'm frequently here from nine in the morning till 10 or 11 at night. I have more to do than I'm capable of doing properly. At the same time this arises from the number of things which I am obliged to attend to personally, especially in connection with the Overland Telegraph. My feeling is that, in the course of time, I should transfer, as far as I can, all the mere routine duty of the telegraph department to Mr Cunningham and all the routine duty of the post office to Mr Hurst, so that I may be relieved as much as possible.[33]

Todd was keen to justify these proposed changes in view of 'the large number of extraneous things which occupy my time,' not only his observatory work which demanded he prepare for the upcoming transit of Venus observations. He was also, in his role as scientific adviser to the South Australian government, responsible for organising the manufacture, import and installation of a Post Office clock. In a thinly veiled criticism of his predecessor Lewis, whom he believed was harbouring ambitions of returning as head of a separate postal department, Todd remarked not without irony: 'I do not suppose that my predecessor would ever have been asked to draw up a plan for the Post Office clock'.[34] He went on to explain that, with so many different telegraphic projects under way, not least a link to Western Australia, that the work 'which presses most hardly on me, and prevents my exercising the supervision I feel to be necessary, is in the telegraph, and not the post office side'.[35] His correspondence of that year with Chief Secretary Blyth[36] confirms that Todd was still proceeding with ambitious cable projects, not only to Fowler's Bay on the Great Australian Bight but on the southern coast of South Australia, where land and underwater cables were planned to connect existing lighthouses on Kangaroo Island, while another line would proceed beyond Moonta down the Yorke Peninsula to Cape Spencer.

The upshot of the protracted Post Office Inquiry proved more favourable to Todd than his critics anticipated. In its long-awaited report of late

November, the 1874 Commission upheld the economic and administrative value of an amalgamated post and telegraph department, but sought to alter its existing management by recommending the immediate appointment of a new Deputy Postmaster General with combined oversight of both the postal and telegraph sections, rather than continuing with separate arrangements. In view of widespread concern about the state of the postal service this was its immediate priority, with the result that Todd was not relieved of routine telegraph work as he had wished. Instead, Edward Squire, an officer from the telegraph section who had made his reputation overseeing demanding border stations at Robe and Wentworth, was transferred from Gawler to Adelaide and promoted as Todd's Deputy Postmaster General in early 1875. Having demonstrated both financial acumen and organizational ability, Squire also assumed the dual role of Assistant Superintendent of Telegraphs six months later,[37] after the death of Todd's close colleague William Cunningham. It was the beginning of a decade of stable and productive management, as the department continued its astonishing rate of expansion, with as many as 390 new post and telegraph offices established[38] in a short space of time. Together, Todd and his new Deputy, who became equally renowned for his fierce loyalty to the department, turned back the tide of criticism, sharing public responsibility for investigating further internal incidents, and issuing explanations and rebuttals when criticism of their department resurfaced from such bodies as the Chamber of Commerce.[39]

In Todd's judgement, the combination of long hours and routine work within the postal service was exacerbated by the routine loss of promising young staff to other departments of the public service. During his lengthy appearances before the Commission, he took the opportunity to complain bitterly about the issue, citing the recent removal of his fifth class clerk[40] as but one instance of an established trend which not only deprived him of much needed staff but demoralised the department, which was perceived within the service as 'weak' and uninviting for ambitious and talented young recruits.[41] Only weeks prior to the Commission, he had addressed a confidential letter of protest to the government concerning the loss without notice of his 'most experienced and reliable' clerk declaring it 'a suicidal step' at a time when 'the Department is weak in field officers' and 'in public esteem,' with 'the possibility (I don't like to say probability) of changes being necessary'.[42] Alert to the case of his own nephew Griffith George, who on returning from the Northern Territory, chose not to remain with Posts and Telegraphs, Todd knew that his was much less attractive than other departments such as engineering, audit or survey.

The Commission was prepared in its final report to concede Todd had been placed 'in an unfair position'[43] but made only general reference to the problem, leaving Todd to articulate his ongoing opposition to the practice. In official correspondence, Todd reiterated that 'frequent changes are to be deprecated and should as far as possible be avoided by making the service sufficiently attractive to induce its best men to remain in its ranks'.[44] Yet he knew that such an accepted practice would be difficult to eradicate, without stronger support from his own Minister of Education.[45]

Todd was quick to seize on the Commission's concessions in a bid to increase staffing which he documented thoroughly when acknowledging the final Commission report. In particular, he considered that the letter branch of the GPO was in need of 'immediate relief,'[46] and that staffing in the GPO should be increased from fifty to sixty workers.[47] While the Commission concurred with many of Todd's recommendations, it left the Postmaster General to provide the necessary details for consideration by the executive. On the critical issue of the GPO's design, the Commission also stopped short of supporting Todd's specific recommendations for the creation of an open working area in place of the numerous cramped offices then currently in use. Such a change would have necessitated depriving the public of the great hall, one of the architectural features of the building, with the result that Todd's desired changes were never fully put into effect.[48]

There is nevertheless, little evidence to suggest that Todd's workload declined in the wake of the Commission's recommendations, if that had been his intention. Staffing remained a troubling issue. The loss of his private secretary at short notice could be even more difficult, as Todd explained confidentially to Henry Ayers a few years later. On that occasion, in 1877, Todd was seeking to employ a second clerk in the correspondence office, at a time when he was receiving as many as sixty to eighty incoming letters a day. The appointee had been 'drawn away to the Audit Office,' with the prospect of rapid promotion and twice the salary for 'commensurate' duties. In a reprise of his protestations before the Commission, Todd declared:

> It is certainly disheartening and not calculated to promote efficiency in a very important branch of the public service. And when I assure the government that I require a Clerk of certain qualifications, I do think after many years of faithful service, my word should be taken and my recommendation should have some weight.[49]

Such incidents confirm that Todd was keen to make the postal service a more attractive career path for talented young civil servants. But the same incident also cast light on the tremendous workload which Todd sustained, often without adequate support, throughout the hectic 1870s. Nor did his office hours appear to ease in subsequent years. In early 1883, when a fire broke out in the crypt of the Adelaide GPO,[50] Todd was already on hand, having arrived at the office before 6 o'clock that morning.[51] At the time, there was still little equipment in place to deal with such emergencies. The damage, though contained, was sufficiently serious for the Postmaster General to rapidly introduce fire-proof compartments throughout the South Australian service thereafter.[52]

If Todd's sprawling portfolio lacked status – some described it as a 'service within the civil service' – Todd put politicians and his fellow administrators on notice that he would not be easily bypassed or overruled in future. When the Commission singled out Hurst, his former postal deputy for censure over the robbery, forcing his reassignment and replacement by Edward Squire, Todd was quick to point out that Mr Hurst has simply had 'far too much to do'.[53] There was invariably, in his public defence of staff, a fierce loyalty to his own employees, one which helped to lift morale and gain the post office some of the respect which the telegraph department already possessed. A few years later, Todd again took up the cause of his senior staff, many of them in the postal service, when the South Australian government contemplated removing retirement allowances at the time of the Civil Service Amendment Act in 1881.[54] It marked the beginning of his long involvement on the executive of the Civil Service Commission and his enlightened advocacy of a compulsory assurance fund – akin to the superannuation policy of today.

In spite of ongoing frustrations, Todd expressed his satisfaction when the Commission had tabled its report, concluding in his response of the following month that:

> Adversity is not an unmixed evil when the lessons it is intended to convey are properly apprehended and utilised. The robbery, which so rudely disturbed our repose, will prove to be a blessing if the enquiry it has invoked is productive of the reforms necessary to give greater efficiency to the administration and working of so important a Department of the public service as the General Post Office.[55]

Todd, though still lacking in funds, had already begun to transform the postal service and relieving his hard-pressed work force of the opprobrium cast upon it by introducing iron safes and locked pigeon holes as well as improved night security in the wake of the 1874 robbery. When the Adelaide *Register* published a letter in mid-1877, accusing postal staff at

Callington in the Adelaide Hills of theft, Todd, alerted the police and instituted his own departmental investigation. On this occasion, it did not become a public one, for he was keen to avoid a repetition of the 1874 crisis. Although he had been pleased that the Commission had relieved him of inspectorial duties and created a separate position for the task, Todd still did not wish to be confined entirely to his King William Street office, observing that 'I may occasionally take this duty myself'.[56] In his evidence to the Commission, Todd had succeeded in rebutting many of the complaints levelled at his department, providing documented cases of carelessness, loss of money and lack of understanding on the part of public. In the course of the Callington complaint, he remained willing to listen to and defend his staff, reporting subsequently to his Minister that 'I should certainly hesitate in attaching any suspicion ... in this instance, without stronger evidence before me ... Nor do I feel justified in suspecting any of the other persons concerned'.[57] For he was more inclined to support his staff than acquiesce to pressure from hostile politicians or business figures.

Nor did he as Postmaster General lose touch with country postal staff, many of them women, whom he characterised before the Commission as drawing 'but a small pittance,'[58] and in some cases, 'serv[ing] gratuitously' for extended working days of more than 12 hours.[59] Having successfully delegated his predecessor's inspectorial role, Todd set out to build more positive relations with staff outside Adelaide, opening new offices in country districts and speaking at staff farewells or funerals. He remained its paternal figurehead, receiving delegations and petitions from across South Australia, and increasingly adopting the ceremonial and public role which he continued to perform in later years. When Ororoo, a small settlement in the Flinders Ranges sent a deputation to Adelaide seeking a local post office, the Postmaster General, before acceding to the request, quipped famously: 'it's only got two letters!'[60] When Todd subsequently visited the township to officially open the new office in 1880, the 'Punmaster-General,' as he came to be known in civil service circles, received a warm welcome. The town was gaily decorated, and a holiday declared to mark the auspicious local event.[61]

7

The Trials of a Colonial Astronomer: Observing the Transits of Venus (1874 and 1882)

The intense effort involved in completing his greatest telegraph project not only removed Todd from his demanding post and telegraph portfolio, but threatened to bring his astronomical work to a standstill. Before departing for the Northern Territory, Todd delegated his departmental responsibilities to his senior officials; but systematic observatory work remained impossible without the aid of an assistant. Invariably, opportunities for astronomical observation and collaboration passed him by at this high point in his career. One such instance occurred in April 1871, when Victorian astronomer Robert Ellery wrote to the Adelaide Philosophical Society proposing a joint expedition to northern Australia at the end of that year in order to view an eclipse of the sun.[1] Todd, who was grateful to Ellery for the loan of a transit instrument, would normally have seized the opportunity, for a full eclipse would not recur for the rest of the century.[2] But when the eclipse expedition took place in mid-December, Todd, about to embark on a rescue mission of the northern telegraph expedition, could hardly hope to observe it with the naked eye through monsoon cloud.

During his absence from Adelaide, where the solar eclipse was only partial, scientifically-minded staff at the *Register* newspaper took local observations, while the rival *Advertiser* voiced Todd's own regret that 'under the pressure of work that has fallen on him, [he] cannot spare time to observe the eclipse or even enter into calculations'.[3] Expressions of disappointment at the lack of time left for astronomical observation became a regular theme of Todd's correspondence during the 1870s, not least because astronomy was entering an exciting new phase. In the Australian colonies, the transit of Venus expeditions across the globe and a series of other astronomical events attracted widespread colonial interest into the early 1880s.[4] Under-resourced and underprepared as he often was, Todd might well have let such opportunities slip away. But he continued to use his early training and networking skills to good advantage in order to maintain his scientific reputation and astronomical credentials.

The prospect of resuming work in the Observatory was attractive for Todd by 1873, after such a strenuous period of telegraph construction. The South Australian government, in recognition of his efforts, now looked more kindly on his requests to equip the Observatory for purposes other than meteorology. Acknowledging Airy's congratulations in early 1874 on the completion of the overland telegraph,[5] Todd declared his professional obligation 'to maintain the credit of the Royal Observatory in this part of the world'. In the same letter, he proceeded to discuss plans for new equipment and collaborative projects with the Astronomer Royal. Seizing the moment as the recent recipient of a Companion of St Michael and St George (CMG) award, Todd lobbied the South Australian government 'to get a vote for an astronomical observatory' and to secure a much-needed assistant. Instead of replacing the transit instrument on loan from Ellery, he decided on the acquisition of a new 8 inch refractor at an estimated cost of £850.[6] Resting on a sophisticated mechanism with a dome capable of rotating horizontally on cannonballs, the equatorial telescope was designed to track the movement of planets, comets and stars and would greatly enhance Todd's capability as an observer.[7] A specially designed dome would be required to house it at an additional cost of £500, but Todd knew that it would be an important acquisition.[8] For an astronomical event of far greater significance than the 1871 eclipse was now approaching – a transit of Venus in December 1874.

Historically, the transit of Venus was bound up with Australia's colonial past. In 1769, Captain Cook had been sent to observe it in Tahiti before reaching Australia's eastern coast in the following year. Renowned British astronomer, Edmond Halley had previously postulated that transits of the planet Venus, could be used to measure the distance from the earth to the sun, if the time of transit was measured simultaneously from multiple locations on the earth.[9] Cook's voyage was only one of a number of ambitious 18th century expeditions by Europeans to different parts of the globe, in order to view and record the transit of Venus across the sun. A century later, astronomers continued to use observations of the transit of Venus to calculate the distance between the earth and the sun, and thereby establish the size of the solar system: the 'astronomical unit' as it was known.[10] This was determined using triangulation to measure horizontal and vertical triangles from a baseline of known sites on the earth.[11] Transit observations in 1862 suggested a figure which was much lower than the astronomical unit estimated from Cook's and other 18th century observations. Consequently, an expectation prevailed among Todd's contemporaries that the transits of Venus due to occur in 1874 and 1882, would give a more accurate determination and resolve previous inconsistencies.[12] Preparations for the 1874 event were undertaken on an unprecedented scale, as scientists from Germany and the United States joined with their British and French counterparts in organising expeditions to different points of the globe.[13]

At the centre of Britain's intense preparations stood George Airy who, as Astronomer Royal, assumed responsibility for organising and equipping expeditions as well as for directing observers to suitable sites to record Venus' different phases of entry (ingress) and exit (egress) from the sun. Airy estimated that the Asia-Pacific region would be the best location from which to observe its ingress, while India and the Middle East would be superior vantage points for recording its egress from the sun.[14] It presented Australian and New Zealand astronomers with an exciting opportunity and encouraged competition between colonies. Todd, preoccupied with postal and telegraphic matters throughout the early 1870s, recognised it as a situation in which professional reputations could be made. He also knew that the Melbourne and Sydney observatories, directed by Ellery and Russell, were better resourced and had gained a head start. Yet Todd's scientific training and sense of duty to Airy were such that, despite the relentless pressures of his expanding portfolio, he would not forgo such a challenge.

1874 augured well for Todd's astronomy. The South Australian government had approved his observatory requests and its Agent General in London, Francis Dutton[15] placed an order for an equatorial with Airy in October 1873. Dutton, like Todd, knew that a year was in reality a tight time frame within which to design, build and ship such a complex instrument across the world. There were moreover, a number of complications which militated against its timely dispatch. Firstly, Airy, under 'sharp pressure of business'[16] over the upcoming transit of Venus expeditions, had to expedite its manufacture by northern England's highly specialised instrument makers, Cooke and Son, at a time when demand for their telescopes had never been greater.[17] Todd's was but one of numerous requests sent to British workshops by amateurs and professionals eager to observe the celebrated transit of Venus in early December. By July of 1874, this combination of circumstances produced a series of delays and became a source of anxiety both to Dutton, writing to the various parties from London, and to Todd who waited anxiously for news of progress in Adelaide. In August, Dutton wrote to Cooke and Son 'most earnestly requesting that the necessary inspection may be accomplished at the time stated'.[18] Airy was prepared to give up precious time to test the instrument before its dispatch, but Dutton feared that further delays would be incurred should the telescope be sent to Greenwich for inspection, with the real possibility that it would have to be sent north again for final adjustments. To obviate this, Dutton pressed Airy to travel to York himself and undertake the inspection on site, offering to reimburse him for his time.[19] A month later, Cooke kept Dutton on tenterhooks after he telegrammed Airy from York requesting that the necessary inspection be delayed for five days, so that shaking in the mechanism and disturbance to the lenses could be rectified.[20] When Airy eventually arrived from London in August, he still had to wait for the equatorial to be reassembled before his successful inspection, after which it was packed and transported to Southampton for shipping by the end of that month.[21] Only then, with some seven weeks remaining, could Dutton reassure Todd that his telescope would reach Adelaide by 18 October. It had been a tighter than expected timeframe in an unusually crowded year.

It was fortunate that Dutton had assumed responsibility for the acquisition of Todd's equipment. For the Postmaster General himself was engaged on a number of fronts throughout 1874. He was planning to extend telegraph lines south to the coast and across to Kangaroo Island, but the Post Office robbery and Commission usurped most of his time. By late 1874, the Commission was also subsuming his observatory work and threatening to disrupt preparations for the transit event. Amid excitement at the prospect of acquiring 'such a fine instrument,[22] Todd grew increasingly anxious about arrangements for housing his new acquisition and making adjustments to it by December. Although he had finally succeeded in recruiting Alexander Ringwood, a former surveyor on the Overland Telegraph Line as his assistant, he lacked sufficient time to train him, confiding to Oppenheimer in October:

> I am anxious about my equatorial which will be landed next week ... With my hands so full I shall hardly be able to do much for the Transit of Venus.[23]

Fearing damage on its arrival at the wharf and during the construction of the rotating dome in which it was to be housed, Todd meticulously supervised its removal to the Observatory and had it covered to avoid mishandling on the site. By December he had the equatorial mounted and in use, but was still making ongoing adjustments, some of which were not completed until after the transit occurred.[24] Although the Post Office Commission had by now tabled its report, Todd was still busy addressing its recommendations in a detailed response until the New Year. Moreover the sustained pressure of his departmental responsibilities, combined with soaring summer temperatures were taking their toll on his patience. Amid busy preparations, he reported a serious setback to Dutton when the coloured glass of the optical filter, which he needed to install to safely observe the sun, 'shattered in my face' and 'nearly blinded me'.[25] Nor was he able to proceed with systematic plans to photograph the transit, at a time when both Ellery in Melbourne and Russell in Sydney had installed sophisticated photoheliographs capable of capturing and enlarging images of the sun.[26]

One of the attractions of the transit of Venus for Todd and his fellow Australian observers was its renown as a truly international event. Late on the morning of 9 December 1874, a host of astronomers at a multiplicity of sites trained their telescopes on the Sun, waiting for Venus to begin its transit over a period lasting almost five hours. Many of them including Todd were disappointed by the cloudy conditions which obscured their view of its entry and delayed contact. In Adelaide, the extreme heat experienced by Todd during the preparatory period gave way to 'disturbed conditions' and a 'south-west wind,' so that he at first 'very much feared that we should not get even a glimpse of the sun'.[27] When the hot sun did eventually break through the clouds, Todd reported, 'it was only occasionally that either the sun or the planet were steady or sharply defined'.[28] Under these frustrating circumstances, Todd and Ringwood performed creditably, using photographic equipment loaned by the Surveyor General, G.W. Goyder, to take several pictures of Venus after mid-transit, as well as making several sketches. Their most useful contribution comprised micrometric readings of Venus' changing position, taken with the equatorial and a sidereal clock, including its exit from the Sun's face.

Refracting telescope by T Cooke and Sons of York, 1871

One phenomenon which intrigued observers of the transit during both the 19th and 20th centuries were earlier reports of a mysterious 'black drop' visible at the times of ingress and egress from the Sun. During these phases of the transit, the sudden drop in light created an impression that the limb of the sun was making preliminary contact with the visiting planet. Todd looked closely for signs of the black drop, of which 'so much has been written' that it was 'calculated to bias my judgement'. Instead, as Venus approached egress, he observed only 'a very slight disturbance' with 'little distortion'.[29] What he and Ringwood did report this time was 'a faint purplish hue' surrounding the Sun which they interpreted as evidence of Venus' atmosphere.[30] At Adelaide, several amateur astronomers also observed the famous transit: a Mr Smeaton at North Adelaide who used an excellent Cooke and Son equatorial; Mr Dobbie, an instrument maker residing to the north-east of the Observatory, and Mr F.C. Singleton who recorded its times of egress in the Adelaide Observatory grounds. Yet despite the advantage of additional observers and the absence of the black drop to complicate observations, Todd still expressed uncertainty about the precise time of egress, based on the local data he recorded. It was almost a year before he had time to compile a report for Airy at Greenwich as part of the Astronomer Royal's larger undertaking to sift and analyse the mass of incoming observations over the next five years. In spite of Todd's difficulties and his limited success on the day, the 1874 transit of Venus rekindled in him a youthful passion for astronomy over the next decade.

While 1875 was largely taken up with implementing major departmental changes and with planning an ambitious new telegraph route across the Great Australian Bight to Western Australia, Todd found time for his scientific correspondence from London and received minutes of the Royal Astronomical Society meetings. He was in close contact with Robert Ellery and complained to Dutton that while Ellery and Russell were enjoying visits to England, he was 'overworked' and 'a slave' to his Adelaide office at the GPO.[31] Todd particularly wanted 'to get away,' as he put it, to attend the bicentenary of the Royal Observatory, at which Ellery and Russell acted as Australian representatives. In the wake of the transit of Venus, Todd followed professional developments in Britain closely at a time when George Airy faced harsh criticism in the Royal Astronomical Society from Richard Proctor over his calculations and organisation for the transit expeditions. In a letter to Ellery in February 1875,[32] Todd bristled on behalf of his former employer, labelling Proctor 'vindictive' for attacking 'a grand old man who cannot reply to his rash assertions,' and trusted that 'my old friend' Dunkin had not endorsed the 'wrong feelings expressed'. In the following year, Todd took the opportunity to renew his acquaintance from Greenwich days with Dunkin, destined to become President of the Royal Astronomical Society, informing him of his recent observations of the transit of Venus at Adelaide with the newly acquired equatorial telescope.[33]

In spite of Todd's best efforts during 1874, Ellery and Russell stood to benefit most from their participation in the transit of Venus event. They had been well prepared and more fortunate than Todd in enjoying better weather and viewing conditions on the day. As Todd subsequently admitted to Airy, 'my friends Mr Ellery and Mr Russell ... have their own complete appliances,'[34] capable of more extensive photographic observation than his own. Russell, celebrating the 'great success' of his photographic observations, subsequently claimed that they were 'much greater than that of any other party of observers ... of first rate quality [and] numerous of ingress and egress'.[35] All of which scarcely concealed Todd's professional concern that he was being left behind in the astronomical field. The timely visits of his professional colleagues to England proved to be of professional importance. For the photographic reproductions and transit observations which they took overseas with them gained them considerable recognition. Russell's contribution earned him an enviable reputation for stellar photography and he was chosen to represent the Australian colonies at an international astrographic conference in 1877.[36] Ellery, already a member of the prestigious Royal Society, attended the historic Greenwich gathering of astronomers in August 1875 at which Airy paid him a personal compliment, describing the Melbourne observatory catalogue of southern hemisphere stars as 'the best ever published'.[37] Todd, who could only watch from the sidelines, sent Ellery belated congratulations, asserting that had he himself been present, 'I should have liked at the dinner to have expressed my estimation of the observatory under your charge'.[38] His was a genuine compliment but one tinged with a good deal of frustration and professional regret. Of Greenwich, he went on to confide: 'I worship the very ground as hallowed by old association'. He knew the venue well from his days as a young computer.

In touting his longstanding credentials as 'an old Greenwich astronomer' in colonial circles, Todd irritated Ellery and Russell on more than one occasion, forcing him into moments of written apology.[39] At a time when earnest discussions had begun concerning the establishment of a university in Adelaide,[40] Todd still nourished high hopes that the Adelaide Observatory might become an educational institution operating in conjunction with the South Australian Institute under the patronage of the Royal Observatory.[41] His eastern colleagues however considered such confidence misplaced after their successful visits abroad. When Ellery reported critically after his Greenwich visit that he was 'not quite pleased with the cleanliness and order prevailing there,' Todd could only demur, explaining that like all such reminiscences, he saw his early workplace through a different coloured prism. Underpinning Todd's letters to Ellery and Airy at this time, were moments of self-doubt. Fearing that the Adelaide Observatory might yet be reduced to an insignificant backwater unworthy of intercolonial visits, Todd pressed Ellery to make the journey to Adelaide after his return from England, painting his establishment and its newly planted grounds in positive terms.[42] In spite of his great telegraphic work, Todd was painfully aware that an opportunity had gone begging and that his astronomical credentials hardly ranked in England.

Even Dunkin, who knew Todd well from their Greenwich days appeared to subscribe to this view. In his popular astronomical work *The Midnight Sky*, published in 1879, Dunkin who had by then entered the inner circle of British astronomy, made no mention of Todd or of Adelaide, ranking only Ellery's Victorian and Tebbutt's New South Wales establishments as comparable with the established observatory at the Cape of Good Hope.[43]

Todd, with personal knowledge of Airy's situation, knew that the Greenwich bicentenary had occurred at a particularly difficult time for the Astronomer Royal. With the protracted dispute with Proctor still simmering and his board of visitors taking a firmer stance against him, Airy had begun to grapple with the mass of incoming data generated by the transit of Venus expeditions. Comprising some two hundred volumes in extent, it was as yet in unbound form and awaiting years of close analysis. Little wonder that after its central role in the project, the Greenwich Observatory appeared disorganised to colonial visitors. Compounding Airy's difficulties at this period was the poor health of his wife, Ricarda who, having suffered the effects of a paralytic stroke five years before, died a few days after the bicentenary celebrations.[44] Her death cast a long shadow over the Observatory where she had lived and been revered by its staff. From personal memory, Todd learned of Lady Airy's passing 'with much pain' and communicated his sentiments to Airy, albeit in the usual formal manner.[45] Having spent long years in the Observatory as a computer, he had come to look on the Airys as family. For despite his strict discipline, Airy took a personal interest in his young staff.

In the same letter of November 1875, Todd enclosed a detailed report of his transit of Venus observations from Adelaide, enumerating the serious difficulties he had experienced in the preparation and observation phases. His opening apology for the late arrival of the report, delayed by the breakdown of a mail steamer, set the confessional tone for what followed. In keeping with Greenwich days, he reverted to the role of humble assistant, excusing himself in the first instance for the lateness of his results due to 'urgent official duties' and the Post Office Commission.[46] Apart from positive news about his telegraphic projects, his lengthy report exuded frustration and disappointment with his astronomical endeavours. Not only did he dismiss his photographic negatives, in contrast with those of Russell and Ellery, as 'possessing little practical value,' he had since discovered a problem with the micrometer wire, used to track the transit. It cast further doubt on the value of his contribution, though 'he had since remedied it ... I did not notice [it] before... observing the transit of Venus. I should have discovered it when taking coincidence'. All in all, he recalled, it had been a 'most trying season with so much to do – too much to do it satisfactorily'. In a contrite mood, he promised to do better, secure in the knowledge that 'my equatorial is magnificently steady' and 'I hope to have some time next year'.

Whatever Todd's misgivings about his own performance of the previous year, there was no doubting his loyalty to Airy at a period of deep division within British astronomy. Not only had the Astronomer Royal given of his valuable time to ensure the quality of Todd's equatorial, he also provided Todd with useful advice about projects he could undertake in the southern hemisphere. Since Todd had also acquired a spectroscope, capable of separating and analysing starlight, Airy recommended he observe the nebulae and southern stars. The double star of Centaurus was also 'worth watching,' he advised and 'let me put in a word for the phenomenon of Jupiter satellites'.[47] Close examination of Jupiter's atmosphere and its four Galilean moons would preoccupy Todd and his growing observatory staff over the next decade, capturing public interest in the process and gaining them professional recognition through published papers and high quality sketches.[48] By mid-1877, the Adelaide *Advertiser* was proudly reporting that the Observatory's large telescope was being regularly deployed for 'the occultations, transits and eclipses of Jupiter's satellites... at the special request of the Astronomer Royal,' with Todd and his staff 'constantly watching its cloud formations for sudden changes produced by storms of great magnitude and fury' in the vicinity of its great red spot.[49]

Regardless of professional opinions about the Adelaide Observatory in British or colonial circles, the Astronomer Royal continued to engage Todd in collaborative projects, requesting he participate in observing the total lunar eclipse of 1877 and the transit of Mercury in the following year.[50] Although Mercury's transits across the sun were more frequent and deemed to be of less astronomical significance, Todd was better prepared for the occasion and the brief notes he sent to Airy were more positive and enthusiastic than his report of 1875. On this occasion, he enjoyed 'very favourable conditions' with a 'very fair definition of egress.'[51] As previously he saw no sign of the famous black drop after the planet left the face of the sun, but contrasted Mercury's invisibility in 1878 with his 1874 observation, at which time 'the whole disc of Venus was plainly visible'.

The prospect of a second transit of Venus in 1882 made the reduction of the 1874 observations at Greenwich a high priority. But the task would prove a daunting one. According to Airy's senior assistant, Edward Dunkin, it would take seven years to complete.[52] As Airy and his assistants set about their mammoth task, they encountered 'ongoing difficulties' with the determination of sidereal times; 'some of the observations books submitted to them still required 'extensive transcription,' while 'some instrumental errors' gave rise to uncertainty.[53] By his own admission, Todd's data fell into the latter category. There were general and technical problems to be addressed as well. Despite the widespread effort expended on photographing the transit, the wet plate process then in use introduced distortion, so that many photos taken at ingress and egress had to be discarded. In this respect, the contribution of Todd's colleagues, Russell and Ellery, along with those of Indian observers were noteworthy in achieving greater clarity than observations from elsewhere.[54]

Once incoming observations had been confirmed or discounted by Greenwich, colonial contributions were merged with British data to produce a mathematical value of 8'.846 for the solar parallax,[55] an estimate somewhat lower than 18th century observations.[56] Amid general disappointment at the widespread inconsistency of the 1874 observations,[57] Airy, on the advice of the Royal Society's transit of Venus committee,[58] proposed 'more careful preparation' for the 1882 event by confining observations to 'simple telescopic observations or micrometric observations at ingress and egress, if possible at places whose longitudes are known'.[59] For the ageing Astronomer Royal was convinced that 1874 observers had paid insufficient care to identifying their own positions and longitudes. Although he would retire as Astronomer General in 1881, a year before the second transit took place, Airy was still responsible for putting preparatory arrangements into effect. His criticism of the 1874 results was tempered with optimism that the ever-expanding telegraphic network outside Britain would provide the means of determining longitudes more precisely, especially in distant countries like Singapore and Australia.[60] Moreover, the Astronomer Royal was now looking to colonial co-operation with incoming British and American expeditions in order to undertake a definitive determination of local longitudes in conjunction with the 1882 event. It was no small task given his own admission that the determination of longitudes had proved to be 'the most laborious and most expensive part of the transit of 1874'.[61] Yet it was a fresh challenge for which Todd was particularly well suited, having presided over the expanding telegraphic network in Australia including the recent arduous link to Western Australia. With his Adelaide Observatory now properly staffed and in possession of its own transit telescope, Todd was better placed to make a positive contribution than in 1874.

If Airy was looking to a more accurate determination of longitudes as a means of improving results for the second transit of Venus, local developments in the colonies encouraged Todd to pursue a similar course. In mid-1877, five years before the second transit was scheduled to occur, he penned Airy an enthusiastic letter seeking cooperation from Greenwich on the clarification of South Australia's boundaries.[62] As if to dispel lingering doubts about his colonial performance, Todd's self-assurance on this occasion made it clear that he was not simply following instructions or indeed apologising for his previous efforts during 1874–75. Rather, he was proposing a bold plan of action in keeping with his growing reputation as an administrator of vision and energy. In this vein he proceeded, as if to anticipate the Astronomer Royal, 'I think you have already in connection with the transit of Venus made a determination of the differences of longitude between Greenwich and Alexandria'. Now he wanted to extend this work into north Australia, anticipating the new wave of visiting British and American observers. Nor was he simply waiting for Airy to issue him with instructions but took the matter into his own hands. It marked a significant shift in the tone of their correspondence and ushered in a period of renewed self-confidence as a colonial astronomer and collaborator. In order to extend South Australia's survey northward, Todd proposed to divide the telegraph circuits into sections, extending beyond Port Darwin to an Indonesian sister station at Banyuwangi. He further announced his intention to communicate with the Dutch government and with astronomers at Batavia for this purpose, while 'inviting your valuable cooperation in this important matter'.[63]

Although the second transit of Venus was not yet imminent, there were sound reasons for proceeding with a further determination of South Australia's boundaries as Todd was proposing. Ten years earlier, in close consultation with Sydney and Melbourne astronomers as well as members of his survey department, he had embarked on an earlier initiative during construction of a direct telegraph link from Adelaide to Sydney via the border settlement of Wentworth. In July 1867, he communicated his intentions to Airy, stating that 'after I have fixed the East Boundary of the colony I intend verifying some of our outlying surveys'.[64] At that time Todd was seeking to establish the exact location of South Australia's eastern boundary on the 141st meridian of longitude. From a field observatory near the border, he had arranged with astronomers in Sydney and Melbourne to undertake simultaneous observation of the transits of stars on particular evenings and to exchange signals at prearranged times.[65] His controlled 1867 experiment on the north bank of the Murray River had yielded surprising results. Todd concluded that the actual boundary lay 2¼ miles further to the east and constructed a cairn to mark the revised boundary line between the two colonies.⁶⁶ Despite his collaborative approach, the 1867 boundary survey fuelled ongoing controversy between South Australia and Victoria. Ten years later, with no signs of agreement over the boundary with Victoria, Todd was keen to re-examine the question by taking up Airy's appeal to colonial astronomers to determine Australian longitudes for the 1882 transit of Venus. Not only did the systematic determination for Australia and its northern locations promise a more consistent result than in 1874, it also gave Todd the opportunity for 'a good check to the assumed longitudes,' including the vexed 141 meridian.

While at Cambridge, Todd had gained previous experience of determining longitudes by means of the telegraph. But the ambitious attempt to calculate Australian longitudes in conjunction with 1882 transit of Venus was logistically more complex than anything which he had previously attempted. Undertaken across multiple sites both within and outside Australia, it required not only co-operation with Russell and Ellery in Sydney and Melbourne but involved prominent members of Airy's Royal Observatory network. For although the Astronomer Royal, was wearied by the 'long continuous drag of the transits of Venus work' and due to retire in August 1881,⁶⁷ Todd's stated intentions to him had not gone unnoticed in British circles. One leading overseas participant, due to come to Australasia before the 1882 transit, was Colonel George Tupman, who had helped Airy to organise the 1874 British expeditions and labored for four years on the 1874 reductions.⁶⁸ Todd was also in correspondence with Edward Stone, another former Airy assistant.⁶⁹ By now head of the prestigious Radcliffe Observatory at Oxford, Stone was poised to play an important role as a member of the British Commission advising the government on the best methods for observing the 1882 transit. By late November 1882, Todd reported to Stone that he had arranged for exchanges of longitude signals between Singapore, Port Darwin, Adelaide, Melbourne, Sydney and New Zealand.⁷⁰ As ever there were complications when Todd, busy laying a cable in the Gulf of St Vincent missed Colonel Tupman, arriving in Australia by steamer to participate in the operation. Using independent observers at each of these locations, the joint operation first required they take transit observations of selected zeniths over each meridian and establish 'personal equations' or individual variations.⁷¹ Beats were then exchanged automatically and recorded on chronographs, Todd recommending the use of a mirror galvanometer as the optimal method for recording the timing of the signals. His familiarity and technical knowledge of these instruments dated from his later Greenwich years when Airy had recalled him from

Cambridge and promoted him to head the Royal Observatory's new galvanic department.

In directing what was a complex process, Todd was clearly a key player, not least because, as South Australia's Postmaster General, he was able to secure free use of the Eastern Extension's telegraph wires between the chosen sites and facilitate access for visiting observers through his long serving Port Darwin postmaster, J.A.G. Little.[72] Alert to the possibility of limited battery power, Todd conducted a trial exchange between Port Darwin and Singapore before recommending 'the use of simple time signals,' whereupon 'they came through well both ways with very little additional battery power' required.[73] While limited battery power over long distances had been a challenge along the lengthy Overland Telegraph Line, he was by now having to use 'only one translating station at Alice Springs between Adelaide and Port Darwin'. Aware that the exchanges were scheduled to take place during the summer of 1882–83, 'a bad season for the overland telegraph in the tropics,'[74] Todd took the precaution of alerting Stone to possible delays, although he hoped 'to finish everything in January' shortly after the transit of Venus in early December. Careful to acknowledge Ellery's assistance, Todd, in concluding his preliminary report, trusted that 'his own efforts would meet the approval of the commission'. In 1874, he had missed a valuable opportunity to renew his British connections, especially with Airy and the Royal Observatory, but he would not do so again. Writing to Dunkin shortly afterwards to congratulate him on his election to the Royal Society, he confessed that 'he was so overwhelmed with work and correspondence ... I fear I've sadly neglected many old friends'.[75]

As an observer with experience of tropical weather conditions Todd was having second thoughts about travelling to Port Darwin in early December when the transit of Venus would become visible. Rather than run the risk of disappointment a second time, he decided 'at the last minute' to travel by train and steamer to Wentworth, situated at the Murray Darling junction, in the hope of better conditions. He was indebted to Ellery for sending an assistant to replace him at Port Darwin where he was scheduled to participate in the signals exchange with Tupman.[76] At the time of the 1882 transit of Venus, Todd was still awaiting the arrival of a new transit circle[77] which he had purchased for the Adelaide Observatory in 1881.[78] To avoid a repetition of his 1874 problems, Todd put his trust in a 4½ inch equatorial telescope purchased from Benjamin Babbage, an Adelaide scientist and friend. He was already familiar with this instrument, having used it in the previous year to observe the transit of Mercury with Ringwood.[79] The equatorial had passed to Benjamin from his famous uncle, Charles Babbage, and was reputed to have been used by none other than Sir William Herschel.[80] Todd, with his fascination for old astronomical and scientific instruments, must have guarded it zealously on the long journey to Wentworth. His return to the border town where he had made his earlier boundary determination some 15 years ago marked another historic moment in his career as a colonial astronomer. It was a calculated risk to travel inland, but one which proved professionally rewarding on this occasion. To establish his temporary observatory, Todd chose a site a mile from the town near the gaol and constructed an iron fence for the equatorial, with a brick pier in the perimeter for the azimuth transit telescope.[81]

Observers situated on the Australian eastern coast experienced mostly cloudy conditions during the 1882 transit, while Adelaide observers were frustrated by 'a band of cloud over the Mount Lofty range'. With little time to take meridian observations, Todd relied on telegraph signals from the Adelaide Observatory to determine his time and position. He was however able to report 'a fine clear sky' at Wentworth on the morning of 7 December, ideal for viewing Venus both at ingress and egress.[82] In the first phase, he reported seeing 'a few very fine ligaments … connect[ing] the limb of the planet with that of the Sun,' before observing the subsequent phases and successfully recording the times of Venus' internal contact with the Sun.[83] The value of his observations, as noted in his report of late December, was enhanced by the fact that Wentworth constituted the 'most western egress station'[84] for the co-ordinated transit exercise. As Edwards notes, 'he was at one end of a very long baseline, viewing the egress shortly after sunrise, with American observers at the other, and his observations were considered of some importance'.[85] Not that Todd had much time to savour his success. No sooner were the observations made than he had to 'hurry away, having many hundreds of mail tenders coming in … which required my personal attention'.[86] The pressures of his expanding post and telegraph department were a constant refrain of his scientific correspondence, but some of the intense frustration of the mid-1870s was now dissipating. For although he had been forced to wait until after Airy's retirement, he rightly sensed that his reputation as a colonial astronomer was now in the ascendant.

Stone's subsequent reduction of the 1882 observations and calculation of Venus' egress would await the determination of Australian longitudes, completed a few months later in early 1883. In March of that year, the results of the signals exchanged between the various sites were relayed to Stone and to Todd himself. Well before Russell and Ellery filed their report on the joint project in 1886, Todd had every reason to be gratified with the results of the Sydney and Melbourne exchanges, and promised 'to make another determination with my new transit circle in a few weeks'.[87] For while the new longitude calculations were marginally less than his survey results of 1867, they confirmed his claim that the South Australian – Victorian border was well to the east of the existing boundary line and upheld his professional reputation both within and beyond South Australia. In his 1899 report on the landmarks of his Adelaide observatory, Todd nominated his initial determinations, taken at Wentworth in 1867 as one of his earliest and most important achievements.[88]

8

Mapping the Climate, Settling the Land

By the mid-1870s, amidst the rush of postal and telegraphic business, Todd turned his new communications network to scientific advantage by training his scattered observers and departmental staff to record and collect regular rainfall, temperature and barometric data across South Australia. Despite the Observatory's limited staff and lack of instruments, Todd used his official influence as Postmaster General to recruit an assistant and a cadet to begin the task of organising the 1870s data which he had gathered in conjunction with a motley collection of untrained observers and novice officials. To assist him, he chose Alexander Ringwood, a surveyor with a military background and experience on the overland telegraph. Ringwood, who proved to be 'a valuable officer,'[1] was one of a number of officials in South Australia to benefit from Todd's organisational skill and mentoring at the Observatory. As the new cadet, William Cooke, a local university graduate of high mathematical ability,[2] also stood to benefit from Todd's supervision after Ringwood departed in 1883.

At the time of these new appointments, there was still much to be done. The *Register* newspaper, which was scientifically minded, noted with some anxiety that there had twice been delays in the publication of Todd's meteorological reports.[3] This situation was subsequently rectified in 1881, when Todd published detailed rainfall records for 1878 and 1879, including the first map of average annual rainfall for the colony and the Northern Territory. Accompanying these statistics was a photograph of 'thermometer house' at the back of the West Terrace Observatory, where the duplicate weather instruments were located.[4] To the north of the thermometer house in the Observatory complex were the original weather instruments which Todd used to gauge temperature and barometric pressure. This set of readings was routinely compared to those taken on the Greenwich meteorological stand located outside.

While the Observatory remained the site of Todd's Adelaide meteorological observations, the expanding use of the telegraph network meant that much of the work in preparing rainfall reports shifted to the main Post Office. Here a weather clerk was stationed in a room adjacent to the main office in order to collect the reports of local weather dispatched each morning from the growing number of telegraph stations around the colony. By 1 pm each day, Todd, in consultation with Ringwood, drafted a weather report for publication in the afternoon papers. Weather charts were also posted daily at the central Post Office as well as major commercial outlets including Port Adelaide.[5] As Postmaster General, Todd was better placed than his colonial counterparts elsewhere to accord such reports the highest priority and to guarantee their reliability and currency. But it was, above all, the geographic spread of South Australia's stations, as many as 250 by 1883,[6] and the transcontinental reach of the Overland Telegraph Line, which guaranteed them widespread colonial interest. Indeed, a recent South Australian writer argues that by the early 1880s, the unprecedented scope of the Observatory's weather data, over 'a land mass as great as Europe or the lower 48 states of the continental American union,' placed Todd at the forefront of colonial meteorological science.[7]

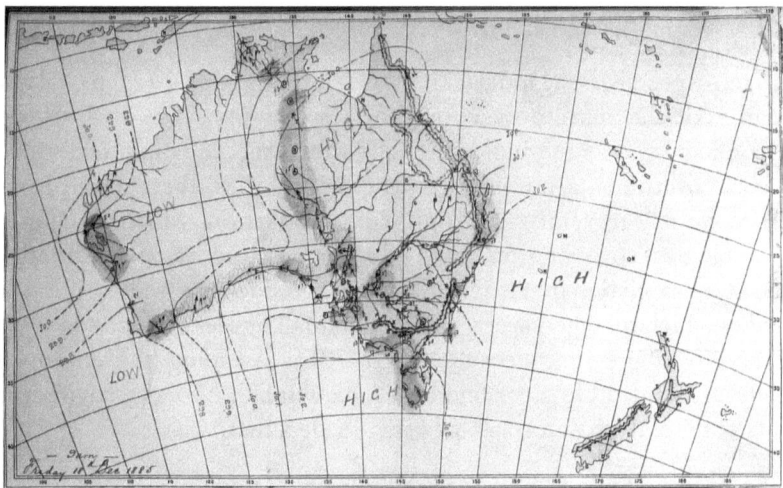

Todd Weather Map showing OT Line and continental coverage, 1885

Throughout this period of consolidation, Todd was also pursuing technical improvements to protect the Line from the damage inflicted on it by seasonal storms and lightning strikes. Regular inspections by linesmen and the reports of station masters identified a number of reasons for these interruptions, among them termite damage and Aboriginal interference.[8] Yet the most serious incursions remained those of the monsoon which flooded adjacent catchments and disrupted telegraphic communication when lightning strikes damaged the insulators and brought down poles. To his British business contact and family friend, Joseph Oppenheimer, Todd, wrote in 1878 of his anxiety 'to know what you think of my new insulators for iron poles. We must do something – the interruptions from broken insulators are fearful'.[9] In May 1880, having already drawn upon Oppenheimer's considerable knowledge of iron poles in order to eliminate termite damage, Todd wrote to him with renewed confidence, adding:

> I fear you will be sick of the subject [but] it is too important to be treated lightly [and] worth all the trouble.[10]

The technology of his telegraph was improving, but conditions in the Northern Territory, coupled with the recent completion of an Adelaide to Perth line across the Great Australian Bight by mid-July 1877 continued to test Todd's ingenuity. By 1884, he had also begun to extend his network of weather stations along the southern coast as far as Eucla, where South Australia established a joint telegraph station with Western Australia. For he rightly argued that a network of stations along the south west coast offered the potential to alert shipping to imminent changes from the Southern Ocean.

In retrospect, Kirsty Douglas rightly identifies Todd as 'a meteorological avatar' and 'the narrator-scientist' for the colonies,[11] at a time when meteorology was emerging as a significant preoccupation not only of colonial governments, but also of their communities. There were practical and economic imperatives of primary production which encouraged meteorological co-operation. Todd took pains to interest horticultural and agricultural societies in his weather work, producing carefully published analyses which matched average annual rainfall figures against wheat yield per acre over previous decades (1861–78).[12] Avoiding the controversy which surrounded Goyder's line of reliable rainfall,[13] Todd recognised the limits of his statistical records, advising readers that:

> Mere inspection of the tables is of little use in leading to just conclusions; the benefit of the rainfall depends, but so much on the quantity

during a given month, as the rapidity or otherwise of its fall, as well as the season of the year.[14]

Steady soaking falls, rather than violent ones, he advised, were preferable for agricultural purposes, and he nominated specific months which were preferable for farming, viticulture and orchards. He was as yet unwilling to issue local forecasts of future good seasons, erring on the side of caution in stating that:

> To be forewarned is to be for forearmed. If men cannot alter the laws of Nature, correct knowledge of them often serves to mitigate their effects.[15]

A further outcome of Todd's enlarged weather network, critical for tracking the movements of the tropical monsoon, was a scientific preoccupation with achieving more accurate information for monthly and annual reports which appeared in the press as well as the *Government Gazette*. In his Observatory report of 1875, Todd recommended 'a system of photographic registration of temperature and atmosphere,' in preference to simple visual observations, and the acquisition of 'a more sensitive anemometer' to record the velocity and direction the winds.[16] By the late 1870s, colonial newspapers paid tribute to Todd's exposition of South Australia's climate. The *Sydney Morning Herald* commented favourably on Todd's accumulating statistics, noting the dryness of the South Australian climate which, according to Todd and George Strickland Kingston averaged only 21 inches of rain annually over the previous 26 years. For the edification of its own drought-affected readers, the *Herald* went on to observe that:

> In New South Wales we should consider this a wretchedly small supply; but the South Australians are used to it and manage to get along very well with that average. They only call out when the rainfall is considerably below this.[17]

Accolades also came from further afield. When the science journal, *Nature*, favorably reviewed Todd's systematic rainfall returns in 1877, the Adelaide *Register* editorialised that greater government funding should be provided for the staff and instruments of the Observatory.[18] In particular there was a need for new self-registering instruments, less prone to human error than existing methods, in order to guarantee the Adelaide Observatory improved status as a first class meteorological station by the international standards of the day.

Though it was previously deemed premature, Todd helped revive the initiative of inter-colonial meetings to discuss meteorology on a regular basis. As a hallmark of respect for his illustrious German colleague Neumayer, Todd retained in his library a personally signed copy of his definitive meteorological study of Victoria[19] for reference in ongoing discussions with Ellery and other colonial colleagues. The first in a series of meteorological conferences was held in Sydney in 1879. Convened by Henry Chamberlain Russell, George Smalley's successor, it marked a new phase in co-operation between the colonies, one which endured until the end of the century. Russell, who had made a name for himself over the transit of Venus observations, was bent on expanding New South Wales' meteorological services, having published a synoptic chart in the *Sydney Morning Herald* two years earlier.[20] The 1879 conference upheld Todd's preoccupation with agricultural and climatic observation, adding the need for storm warnings to coastal shipping as a second scientific imperative. Those present had to grapple with the need for agreed standards on the types of instruments in use, as well as on times of observation across the colonies.[21] In spite of abundant anomalies, the Sydney conference went about its work vigorously for the best part of a week, adopting 26 resolutions against which each delegate subsequently reported at a follow-up Melbourne event in 1881. Perhaps the most critical omission was the absence of wider participation on the part of other colonies. Queensland and New Zealand, in particular, were identified as essential in providing their neighbours with weather trends and early warnings of storm events.

At face-to-face gatherings, Todd, with his careful preparation and grasp of detail, was characteristically in his element. Though often lacking the resources and staffing of his fellow meteorologists, he was more than able to hold his own in discussions with representatives of the more established colonies. Reporting on the 26 resolutions of 1879 at the second gathering of April 1881, he confirmed the acquisition of self-registering instruments at the Adelaide Observatory as well as a dramatic expansion of weather stations. He boldly added further resolutions to those of 1879, with a view to obtaining 'a standard set of instruments across the four colonies'.[22] Prior to the 1881 event, he had already been in correspondence with Ellery's Victorian deputy about standardising observations between the colonies and took the opportunity on this occasion to press Charles Russell of New South Wales to rectify inconsistencies in the times of observation of the telegraphic data exchanged between them.[23] After a further request by New South Wales to approach Queensland about joining the conferences,[24] Todd went on to prescribe the conditions and nature of the observations to be taken at future meteorological stations established in the centre and far north of the continent. Victoria, under Ellery was already well organised for such collaboration, but whether New South Wales or Tasmania, let alone Queensland or Western Australia, would proceed with such measures, dependent as they were on government support, remained to be seen. For the moment, however, Todd's capacity for organisation, allied to scientific precision, confirmed his professional and administrative prowess in the company of other leading figures and fellow public servants.

In the wake of his overland telegraph exploits, Todd remained something of a risk taker. For while issuing cautious advice to settlers and farmers, much of it disregarded in the wake of the Goyder's controversial line of rainfall recommendation, Todd persisted in the optimistic belief that South Australia's northern stock owners, including family, had learnt the harsh lessons of the 1860s drought and were less vulnerable than their counterparts elsewhere. A few years later, Todd himself decided to invest in 'sheep farming,' as he described it, motivated in part by the desire to assist his young relatives, especially his niece Fanny who, after marrying Charles Willoughby Davies in 1871, took up land in the north-west of the colony.[25] According to his own diary,[26] Charles Willoughby acquired his early sheep farming experience in the Gawler ranges and had visited the Mattawarrungala property as early as 1863, eight years before he married Frances. Confident of its water supply, he established a three-room homestead there, leaving it in the hands of a manager. Todd's own interest in property may have been kindled during his return trip across the continent in 1872, at which time he visited Charles and Fanny at their Mattawarrungala station in the Flinders Ranges. By the end of the decade, he would encourage the use of his overland telegraph stations, including Alice Springs, as experimental sites for sheep farming in inland Australia.[27] When Charles Willoughby Davies decided, in 1877, to purchase a second property Moonarie station, in the Gawler Ranges, Todd joined him as a partner in the enterprise which traded as Davies Todd and Coy, and purchased a one-third stake in Mattawarrungala with his nephew by marriage.[28]

Fanny Todd, c.1865

Friendship and family loyalties aside, how might one explain this unlikely investment by Charles, the civil servant, who observed careful domestic and departmental economies and whose investments had previously been confined to banking and other urban enterprises? In the first instance, the material circumstances of the Todds were, by the mid-1870s, better than they had ever been, despite the birth of their fourth daughter, Lorna in 1877. Moreover, as Postmaster General and Superintendent of Electric Telegraphs, Todd was now one of South Australia's best paid public servants on the comfortable salary of £950 per year.[29] Additionally, for his strenuous efforts in completing the Overland Telegraph Line under such difficult circumstances, he had been granted a bonus of a £1000 by the South Australian parliament.[30] On his return from the north in 1872, Charles and Alice initially planned a holiday to Tasmania, but owing to the demands of his expanded portfolios, this trip did not eventuate, nor indeed a subsequent plan to visit the United Kingdom. Given these circumstances, it is not altogether surprising that Charles and Alice considered investing in the Moonarie property, located some 450 kilometres distant from Adelaide. Alice too, had been a beneficiary of the Bell family will by this time, after her mother Charlotte died in her care at the Observatory in mid-1875.[31]

Although their financial position had been secure, it proved a difficult time for both her and Charles, when a family legal dispute broke out with Edward Bell, the eldest surviving son, over his claim on the family will,[32] compounded by the sudden death of Charles' Assistant Superintendent of Electric Telegraphs, W.J. Cunningham from apoplexy.[33] Cunningham, recently promoted to Deputy Postmaster General, had provided the Todd family with much-needed support during Charles' protracted absence in the Northern Territory, including advice to Alice on financial matters and post office business.[34] Thereafter, he was regarded as a family confident as well as Charles' trustworthy Assistant. In protecting Alice's interest, Charles dealt firmly but fairly with the matter of the will, explaining to various legal parties how the Adelaide family had supported Mrs Bell at their expense during her long illness at the Observatory, one which necessitated the employment of a full-time servant to care for her.[35] Instead of returning to England on the death of her mother, Alice remained in Adelaide, nursing Lorna and comforted by Charles and her own growing family.

After Charles' pastoral investment in 1877, his daughters Lizzie and Gwendoline, who had befriended Frances when she lived and worked in the Todd household, paid visits to her and her children at Mattawarrungala.[36] According to a comprehensive study of the Adelaide colonial gentry,[37] ownership of pastoral property was well regarded among established Adelaide families and its acquisition represented a significant moment in the gentrification of the Todds. By now, the Observatory had acquired its own roomy stables and the older children took morning rides, albeit not without risks in the busy city environment. In August 1877, the local *Register* reported a dramatic 'double accident' after Maude's horse bolted and carried her from the Observatory at West Terrace into the city centre, with her elder brother Hedley in hot pursuit. The *Register* noted at the time that 'Miss Todd, being a good rider, had kept her seat' through the ordeal, until the runaway horse finally threw her onto the roadway in King William Street, 'shaken but unhurt'.[38] Lorna later claimed that Maude had in fact been 'dragged by one foot in the stirrup over newly metalled roads' and that she suffered more serious injuries than the *Register* implied.[39]

Hedley, who had collided with a pedestrian in the pursuit of his sister aged 12 at the time of their publicised incident, continued to develop his riding skills to a high standard, earning him regular membership of the Adelaide Hunt Club in keeping with the family's rising social aspirations.[40]

Among their wide ranging social contacts in Adelaide society, the Todd family boasted established members of the medical fraternity, including Charles Willoughby's father, Dr Charles Davies a close friend of Todd who had been a neighbour after they arrived in Adelaide. Of Welsh extraction, Dr Davies had established a 'large and lucrative medical practice' over several decades in the city,[41] while actively pursuing other professional and cultural interests. These included serving on the Adelaide Hospital Board, involvement with the Botanic Gardens and a seat on the Legislative Council (1857–64). A noted French scholar, keen biographer and historian, Davies contributed articles to the *Register* before he retired from North Adelaide to Beaumont. Apart from active civic involvement, Davies shared with Todd a passion for museums, and some of the items which made up Davies' private museum may well have passed to his longstanding friend when it was broken up prior to his death in the late 1880s.[42] Davies had previously sold the Mattawarrungala property to his eldest son, Charles Willoughby Davies, who was also educated in languages and interested in colonial science. During the mid-70s, Charles Willoughby took Fanny and their young family to Adelaide, Melbourne and Sydney, visiting the New South Wales Observatory 'where Mr Russell was very attentive and showed us all over it ... it was magnificent'.[43] By colonial standards, he was a liberal thinker, disparaging the Ten Commandments as 'the work of a man' at an age 'when women were looked upon as little more than slaves and as inferior beings'.[44]

The success of close associates like Dr Charles Davies fuelled the Todds' own social aspirations during the late 1870s. Another eminent Adelaide doctor, Edward Stirling, gave Charles professional advice concerning the education of his elder son, Charles Edward. In 1876, Todd had already placed his younger son Hedley, with Elders, the leading South Australian pastoral company;[45] but 'Charlie', more academically gifted and restless for England, was destined for the ranks of the medical profession. After he won a scholarship at St Peter's College, Todd, on Stirling's advice, paid for him to train as a surgeon in London. Upon Charlie's arrival in 1878, Stirling, who was lecturing in London at that time, undertook to 'befriend him and... help him in the way of taking the necessary steps at the Royal College of Surgeons and studying at St George's Hospital'.[46] Stirling's close involvement was further evidence of the Todd's family's social standing, but Charles' London training incurred sizeable expenses which had to be met at a time when Todd's pastoral investments had not yet realised a profit.

In the course of his son's medical training, both in London and subsequently on the continent, Todd turned to his business associate Joseph Oppenheimer, to oversee the necessary financial arrangements and for news of his son. During the early 1880s, their regular correspondence alternated between technical discussions of telegraphy and electricity, and more personal matters, including his aspirations for Charlie and his own new-found interest in sheep farming. Charles, who was sending Oppenheimer Charlie's living allowance in regular £50 instalments, recognised the importance of his son's success for the entire family. In a letter of October 1881, he thanked Joseph for taking his son on a trip to the continent, expressing pleasure at the news that 'he is reading diligently. [I] hope he will pass his next exam with flying colours'.[47] Deferring once more to Stirling, he suggested in the same letter that Charlie undertake 'some hospital practice as a junior house surgeon' while in Europe, deferring to the former's advice that:

> If he can obtain some other position with pay, it will be a very great thing. It is important that he come home as a tried man.

Charlie did not disappoint his father. By 1881, he had been awarded several medical degrees in London, gaining further qualifications and experience during 1882 at Brussels, where he obtained a Doctor of Medicine.[48]

While supporting Charlie in Europe, Todd with his partner Charles Davis Jr increased capital investment in Moonarie in the expectation of better returns. Writing to Oppenheimer in 1882, he expressed confidence that 'we can work the two stations more economically than one and we shall shear 30,000 sheep this year and next year I hope we shall shear 40,000'.[49] Todd and Davies appear to have learned some of the harsh lessons of the 1860s drought in the Gawler Ranges for they demonstrated an enlightened approach to improving the land.[50] In the following year, Todd confided to Oppenheimer that he would have to defer his journey to England because of the additional costs involved in fencing, sinking wells and making other improvements.[51] All of this incurred considerable expense and necessitated substantial loans from the Commercial Bank of South Australia, amounting to almost £10,000 by the mid-1880s.[52] Whether Todd had agreed to borrow this entire sum before his departure for England is unclear. But the family's pastoral investments appear to have weathered the difficult start-up conditions and were, in Todd's own words, 'fairly profitable'.[53]

Todd identified the figure of 40,000 sheep as the number of stock needed to put Moonarie on a firm footing. However the business was not progressing as rapidly as he had hoped when he left for England; lambing was less satisfactory and bank charges were draining the family company's finances amid the growing prospect of renewed drought. Buoyed by Charlie's successful return from Europe and by the prospect of sharing his plans with Oppenheimer in person, Todd could delay his promised trip to England no longer. Preoccupied with departmental matters before his impending departure, he did not visit the property in person; nor did Charles Willoughby at that time take an active role on Moonarie, preferring to employ a series of on-site managers. The sharp recession in primary production during 1886–87 confirmed that the family firm had overreached itself. The renewed involvement of Charles Davies senior in the Moonarie company, which traded in its later years as Davies, Todd, Davies,[54] confirms the heavy ongoing capital demands which the station was placing on its owners. The company continued to lose money, accumulating a large debt to the Commercial Bank of South Australia repayable at high rates of interest.[55] Mattawarrungala, already unprofitable,[56] had been disposed of, but the firm's heavy debts on the Moonarie runs, amounting to no less than £18,000, were still outstanding. Of the £7000 which had to be paid back to the bank promptly in September 1887 under the terms of settlement, Todd's share was an estimated £2764.[57] More onerous still was the outstanding £10,000, a huge sum of money, expected from the owners only a few months later. It was a crisis which threatened to engulf every member of the Todd family.

The only solution was to resort to creditors who, after satisfying the Bank's demands, would in turn demand repayment with interest over a more protracted period. The identity of the individual creditor who was responsible for discharging such a large pastoral debt was not widely known beyond the immediate family. Described only as 'a family friend,'[58] he was none other that Henry Scott, a former Adelaide Mayor and Legislative Councillor with pastoral investments and extensive experience as a wool merchant. That Scott, with substantial holdings at Glen Osmond near Adelaide, entertained the South Australian Governor and other dignitaries, was proof of his social standing.[59] The Todds do not appear to have been part of Scott's inner circle. Rather, it is likely that Henry Scott, as a sheep farmer, became acquainted with Todd through their business interests and may have sold him stock before the crash. Certainly Scott, whom Todd later described as a 'kind creditor,'⁶⁰ did more than could have been expected of him in the immediate aftermath, offering the Todds and Davies a large loan on generous terms and even assuming one third of the reconstructed company's future liability.⁶¹ Yet business records show that Scott was not always so generous towards his clients and was not averse to compounding their debts by adding the costs of Supreme Court actions against them if they failed to maintain timely payments.⁶² Neither this additional expense nor the adverse publicity accompanying it was desirable for someone of Todd's position.

Notable, too, in the course of the episode was the central role assumed by Todd's eldest son, Charles, who, having returned from Europe and established a successful Adelaide practice as a surgeon, acted as financial guarantor for the family interest under the terms of the new agreement. It was to Charles Todd junior that Scott lent £2000 on generous terms ⁶³ to assist the Todd family, when it was unable to meet the initial sum required by the Bank. Of the £10,000 still to be repaid, an estimated £3600, with additional annual interest of £200, fell upon the Todds themselves, most of which would come from Todd's lucrative annual salary of £950 per annum. Within the immediate family circle, Lorna, the youngest was inclined to blame both her father and her relatives for the imposed austerity which she claimed endured until the end of the century, by which time the full sum had been paid off. As she recalled, not without irony:

> In the terrible droughts and early eighties, so many of the banks failed and station owners suffered heavily. We were not out of debt until I was twenty. In spite of this financial disaster, I never remember money being spoken of in our family. Perhaps because there was none to speak of! ⁶⁴

Yet her further complaint that both Hedley and Charlie's careers were adversely affected by the family's financial situation appears overstated, since both had secured their positions before the family company's collapse. Clearly though, the family's aspirations and social status had received a substantial setback. George Symes, Todd's early biographer, after a searching examination of the episode, could only conclude 'there must have been some economies, but they do not appear to have affected the family lifestyle unduly'.⁶⁵

In the aftermath, the Davies family who had partnered Todd in Moonarie, bore the greatest share of the financial burden, only some of which was met before Todd's close friend, Charles Davies senior, passed away in 1889. Neither Charles nor Alice appear to have blamed the Davies for their loss, and they maintained contact with Fanny after that time. It was undoubtedly a salutary lesson which left its mark on Todd's administrative style throughout the 1890s. For Fanny and Charles Willoughby, who managed Moonarie for another decade after the debt crisis, life on the land became a protracted physical and emotional struggle. The dry conditions of the 1890s helped to end the rabbit plague, but renewed drought, coupled with the cost of fencing to deter dingoes, proved exorbitant at a time when few properties were making a profit. Moreover, Charles Willoughby, despite his energy and experience, suffered more publicly than Todd. Their eventual return to Adelaide must have been a relief for Fanny, who died before her uncle Charles in 1909 at 58. While on the land, she had given birth to seven children, but was predeceased by four of them, three as babies.[66] Such were the hazards of colonial life on the land. By the time the Davies had finally paid off the debt at the end of the century, drought had taken on a dramatic new dimension across the colonies in the form of a triple El Nino of unprecedented intensity.[67]

The risky sheep farming venture provides a fresh perspective on Todd, the settler, but what of the scientist? As a meteorologist, he may well have been 'forewarned', but personal factors including family connections and his commitment to inland settlement came into play, overriding his natural caution. Although he had documented the rainfall of the colony for several previous decades, including seven-year averages for its pastoral stations, this had ultimately little mitigating effect on the Todd Davies company losses. That Mattawarrungala station's annual rainfall declined from 11 to 6 inches by 1880, or that the Moonarie runs recorded only 4.5 inches in 1886–87,[68] appears to have played little part in his or his nephew's business decision. As family historian, Alice Thomson, would later contend of Todd's failed pastoral venture:

> He must have begun to realise that they'd been the worst bet of his life. By the early 1880's, the region's lakes had turned to salt, and the properties were worthless.[69]

Drought had not been the only cause of the setback. On Moonarie station,[70] like Mattawarrungala, 'the increase in dingoes, the absence of vermin [rabbit] fences and the low price of wool,' all played their part – factors which were largely beyond the settler's or the scientist's control. According to one contemporary witness in evidence to the 1893 Vermin Proof Fencing Commission, the onset of rabbits was responsible for reducing stocking levels on sheep properties in the Gawler ranges to as little as a quarter of their previous numbers.[71] The Todds were not destined to enter the ranks of the gentry, with ongoing links to the land, but they remained distinguished members of Adelaide's professional middle class.[72]

What do Todd's own meteorological notebooks tell us about this critical period? In early 1884, he wrote that the climate had been a mixture of 'extreme heat all over the colony' and 'almost wintry weather' with 'low temperatures and wet days'.[73] By the middle of that year, South Australia's rainfall had fallen well below the annual average, both in Adelaide and in northern pastoral areas.[74] Todd's meteorological description of drought within the colony at this time encompassed a number of indicators, not merely heat and rain, but barometric pressure and 'a remarkable absence of wind'.[75] At the Observatory, he began to scan the rainfall figures with growing apprehension, writing to William Preece in 1889:

> I sent you some notes on rainfall for 1888 – probably the driest year on record. I am anxiously waiting for rain, and unless it comes soon we shall have another bad lambing.[76]

By the 1880's, Todd, as South Australia's observer, was adept at meeting public demand for weather forecasts, but the issue of seasonal prediction was far more complex. Moreover, his views on the subject differed from those of his professional colleagues. When interviewed by the Melbourne *Argus*, amid fears of an impending drought, neither Todd nor Ellery were willing to stand by the accuracy of their weather forecasts beyond a few days, unlike Henry Russell who proposed a complex ten year weather cycle as a means of predicting drought.[77] The *Argus* reporter, unaware of Todd's own predicament, applauded his 'winning modesty', but was conscious that pastoral settlers required scientific information 'in advance for stocking purposes', and farmers 'for manure and pest prevention'.[78] In the following year, Russell's New South Wales colleague, Charles Egeson, who championed cyclical prediction, proposed a 33 year cycle of weather change.[79] Amid a new willingness on the part of the press to enlist both sunspot and cyclical theories in the interests of colonial meteorology, the Adelaide *Register*, like the Melbourne *Argus*, devoted a long feature article to cyclical theory, attributing its colonial origins to Russell's 1876 paper.[80] When questioned about cyclical theory, Todd responded cautiously, intimating that more research would be required. Writing to Russell to congratulate him on his recent appointment to the Royal Society, Todd voiced his private opinion of Egeson as a mere populariser and 'faddest of the extreme order'.[81] Subsequently, he responded publicly to Egeson's further predictions of a three-year drought, claiming that, on the basis of the existing rainfall record, he could see 'no justification' for such a prediction.[82] Whereupon, the *Register* turned Todd's critical remarks into the positive but misleading headline: 'The Predicted Drought: No Cause for Alarm'.[83]

Despite such public statements, Todd was not entirely sceptical or dismissive of contemporary meteorological theory. Rather, he and his assistant William Cooke put cyclical theory to the test. After a careful study of fifty years of South Australian and New South Wales climate data, they concluded that the unusual weather events of 1875–76, during which the wettest year abruptly shifted to the driest, undermined the assumptions of cyclical theorists and the proposition that 'years in succession gradually get wetter until they reach a maximum [and] a minimum is reached when the cycle begins again'.[84] Stimulated by Henry Blanford's regional study of the Indian climate and his observations of high barometric pressure in the Indian Ocean during the monsoonal failure of 1877–78,[85] Todd had also begun to look beyond immediate colonial conditions. Though little publicised or understood at the time, these important insights appear in his 1888 *Argus* interview, when he explained that:

> Comparing our records with those of India, I find a close correspondence of similarity of seasons with regard to the prevalence of drought and there can be little or no doubt that severe droughts occur as a rule simultaneously over the two countries.[86]

Only a century later, with greater scientific understanding of the ENSO (El Niño Southern Oscillation) would Todd's part in identifying teleconnections – 'associations or linkages between climate anomalies in different parts of the world'[87] – be fully acknowledged. It was a valuable insight, guided not solely by close and persistent local observation, but by Todd's willingness to collaborate and communicate with observatories further afield in India and Singapore. Nor was this mere posturing on Todd's part; for he would continue to pursue teleconnections between Australia and India, proposing a few years later that 'a thorough investigation' be conducted of 'past numerical data regarding pressure, rainfall and droughts and comparison of these with elements over the Indian, Javan and Cape areas at the same time'.[88] Here was firm evidence, of important meteorological work undertaken on the periphery of empire, with the potential to guarantee colonial science an important ongoing place in public affairs and policy.[89]

9

Renewal and Recognition: The European Tour of 1885–86

Todd's energetic tour of Europe, undertaken during 1885–86, after thirty years in office as South Australia's Superintendent of Electric Telegraphs and scientific Observer, and fifteen years as its Postmaster General, marked an important moment in his eventful public career. Despite sporadic ill health in early 1885, Todd had sustained relentless administrative schedules since the 1870s. Until the time of his departure for Europe, Todd was working on an extensive report of his multiple portfolios, including one which encompassed the achievements of the Overland Telegraph and West Australian lines. Additionally, he documented South Australia's expanding communication network, comprising not only local and intercolonial telegraph lines, but also hundreds of new post offices and an embryonic telephone network, opened in Adelaide during mid-1883.[1] Todd's meticulous passion for departmental statistics was offset in his monumental report by a first person narrative which addressed his readers in a condensed and at times disarming style. He was undoubtedly ruminating as he wrote up the events of previous decades. What began as a 'mea culpa', based on an admission that previous departmental reports had appeared only in the form of parliamentary papers, ended with a note of quiet satisfaction and the philosophical declaration that 'my task is finished. I have dug deep and turned the Department inside out. I've shown it as it is with all its spots and wrinkles and blemishes,' coupled with the request that 'we may be compared with similar institutions elsewhere and, so judged, we shall at least pass muster'.[2]

Many fellow South Australian colonists believed that Todd had done much better than this. After announcing a 'trip home ... to take in America' over some eight months, he was showered with compliments. Charles Kingston, then Attorney General, spoke to the first full gathering of Todd's departmental officers, some 1300–1400 in number, urging him to 'throw off the cares of office and thoroughly enjoy himself,'[3] while the Mayor of Glenelg applauded his public mindedness and respectful attitude to his women workers. Responding to well-wishers, Todd attributed his success to the diligence of his own staff, commending in particular Edward Squire, 'his able and affectionate colleague,' who would administer the Post and Telegraph department in his absence, while William Cooke maintained the Observatory.[4]

Although his plans were by no means finalised, Todd had planned to return to Europe for decades; his inability to do so was a regular theme of his correspondence. His motives for doing so now were complex and not simply about relaxation, although he would prove to be a keen tourist. To his close friend and correspondent, Joseph Oppenheimer, Todd had written excitedly as early as 1866 of 'a trip to Europe especially with the pleasure of your company,' since:

> I need hardly say that one becomes rusty in a scientific manner after living in a small colony like South Australia for upward of 10 years.[5]

Since ordering electric lamps from Oppenheimer in preparation for the Prince of Wales' visit to Adelaide in 1867, Todd had maintained their enthusiastic correspondence on telegraphic and electrical matters, but also increasingly on family affairs.[6] It was therefore not surprising that Charles, though a Londoner by birth and education, intended spending considerable time in north England close to Oppenheimer's residence at Stockport, Manchester, in order to join him in inspections of the cable and engineering workshops concentrated around industrial Manchester and Liverpool.

The prospect of a long trip to Europe beckoned as early as the 1870s, when on completing the Overland Telegraph Line, Charles announced to Harry Squires, a close Cambridge relative, that he planned an overseas trip 'to see as much of the world as possible,' returning via California at a cost of £500.[7] To Francis Dutton, South Australia's Agent General, Todd confided in 1873 that:

> I am being persuaded to visit Europe this year – leaving about May but I fear it would not be wise to leave my department so soon.[8]

Two years later on, Todd complained that 'it will be impossible for me to get away' and that he had 'never worked harder ... nor had he been less thanked or thought of'.⁹ He further contended to Dutton in London that:

> The entire absorption of my time on purely departmental matters has operated greatly to my injury in reputation. Had I visited England immediately after my completion of the Overland Telegraph, I should no doubt have secured my election on the RS [Royal Society].¹⁰

At that time, there had been encouragement from the local press and in England from Professor John Couch Adams at Cambridge and George Airy at Greenwich, but Todd, still intensely busy with telegraphic and postal matters, had been unable to 'seize the moment' or even the prospect of a short holiday in Tasmania with Alice and daughter Elizabeth.

Now in the early 1880s, Todd was sufficiently established to reconsider his situation, after renewing contact with former Greenwich colleagues upon whom he could rely in gaining professional recognition. Well aware that correspondence alone would be insufficient, he began to lobby both old and new acquaintances in person to achieve what he still regarded as the pinnacle of scientific achievement – election to the prestigious Royal Society of London. Even so, there was lingering uncertainty as late as July 1884, when he inquired of British scientist and Royal Society Fellow, Edward Stone:

> Do you think I should have any chance of again nominating to FRS? Professor Adams and some others nominated me many years ago before I had completed my chief work, the erection of the telegraph through Australia.¹¹

Clearly, the European trip of the following year was about fulfilling the lost opportunity of an FRS, and putting both himself and South Australia on the same professional footing as New South Wales and Victoria, while seizing a rare personal opportunity to visit the workshops and observatories of Europe.

Despite the weight of these expectations, Todd's trip also included personal considerations. Apart from regular summer holidays spent at Port Elliot and Henley Beach, Charles and Alice had spent little time away from the Observatory together. Unlike Charles, whose parents were by now deceased, Alice had previously returned to England to visit her family in 1862, and no longer felt the need to do so again. Her father, Edward Bell, had died a few years after her visit in 1865, and her eldest sister, Sarah Squires (née Bell), with whom she had corresponded in the early Adelaide years, had passed away in 1868,[12] while her ailing mother, Charlotte, who had come to live with her at the Observatory, had succumbed in January 1875.[13] Instead of Alice, it was to be Elizabeth, their eldest daughter, who accompanied Charles on his travels abroad. As a young child, she had visited the Bells in Cambridge with her mother, but was now ready to follow in her brother Charles' footsteps and return to England for a more protracted European tour. Well educated, independent and at ease in society, Elizabeth had played an important part in the upbringing of her younger sisters, a role not lost on Charles who referred to her in correspondence as 'the same dear girl and ever a help to Maud and Gwenny'.[14] Lorna, though 21 years her younger, regarded Elizabeth as a 'wonderful sister' and 'daughter to the whole family'.[15] For it was Lizzie who had nursed Maude after her well-publicised riding accident and given Lorna the time she craved during her mother's busy social and church routines.

Now approaching thirty, Elizabeth had not yet married, and Lorna hinted that a 'personal disappointment' in Adelaide society had led her to withdraw from subsequent involvements.[16] Alice and Charles may have considered that such a trip would distract his cherished daughter from contact with Adelaide society and her family duties, though he could not have foreseen the consequences of her entering London and European society. For the purposes of travel, Elizabeth was to be accompanied by an older woman, in this instance, a friend of the family in place of Alice. Charles, despite his many professional commitments and activities, would spend considerable time in concert going and sightseeing with Elizabeth and her various travel companions. For he enjoyed mixed company, especially among fellow scientists, and proved adept throughout their European travel at working social and tourist engagements into his taxing professional schedule.

On 24 April 1885, Todd, 'in the seve and yellow leaf of old age'[17] as he then described himself, embarked from Adelaide with Elizabeth on the *Khedive*. Compared to the Adelaide voyage of 1855, their return journey thirty years later was relatively short, lasting only six to seven weeks. Todd enjoyed the sea and was adept at tracking the stars and the longitude. Even so, the return journey must have felt strange after his usual strenuous office routine, which stretched from morning until evening, followed by his observatory work. No personal record of their early weeks on the *Khedive* survives, until September when Charles began a travel diary. No doubt the recent completion of his monumental departmental report had temporarily curbed his prolific report writing, though not his correspondence which he continued actively while at sea. Subsequently

Todd divulged that their vessel stopped for several days at Colombo *en route* to Europe, where they visited former South Australian Governor, Major Fergusson, dining with him at his residence in the Cinnamon Gardens. Fergusson had been Governor at the time of the Overland Telegraph Line's construction, and Todd found that he 'still took a deep interest in all matters concerning South Australia' including its overland telegraph network.[18]

Apart from the company of Lizzie and the other passengers, Todd still had administrative matters to ponder. The South Australian government had requested his attendance at an international telegraph conference, to be held in Berlin in September, while the intercolonial post and telegraph conference of 1883 had relegated to him the task of negotiating with the British Post Office on its behalf. Newspaper reports make it clear that Todd's first weeks in London after his arrival set the pace for what followed in coming months. Once in the capital, he lost no time in opening negotiations on several fronts, notably with British postal authorities for a parcel post to the Australasian colonies. Postal authorities in India and Hong Kong had previously mooted such a service between the Far East and Britain, but it was left to Todd to pursue the matter, which he did so effectively once in London.[19] Secondly and more critically, he was looking to urgently negotiate the reduction of telegraph costs to Australia, with potential implications for South Australia and its transcontinental landline. For, in the event of success, it too would be required to lower its transit rates and incur additional financial loss. Unlike his previous cable business, the London talks involved him in face to face discussions with Eastern Extension (EE) Telegraph Company's powerful British directors, John Pender and James Anderson, and with the colonial Agents-General based in London as well as with conference delegates arriving for the upcoming Berlin event. In view of the number of interested players, there would be much hard bargaining before any solution was forthcoming. In particular, Todd, as the go-between for the Eastern Extension and the Australasian colonies, was keen to reach an agreement with the EE, to which the Overland Telegraph Line was linked, on a price structure for different classes of telegrams: firstly, for private cables, still expensive at 8s 8d a word and also for press cables, at a more moderate 2s 8d per word.[20]

Amid these preliminary negotiations, Charles took time to revel in the food and company on offer in London, 'out-heroding Herod,' as one London corresponding put it, and 'boasting two dinners in one evening'.[21] One initial source of enchantment in London for Todd were the illuminations. He had long studied such developments while in South Australia and, prior to his departure, advocated the use of electric lighting in Adelaide's public buildings; what he now saw at the Invention Exhibition proved overwhelming. Thousands of incandescent lights illuminated the galleries, grounds and fountains of the Exhibition – a foretaste of subsequent European expositions. Here was science at its most worthwhile, he would recall, 'improv[ing] the public taste, foster[ing] morals and science, and prevent[ing] people from crowding into the gin parlours'.[22] The memory of such spectacles encouraged him in turn to emulate their grandeur upon his return, whereupon he advised the South Australian Executive Council on an electrical lighting plant for Adelaide's Jubilee Exhibition later in the decade.[23]

A number of Todd's London dinners were hosted by professional organisations, among them the Royal Society as well as the Royal Astronomical Society and the Meteorological Society, where he was invited to speak on behalf of South Australia. As if to confirm Todd's longstanding colonial reputation, further invitations were received from the Society of Telegraph Engineers of which Charles was already a member, the Society of Arts and the Reform Club. Additionally, Todd was paying visits to notable figures in the field of British telegraphy, among them John Pender and Cyrus Field. He also made the first of several visits to William Preece,[24] previously known to him when working at Greenwich in the 1850s, along with Latimer Clark. One of the outstanding researchers of his generation, Preece was already a Fellow of the Royal Society and would later become President of the Society of Electrical Engineers. During the 1880s, his interests in telephony and lighting paralleled those of Todd, and he would remain an important professional source of information after Charles returned to South Australia. Todd, better than most colonial visitors, understood the value of patronage, having practised it extensively in the colonies. He would rely on prestigious figures such as Airy and Preece to gain the recognition he deserved. Not only was Preece prepared to support Todd's bid for election to the Royal Society, he continued to show generosity to members of the Todd family when they visited Britain, either for the purposes of research in the case of William Henry Bragg, or in a social capacity in the case of both Elizabeth and Maude.[25]

Some of Charles' short visits in and out of London were of a personal nature. In late June, he travelled to Cambridge to meet his younger brother Henry, now assistant astronomer at the Observatory. Before leaving for Australia, Charles had 'looked out' for Henry, ten years his junior, training him for employment as a computer at Cambridge, and had written to Professor James Challis on Henry's behalf.[26] The path of professional advancement had been slower for Henry, who had been able to find only temporary employment as a computer at Greenwich. After their mother's death, Henry continued to live with their father in London, under the same roof as Griffith Todd's young second wife and family.[27] As the youngest member of Griffith's first family, Henry felt the need for financial independence keenly, but regular entreaties to Challis[28] for employment brought Henry only partial relief, until he obtained a more permanent situation under Challis' Cambridge successor, John Couch Adams. Thereafter Henry's fortunes improved; he moved from London to Cambridge, where he married Emma Squires, a close relative of the Bells, and they began a family of four.[29] Subsequently, correspondence with Charles dwindled, although the two brothers clearly enjoyed common professional interests, and a similar boyish sense of humour. According to Charles, on the occasion of his arrival from London in 1885, Henry came to meet him at Cambridge station, but missed him in the crowd, expecting 'a grey-haired old man… we never found one another until I ventured to address him,' Charles chuckled after the event, recognising the 19-year-old youth he had farewelled some thirty years earlier.[30]

No less nostalgic for Charles was his return to Greenwich, where he and Henry had boarded prior to his departure for Adelaide, and the site of his early education and scientific training under Airy's demanding direction. Now aged 85, Airy was no longer Astronomer Royal, having been recently replaced by William Christie. He greeted Todd like a long lost son and 'insisted upon taking me and showing me personally the improvements which had been effected in the Royal Observatory since [I] had left it to go to South Australia'.[31] A decade earlier, Todd's Victorian colleague, Robert Ellery, had been critical of Airy's microscopic management of the Greenwich Observatory. Todd, who was by then looking at a revitalised workplace under Airy's successor, recorded no such reservations, although Burnett notes that:

> Airy's overdeveloped sense of duty … made him reluctant to spend public money. When he retired, the Observatory was not in a good condition and urgently needed refurbishment.[32]

Four years previously, William Christie, with whom Todd was also on good terms had begun this task. But Airy's welcome remained a special honour for Todd. Despite their different temperaments, Todd had earned the respect of the former Astronomer Royal, not only for his extensive telegraphic work, now renowned, but also for establishing the astronomical workings of the Adelaide Observatory in correspondence with Airy over many years.[33] It was one of several visits which Todd made to Greenwich in the course of the trip, not only to familiarise himself with the current work and equipment of European observatories, but to reacquaint himself with old Greenwich colleagues among them William Ellis and Edward Dunkin, with whom he had served and continued to correspond.

The 1885 telegraphic conference, held in Berlin during August and September, had become a major international forum of its kind, at which both the cable companies and an increasing number of governments were represented. Todd, enmeshed in administrative matters, had declined an invitation to attend a similar event held at St Petersburg in 1875, although he took care to read revised regulations emanating from the 1875 event concerning the service requirements of providers like the EE and South Australia.[34] For at that time, interruptions to Australasian cable traffic were on the increase, prompting calls from critics for a second independent line. In private, Todd had then urged Eastern Extension's director, John Pender, to lay a duplicate cable to Port Darwin as an effective means of 'shutting out all opposition and rival schemes'.[35] On the basis of such a recommendation, one telecommunication historian, Livingston, has described Todd's action in supporting an EE monopoly as akin to that of 'a private agent of the EE in Australia,'[36] though it is clear from correspondence that senior directors of the company, like Pender and Anderson, directed their enquiries to him on the basis of his overland telegraph achievement and held his financial and technical prowess in high esteem.[37] Certainly, the prospect of increased losses on the Overland Telegraph Line was Todd's prime concern in the event of competition, while he was equally committed to fighting internal revenue battles with successive South Australian administrations in order to maintain its efficiency.[38] During his London talks and the Berlin conference, Todd was at pains to remind Eastern Extension and the British public[39] that South Australia, while sustaining ongoing losses on its leg of the service, was prepared to play its part in any subsequent reductions, but that other governments, both within and outside Australasia, would also be expected to contribute.

Although in-principle agreement was reached on significant rate reductions on the part of Eastern Extension, there was as yet no clear-cut agreement with the Australasian colonies, and the 1885 conference outcome was seen at the time as a victory for the status quo.[40] Despite a degree of professional rivalry with Todd since his appointment as New

South Wales Superintendent of Telegraphs, Charles Cracknell remained a close colleague of Todd and a supporter of the Eastern cable company. Both men were on good terms with the EE's London staff, though there was little doubt whose opinion carried the greater weight in company circles. As influential colonial administrators, each was lobbied strongly by company representatives after the Berlin event. Reunited in London after their years of early service together in South Australia, Todd and Cracknell paid visits to manufacturing establishments together, travelling as far afield as the Liverpool telephone exchange. No doubt the EE expected their ongoing support and approved of their friendship, lest New South Wales might in time become allied with independent Queensland on the cable question. Their friendship was more than a political alliance, for Cracknell had previously been selected and trained by Todd as his initial associate in Adelaide. Here then was another old friendship in which Charles could take considerable pride and pleasure.

For Todd and the other Australasian delegates who attended the Berlin gathering, the telegraph conference raised as many questions as it had resolved, especially in relation to British interests and its telegraphic network in the Asia-Pacific. However, before returning to London for further talks, Charles and Elizabeth toured Germany *en route* to Paris. Elizabeth, in the company of Mrs Cracknell whom she would have known as a child in Adelaide, had by then passed a fortnight in Berlin inspecting its 'wool shops, beautiful leatherwork and furniture,' as well as visiting the 'palaces of the Royal family and nobility'.[41] Charles, when he was able to find time away from his committee work and speechmaking, had joined them. On one such occasion, he was reputed to have been combing Berlin's well-stocked bookshops when he found 'a description of the construction of the Overland Telegraph line ... and a complimentary reference to himself, of course in the German language'.[42]

From Berlin, they travelled to Dresden, 'a fine old city' Todd noted, now 'rebuilt with handsome new houses as elsewhere in Germany,' and visited its renowned art gallery, where he thought Raphael's Madonna 'magnificent,' but liked Holbein's less, though 'his portrait of Thomas Morris is very good'.[43] During their journey through Germany, Todd was aware of its renewed prosperity and military power, heightened since the outcome of the Franco – Prussian War.[44] His familiarity with the expertise of German companies like Siemens in electrical engineering, not to mention German science and astronomy, led him to conclude favourably that 'the Germans are great hero worshippers and they have a special regard for men of letters, music and science'.[45] At times, Charles' and Elizabeth's itineraries diverged.

At Cologne, Lizzie booked a tour of the cathedral, while Charles preferred to visit a large wire and fencing factory at nearby Karlsruhe capable of turning out 'one hundred tons of fencing steel wire in a day' and entered a description of its machinery in his journal.[46]

In the last week of September, they reached Paris and made for the Louvre, taking in Notre Dame and St Cloud on the following day. Unimpressed by the tram system, Todd was more taken with the Paris Observatory's 'fine collection of ancient instruments' and its working telescopes, comprising several large refractors and reflectors.[47] But the most detailed of Todd's entries, while in France, concerned the workings of the central telegraph office and telephone exchange at the main post office. Telegraphy was becoming more sophisticated with the introduction of duplex and quadruplets machines, soon to be imported into the Australian colonies during the 1880s and 1890s. Impressed by their output, Todd noted the number and type of telegraph machines in use there, along with staffing requirements. As Postmaster General, he was also interested in lighting arrangements for his night workers and recorded the relevant details, as well as the machinery and voltage required to drive them. Telephony too had been an important consideration at the Berlin conference, and Todd spent almost as much time inspecting the telephone exchange,[48] noting among other things, its switching capacity, the padding of telephone booths and overall subscriptions, still relatively small at between three and four thousand. Finally, there were letter departments to visit and inspect, the cost and weight of letters, postcards, money orders, delivery and clearance: the essential workings of the modern post office, all of which were carefully recorded. In Paris as elsewhere, Todd was able to move seamlessly between the conventional and cultural tourism enjoyed by Elizabeth and her female companions, and the technical detail of professional visits which never ceased to stimulate and intrigue him while abroad.

From his hotel, Charles wrote Alice postcards and received updates on telegraph developments in South Australia from Knuckey and Giles.[49] Within his immediate family circle, Hedley, now aged 25, was assuming increasing financial responsibilities, informing his father of local developments, at a time when the South Australian economy was teetering on the brink of recession, lacking in manufacturing and reeling after poor seasons which reduced primary exports.[50] Such sombre news, confirmed by Alice's observation that 'people are very hard up, nearly everyone is you can mention,'[51] did not deter Charles from his regular visits to all parts of England, but may have had a dampening effect on his enthusiasm for ordering much-needed new departmental equipment. Despite his London-based engagements, Todd had not forgotten Joseph Oppenheimer, nor his ambition to accompany him on a tour of manufacturing workshops in northern England. One of the unsung heroes of the overland telegraph saga, Oppenheimer played a crucial role in the preservation and maintenance of the telegraphic line, using his German and continental business connections, as well as ingenious patents to salvage the early wooden built line from the ravages of weather and tropical termites.[52] The iron tubular and telescopic 'Oppenheimer' poles, which Todd used to systematically replace the original wooden ones, represented, along with their special insulators and wiring, nothing less than 'a symbol of human ingenuity'[53] in solving the ongoing problems associated with the harsh inland route. Oppenheimer having spent time in Victoria as a cable contractor during the 1850s, before returning to northern England, continued to support Todd's major telegraph projects both in the Northern Territory and Western Australia.[54]

In mid-October of 1885, Charles travelled to Liverpool with Lizzie and, after several days of sightseeing there, teamed up with Oppenheimer and Cracknell to inspect local steelworks. He returned afterwards to Oppenheimer's residence at Stockport, where Lizzie and a female companion, Ethel Harley, awaited them. During October, they spent several days at Manchester and Liverpool, sightseeing together in dull and rainy conditions. As winter approached, Charles continued to base himself in the north, combining amusements such as opera going with ongoing professional matters, while writing home to Alice and Edward Squire, at the post office. One professional visit was to Horace Lamb, who had recently left the University of Adelaide to take up a position as Professor of Mathematics at Owen College in Manchester.[55] Charles, who played a small part in the selection of Lamb's Adelaide replacement, was not to know that the successful applicant, William Henry Bragg, would become his future son-in-law.[56] The visit to Lamb was not entirely altruistic on Todd's part, for Lamb, now a distinguished Fellow of Trinity College Cambridge, was well placed to advance Todd's own Royal Society ambitions.

Although the October weather was becoming inclement, Charles and Lizzie remained at Stockport, partly at their host's insistence. Elizabeth remembered Oppenheimer, expansive in his hospitality to Charles as well as his family, as an enigmatic figure – a wealthy flamboyant middle-aged bachelor who, 'for his summer holidays … would go on a continental tour, taking with him three attractive young women and enjoy walking around ballrooms with a different girl on his arm each evening'.[57] In some respects, the well-travelled Oppenheimer represented the antithesis of the close Cambridge professional circles in which the Todds, Bells and their children were to move. Yet some of Joseph's roguish charm appears to have 'rubbed off' on Charlie, Todd's elder son whose 'love affairs', upon returning to Adelaide, were duly reported by his father in letters to Joseph.[58] Both Charles and Alice, concerned for Charlie's moral welfare in London, remained intensely grateful to Oppenheimer for his interest in their eldest son. It was also a mark of his influence, a few years later, when his wish prevailed for Elizabeth's marriage to take place at his spacious residence at Stockport.

Even with winter advancing, Charles excited by long-awaited expectations, did not take a much-needed opportunity to rest at Stockport. He had, by now, been travelling almost continuously since late April, and the pace was beginning to take its toll on his generally robust constitution. After a short excursion with Lizzie to Wales, he returned to London where he, Blyth and Cracknell lunched on board the EE's newly constructed cable ship with its staff, including Captain Halpin who had brought the *Investigator* to Port Darwin in overland telegraph days. He was back in the capital only a few days, however, when his schedule came to an abrupt halt. In early November, Charles suddenly experienced 'great pain' and was simply 'unable to go out'.[59] He had succumbed to what was, in all probability, a severe bout of influenza, then relatively common but nevertheless serious. Ten days later, he managed to attend a Royal Society dinner in the company of Preece and Christie,[60] in anticipation of his critical nomination as a Fellow. A week later, he attended a Royal Astronomical Society dinner as the guest of Christie,[61] Airy's successor at Greenwich. According to Edwards,[62] Todd spoke briefly about a nova he had observed in August, presumably at the Berlin Observatory, although he did not record this in his diary. For almost six weeks, his terse journal entries ceased, after which he simply noted on 18 December that he had been 'almost entirely confined' and 'in great pain' throughout this period.

For such a gregarious nature as Charles,' there can have been little more frustrating than such protracted confinement, after waiting decades to enjoy his time in Europe. Alice, in her letter of January, gently chided him for 'doing too much' and 'not taking proper care of yourself,' adding that 'we are all hoping that the quiet change at South Cliff will set you up in health'.[63] For Alice, Charles' prolonged absence from Adelaide paralleled his protracted absence in the Northern Territory a decade earlier; but she was now less anxious and isolated than on that occasion and more comfortable in the company of her adult children. In contrast with Charles who was enduring his first European winter in thirty years, Alice stated that Adelaide had been experiencing extremes of heat with 'many deaths by apoplexy,' so that 'the girls do all the shopping for me'. Like Charles she was confined by day, but cheerful, and looking forward to the time when 'we shall have you with us again and what a lot you will have to tell us'.[64]

While he admired the 'white mantle of snow and hard frost' outside,[65] Charles, was now feeling the 'very cold weather,' but managed to retreat to Stockport in the north, staying there until mid-January, while Lizzie travelled on to Cambridge[66] It was to prove an important journey for Lizzie who, while visiting the Bells, met her future husband in Charles Squires, a mild-mannered Cambridge solicitor, related by marriage to her mother's family. In contrast with the reserve of her future husband, Elizabeth impressed her Cambridge hosts as a 'much travelled young woman,' blessed with an 'easy social manner' and a 'romantic Australian background'.[67] There was even a little of her father's and Alice's romance in the new friendship, complicated in each instance by the prospect of travel to distant Australia. Charles, who was steadily recovering, rejoined his daughter at Cambridge, where they attended services and concerts held at the Great St Mary's and at Trinity and King's Colleges. Thanks to Professor Adams, Challis's successor at the Cambridge University, Todd had been nominated by the University for an honorary Masters degree and would return there to receive it a month later. It proved an intoxicating visit for both of them. Though preoccupied with his own health and professional matters, Charles had by this time purchased a house at Cambridge in Catherine Street off Mill Road, possibly with Lizzie in mind.[68] But whether, he had, as yet, noticed his daughter's new friendship is unclear.

By mid-January, Charles was strong enough to return to London, where another special pleasure awaited him – a reunion with his sisters, Mary and Elizabeth and their families. Unlike Henry and Charles who had gravitated professionally towards Cambridge, Mary and Elizabeth stayed in the Greenwich district, where they had married and lived comfortably. Mary, who was several years older than Charles, had married Samuel King a year after his departure to Australia, and moved to neighbouring Blackheath, before locating to Kent and mothering a family of six children.[69] In her youth, Mary had been a gifted pianist reputed to have performed before Queen Victoria and able to earn a living teaching other aspiring young women.[70] Elizabeth, who was four years younger than her brother,[71] and who saw Charles on several occasions, had already married and given birth to a son before his departure to South Australia. A teacher like her sister, she partnered her husband, Samuel Bishop in a small school at Greenwich, while bearing him eleven children.[72] From Cambridge, Charles and daughter Lizzie had returned to London[73] with a group of female companions, some of whom were known to Charles from his early years there at the Observatory.[74] There was excitement in the air and the mixed pattern of professional and factory visits by day, and dining engagements and concerts by night, resumed without any immediate strain on Charles' health.

Todd was now able to resume negotiations with Eastern Extension over its proposed reduction to cable rates. On 25 January, he met with the EE director and a number of Australian officials at Pender's Arlington mansion to consider the Company's new proposal, returning with Lizzie a few days later to dine there.[75] During these protracted negotiations which included the Australasian Agents General, Todd replaced Blyth as South Australia's representative with Murray-Smith of Victoria convening. They found short-term agreement with Eastern over the need to press the Indian administration to reduce its high transit charges on Australasian through-traffic. But by the end of January, it was clear that neither the efforts of the cable company nor the Colonial Office could induce India to change its position.[76] In the interim, the Agents General were presented with a fresh Eastern proposal which offered them immediate reductions of 1s 4d on public messages, but made any further reductions contingent on the colonies signing up to a collective subsidy for the next twenty years. There was much at stake, since ongoing opposition from Queensland, Tasmania or New Zealand would leave the other colonies to shoulder most of the financial burden. Todd, on behalf of South Australia, offered to reduce its transit charges on the overland route by 3d per word as part of EE's overall reduction of 2s 6d per word, though considerably less than its critics had hoped for.

It was in the course of these ongoing negotiations that Todd, in early February, delivered his landmark address, *Telegraphic Work in Australasia* to the Royal Colonial Institute, before such notables as Sir Henry Barclay and Sir Andrew Clark, as well as senior cable business figures and the assembled colonial Agents General. Todd's initial reluctance to present at this forum reflected lingering concern about his professional credentials as a prospective candidate for the Royal Society; for he initially considered the lecture more appropriate to the Society of Telegraphic Engineers.[77] After reassurances, he prepared a detailed account of South Australia's telegraphic development, supplemented by accounts of similar work in Queensland and Tasmania. By way of enhancing his colony's moral claim in relation to the overland line, Todd produced comparative figures which confirmed that South Australia had spent larger sums on its own network than any of the other colonies, while its revenue was considerably lower than those of either New South Wales or Victoria. In his outline of the Overland Telegraph Line, Todd was careful to acknowledge Stuart's pioneering exploration and to recognise the initial enterprise of Samuel McGowan in Victoria.[78] He chose not to elaborate on the sensitive question of rivalry with Queensland, adding simply that South Australia had 'undertaken to construct at her own cost and risk, a line across the continent from Adelaide and thus relieve the company for that part of the scheme'.[79] Anticipating previous arguments over Queensland's superior northern location, Todd went on to point out that 'the direct southerly course of Stuart's route ... sooner carried the line beyond the adverse atmospheric conditions during the prevalence of the north-west monsoon and into the dry interior'.[80] Before proceeding to describe the rigours associated with the construction of the West Australian line, characterised by drought rather than by the monsoon which dogged the Northern Territory expedition, Todd concluded his review of the overland saga in optimistic fashion, emphasising the improved technology of the duplicated overland Australian cable, its system of inland stations, 'with only one automatic translation at Alice Springs,' the development of pastoral settlement and the likelihood of a railway from north to south along the route of the telegraph line.[81] His was an expansive vision, likely to appeal to Colonial Institute members who maintained a keen interest in the progress of Britain's colonies. Todd was duly commended by most of the Agent-Generals who attended – Malcolm Fraser on behalf of Western Australia; Samuel Saul of New South Wales, for leading the way and sending his deputy Cracknell to work in the east; Murray-Smith of Victoria, for his heroism and modesty.

Of the Agents General in attendance, only J.F. Garrick, representing Queensland, revived earlier bitterness over the construction of the line, when he accused South Australia of stealing a march on Queensland and deprecated the Company's prohibitive charges and poor performance. At this point, James Anderson, an influential EE director weighed into the discussion, defending the rights of his shareholders and the 'modest dividend' accruing to the company on its Eastern operations.[82] Garrick's outburst, in which he reiterated Queensland's intention to seek an independent cable, effectively pre-empted negotiations over Eastern's new proposals, and made any colonial consensus over the Company's subsidy proposal unlikely. Todd, in rounding off the animated discussion, joined Anderson in warning against Queensland's proposal to spend 'millions on another cable'.[83] Instead he called for colonial co-operation and reiterated South Australia's offer for Queensland to join its cable system to the existing overland line.

Further visits to Cambridge and Greenwich provided some relief for Charles from the robust cable discussions occurring in London. Not only was he closer to family members, but he was more at ease with the scientific fraternity and the steady rhythm of their observatories. These visits served a number of purposes: on a professional level, they allowed him to renew early friendships, while garnering support for his future election bid to the Royal Society. By March, an important stepping-stone was in place with the ceremony to award him an honorary Master of Arts in recognition of his many distinguished achievements. Todd's brother, Henry, a long serving astronomical assistant at Cambridge, was well informed about the award. When Charles returned there on 10 March to consult with the University Registrar, Henry went again to the station to meet him and they dined together before Charles went on to visit Professor Adams at the Observatory and spend the evening with Alice's family.[84] The award ceremony was held on the following afternoon and conducted in Latin by the public orator who lauded Todd's combined achievement in 'observing the heavens,' while also attending to 'things of the Earth'.[85] If lingering contention remained about Todd's having been the 'first to suggest' an overland route, there was no doubt about who had 'carried out the work' with 'energy and success,' as the orator described it. Todd's corresponding entries of 10 and 11 March were characteristically brief, although his photo, taken on the occasion in his graduation gown – bespectacled and with hair and beard carefully cropped – undoubtedly marked a personal highlight of the European trip. As a young assistant to Challis in mid-century, Charles had not been a fully-fledged member of the Cambridge University community; for he lacked a College affiliation, or the prestige of scholarship, let alone the degrees later conferred on some of his fellow workers. Indeed, his family background and Nonconformist denomination made it unlikely that he would have ever been able to enter university and gain such a distinction. Now, at age sixty, his contribution had finally received formal recognition from a prestigious British institution.

At the March graduation ceremony, Charles' appearance was more gaunt than usual, for he continued to feel the effects of a heavy cold during most of March.[86] None of which prevented him from returning promptly to London to meet with Preece, and attending a Royal Astronomical Society dinner, at which William Christie proposed a toast to his health.

With Preece's support, Todd's bid for election to the Royal Society of London was now firming, but he would also need the backing of Christie and the scientific establishment which constituted the majority of the Royal Society for his election to be secure. A great deal of his time in England had been spent in telegraph and engineering workshops; yet Charles, recognising his professional support base also paid visits to observatories in Berlin and Paris; and in Britain to Cambridge, Greenwich, Kew and Oxford.[87] He had already been elected a Fellow of the Royal Astronomical Society in 1864 and to the Society of Telegraph Engineers, ten years later;[88] but election to the prestigious Royal Society was more complex, requiring written recommendation by six or more of its existing Fellows, of whom three had to sign on the basis of personal knowledge. By the time his nomination had been submitted for a new election round in January 1887, Todd had gained the sponsorship of no fewer than fourteen Fellows, of whom twelve were from personal knowledge.[89] Six of these were also Fellows of the Royal Astronomical Society, but only two were Electrical Engineers.[90] Moreover, in direct contrast to the wording of his Cambridge award, the FRS recommendation which led to his eventual election two years later in June 1889, elevated both his astronomical observations and meteorological work, including written treatises and papers to the Royal Society of South Australia, above his extensive and better known telegraphic achievement. On this occasion, it was what Todd himself would have wanted. As the time of his departure approached, however, he cannot have been entirely certain of success, and he later described himself to Ellery as 'an unworthy fellow'.[91] Yet, despite his professional isolation and shortage of time, Todd's achievements as an astronomer were by no means inconsiderable. In addition to his determination of Australian longitudes and his observations of the two transits of Venus, of which the 1882 results were deemed the more remarkable, he had contributed to the Royal Astronomical Society's monthly newsletter since 1868 and participated in observations of the stars after the acquisition of a transit circle instrument in 1881.[92] Additionally in 1880, he had been one of the first Australian observers to report on the great southern comet,[93] and in 1882, observed Wells' comet in conjunction with Ellery and Russell.[94]

As his journal entries in the last few weeks of his trip confirm, Charles showed no let up in his professional activities, but he had also become caught up in personal and family matters. For although Elizabeth had spent a considerable part of the trip independently in the company of female companions and family friends, it was becoming clear by February that her attachment to Charles Squires was now a serious one, which Charles also needed to consider. Brief journal entries of March confirm his growing awareness, starting with a record of the visit to Charles Squires at Cambridge[95] prior to the degree ceremony, followed four days later by lunch with Squires 'who spent the evening with us'.[96] Contact intensified in early April, when Squires met them both and took Lizzie to Westminster Abbey,[97] while Charles continued his London rounds. Three days later, Squires having already visited the Albert Dock to look over the *Valetta* on which they were to sail, continued to accompany them, as they packed for the return trip to Adelaide.[98] Contrary to family reminiscences,[99] Squires had by this time proposed to Lizzie and she had accepted him, with the mutual agreement that she return to marry in Cambridge. Busy in the lead up to the departure, Charles appears to have been fully apprised and supportive of these decisions, although the thought of Lizzie's return to England, along with the knowledge that he himself might not be returning to 'old England,'[100] constituted an undoubted 'wrench' after their happy time together.

On the return trip to Australia there was still ample time for Charles to spend with his cherished daughter. The *Valetta*, on which they set sail on 8 April 1886, experienced rough weather before tracking down the Spanish coast and entering the Mediterranean to calmer conditions. Charles, who had conducted Sunday services on the *Irene* coming out thirty years ago, now deferred to a young Cambridge clergyman whose prediction that 'we may be sent to other worlds' inspired renewed thoughts of astronomy in Todd. He noted it in his journal as a 'novel idea,' adding wryly 'I may volunteer to go to Jupiter'.[101] More relaxed than at any time on tour, he played chess with the passengers, improving with time but performing poorly at tennis.[102] Back in his cabin, Charles sustained a vigorous correspondence both with England and Australia,[103] while devouring Froude's *Oceana*, a popular travel account of the colonies whose author mooted the idea of imperial federation as an alternative to colonial nationalism.[104] Whenever the opportunity arose, Charles and Lizzie disembarked with her travel companions for dinners and visits, firstly at Malta then at Port Said a few days later.[105] Having already experienced a change to its Mediterranean schedule, occasioned by an outbreak of cholera, the *Valetta* experienced a more serious delay after it ran aground in the crowded Suez Canal on 22 April, and was forced to offload and reload its cargo over the Easter period. Undeterred, Charles and Lizzie disembarked by barge at nearby Ishmalia, picnicking in the gardens before Charles resumed letter writing in the evening.[106]

For the first time in months, they were experiencing hot conditions and Charles thought of home, inspired in part by the sight of the Southern Cross, which 'seems to bring us near to the beloved ones at Adelaide'.[107] At Colombo which they reached on 7 May, Todd collected a number of letters and renewed old acquaintances, dining with Major Fergusson and a former Cambridge colleague of Henry's, before accompanying Lizzie to a Buddhist temple and the Cinnamon Gardens. Additional passengers for Australia boarded at the same busy port, among them Professor Threlfall, a new appointment in physics at Sydney University and one of a generation of talented scientists to arrive in the Australian colonies at that time. Threlfall would become a close associate of Lamb's Adelaide successor, William Henry Bragg.[108] By the second week of May after a month at sea, the *Valetta* was driving into the south-east trade winds while its passengers amused themselves. Lizzie figured prominently in musical entertainment, borrowing her father's Cambridge cape for the fancy dress, and playing the part of Lucy opposite Threlfall in the farce, *A Fish out of Water*.[109] On 19 May, the *Valetta* passed Cape Leeuwen, reaching Adelaide on 25 May. Although Charles' long-term plans to visit America had not materialised, it was his longest absence from Alice and Adelaide, surpassing even the momentous ten-month sojourn of 1871–72 in the Northern Territory.

For Todd, the strenuous European voyage brought unprecedented recognition by British professional societies adding to his now impressive list of overseas qualifications. The Royal British Meteorological Society (FRMS) bestowed a Fellowship on him in November 1885, before his election to the prestigious Royal Society a few years later. Before long, the European trip also advanced Todd's local reputation, bringing further honours in its train. The University of Adelaide Council, amid embarrassment at its failure to reappoint Todd to the Senate in his absence, promptly awarded him an honorary Masters qualification ('ad eundem gradum') in recognition, not only of his 'distinguished achievements,' but also of his 'great public service to the colony'.[110] By now his career momentum appeared unstoppable. With the confirmation of his FRS in 1889, and the prospect of further awards, he was destined to become the 'Grand Old Man of South Australia'.[111]

In the meantime, a press of departmental duties brought Todd back to colonial reality, compounded by his deputy Edward Squire's leave, on the grounds of illness. On a personal level, Charles was now grappling with the prospect of deepening debt and with Lizzie's imminent departure and marriage in England. Lorna recorded that the news dealt a 'devastating blow' to family life at the Observatory, since Lizzie had been 'the mainstay of the family' and 'a wonderful sister'.[112] Charles also alluded to it after his return, writing to Preece in January 1887:

> My daughter leaves us in March ... [It] is a dreadful wrench for us. You will take care to see her. She writes in [sending] kindest regards.[113]

Reflecting the mood of his own household, Charles again revealed his close feelings in the following month to Oppenheimer, who was assisting the family with Elizabeth's marriage arrangements, complaining that 'Lizzie prepares to leave – I shall never see her again. This is awful'.[114] When the time came for her to depart on 12 March, Elizabeth, accompanied by Alice's parlour maid as her travelling companion, was escorted down to the wharf by Charles and her brothers. That evening, Lorna, distraught at the loss of 'Cis', had to be comforted before bedtime by her father, who observed to his youngest daughter: 'I shall miss her far more than you, for I have lived longer and loved her more'. Whereupon, he 'ordered all onlookers to go to bed'.[115]

Although family life changed significantly with Elizabeth's departure to Cambridge, close ties were maintained during the following decade by a series of visits to England and to Cambridge. The first to visit in 1891 was Maude, one of Lizzie's younger sisters, who kept her parents informed from Cambridge of Lizzie's and Charles Squires' new life at Vale House in Cherry Hinton Road. It constituted the renewal of a longstanding Adelaide-Cambridge family connection, starting with Alice and Charles in the mid-nineteenth-century, continuing through the twentieth century to the present day. Like Charles, Alice responded enthusiastically to the prospect of a visit by the Squires, directing Maude to:

> Tell dear old Charlie and sweet Lizzie that they must be careful and save now, so that they can come out here for a time ... the voyage would do them good ... oh how we should love it.[116]

Nor did their eldest daughter forget her father or family, returning to Adelaide to a rousing welcome a decade later. At the time of her arrival,[117] Charles and family excitedly went out to meet her by launch. Lizzie stayed at the Observatory for six weeks during which time she attended a number of social events and renewed her ties in Adelaide society. A formal family photo, taken in the Observatory grounds to mark the occasion, shows her surrounded by her parents and assembled Adelaide family, now much larger in number. For her talented younger sister Gwendoline and both her brothers, Charles and Hedley had also married by this time, while Charles and Alice had become grandparents.

Todd Family group at the Adelaide Observatory for Lizzie's 1897 visit.
L to R, back row: Elsie, William Bragg, Maude, Elsie's sister (Mrs Tower), Hedley, Lorna; centre row: Alice, Gwendoline, Charlie, Lizzie, Jessie, Charles; front row: Willie Bragg, Tower daughters, Bob Bragg

Part III

Contested Ascendancy: The Illustrious Civil Servant (1887–1910)

10

'The heat and burden of the day': Todd's Cable Diplomacy Before Federation

During 1886–87, despite the announcement of Pender's knighthood, the Eastern Extension Telegraph Company (EE) was attracting growing criticism in Britain over its excessive profits and anti-competitive practices. Back in Adelaide, Todd missed the London jubilee conference of 1887 which celebrated fifty years of British telegraphy and honored Pender as its reigning champion. While in England, Todd had played a part in lobbying the EE to reduce its Australian cable rates by as much as 2s 6d a word, amid complex negotiations with the other Australian colonies. But in Berlin and London, he also met Pender's arch critic, Henniker Heaton, a former Australian journalist with a seat in the British House of Commons. As a guest at Heaton's Kensington residence,[1] he heard his host at first hand rail against the EE's stranglehold on cable business, likening it to an octopus with tentacles spread around the globe.[2] During his Colonial Institute address, Todd had made his own position clear. In the face of calls by Queensland's Agent General for cable competition and the laying of a Pacific cable to reduce Eastern's exorbitant cable rates, he questioned the prohibitive cost of such a project.[3] As the cable debate assumed greater intensity, Todd's key role in making the case for a single Australian carrier aligned him publicly with the EE and its directors. The political and financial realities were, however, more complex.

In view of his previous achievements and the respect he commanded both at home and abroad, Pender regarded Todd as a natural ally and was pleased to be able to delegate to him much of the hard bargaining between the colonies over cable breakages and subsidies. As South Australia's representative and the acknowledged Australasian authority, Todd enjoyed a co-operative relationship with Pender, albeit one which remained formal and was rarely conducted on an equal basis. For it also fell to Todd, as Australian negotiator with Eastern, to propose outcomes which were compatible with South Australia's heavy commitments, not to mention those of established colonies like New South Wales and Victoria which accounted for the lion's share of Australia's overseas cable traffic.

In the course of his Colonial Institute address, Todd had produced figures to support his contention that South Australia had consistently outlaid more on the Overland Telegraph Line than other Australian colonies. Unlike Eastern Extension which possessed deep capital reserves and could sustain ongoing reductions to its tariffs, South Australia, he pointed out, was running the overland line at a substantial loss and stood to lose even more heavily once the Eastern's promised reductions came into effect. Todd's annual figures, subsequently tabled at the intercolonial post and telegraph conference[4] of 1888 confirm that, while its revenue narrowly exceeded working expenditure over the period 1873–87, South Australia was still burdened with annual outlays of £25,000 per annum to service its original construction loan. So when Arthur Blyth, its London Agent General, insisted that his colony had borne the 'heat and burden of the day'[5] in single-handedly constructing the overland link, he was not simply referring to the manpower required, but to its onerous financial commitments and the immediate prospect of further losses once its transit rates were reduced in line with Eastern's concessions. Subsequently, this catchcry was taken up by Todd and other South Australian representatives at intercolonial conferences when questions of cable subsidy reduction were being debated. South Australia continued to advance the moral argument that it had initiated a national work for which, several decades later, it had never been fully compensated. After 1888, Todd, who attended these gatherings, lent South Australia's case considerable weight and authority, not only as one of the 'permanent departmental heads,' but as the person responsible for building and administering the Line. While prepared to let his politicians do most of the talking, it was he, throughout the 1890s, who provided them with the necessary statistical documentation and briefings to make a strong case.

Despite Todd's impressive telegraphic knowledge and achievements, there was little scope for complacency. If successive conferences served to consolidate both Eastern's and Todd's influence on cable matters, there was nevertheless ongoing criticism of the service they provided. After protracted delays and protests in the late 1870's, a duplicate cable was laid in 1880.[6] But, with renewed criticism of Eastern and the international cable service, protracted interruptions became a political matter which served to justify the introduction of competition. In 1888, for example, six interruptions occurred along the land route, most of these from natural causes.[7] In a later instance, the line was deliberately cut by a stockman to save him from dying of thirst. For explorers in the outback, the Overland Telegraph remained a vital point of contact, for Todd and his staff were generally hospitable to those in difficulty. Although repairs were time-consuming and expensive, Todd himself felt that such extraordinary behaviour as cutting the line was justified, because 'a man's life is of more consequence than a chunk of cable lines'.[8] Over the following decade, as cyclists and tourists began travelling the Line at their leisure, deliberate interference under less than dire circumstances attracted censure and the prospect of fines or even imprisonment, such were the pressures of increased cable traffic.[9]

More troubling and difficult to locate, however, was the disruption which continued between Java and Port Darwin to the underwater cables upon which the service relied. During the 1880s, an upsurge of volcanic activity disturbed the ocean bed and threatened cable communication to Australia and New Zealand. Although the Overland Telegraph stations registered tremors on the mainland, the land route was never as vulnerable to this kind of interruption as its offshore connection. When one such disturbance severed the Australian ocean cable in late 1888, Eastern dispatched the SS *Recorder* to undertake urgent repairs. The ensuing dislocation to the international service highlighted the problems of maintaining underwater cables in tropical conditions, where they tended to lose strength and drift for several miles under the influence of local currents.[10] With a duplicate underwater cable in operation nearby, care had to be taken to identify which of the cables had been damaged before the tasks of grappling and lifting the damaged line could begin, a difficult and time consuming task in unstable weather conditions.

Back in Adelaide, it was Todd, rather than Eastern's Adelaide-based management, who generally bore the weight of such protracted disruptions despite the fact that the underwater operation was not his responsibility. When local users became impatient, Todd would contact the Port Darwin office whereupon J.A.G. Little would collect and ferry delayed messages across from Java. Responding to concerns voiced in mid-1888 by the

Argus, a prominent member of the Australian Press Association,[11] Todd confirmed that the disruption was due to volcanic activity. At the same time, he reassured the colonial public that Eastern's repair ship was now in place and promised that communication would be restored 'in a few days'.[12] Readers were, however, sometimes disappointed, for the new cable also failed in October of that year after a more widespread eruption occurred. Despite J.A.G. Little's efforts at the Port Darwin office, the cable remained ominously silent during most of October.[13] However diligently Todd and his departmental officials responded, they could not guarantee the reliability of the underwater cable or of the tropical conditions during periods of disruption.[14] Even Pender, Eastern's managing director, recognised the seriousness of the situation in 1888, and immediately announced the laying of a third cable from Java, this time to Roebuck Bay on the north coast of Western Australia. With Queensland still unwilling to entertain a cable link to its northern shores from Java, even at Eastern's own expense, Pender negotiated a new cable line with the Western Australia government, and the third connection was completed rapidly by April 1889.[15] Nevertheless, such episodes fuelled colonial speculation about the risk of depending on a single international line, since all three of Eastern's cables ran from the unpredictable Java coastline.

Despite ongoing resistance from Queensland, a decision was taken at the 1890 post and telegraph conference to compensate South Australia through annual subsidy arrangements. It constituted a significant victory for Todd, the civil servant and diplomat, amid ongoing recognition of his personal achievement. Nor was Todd simply putting South Australia's subsidy proposal on behalf of Eastern; for the recommendation of the conference had yet to be considered by the Company chair. In mid-May of the same year, Pender wired back his approval, acknowledging Todd as the architect of the arrangement and proposing that 'if at the end of the first year, no serious loss is involved, the Company might not object to continue the experiment for another two years'.[16] A judicious compromise, it was designed to ease tensions between all parties, albeit one which had yet to stand the test of time. Todd's reputation at home and abroad had given South Australia a decided advantage in these complex negotiations and continued to win his colony significant resources at a time when looming depression placed a still heavier strain on colonial revenues. At the time, all of the parties involved in the arrangement acknowledged that Todd's role, while often behind-the-scenes, was much more than that of any colonial Postmaster General.

As Australasia's acknowledged negotiator, Todd was poised to begin a long period of cable diplomacy, in which he enjoyed influence as 'a powerful, if not the most powerful communication technocrat in colonial and federating Australia'.[17] Despite advancing years (he was 65 in 1891), Todd embarked, with fellow civil servants and South Australian politicians, on a hectic schedule of continuing negotiations during which he attended more conferences than any other colonial representative. His relentless endeavours to ensure the viability of the Overland Telegraph Line were both a personal investment as well as a public duty. Such was his grasp of the portfolio and of the wider issues, that the Adelaide press was inclined to defer to its Postmaster General ahead of his own Ministers, for their Education and Agriculture portfolios appeared to have little direct bearing on either cable or postal issues. At a subsequent round of scheduled conferences in 1891, the Adelaide *Register* observed that although South Australia's only representative was Sir Charles Todd, 'the colony did not sensibly suffer through the absence of a ministerial delegate,' declaring that 'the erudite knight is ... probably the greatest authority in Australia on postal and telegraphic matters'. It went on to assert that, unlike South Australia's departmental heads, 'short-lived ministries know nothing of their departments when they take charge of them and are not so fully informed respecting them when they leave'.[18] Throughout Australasia, post and telegraph negotiations featured prominently over the next decade, as numerous forums were rotated among the colonial capitals, including Wellington in New Zealand. According to Livingston, all of the Australian capitals, except Perth, hosted at least one conference during the 1890s[19] and conferences extended over one to two weeks of almost daily meetings, as representatives 'work[ed] through some of the most significant areas of "practical federation"'. Certainly, during decade-long negotiations around federation regarding the amalgamation of posts and telegraphs, senior civil servants like Todd, with their extensive knowledge of colonial systems, held a decided advantage.

With Todd and his Ministers committed to saving South Australia much-needed finance and maintaining its position as a colonial communications hub, there were also a series of personal milestones for him to celebrate. On the occasion of his fifty-year jubilee in government service, newspapers and public figures from around Australia joined in congratulating Todd for 'abley, zealously and faithfully' discharging the onerous duties of his multiple departments. His own staff presented him with an illuminated address to this effect, and in the course of the same week, the Adelaide GPO was filled to overflowing with well-wishers, as cables of congratulations arrived from Ayers, Playford, Governor Kintore and New South Wales' Governor, the

Earl of Jersey. A general view was expressed at the time that Todd still had much to offer the wider community. Even Pender's cable for the occasion departed from his customary brevity in heartily congratulating Todd for his services to 'telegraphic enterprise' and 'electrical science,' while wishing him long life in order to see something of the future developments in the field.[20] Still more satisfying for Todd was the belated award of a knighthood in mid-1893. He was not the only South Australian to be so honoured on this occasion; Dr Edward Stirling, an eminent natural history researcher and longstanding professional acquaintance who served with Todd on the University Senate and had been elected to the Royal Society, equally received a KCMG.[21] The local *Register*, observing that 'Professor Stirling is not so well known as the Postmaster General,' and acknowledged Todd as 'the most popular figure,' endorsing the 'opinion … freely expressed that he ought to have had a knighthood before'.[22] At the time of the 'great work,' the Premier, Henry Ayers, had won this distinction ahead of Todd who received a lesser award, though he expressed little disappointment at the time. Twenty years later, he owed his knighthood to the patronage of South Australia's Governor Kintore. For, though Todd had befriended a series of Governors and acted as their scientific adviser, his relations with Kintore, who was not a military officer like his predecessors but a British aristocrat, assumed a more personal and political character. Several years earlier, after his arrival in South Australia in 1891, the new Governor had travelled with Dr Stirling down the Overland Telegraph route from Port Darwin as far as Oodnadatta, returning by train to Adelaide after an arduous four-month trip.[23] Consequently he was well aware of Todd's earlier achievement and keen to recognise his contribution in establishing and maintaining direct communication with Britain.

Todd had always been a regular guest at government house and at levees held there for the Queen's Birthday. But by the 1890s, the entire Todd family became part of Kintore's social milieu. The successive marriages of Charles, Hedley and Gwendoline in a relatively short space of time ensured that the Todds maintained an unusually high social profile in Adelaide during the early 1890s. Their eldest son, Charles married Elsie Backhouse, the daughter of a wealthy Sydney family; the couple then became socially active in Sydney circles as well as in Adelaide, where Charles maintained his busy medical practice. In October 1891, Dr Charles Todd and his wife were also listed as attending entertainments at Government House. The Todd's third daughter, Gwendoline, married William Henry Bragg, after a brief but awkward period of courtship in which Alice played a counselling role. A Cambridge graduate and Adelaide University physics professor,

Bragg was destined for a brilliant scientific career. For the next two decades, the couple settled in north Adelaide where 'Will', as the family knew him, became active both professionally and socially on behalf of the University.[24] Even Lorna, the youngest daughter of the family was persuaded to join a dancing class at Government House and attend a fancy dress ball at the town hall. Recalling the arduous preparation before the event she wrote of the end of the evening:

> I felt so important at hearing Mr Charles Todd's carriage being roared for by the commissionaire with all his medals. 'Ought I to tell him it is really Charlie's?' I whispered to my mother [who] laughing pulled me after her.[25]

Both parents and children maintained strenuous social rounds. At a Lord Mayor's Ball, Sir Charles and Lady Todd could also be seen, Alice wearing 'a rich black satin dress, trimmed with lace'[26] and paired with Sir John Downer for the first dance of the evening. In the face of South Australia's lingering recession, Sir Charles in particular maintained his unusually active presence as patron of numerous associations including the sailing club, cricket association, chess and photography groups and public service organisations. It was indeed a hectic round, given his heavy work commitments, and one which was put at risk as his conferencing commitments beyond Adelaide intensified.

Events in late 1893 confirmed that Todd's association with Governor Kintore was more than a social one. It became distinctly political when the Governor's entourage was targeted by the Kingston government for significant funding reductions. While it was not unusual for senior civil servants and politicians to frequent Government House, it was less common for Governors to dine with civil servants as Kintore began to do at the Observatory.[27] At a time of continuing economic uncertainty, the new South Australian Premier, Charles Kingston, a radical liberal 'with a vindictive streak'[28] introduced controversial legislation aimed at slashing Kintore's salary and staff by as much as £1500. It provoked heated debate in both Houses of Parliament and raised delicate constitutional questions as to whether the Governor himself could ignore the advice of his ministers and refuse assent to such legislation. During the ensuing furore over the Bill before its sensitive clauses were excised, Todd became a Kintore ally[29] and lent his authority to the anti-Kingston faction, risking the ire of the Premier who enjoyed a political fight and was dubbed by one British critic 'the most quarrelsome man alive'.[30] In late 1893, Kintore took six months leave in England, returning to serve his full term as Governor until 1895.

According to his biographer, the Governor 'scrupulously observed the correct constitutional and social conventions and, in official correspondence, never commented on Kingston personally'. Though in a private letter to the Colonial Office, he warned one of its officials that 'in dealing with Kingston you are dealing with an able but absolutely unscrupulous man'.[31] In the course of the dispute, Todd's experience and temperament proved adequate to the challenge, but his pointed quip in the presence of the irate Premier: 'In me, sir, you Observe – a – Tory,'[32] risked putting him out of step with radical Kingston administrations which would shape the colony's direction over the pre-federation decade.

Todd's opposition to Kingston's 1893 legislation was also bound up with proposals, contained in the same Bill, to reduce the salaries of senior public servants as part of the government's economy drive. Targeting those in receipt of high salaries, these economies were less drastic than those intended for the Governor. But in subsequent years, as more extensive economies were introduced, salary reductions of up to 25% for civil servants on wages above £600 were proposed.[33] During periodic debate over senior civil servant salaries in the Legislative Council, some members argued they were 'too large', while others maintained that 'the few receiving high salaries had a right to some consideration'. As a civil servant and departmental head on £1000 per annum, Todd would have experienced a reduction of £250 per annum to £750, had this measure passed. Eventually, as part of a compromise, it was decreed that 'no public salary in excess of £1000 should be paid except to a person already in receipt'.[34] For the time being at least, Todd's salary would be capped rather than reduced. In his case however, this concession came at a cost of longer hours; for when his deputy Edward Squire was tragically killed in a riding accident in late 1893,[35] he was not replaced, leaving Todd to administer his dual portfolio alone.[36]

In spite of his differences with Kingston, Todd's position remained solid in the wake of his knighthood. Not only had he reduced South Australia's debt on the Overland Telegraph substantially through skilful colonial diplomacy, but he presided over his departments with unmatched efficiency, returning a profit and earning the accolades of the press in 1893 on the grounds that:

> Notwithstanding the liberal concessions to the public in recent years in reduction of costs of postage and telegrams, the Department under Sir Charles Todd is being worked at an increasing profit to the state. The revenue exceeded expenditure out of the general revenue by £8,817 in 1891–92 and last year by £12,894.[37]

Though mistrustful of the fiery Kingston, Todd enjoyed better relations with John Cockburn, to whom as Education Minister he was answerable, as well as with Kingston's political mentor, Thomas Playford, who replaced Blyth as Agent General in London. In the following year, the new Agent General reproduced Todd's figures at the Ottawa conference in order to justify South Australia's opposition to the introduction of cable competition across the Pacific. Formerly a South Australian Treasurer, Playford used the same strategy advanced previously at intercolonial conferences and identified Todd as his source, to whom:

> I am deeply grateful for the full information he supplied me, which enabled me to obtain a good grasp of the facts and place the case for South Australia clearly before the conference.[38]

It was ongoing proof of Todd's abiding influence on government and on cable politics at both local and international forums, and helps to explain why there were so few calls for him retire in his seventies.

In the course of his cable diplomacy, Todd encountered notable rivals as well as supporters. The most prominent of these was Sir Sandford Fleming, a Canadian engineer and Pacific cable advocate. In Fleming, Todd recognised a worthy rival, for their expertise and remarkable careers were similar in many respects. Unlike Todd however, who was increasingly of the view that large underwater cable projects such as the Pacific proposal should be left to private interests and wealthy capitalists, Fleming was a 'constructive imperialist'[39] who believed that the modern state had a role to play both in the cable industry and in the market more generally. Their differences reflected ongoing debate within the ranks of the British Conservative party which was strenuously lobbied by Pender and Anderson on one hand, and by Fleming and his allies on the other. When Fleming visited Adelaide with a trade delegation in late 1893,[40] Todd attended a dinner with senior politicians and other public servants at Government House to mark the occasion. Despite common professional interests, his relations with Fleming remained distant. Closely allied with Eastern, Todd undertook to write to Pender in late 1894 informing him of renewed Canadian efforts to interest the Australian colonies in a joint subsidy for a Pacific cable. In a display of loyalty and influence, he went on to reassure Pender that:

> I lost no time in placing the matter before my government and have pointed out that the Pacific cable is not required for commercial purposes.

In his dealings with the Canadian delegation, Todd claimed to speak on behalf of the Australian colonies when insisting that:

> Owing to the present state of trade, the colonies at the present time are not in position to incur further liabilities to support a sentimental cable not required by the traffic'.[41]

While he was careful to distance himself from Fleming, Todd developed a more personal rivalry with New Zealand's Pacific cable exponent, Joseph Ward. They 'crossed swords' on several occasions at post and telegraph conferences, where Ward represented New Zealand. Both were talented administrators, presiding over multiple portfolios, extending in Ward's case to the powerful position of New Zealand Treasurer, as well Postmaster General and Commissioner of Telegraphs. A fluent speaker and animated debater, Ward proved a more formidable rival than any of Todd's Queensland critics and an effective advocate of cable competition at these regular inter-colonial gatherings. In spite of their rivalry, the two men shared common interests. Ward had learned Morse code as a young telegraph boy and delighted visiting dignitaries including Todd by typing out his own messages during tours of the post office. He also shared Todd's interest in sheep farming as well as a mutual 'fascination with new technologies'.[42]

Nevertheless, their fundamental differences in outlook and policy were soon apparent. For Ward championed Henniker Heaton's campaign for the introduction of penny postage in the Australasian colonies and became the first colonial Postmaster General to introduce it into New Zealand by 1901. At the 1891 conference, their relations began well enough. Ward joined with Australian representatives in complimenting Todd on his motion for the introduction of hour time zones across the colonies.[43] He was also prepared to acknowledge Todd's longstanding contribution to Australasian telegraphy by acceding to South Australia's request for subsidies from its fellow colonies as a means of recouping losses on the Overland Telegraph Line. But Ward baulked at Todd's opposition to a second cable across the Pacific and concurred with Fleming in speaking out against Eastern's expensive cable monopoly. At a follow-up conference held at Brisbane in 1893, Ward disputed Todd's figures on the subject as 'somewhat misleading'.[44] When Todd responded that he was only giving 'the promoter's [Fleming's] own figures,' Ward retorted: 'my friend Mr Todd has taken figures which were furnished several years ago ... He is remarkable, he is drawing a red herring across the trail'. When a motion was subsequently put and passed in favour of lobbying the British government for a new cable via Vancouver,⁴⁵ South Australian and Western Australian representatives abstained from voting. Todd's rivalry with Ward continued across the Tasman at the 1894 post and telegraph conference in Wellington, where discussions again turned to Heaton's call for penny postage in the colonies. As chair of the local event, Ward went out of his way to complement Todd on the 'acquisition of his knighthood'. Though he soon returned to the vexed theme of cable competition, advocating an independent Pacific cable and citing the advantages, since:

> Amongst them will be an increased facility of communication and somewhat reduced rates for telegrams, the abolition of some vexatious interruptions as may occur through an earthquake, or simple breakage of existing lines.⁴⁶

The Adelaide press in defence of Todd observed that 'two strings to our bow are doubtless better than one, but what if the second string cannot be afforded?'⁴⁷ In spite of their divergent positions on both cable and postal matters, Todd recognised Ward as a worthy adversary, and their relations remained cordial at a time when New Zealand was still considering federation with the Australian colonies.⁴⁸

Increasingly as he approached seventy, Todd experienced the loss of senior colleagues, often in difficult circumstances. His Sydney visit to the 1891 post and telegraph conference was one such instance, when his own Minister, David Bews died suddenly. Earlier in 1893, he learnt of the death of Edward Cracknell, his former South Australian assistant, who had risen, on his recommendation, to become Superintendent of Electric Telegraphs for New South Wales.⁴⁹ They had become close again during his protracted European visit, when they agreed to support the Eastern Extension Company, while introducing updated cable technology in their respective colonies. According to Livingston, the death of E.C. Cracknell in January 1893 'removed Eastern's powerful, long-standing ally from the scene'.⁵⁰ If Todd's professional circumstances and network were jeopardised by such untimely losses, he was steadily building new ties across the colonies, most notably with Western Australia. As noted earlier, Western Australia joined South Australia at the 1893 Brisbane conference in abstaining from voting, when a resolution of support for a Pacific cable was put.⁵¹ An irony of the Pacific scheme, one which was not lost on Todd, was that the Western Australian goldfields were by then developing rapidly in defiance of the colonial recession.

After laying a lengthy cable across the Nullarbor Plain in the late 1870s, Todd had given the western link little sustained attention, since the bulk of colonial traffic came into Adelaide from the east before travelling up the international link to Port Darwin. While initial West Australian traffic earned his South Australian department considerably less revenue in transit charges than from eastern colonies, the new gold rush and exponential growth in cable traffic between the two colonies by the mid-1890s made Adelaide a central hub for mining communication and business. In 1896, Todd confirmed the dramatic scale of this increase, after the number of messages between the two colonies rose fourfold in two years (1893–95) and revenue to South Australia quadrupled over the same period.[52] If South Australia itself had little to offer in the way of gold, Todd was nevertheless reaping timely rewards for his colony.

Before this dramatic upsurge began, Todd had already initiated professional contact with his Western Australian counterpart, R.A. Sholl. Armed with superior technical expertise, Todd was well placed to offer Sholl ongoing advice, and spent considerable time in discussions with him at the 1894 New Zealand conference. Their association undoubtedly provided a measure of consolation for Todd after the loss of Cracknell. But his professional relationship with Sholl recalled his earlier friendship with Victoria's early Superintendent, Samuel McGowan. McGowan, armed with overseas experience, had acted as colonial mentor to Todd after his arrival; now it was Todd's turn to advise his Western Australian colleague at a time when its telegraphic network, like Victoria's in mid-century, was experiencing sustained pressure from goldfields investment and mining speculation. It was further evidence of Todd's shrewd diplomacy, for it ensured that the neighbouring colonies would continue to vote as a block on the issue of the Pacific cable, with Todd providing most of the necessary statistics and information. Nor was Todd averse to recommending some of his own officers to Sholl, lured as some were by improved prospects in the goldfields colony.[53]

In the Western Australia's Premier, Sir John Forrest, Todd also found a valuable political ally. The western goldfields had benefited from increasing international traffic into Australia as well as from neighbouring colonies, strengthening Forrest's political influence and providing much needed relief for the other colonies from their financial obligations to Eastern.[54] Forrest had personally benefited from the hospitality of the Overland Telegraph stations after his arduous exploration of north-west Australia in the 1870s, and written admiringly of Todd's telegraphic achievements.[55] But the challenges associated with the simultaneous increase of colonial and international traffic along Western Australia's telegraphic network were of no mean order. Accordingly, Todd sent Richard Knuckey, his senior telegraph inspector to advise on the weaknesses and strengths in the West's network which included its own international link to Roebuck Bay, with an overland connection from the far north western coast to Perth. Knuckey, who had been largely responsible for supervising the construction of the cable west to Eucla,[56] agreed with Todd's previous assessment that the existing line via Port Lincoln had been built too close to the coast on the express wish of the local inhabitants, making it vulnerable to the high winds, salty air and mists which haunted the Great Australian Bight. It would require a combined effort on the part of both colonial governments and their Postmasters General to relocate and upgrade the entire line both east and west of Eucla, at a time when pressure from users and the press had never been greater.

Todd kept in close touch with his Western Australian counterpart throughout the mid-1890s, providing most of the media publicity on much awaited upgrades and responding to complaints from the press in eastern Australia. In the face of complaints from Sydney and Melbourne dailies, the South Australian Postmaster General took care to place the true state of affairs before readers, attributing interruptions to the 'enormous amount of words which were now being sent through,' and explaining that 'when any break occurs, the work accumulates so fast that the operators were kept at it day and night trying to overtake arrears'.[57] Before Todd's recommended changes could be put in place – the replacement of wooden poles by metal ones and the introduction of duplex and automatic repeating systems – the situation risked deteriorating to the point where the line to Eucla on the southern border fell silent for several days at a time.[58] In the face of criticism from both the Western Australian and South Australian press, each of which accused the other colony for the delays, the two Postmasters General maintained friendly contact by wire. Sholl was in a position to repay South Australia's assistance after Todd secured an agreement with Pender, to reroute incoming international messages via Roebuck Bay when serious breakages occurred along the Overland Telegraph. Financially and politically, Todd, the cable diplomat, appeared to have chosen his allies well, both in neighbouring Western Australia, and abroad, in the powerful Eastern operation.

As part of his wider diplomatic role and as a sign of his public friendship with Sir John Forrest, Todd travelled to Perth in mid-January of 1896 to attend a banquet in honour of the longserving Western Australian Premier.[59] There, he was Forrest's personal guest and dined with him at government house. It provided a measure of respite from what would prove a difficult year. While in Perth, Todd also inspected and recommended a site for the future Perth Observatory as well as consulting with Sholl on plans to upgrade the existing Perth to Adelaide telegraph route. Although Western Australian traffic was lucrative during 1894–96, it required protracted upgrades which diverted much-needed resources from the Overland Telegraph Line itself. For the most part, Todd took such criticism in his stride, but there were occasions when he was prepared to intervene directly in the affairs of the Western Australian telegraph department, notably when its staff struggled to install new duplex systems for the South Australian line.

Subsequent complaints about interruptions to the Port Darwin line by the *Sydney Morning Herald* and Melbourne *Argus*, both of which derived significant profits from distributing London cable news,[60] in turn fed political arguments in favour of international cable competition. Natural causes continued to play a part in these breakages. In early 1895, major flooding washed away part of the cable near Strangways Springs, including the railway and telephone service, at a time when the line north of Perth was also experiencing disruption.[61] Several days later the Melbourne *Argus* complained that there was 'no cable business at present'.[62] Even the local *Register*, which reported on the renewed efforts of Todd's teams to reach and detect the fault with the aid of a ballast locomotive engine, grew impatient. A few days later, when cataloguing the history of interruptions to the Line since its construction, the *Register* claimed that the ensuing six-day breakage was the most protracted to date, 'longer than the lightning strike, the previous year, which lasted 39 hours'.[63]

Todd's commitments in Western Australia meant that he did not attend the Sydney post and telegraph conference in January 1896, leaving his Minister, Joseph Cockburn to defend the inter-colonial subsidy which South Australia had requested to maintain its Overland Telegraph Line. Like Todd, he was at pains to point out that his colony had experienced more 'lean years' than 'fat years' during the 1890s.[64] Todd's own departmental report of 1896 confirmed that an upsurge in international telegraph business in the early 1890s had been short-lived and that, in one year only, 1893, had the transcontinental line registered a substantial profit.[65] Cockburn continued to rely on Todd's statistics in rejecting accusations by Queensland that South Australia had built the Line solely for its own benefit.

Todd's absence from these gatherings was unusual, especially at such a critical time. He was nevertheless monitoring new developments in the United Kingdom where the incoming Chamberlain administration had decided, contrary to advice from Eastern and its supporters, to review the potential for a Pacific cable. Representatives of the eastern colonies in Sydney, buoyed by the recent news from Britain, were now calling on South Australia to contribute to the Pacific cable project on an equitable rather than on a population basis. It was a principle to which both Todd and Cockburn objected as inconsistent with previous intercolonial financial agreements. After several days of hard bargaining, Cockburn still insisted that the existing inter-colonial subsidy be honoured and that, should a Pacific cable proceed, South Australia 'be given some guarantee that she would not be left with an unprofitable line on her hands'.[66] The second option canvassed by South Australia's representative was that the transcontinental line should become a federal undertaking. The political momentum towards federation was now such in both the eastern colonies and South Australia itself, that the prospect of a federal takeover of the Overland Line looked increasingly likely.

For reformers like Heaton and Fleming, 1896 marked a potential turning point in their protracted campaign for a Pacific cable. With the recent death of its most powerful lobbyists and executives – Sir John Pender and Sir James Anderson, Eastern had lost significant ground and influence with conservative administrations. Todd, who had long known and cultivated its powerful directorate, was undoubtedly dismayed at this turn of events. He estimated that, should the Pacific cable now gain British government backing, it would deprive the transcontinental line of as much as fifty percent of its existing revenue, and endanger the viability of the international link to Roebuck Bay in Western Australia. These overseas developments help to explain Todd's Perth visit as part of a diplomatic attempt to ensure that South Australia would remain allied with Western Australia and not become isolated. At the same time, Todd's Minister, who travelled to Sydney in the same month, was seeking to enlist Tasmania to his cause. Todd's private discussions with Premier Forrest, who had represented Western Australia at a number of post and telegraph events, provided him with an opportunity to broach the Chamberlain government's new position on the Pacific cable as a matter of priority for both colonies. With the stage now set for a deepening colonial divide on the all-consuming cable question, Todd returned to Adelaide at the end of January 1896, secure in the knowledge that he could still rely on the support of Forrest and the buoyant Western Australian economy.

When an Imperial Pacific Cable Committee, comprising British and Canadian representatives, met in London to take evidence in June 1896, South Australia's Agent General, Thomas Playford, protested on the grounds that the scheme would compete with and potentially compromise the existing international line. In addition to Eastern's representatives, the British Post Office sent its most senior electrical engineer, William Preece, to report on the technical difficulties of laying the Pacific cable over such long uninterrupted distances. Preece was, at that time, one of the most respected electrical engineers in Britain, and it was he who had been responsible for Todd's nomination to the Royal Society in the previous decade. Preece and fellow Post Office technician, J.C. Lamb, testified as independent witnesses that reduced speeds of transmission over a single stretch of line three thousand miles long would ultimately impact adversely on the financial viability of the Pacific project.[67] Eastern's new director, the Marquis of Tweeddale, in support of Playford's concerns, estimated that the new cable would reduce Eastern's messages, most of which passed along the Overland Telegraph, by as much as one third, after Sandford Fleming, its Canadian promoter, sought to convince the Committee that a Pacific link would account for as much as fifty percent of incoming international messages into Australasia.[68]

Todd brought similar arguments against the Pacific scheme, disputing Fleming's estimates of its early potential revenue as 'much too sanguine', and concurring with Eastern's estimates of the potential loss to existing business.[69] While Preece and other British post office witnesses raised technical questions about Fleming's scheme, Todd's concerns were directed primarily at its financial aspects. In the eyes of Eastern's resolute critics, many of them Australian nationalists, Todd was on the wrong side of the fence in the long cable debate. Yet his convictions on the Pacific cable question were not entirely misplaced. For, although the technical objections raised by Eastern and its allies to the Pacific cable, including doubts of its length and depth, were discredited once work began on the project during 1901–1902,[70] Todd's major misgiving about its cost proved more accurate than Fleming's inflated predictions about its potential revenue. Recent cable historians, Winseck and Pike, confirm that the hopes of progressive imperialists like Fleming about the performance of the new cable would prove to be 'wildly optimistic'.[71] At the same time, Todd was becoming aware of his declining influence on the Pacific cable question, expressing the regret to Cockburn, now serving as South Australia's Agent General in London, that:

> my reports [which] show the loss unfortunately do not come before the public ... I'm hoping that at least Victoria, New South Wales and Tasmania in view of the loss, will defer the matter till Federation is accomplished.[72]

During 1898, statistical debate over comparative cable costs and tariffs intensified, amid complaints over constant interruptions along the Overland Telegraph Line. In this spirit, Melbourne's Chamber of Commerce sent a delegation to its own Postmaster General, asserting that 'the Overland Telegraph line was always out of order' owing to the monsoon, to which Todd replied that 'he could remember only four occasions' when interruptions had been caused by flooding between Port Darwin at Alice Springs.[73] At the Hobart post and telegraph conference of the same year, New South Wales representative, Joseph Cook, returned to the same theme, complaining that the eastern colonies were being forced to subsidise an inefficient line. Cook, when stressing the serious implications for business, cited as many as '38 specific delays in the cable business... last year they were over 60'. Todd was on hand to rebut his outspoken critic, explaining that frequent hours of delay between Adelaide in Sydney arose from 'pressures of the line' and that a direct duplex line between the two colonies would be completed 'in about six months'.[74] Todd continued to fend off criticism of the Line by distinguishing between delays and breakages. The *South Australian Register*, coming to his defence, mused that 'while rival colonies were quick to castigate South Australia, nobody seems anxious to bear the heavy cost of constant upgrades'.[75]

If a series of 1898 conferences kept the cable issue alive, 1899 brought with it dramatic new developments which not even Todd could have anticipated. In mid-1899, as Todd pondered the implications of the Cape Cable, came the disturbing news that the incoming Chamberlain administration in Britain, after offering only minimal support for the Pacific cable in April, had bowed to colonial pressure in mid-year, and was now pledging its full co-operation to establish a provisional cable commission which would 'begin the processes for the construction of the cable'.[76] If colonial proponents of a Pacific scheme were elated, notably in Queensland and New Zealand, Todd was incensed. After reading of it in the London *Times*, he condemned it to Cockburn as 'a disgraceful act'.[77] In mid-November, he enclosed a copy of his own 1899 report to Eastern's secretary F.S. Hesse, confirming that 'I have supported your claim in the other colonies and hope the Pacific scheme will fizzle out'.[78] Nor did Todd confine his efforts to known allies. For he considered his report to be a definitive assessment of the subject, sending a copy to none other than Henniker Heaton, Eastern's arch-critic in the British Parliament. In an accompanying letter, Todd stated confidently that 'in the eyes of all the businessmen I have shown that the Pacific cable must end in a serious loss,' reminding his rival that 'it will have no feeders after leaving Vancouver, and, in the eyes of the Admiralty, it possesses little or no strategic value'.

The facts, as Todd saw them, were irrefutable and he finished his long, yet amicable letter with the remark: 'I feel quite sure you will go with me after careful reflection'.[79]

Todd's views did not go unnoticed overseas. When the *Electrician* in London reprinted his objections to the Pacific cable on the grounds of cost, the recently knighted Sir Sandford Fleming took umbrage at his remarks, including the claim that, in view of its unusual length, the Pacific cable would need to be duplicated from the outset, thereby rendering it exorbitant to construct.[80] Nor was Heaton to be swayed by Todd's figures, for he renewed his parliamentary attacks on the 'Eastern octopus' at the time of the passage of the Pacific Cable Act in 1901, condemning the Company for perpetuating 'the greatest monopoly the world has ever seen'.[81] Todd had indeed lined up with an aggressive monopolist in the course of the longstanding debate. Yet, he also continued to believe, as an influential civil servant and cable authority, in his responsibility to alert governments to potentially debilitating cost blowouts, at the risk of being labelled divisive and parochial. Todd's correspondence on the eve of federation makes it clear he also looked to the new Commonwealth as a means of rationalising South Australia's debts on the transcontinental line.

His alignment with Eastern was founded on the belief that Britain's international influence should be buttressed by superior cable technology at a time of growing challenge and 'new imperialism'. Rather than embracing the ardent views of progressive imperialists like Sandford Fleming who exhorted Britain's colonies to establish an 'All Red' cable route around the globe, Todd was inclined to dismiss the Pacific cable as a 'sentimental project'.[82] As a pragmatist and strategist, he had come to believe that British interests abroad were best served by large private companies like the Eastern Telegraph Company and its affiliates. On such matters, he was clearly at odds, not only with Fleming, but also with global reformers like Heaton and with liberal nationalists in Australia who argued that intervention and competition in the public interest were preferable to monopoly, however lucrative or efficient.

11

'Time Lord': Todd's Elusive Pursuit of Standard Time in the 1890s

In 1891, at the time of his fifty-year jubilee in government service, Todd's public reputation was still closely bound up with the building of the Overland Telegraph Line, an adventure narrated tirelessly by the press in England as well as in Australia. Twenty years after the event, the *St James Gazette* joined with Adelaide and other colonial newspapers in highlighting the now famous episode, yet chose in the same article to devote only one sentence to Todd's capacity and services as government astronomer and meteorologist.[1] It must have seemed strange indeed to Todd, now age 65, and still engaged as he was on so many fronts. While his association with the Overland Telegraph Line endured at the turn-of-the-century on the basis of his adroit cable administration and diplomacy, his collaborations in other related fields guaranteed him a voice at a multiplicity of inter-colonial forums in the early 1890s. By this time, he was resented in some quarters, as wielding preponderant influence on behalf of South Australia at Queensland's expense. But a wider view of Todd, the scientist,[2] encompassing his multifarious activities, should equally acknowledge his contribution as an energetic moderniser.

As a scientist who collaborated with other colonial observers on a regular basis, Todd promoted standard methods of recording and measurement. These principles, underpinned by a continuing allegiance to Greenwich scientific practice, had long been fundamental to his meteorological and astronomical activities. So it would prove on the critical issue of calculating and distributing time, a feat for which George Airy and his great transit circle telescope had become renowned.[3] Well before the adoption of standard time across Australia and North America, Greenwich Mean Time had prevailed throughout much of England. By the time of Todd's departure for South Australia in 1855, an estimated 95% of England's population were able to access Greenwich Mean Time on town hall clocks and in post offices.[4] In preceding years when its trial was being perfected, few had laboured harder than Todd, under Airy's stern direction, to perfect the science of time measurement and distribution throughout southern England. Four decades later, however, with colonial time still unregulated, Todd was no longer simply to be one of time's messengers; instead, he was poised, by virtue of his position, to become a 'time lord', with the potential to shape and frame the very manner of its adoption throughout Australia.[5]

Unlike the situation in Britain however, standard time came relatively late to Australia. During the late nineteenth century, the ritual firing of a cannon at 1 pm to alert ships and the town population was replaced by the dropping of a time ball in order to synchronise observatory clocks with those of the town hall and post office. Todd's preoccupation in his early years with South Australia's telegraph network, and his inability to secure the necessary funding, delayed the introduction of the time ball system in Adelaide until the mid-1870s, when he arranged for it to be dropped at Semaphore, a port situated 10 miles to the north-west of the city.[6] An expensive project, costing £620, the Semaphore time ball and tower, recently restored to their original working condition, were manufactured locally and could even be seen in the early years by ships at Port Adelaide on the opposite side of Lefevre Peninsula.[7] Intimately acquainted with time ball mechanisms after his many trips to Deal in England, Todd opted in South Australia for a simple but effective apparatus based on Maudslay's Greenwich instrument. In November 1875, he was able to report to Airy that 'on only two occasions has the ball failed to drop' and 'the time error was no more than two to three tenths of a second, a degree of accuracy nowhere exceeded'.[8] In keeping with the Royal Observatory which supplied the same service to navigators on the Thames, Todd had these local times published daily in the shipping columns of the Adelaide press, along with corresponding Greenwich times. Thus, the time of the Semaphore ball drop in late November 1875, at 1 hour 0 minutes 0 seconds, appeared with its corresponding Greenwich Mean Time of 15 hours 45 minutes 38.7 seconds.[9] This combination of times enabled local ships to establish their position and longitude, using the data prepared and published by the Royal Observatory in its *Nautical Almanac*. Such a tried and tested system with which Todd was long familiar, would also become the basis for international time keeping in the decades to follow.

At the same period, Todd had a clock and chimes shipped from England at considerable expense and installed in the tower of the new Adelaide Post Office.[10] Like the operation of the new time ball, the setting of the Post Office clock by Governor Musgrave marked an important moment in the elevation of time keeping. Yet despite its technical advances, modern time-keeping was often poorly understood by the public. After responding to initial newspaper criticism over alleged inaccuracies with the new time ball, Todd refused to be drawn into further controversy. Yet such misconceptions did not disappear entirely. When the question of standard time resurfaced two decades later, Todd would again be called on to assuage public opinion. Throughout his long career, the introduction of new technologies propelled Todd into the public eye to an unusual extent for a colonial civil servant. It was one reason why his movements and statements were so widely reported across the colonies, initially in New South Wales and Victoria but increasingly in Western Australia and Queensland as well. For it was he, more so than his political superiors, who possessed both the knowledge and capacity to explain their implications both in person and in print. In the case of meteorology, labelled an inexact science by Todd himself, there had been constant challenges; yet it was not the only new development which occasioned public anxiety and confusion. Even the electric telegraph, acclaimed for dramatically closing the time gap between Europe and the Australian colonies, and for transforming colonial news, brought with it uncertainties and frustrations associated with its high cost, limited access and occasional unreliability. More often than not, it was left to Todd to contend with such scenarios in public and government circles.[11]

In colonial Australia, standard time began as a regional issue. Once the Adelaide system set in place by Todd reached regional South Australia along its comprehensive electric telegraph network, local time keeping in smaller centres was adjusted accordingly. However, in settlements located on colonial borders, like Broken Hill, different capital city time systems came into use in competition with local time schedules. In spite of the growing inconvenience of this situation, 'changing old Father Time,' as one colonial politician put it, remained a daunting prospect for any would-be reformer.[12] As one Queensland advocate of standard time predicted in 1891:

> Being conservative in our views, we are prejudiced against any proposed movement involving departure from old-time associations; from interested motives we stoutly oppose infringement of time-honoured rights and endeavour to place all possible obstacles in the way of scientific progress.[13]

Constructed at the time of Todd's overland telegraph, the Adelaide Post Office became the strategic hub for time dissemination to South Australian ports and regional post offices, as well as the source of weather reports and shipping intelligence. Once Todd's overland telegraph network became sufficiently powerful to dispense with the repeater stations initially employed to boost its current across the continent, the time gap steadily closed. Despite Todd's misgivings about its construction, the Adelaide Post Office was a building of both utility and elegance, recognised for its unusual importance by colonial and international visitors alike. But beyond the city's precincts, the Observatory, situated unpretentiously in the West Parkland, provided the essential backup for this complex system in the form of accurate hourly and daily time signals. On daily walks from the Observatory to the Post Office, Todd could monitor the clocks in both centres. A decade earlier, he had come to rely upon an expensive timepiece when negotiating complex railway time-tables throughout Britain. While lacking the accuracy of observatory clocks, domestic timekeeping introduced in the living quarters of the West Terrace Observatory, epitomized the new time consciousness. Only on Sundays, when the time ball did not drop and work ceased, would family life assume a more leisurely course, albeit one governed by traditional regimes of religious observance. Even Alice, despite her outspoken dislike of modern intrusions, could no longer escape the growing time awareness promoted by Charles throughout Adelaide society. By the 1890s, she, like her daughters, was travelling more independently, taking the train from Adelaide to Port Elliott on the coast, to meet up with family members. During protracted retreats to the coast, Todd women and children were sheltered both from scorching summer heat and from the demanding work routines imposed on their menfolk.

As the communication revolution steadily transformed work and leisure in the Victorian period, Todd emerged as an influential moderniser. Not content to push the telegraph across the continent, he used it to extend existing meteorological and astronomical networks as his British mentors had done. But, unlike Britain, where telegraph lines closely followed railways and where companies sold standard time to their populations,[14] Todd's ambitious telegraph lines pre-empted the colonial railway system which remained fractured in the years before and after federation by different gauges and timetables. Elsewhere, in North America, the involvement of railway companies in a new campaign for standard time proved more decisive. Notable among its advocates was Sandford Fleming, an engineer and director of the Canadian Pacific Railway. By the early 1880s, Fleming galvanised a coalition of rail companies and astronomers into lobbying their governments on the issue. No longer was the question simply a local one; for Fleming urged the adoption of an hour zone system across the North American continent and the globe.[15] By 1884, Fleming took detailed recommendations for a universal time standard to an important Washington conference. With the involvement of the United States, Britain and other major European powers, the standard time campaign, was now an international one.

With Europe divided over Fleming's universal time proposal, and Britain reluctant to endorse it, little serious consideration was given to the question of standard time in Australia until 1891. At the postal and telegraph conference of that year, Todd took the local initiative following the receipt from the Colonial Office of memos by Fleming and the Astronomer Royal on the subject.[16] Todd undertook to explain the universal hour zone system to delegates, stressing the 'very great public advantage' to be gained from 'uniformity of action in all colonies'. Conscious that he was speaking to fellow postal officials rather than scientists, Todd did not labour the technical aspects of the time question. Rather his argument for change rested on more practical grounds. Since 'South Australia, Victoria, New South Wales and Queensland were now connected by railways,' standardising colonial time, he stated, would consolidate inter-colonial cooperation along the lines recommended by the Universal Postal Union.[17] Far from being opportunistic, his position on the issue was a consistent one. Recognised as the dominant colonial player on international telegraphy, Todd did not force a decision, recommending only that the conference postpone its decision until Railway Commissioners, Superintendents of Telegraphs and astronomers had been consulted across the Australasian colonies.

Nevertheless, Todd's initial recommendation on standard time went further than Fleming's original proposal. It sanctioned not only an hour zone system, but advocated a uniform standard time for *all* Australian colonies. It is doubtful whether the conference, preoccupied with ongoing matters, gave it full consideration at this early stage. Rather, the recommendation 'lay on the table' pending further review at the Hobart conference in the following year. Nor did Todd, given its complexity, anticipate a prompt resolution of the colonial time question. Most of the 1892 Hobart conference was taken up with more predictable postal matters. However, the issue did resurface a few months later, this time at an inter-colonial conference of surveyors in Melbourne. Its ambitious professional agenda was designed to promote standard practice across the colonies, including the introduction of a uniform system of surveying, the adoption of a uniform standard of length, and a system under which crown land boundaries would be made unalterable.[18] On the basis of his longstanding involvement with the South Australian Institute of Surveyors and active membership of its examination board, Todd attended the surveyors' conference as a South Australian delegate with Surveyor General Goyder. While he considered the issue of the crown land boundaries to be of historic importance in keeping with his ongoing efforts to determine colonial boundaries more precisely,[19] it was the hour zone system which attracted Todd's particular interest on this occasion. A.C. Gregory, Queensland's former Surveyor General, initiated the debate when he moved that 'the true mean time on the 150th meridian of east longitude be adopted as the legal standard of time within the colonies of New South Wales, Tasmania, Victoria and Queensland'.[20] Gregory's conference motion, following Sandford Fleming's hour zone system, identified three meridians of importance for the Australian colonies: the 150th meridian which passed through the eastern colonies; the 135th meridian passing through South Australia; and the 120th meridian through Western Australia. By adopting the 135th and 120th meridians, Gregory continued, South Australia and Western Australia would operate in different hour zones behind their eastern counterparts.

When his turn came to speak, Todd declared the question 'a very important one,' but argued against Gregory's motion in favour of a single central meridian, the 135th, rather than three different time zones for the continent. The *Register* subsequently implied that Todd's primary motive was to protect South Australia's commercial interests, although the *Age* reported that he was equally prepared to countenance the 150th meridian which favoured the eastern colonies in his quest for uniformity across the colonies.[21] Only a few years earlier, Gregory himself had countenanced the 150th meridian for the entire Australian continent as the 'best, and easiest to adopt for the sake of railway uniformity'.[22] In retrospect, Todd's preference for a single meridian, while controversial at the time, was farsighted given the ongoing differences between colonies during and after federation. In declaring for the 135th meridian from the outset, Todd was open to charges of 'chauvinism on behalf of South Australia'.[23] Yet, as events would demonstrate, he was not simply following the advice of the Adelaide Chamber of Commerce, having consulted more widely with Railway Commissioners. According to the *Age*, debate over the time zone proposal at the Melbourne conference was prolonged and animated, before Gregory's motion was adopted. Even so, Todd understood that the standard time question was not fully resolved and that, in future forums, his position still enjoyed the advantages of simplicity as well as uniformity.

A few months later, Todd took the opportunity to reiterate his position at a postal and telegraph conference in Brisbane. On this occasion, he gained strong colonial support for a single time zone, in preference to the three time zones recommended by Gregory. In the course of the discussion, Joseph Ward, one of Todd's strongest cable critics, concurred that its adoption would constitute 'a great advantage for senders and receivers of telegrams,' by eliminating the 'laborious adjustment of each incoming message'.[24] Ward, New Zealand's Postmaster General, had recently taken the important decision to reduce his own colony's chaotic four time systems to one.[25] Victoria's representative also agreed that continuing differences in railway time schedules on either side of the Murray River would remain 'as inconvenient as the break in our railway gauge'.[26] As elsewhere, the railway argument for uniformity was influential in colonial Australian circles. Todd had taken the additional precaution of consulting Queensland's Railways Commissioner who concurred with his South Australian counterpart.[27] Todd also gleaned support in scientific circles, most notably from the Astronomer Royal William Christie. Unlike his predecessor George Airy, who considered the Washington Conference recommendations for a 24-hour day to be a serious obstacle to astronomical work, Christie, after discussions with Fleming, proved more receptive to the prospect of keeping Greenwich as the 'initial meridian of longitude' for the hour zone system[28] and to the possibility of realigning the 12 hour astronomical day with the 24 hour universal day of the time zone system.[29]

From an astronomical perspective, Todd's reservations about changing from a 12 to a 24-hour day, beginning from midnight rather than midday, were based, like Airy's, on the inconvenience it would cause to international navigation. Despite the fact that the Washington Conference had recommended in favour of Greenwich Mean Time as part of Fleming's international hour zone system, the British Admiralty remained as obdurate as Airy on the subject of the civil day. Coupled with opposition from local interests in parts of North America, its resistance helped delay the full adoption of the universal day for several decades.[30] Several years on, Todd was still the only government observer throughout Australasia running with the issue. Among his colonial colleagues, Victoria's Robert Ellery, who had chaired the Melbourne surveying conference, must have discussed it with him at the time without going into writing on the subject. In New South Wales, Russell, like Ellery and other colonial astronomers, appeared more than willing to adopt standard time in line with the hour zone system.[31] By the time of the 1893 postal and telegraph conference, Todd, encouraged by Christie's influential support for 'a single time zone position,' revived the question, citing the Astronomer Royal's prediction that:

> you've done good service by urging the adoption of one time rather than three hours zones which as it seems to me would be only a provisional arrangement. I fancy that in Canada and in the USA they're coming to one time as replacing the hourly zone system, [which], though a great reform, can only be looked upon as a step towards uniformity in time reckoning.

Clearly Todd had been active preparing his case, for he cited not only Christie but the succinct opinion of an English astronomical magazine, *The Observatory*, that:

> From a telegraphic point of view, one time would be a very great convenience to the local mercantile world. A merchant in London would know that every telegram he received from Australia is timed nine hours in advance of Greenwich.[32]

The unanimous 1893 conference resolution secured by Todd marked the high point of his influence on the standard time question. In Western Australia, as in South Australia, the press was generally in agreement, the *West Australian* editorialising in August of the same year:

> There can be but little reason to doubt that we shall yet have one nominal time for Australia, as the time has already come when we have got one currency, and one standard distance area measurement, and will come when we shall have one standard of weights, one postage, one customs tariff and one railway gauge.[33]

Even Sandford Fleming, the Canadian instigator of the universal day, sent Todd a note of encouragement. On the issue of standard time, there was commonality of purpose between these two 'time lords';[34] yet, even on this issue, differences remained. Fleming favoured the application of a gradated hour zone system across North America rather than the use of a single time zone as Todd was proposing. Unlike Fleming's great Canadian

Pacific Railway which spanned no fewer than four hour zones across North America *en route* to Vancouver and the Pacific, Todd's famous cable project bisected Australia from south to north, encompassing only one hour zone meridian. His inclination to accept a single meridian through the centre of the continent, for the purposes of standard time, may well have been influenced by South Australia's strategic location at the centre of Australia's three-hour time zone. But, by the 1890s, his rationale was also underpinned by national as well as regional and international considerations, not least, a pressing need, to establish a coherent system of federal time.[35]

Fleming's visit to Australia a few months later in November 1893, promised to sharpen their differences over the Pacific cable. For when Fleming arrived in Adelaide as part of a Canadian trade delegation, Todd took up a defensive position on the Pacific cable question. They would, however, find a measure of accommodation on the question of international time. After visiting Adelaide and the eastern colonies, Fleming wrote to Christie in early December:

> I'm glad to report to you that there is every prospect of the zone time system being adopted in all corners within a few months.[36]

Whether Fleming, in writing to Todd earlier that year, was supporting the terms of the 1893 conference resolution or A.C. Gregory's 1892 alternative was not made clear. Todd's rivalry with Fleming over the Pacific cable contrasted with the latter's reception in the eastern colonies and may well have reignited opposition to Todd's position on standard time. By the time the colonial Postmasters General reconvened in New Zealand to further consider the question in early 1894, it was clear that the proposal for three distinct time zones, rather than a single time standard, was now ascendant.

In 1894 the Adelaide *Advertiser*, rehearsing the forthcoming New Zealand event, called for more than mere 'abstract expressions of opinion' on the time question.[37] The *Advertiser*, citing Todd's 1893 speech on the subject, anticipated further criticism, since under the system he proposed, the Brisbane day would be an hour ahead the standard civil day, while Perth's would be an hour behind. Todd himself had been at pains to explain that:

> What we do in practical life is to adapt our movements to the duration of the daylight. The sun itself is not a correct timekeeper in one sense. There is a large and varying equation of time ... So long as we make all our arrangements accord with what we know would be the actual hour of the day, whatever the clock might strike, I do not think the differences would cause any practical difficulty. We do not feel any difficulty in South Australia where we have a range of 48 minutes.[38]

In spite of such assurances designed to placate critics of his 1893 conference resolution, Todd would come to recognise that the differences between the solar day and clock day to which he alluded were not well understood by the colonial public. Nor were they by legislators. In the following year, one Victorian parliamentarian referred contemptuously to attempts by a 'few scientific men to make the time of Brisbane and Perth the same,' proclaiming standard time 'a practical matter which affected every man and women in the colony' rather than 'a horological problem interesting only to experts'.[39]

The 1894 New Zealand conference where matters came to a head, was destined to reverse the position of the previous year. In the interim, colonial politicians as well as civil servants were assuming a more prominent role behind-the-scenes. In mid-August 1893, Queensland's Premier Sir Thomas McIlwraith addressed a long letter to the Premiers of other colonies on hour zone time and the Brisbane resolution five months earlier. In it, he regretted the absence of 'full discussion' on the subject and the 'considerable inconvenience' which would ensue should Todd's position be adopted.[40] McIlwraith was no John Forrest, lacking the scientific knowledge of Western Australia's Premier and former Surveyor General, but he had taken advice on the issue before going into print. At a personal level, Davison[41] speculates that Todd's professional rival, the irrepressible Clement Wragge, may have intervened behind-the-scenes, while Sandford Fleming's visit to Australia a few months earlier may equally have encouraged McIlwraith to champion the orthodox hour zone system. But the technical precedent, if indeed the Queensland Premier required one, was A.C. Gregory's motion in Melbourne two years earlier. So adamant was the Queensland Premier in advocating the 150th meridian for the eastern colonies on the grounds of 'the convenience of business arrangements,'[42] that he was even prepared to have a Bill on standard time drafted and submitted to other Premiers of the same opinion. When the South Australian Premier showed McIlwraith's letter to Todd, he reiterated his comments of the previous year, and disputed the inconvenience to which the Queensland Premier referred as 'more imagined than real,' since 'people would become accustomed to the change of hour and go to the office in Brisbane when the clock strikes 8, and at Perth when the clock strikes 10.[43] Recapping the problem of contiguous time zones at colonial border centres, and the views of Railway Commissioners, Todd strongly urged that the question be resubmitted to the other Australian colonies, especially to their railway and telegraph heads before his 1893 resolution was overturned.

In a scenario not uncommon at postal and telegraphic conferences, Todd, after recommending on the detail, let his Minister do the talking. Consequently, John Cockburn initiated most of the conference business on behalf of South Australia when delegates reconvened at Wellington in early 1894. It was an unexpected turn of events, but one for which Todd was prepared, for he spoke only briefly in the course of the debate. Queensland's representative also appeared to be under instructions, as he explained how his Premier Thomas McIlwraith, had personally intervened to overrule Todd's 1893 resolution on standard time.[44] Cockburn promptly moved that the 1893 resolution be reaffirmed, a motion which New Zealand's Joseph Ward seconded. But, without explicit Western Australian support and in the face of Victoria's new-found enthusiasm for McIlwraith's position, Cockburn withdrew Todd's 1893 motion for a single time standard, leaving Queensland's representative to move a new resolution in favour of three hour zones for Australia. If McIlwraith, like Todd, purported to speak on behalf of all the Australian colonies, his prime objective in the prelude to federation was to consolidate the eastern colonies into a single trading bloc.

After the 1894 reversal, the initiative reverted to individual colonies which proceeded to establish three time zones in legislation during 1894–95. In South Australia, where a Standard Time Bill was assented on 21 December 1894, the Post Office clock was stopped for 14 minutes 20 seconds as part of the necessary adjustment to the 135th meridian,[45] the *Advertiser* declaring in anticipation that 'tomorrow is to be the longest day on record … A similar event will take place in Victoria and New South Wales… Queensland set the example of a month ago'.[46] In New South Wales, where Todd's colleague, H.C. Russell proudly informed the Astronomer Royal that 'after today the time ball will drop at 1 pm on the 150th meridian or 15 hours Greenwich Mean Time'.[47] Sydneysiders put their watches forward five minutes to synchronise their time with that of Victoria and Tasmania and Queensland. Nevertheless, the *Daily Telegraph*, in a belated attempt to explain the hour zone system to its Sydney readers, conceded that the chaotic timekeeping situation, to which Todd had previously alluded in centres like Broken Hill, would remain unresolved, since:

> The mines, tradesmen and people generally have decided to adopt Adelaide time, while the government offices, banks and hotels will adopt Sydney time … Between the two times, complications are bound to occur.[48]

Nonetheless, Todd was prepared to follow Russell's example in August 1895, writing to Christie that 'standard time has now been adopted by the colonies of Queensland, New South Wales, Victoria and South Australia ... I hope ere long New Zealand, Tasmania and Western Australia will follow suit'.[49] If the eventual outcome had not been everything he desired, Todd, as the leading instigator at intercolonial conferences, still took most of the credit for its progress through the colonial legislatures, asserting that 'it was mainly through my exertions that standard time has been adopted'. Yet if he, along with most Australian colonists now considered the matter settled, it did not rest there. In his own colony of South Australia, an unexpected backlash threatened to undo the recent legislation, leading more than one member of its government to lament renewed 'legislation against the stars' and 'interference with the rising of the sun and the moon'.[50]

Not that debate over standard time subsided entirely after 1895. In Britain and overseas, the focus shifted to the difficulties of unifying time at sea, one which pitted authorities like Christie and the Royal Colonial Institute against the powerful British Admiralty and Canadian authorities.[51] For informed observers like Todd, these developments had flow-on effects for their own colonies, since they would involve changes to the *Nautical Almanac*, the standard reference for ship captains sailing to the Far East including Australia. Growing international pressure to revert from nautical time to civil time strengthened the case for the hour zone system after 1895 and helps explain the willingness of South Australians, including Todd, to accept the 1894 conference outcome as consistent with developments 'in force throughout the civilised world'.[52] This was not the view of the South Australian business community however, which began to agitate strongly against the existing time standard as prejudicial to its interests. In July 1897, the Adelaide Chamber of Commerce, in the belief that South Australian business was disadvantaged by operating an hour behind its eastern competitors, championed a petition with 246 signatures requesting that the government reduce the time difference from one hour to half an hour, and legislate for the 142.5th meridian rather than for 135th which Todd had recommended.[53] Among those supporting the parliamentary petition was the Early Closing Association, a labour organisation which argued for the new measure on behalf of its factory workers. In vain did D.M. Charleston, a government MP, remind the Assembly that Charles Todd 'had gone very carefully into the matter at the inter-colonial conference' and demanded to know why 'this colony should break faith with the other colonies'.[54] The stage was now set for more polarised debate on the issue.

Once a revised Standard Time Bill was introduced into the South Australian parliament, it seemed inevitable that Todd would again be drawn into public debate on the issue. Yet it was not until early August 1898 that the Legislative Council decided to seek his opinion, and, even then, by only a slender majority. For the Chamber of Commerce, which had clashed with its Postmaster General in the past, appeared determined to proceed with the changes in the face of scientific opinion. The government's motion to consult Todd met with determined resistance in the Upper House, where J.G. Bice insisted that 'the present position affects the mercantile community more than it did the scientists and the nautical community'.[55] Another opposition critic, oblivious to input from the civil service regretted 'a tendency nowadays for parliament to shirk its duty and relegate too much to outsiders'.[56] The motion was carried narrowly by 11 votes to 8, but with the accompanying rider that the views of the Stock Exchange and Chamber of Commerce also be sought. Under normal circumstances Todd would have followed the passage of the legislation through the House and responded promptly to the challenge. But before the Council's urgent request reached him in early August, he was engulfed in a family crisis at the Observatory. Alice's health was rapidly failing. The protracted ordeal of her illness and death only days after the Council debate left Todd temporarily incapable of discharging even the most pressing of his public duties.

Few, if any, in the Adelaide parliament knew of Todd's personal ordeal at this time. Alice had been ill for several weeks, though the seriousness of her condition was kept from the public and known only to the family's immediate circle. Nor was there any hint of it in letters to her daughters. The unmistakable symptoms of breast cancer[57] were in all probability of recent origin. Available evidence suggests that in mid-1898, 'Lady Todd,' as she had become, was not merely intent on keeping up appearances, she was actively pursuing her social rounds including at Government House in the company of family and friends.[58] In early July 1898, less than a month before tragedy struck, Lorna, her youngest daughter, vividly recalled a special moment at Governor Buxton's ball, when Alice shone:

> in her grey evening dress with the soft pink front demurely fastened nearly to the neck, she came down the wide dark wood stairs to the supper room on the arm of the then Governor of South Australia, Sir F. Buxton ... My mother looked especially lovely with her soft white hair and her pink flushed cheeks.[59]

It was no doubt this image which Charles would recall in the weeks to follow. He fully expected that Alice, ten years younger than himself, would outlive him. It was not to be. At the outset of the crisis, neither Charles nor her family were unduly alarmed by Alice's condition. The Todds, father and son, were well known and respected among Adelaide's medical fraternity and could guarantee expert treatment for Alice. Nor were her symptoms so intractable as to necessitate injections, a controversial new form of immunotherapy designed to boost immunity against tumours.[60] Nevertheless complications did occur. The surgical incision she received under treatment triggered an infection which spread to her lungs and induced the coma from which she could not be revived. For Charles and his family, time stood still, as Alice lay unconscious at the Observatory, 'withdrawn from us all'.[61] If Maude remembered Alice's unexpected early death as 'an irreparable loss to the family,'[62] Lorna, steeped in Bunyan's religious vision, saw her father, 'broken and rudderless,' in a different light and recognised the part Alice had played in both his public and private life.[63] One example of her influence occurred in the previous year during the Queen's Jubilee, when Todd called for women to be better represented on a committee established to organise a refuge for destitute Adelaide women.[64]

The *Register*'s report of Alice's death, while omitting any reference to cancer, agreed with Lorna's brief account in stating that:

> The deceased lady enjoyed excellent health until a month ago when she became ill and an operation was performed. Hopes of her recovery were held out, but she gradually sank and died from pneumonia. She had been unconscious for three weeks.[65]

Little wonder that Charles who had kept vigil at her bedside for much of this time, was now incommunicado. A photograph, taken later at the Observatory, captured the protracted grief, which Alice Thomson claims, transformed him into an old man.[66] With the announcement of Alice's death in the press, tributes and condolences began flowing into the Observatory throughout August. Adelaide societies and organisations, unaccustomed to Charles' prolonged absence from society, sent formal expressions of regret and sympathy. Alice's two daughters, Lizzie, resident in Cambridge, and Gwendoline, visiting Lizzie with her family, were soon informed and shared in the family's grief.[67] On 13 August, ten days after the Legislative Council had issued its request to Todd on the Standard Time Bill, the *Observer* reported that Alice's funeral attracted many prominent figures, the Governor and other members of the Buxton family, the Chief Justice, the Premier, and a number of Legislative Councillors.[68] Civil service organisations, respectful of their head of department, attended, while the sizeable contingent of medical and nursing staff reflected Charles

E. Todd's status as a surgeon at the Adelaide Hospital. On a more personal note, the *Register* paid tribute to Alice, acknowledging that:

> Her death will be mourned by many, especially in West Adelaide where her charitable deeds and unostentatious acts of kindness among the poor will not be forgotten.[69]

For most of August, Charles appears to have confined himself in mourning to the Observatory. His only reported public appearance appears to have been outside Adelaide, when he travelled to Port Pirie for the purpose of disciplining junior post office staff there. It was a duty which he found distasteful, but the long 140-mile journey to and from Adelaide afforded him much-needed time alone.

In the difficult weeks following Alice's death, professional support was forthcoming from a number of quarters on the pressing standard time question. In order to comply with the Legislative Council directive, the Astronomical Society of which Todd was President advertised an urgent meeting on 25 August with the intention of framing 'a report on the proposed alteration in standard time' in Todd's absence.[70] The Society would later allude to the agenda item of that month as 'the most important matter to come before it since its foundation' in 1891.[71] The August meeting, attended at short notice by 17 members, began with a letter of condolence addressed to its 'esteemed President' in his 'sad bereavement'. Todd, as its longserving head, had already made known his objections to the Chamber of Commerce measures in the Adelaide press.[72] Whether members of the Astronomical Society would embrace his opposition to the Bill, in view of its widespread support, was yet to be tested. At the outset, one outspoken supporter of the business position urged a motion in favour of 'a half an hour in advance of the present standard time'. But once Todd's assistant, R.F. Griffiths proceeded to dissect the new Bill, labelling as uninformed those 'who suppose that by altering the clock it would in any way lengthen and or shorten the daylight,' the meeting swung solidly behind him. After executive members agreed that the Society should consider the matter from an astronomical perspective rather than a commercial one, the original motion was withdrawn and a subsequent resolution in favour of Todd's position was carried unanimously. The objections to the revised Standard Time Bill raised by Griffiths and the Astronomical Society were substantial, ranging from the legislation's detrimental impact on South Australians living in the west of the colony, to its adverse implications for Admiralty charts and the *Nautical Almanac*, 'already in the course of preparation for the next and following years'.[73] Taking its lead from Todd, the Society further proposed a more simple solution by altering South Australia's hours of business rather than depart from the 'almost universal system' of standard time already in place. On 27 August, the Society sent its report and recommendations to Todd for perusal and signing, after which they were forwarded to the Chief Secretary for consideration by the legislature.

If Todd and his small Astronomical Society appeared to be fighting a losing campaign against local business, the 'no' case also received strong support in the Adelaide press. Although the *Register* generally took the lead on local and scientific matters, the *Advertiser* took the initiative on this occasion, opposing both the Adelaide Chamber of Commerce and the South Australian legislature on the issue. In the following month, with the Bill still under consideration, the *Advertiser* published a long editorial, 'Altering the Clock Again,'[74] in which it reviewed the entire question and came out strongly in support of Todd's position. Alluding to his initial stance on the 135th meridian, it speculated that his proposal for a single federal time might yet receive consideration under the Commonwealth. By contrast, the new South Australian legislation, it protested, was not simply proposing to revert to Adelaide time, but would impose yet another timekeeping system on the colony. Local dissatisfaction with standard time under the 1894 legislation could be met, it asserted without changing the system yet again. Arguments in favour of an additional half an hour of daylight and economies in lighting and gas could be resolved by opening business offices half an hour earlier by the clock, as government departments were already doing. Citing Todd throughout, the *Advertiser* editorial characterised the proposed time difference of an hour and a half between Adelaide and Perth as 'lessening one difficulty ... at the cost of increasing another in the opposite direction,' since regular telegraphic traffic via Western Australia would incur longer delays. Deferring to Todd's long-standing experience as Postmaster General, the *Advertiser* predicted still more confusion for railway and telegraph services, not to mention the *Nautical Almanac* and the international time system. Clearly, the Adelaide daily had gone to the trouble of consulting Todd in producing an editorial which was unusually long and well-reasoned. But were Legislative Councillors listening at this late hour? In the event, the consultation process proved a mere formality and the new Standard Time Bill passed the third Assembly reading in mid-September before gaining the assent of both houses in January 1899.[75]

Though unable to provide public leadership of the rearguard campaign, Todd was heartened by the level of professional and public support he received. The Astronomical Society thought highly enough of the *Advertiser* piece to cite it in its minute book, adding that 'the subject was debated at length, with articles, editorials, and letters to the editor in newspapers'.[76] Led by the *Advertiser*, the Adelaide press deferred to Todd, repeating his earlier adage that 'the name we give to the hour is not of very much consequence. What we do in practical life is to adapt our movements to the duration of daylight'. Such had been Todd's forlorn hope. Yet the *Advertiser* persisted with its 'No' campaign, citing Todd once more at the time of the Bill's third reading in November 1898, before drawing its own conclusion that 'the practical man, it seems, cannot or will not adjust his occupation to the actual duration of daylight, but prefers to be tyrannised by mere figures on a dial'.[77] For Todd, the final phase of the decade-long debate, compounded by his difficult personal circumstances, had proven the most arduous. One personal compensation was the support he received, most notably from the *Advertiser*, which had articulated his position with unusual clarity. Here was confirmation that his public persona was indeed alive and well. Todd thought sufficiently highly of the *Advertiser*'s November editorial to send a copy to the Astronomer Royal, William Christie.[78] Certain passages resonated for both men, especially its reference to the support of 'the highest scientific authorities' for a single federal time at the 135th meridian.[79] But no less telling was the conclusion which the *Advertiser* editorial drew, following the passage of the 1899 Bill, that 'after the South Australian experience ... all hope of federalising the clocks and establishing one time for these colonies must be abandoned'.[80]

12

'Weather Wars': Todd and Clement Wragge

In preparation for his trip to Europe, Todd had taken care to maintain the Observatory's weather service during his prolonged absence. Richard Fletcher Griffiths who replaced Ringwood in 1882 as chief meteorologist,[1] assumed temporary command, while William Cooke, who was showing considerable promise as an astronomer, provided the necessary assistance. They were not the only ones observing the South Australian weather at this time. Unbeknowns to the Observatory, Clement Wragge was establishing his own weather stations in and around Adelaide, independent of Todd's established network. Considerably younger than Todd, Wragge viewed meteorology as a new science distinct from astronomy. His training in the United Kingdom had endowed Wragge with a sturdy Scottish individualism which owed little to the Greenwich Observatory network to which Todd and his colleagues belonged. Noted for establishing high altitude stations, Wragge had famously ascended Scotland's highest peak Ben Nevis, where, as at Mount Lofty near Adelaide, he established meteorological stations using self-registering equipment for atmospheric research.[2] Such a physical approach was in marked contrast to Todd's highly organised methods of information gathering and use of the telegraph, but found a following among colonists who were impressed by his audacity and publicity techniques. Significantly Wragge makes no mention of Todd in his writings on South Australia.[3] Armed with a towering ego, he was less interested in colonial co-operation than in casting his own transcontinental net of stations across the colonies, using low-level volunteers. Here was a vision diametrically opposed to that of

Todd and the collaborative ethos which he had painstakingly nurtured over several decades.

More ominously, Wragge's long and turbulent colonial career was marred by ongoing professional controversy, which thrived on confrontation and self-promotion. Encouraged by Todd's absence, Wragge took the opportunity in mid-1886 to propose the establishment of a Meteorological Society for Australasia to further his national ambitions.[4] The choice of Adelaide for this purpose was no doubt partly personal because Wragge had spent some time there working in the survey department. But it also represented a direct challenge to Todd, whose weather stations were still the most extensive and efficient system of reporting in the Australian colonies. Wragge's provocative proposal met with initial indifference from other observers; this did little to diminish his conviction, despite ample evidence to the contrary, that Todd was overcommitted to his other administrative portfolios, and unable to maintain a comprehensive weather service for his colony. On his return from England, Todd still recovering from illness and overburdened with departmental work, was unlikely to heed let alone respond to such provocations. When Wragge was appointed Queensland meteorologist shortly afterwards in 1887, Todd anticipated official collaboration and a closer working relationship with Queensland. Meteorological dialogue across the Australian colonies had begun well, though it would take considerable time and patience to address all the issues which Todd and his colleagues had previously identified. As yet Todd had not encountered the red-haired Wragge face to face, nor experienced his invective and disruptive tactics at close quarters.[5] It was not until the following year at the next inter-colonial meteorological conference held in Melbourne, that Todd began to understand the serious challenge Wragge represented.

The meteorological conference of September 1888 held out hopes of further unity, since representatives of all the mainland Australian colonies were in attendance, along with participants from Tasmania and New Zealand. On this occasion, the work of previous gatherings in pursuing greater co-operation extended to the production and sharing of weather charts and forecasts.[6] However when Sir John Forrest, on behalf of Western Australia, moved that each colony confined itself to supplying telegrams of its own weather, Wragge, representing Queensland, took umbrage and dissented.[7] It was a highly provocative move, given that all the other colonies present supported Forrest's proposal. Wragge had asserted his independence immediately after his 1887 appointment, by claiming that he had been 'the first to incorporate regular forecasts for all the Australasian colonies'.[8] He was determined to defy the conference recommendation and continue to issue his own national forecasts. The stage was set for prolonged disputation throughout the next decade. In the aftermath of the 1888 conference, the *Sydney Morning Herald* was sceptical of 'that irrepressible and storm-loving prophet, Mr Wragge'[9] and of his Brisbane weather bureau forecasts, now being telegraphed to newspaper correspondents in other colonies in defiance of the 1888 conference recommendation.

Like Todd, Wragge had come to rely on the telegraph to disseminate his weather news, but in a spirit which was more confrontational than co-

Clement Wragge, c.1901

operative. By offering brief weather reports to Brisbane correspondents of the large southern papers, in time for morning publication, he shrewdly extended his influence beyond Brisbane into the southern centres of Adelaide and Sydney.[10] With the characteristic blend of mockery and self-promotion which accompanied many of his public statements, he would also imply that his own 1887 decision had triggered the decision of the other colonies to begin issuing forecasts, rather than the 1888 conference, Alluding to his own pioneering South Australian forecast of 1884, Wragge later derided Todd for his reluctance to issue weather forecasts in his own colony by alleging:

> the story goes that he [Sir Charles Todd] did not care to run the gauntlet of public opinion before, in the case of failures, having remarked that although ninety-nine of his forecasts might be successful, if the hundredth failed, the public would be down on him 'like a thousand bricks'.[11]

If Wragge preferred to exaggerate the reluctance of his colleagues, their dilemma was a real one. Nor was such reluctance confined to Todd and South Australia.[12] The new weather science in Australia, as in Britain, was still an inexact one and prone to be confused in the public mind with the claims of bogus weather prophets. In the United Kingdom, George Airy believed that meteorologists should embrace forecasting in the face of a growing challenge from their American counterparts, while accepting the ensuing risks to their public credibility.[13] As pressure from the colonial press and public mounted, Todd began monitoring the accuracy of the daily forecasts issued by his own department, asserting that 'a good proportion of the forecasts proved correct'.[14] On the more vexed issue of long-range forecasting however, he shared the reluctance of Ellery, his Victorian colleague's to stand by the accuracy of his forecasts 'beyond one or two more days'.[15]

Throughout these preliminary skirmishes, Todd set himself the more complex task of keeping faith with his professional colleagues while gratifying public demand. Bound by the decision of the 1888 conference, he maintained a calm public demeanour and refrained from issuing forecasts for Queensland, though his northern Overland Telegraph network was well equipped to do so. In private, however, he was growing frustrated at the failure to achieve a working consensus after the Melbourne conference, dubbing his Queensland counterpart 'the meteorological Czar of Australasia' and opining to Victorian astronomer, Robert Ellery, that 'Wragge in weather matters acts most absurdly and I think ungentlemanly'.[16] In the wake of the conference, Wragge aggravated an already tense situation by insisting the reports from the other colonies be forwarded to him and accused Todd of withholding South Australian forecasts; whereupon, Todd gave vent to his indignation in a letter to his Sydney counterpart, Henry Russell:

> I'm glad you replied to Wragge's last and enclose a copy of my reply. He is I fear too [insensitive] to feel the snub and too dense to appreciate the closing sentence of my letter.[17]

Like Russell in New South Wales, Todd took umbrage at Wragge's overweening ambition. But it was not long before their dispute re-entered the public domain and Todd would bear the brunt of it.

Wragge's dogmatic attempts to create a Brisbane-based weather bureau, along the lines of Washington in the United States also provoked irritation among his colonial colleagues and drew criticism from the press. The proposed meteorological conference, to be chaired by Wragge in Brisbane during 1893 was cancelled after Robert Ellery, Victoria's representative, declined to attend.

The Adelaide *Register* commented on Victoria's behalf, concerning Wragge's ambitious plan for a national bureau:

> It certainly ought not to be in Brisbane, which has no more qualification for the honour than Hobart or Perth. In Melbourne are collected the best meteorological instruments perhaps in the world ... It is beyond a doubt the most convenient point in Australia, and its meteorological operations are conducted by a distinguished scientist.[18]

Given the intervening events and the state of relations between Wragge and his colleagues, it is questionable whether the proposed Brisbane meteorological conference would have achieved its ends. With its cancellation, the momentum achieved over previous decades was lost, and the dispute now took a more personal turn.

In South Australia, Todd was now facing local accusations of professional jealousy, encouraged by Wragge, for giving priority to New South Wales and Victorian forecasts at the expense of Queensland's bureau. Wragge did not hesitate to intervene personally, drafting a long letter to the South Australian press, justifying his defiance of the 1888 conference decision on the grounds that:

> [such a] crippling regulation would have forbidden this office, even then the chief bureau of Australasia by virtue of the work accom-

plished under the auspices of my government, from issuing any forecast whatever other than those which strictly pertained to the internal interest of my adopted country.[19]

It was one thing for Todd to resist pressure for their publication from outside the colony, but his position on forecasts now came under critical scrutiny from within South Australia. In early 1891, the local Holdfast Bay yacht club demanded access to Wragge's forecasts, disputing Todd's argument that competing forecasts for South Australia would merely create public confusion.[20] The correspondence pages of the *Advertiser*, where lobbying continued, made it clear that, within the yachting community, divisions persisted over the value of Wragge's forecasts. It was not long, however, before Todd was put on the defensive. For the pro-Wragge lobby of 1891–92 was sufficiently energetic to approach the Minister for Education and Culture, under whom Todd's served, with a request for South Australia to publish both the local and Queensland weather forecasts.

Summoned to provide a report on the forecast dispute by his Minister, David Bews, Todd defended himself in the manner in which he was best equipped – the use of statistics. Throughout 1891, he had taken the precaution of monitoring the relative accuracy of both his own and Wragge's forecasts for South Australia. The results, as the press acknowledged when his report was published, 'justified the government in not acceding to the request to make arrangements for the publication of Mr Wragge's meteorological predictions'.[21] Todd's figures undermined public assumptions about the greater reliability of Wragge's local reports, with 82% of Todd's verified against only 35% from Queensland. Todd demonstrated generosity in describing Wragge's record as 'highly creditable' on the basis of the limited information at his disposal, while commending 'the earnest zeal he throws into his work'. At this point the press dispute among weather prophets, as the *Register* labelled it, subsided. The controversy still circulated widely in Adelaide, and in the following year (1893), no less a personage than Sir John Downer called once more for the joint publication of Todd's and Wragge's forecasts on the grounds that Wragge was 'the only thoroughly professional meteorologist in any of the colonies,'[22] an assertion which Todd felt obliged to correct. Although the general accuracy of Todd's predictions was not in doubt, Wragge and his supporters still sought to bring the matter to a head. Todd's monitoring of future forecasts showed that his statements were not as disingenuous as his critics inferred. The issue now became whether the press or the meteorological profession should decide which forecasts were published.

With the cancellation of the 1893 meteorological conference, Todd chose a new and wider forum in which to disseminate his weather work. The formation in 1888 of the Australasian Association for the Advancement of Science (AAAS) by William Liversidge and Charles Russell, Todd's New South Wales colleague, had by then attracted considerable interest across the colonies. One of its prominent proponents in South Australia was Todd's son-in-law, William Henry Bragg, who had married his third daughter, Gwendoline, in 1889.[23] On his arrival in Adelaide as Professor in Mathematics and Physics at the University, he was soon befriended by the Todd family.[24] Charles and William shared a firm belief in science education and understood the need for networking in the colonial science environment. Bragg, having attended the first 1888 gathering of the AAAS in Sydney, wrote enthusiastically of its collaborative potential to Gwendoline:

> I think this association is going to do us a lot of good, especially such as, like me, are willing to work, but don't quite know where to begin. Contact with other and more experienced workers will start us off on the right track.[25]

For the 1893 AAAS event, scheduled for Adelaide, Professors Bragg and Rennie of the local university, were appointed general secretaries and, with Bragg's encouragement, Todd despite numerous other commitments and conferences in that year prepared a survey of meteorological work for one of the conference's sessions. Todd's professional advice may also have been instrumental in the local committee's decision to change the month of the event from January to September in order to avoid the Adelaide heat and entice delegates to the city.

The formation in 1831 of the British Association for the Advancement of Science (BAAS), the forerunner of the AAAS, promised a break from earlier patterns of patronage associated with such institutions as the Royal Society of London.[26] Todd's own training at Greenwich and Cambridge owed much to early nineteenth century scientific culture, and, while his astronomy closely emulated Airy's example, his meteorology had developed a local and regional perspective 'under the Southern Cross'.[27] With this in mind, he presented an informative review of meteorological work in Australia, which was published in the following year.[28] In his home city, Todd had little reason to be on the defensive. In the absence of Henry Russell, who was ill and unable to attend, Todd moved the election of AAAS officers, paying his absent colleague a tribute in the course of his own address. As a long-term advocate of colonial cooperation, Todd had a strong mandate to speak on his fellow meteorologists' behalf. Even Wragge had to admit that his main rival was 'far better versed in the meteorology of Australasia than myself, [having] resided far longer by many years on this side of the world'.[29]

Clearly, seniority counted. For the benefit of visiting AAAS delegates, Todd identified South Australia's three main weather systems. At the same time, he took the opportunity in his address to update his success rate in local forecasts, now estimated at 73% totally accurate, 20% partially accurate and only 7% totally wrong.[30] Meteorology, he went on to explain, was far from being an exact science. At once national and local in scope, Todd's paper not only rehearsed the work of recent meteorological conferences, but also mentioned the early contributions of individuals. He praised the efforts of Ellery and Neumayer in Victoria as 'second to none,'[31] while acknowledging the work of Russell and Tebbutt in New South Wales, along with Griffiths and his own in South Australia. He was no less magnanimous in commending Wragge for establishing weather stations in the Pacific to alert the mainland coast to the approach of cyclones. Although Todd broached the vexed issue of Wragge's Australasian forecasts and questioned their desirability, there was little pointed discussion of this in his paper.[32] For Todd, the advent of the AAAS and the approach of federation demanded renewed co-operation, rather than the professional and public conflict upon which Wragge appeared to thrive. In refraining from open debate, Todd was undoubtedly influenced by his early British training. In private, he admitted to a dislike of public controversy[33] and eschewed the aggression of his Greenwich superior, George Airy who had invariably been confrontational in his dealings with colleagues and with other scientific institutions when he felt his authority was called into question. Although Todd retained a lasting respect for the Astronomer General, he rarely resorted to the intimidation of colleagues or employees for which Airy was feared.

Ironically, in the wake of Todd's notable AAAS address, agitation within South Australia intensified during 1893–94, with renewed calls for access to Wragge's weather reports. Todd's forecasts again became the 'talk of the town'.[34] When interviewed in February 1894, he justified his decision, as superintendent of telegraphs, to withhold Wragge's Australasian forecasts on the grounds that his rival had breached 'professional etiquette' and refused to abide by the 1888 conference resolution.[35] A fortnight later, Wragge, writing to the Adelaide press, confirmed that his forecasts were now sent free of charge to New South Wales and Victoria but not to South Australia, adding ironically that 'my friend Sir Charles Todd needs to explain why our forecasts are not published by him in South Australia'.[36] In its correspondence over the issue, the pro-Wragge Glenelg yacht club drew an unfavourable parallel between the local situation and that which existed in Britain, where meteorologists were prepared to accept American storm warnings.[37] Yet the *Register*, recalling Todd's meteorological address of the previous year, defended the local prophet on the grounds that Todd's painstaking data collection would ultimately 'pave the way for future extensions of the forecast system'.[38] By mid-year, matters threatened to become more personal when Wragge came to Adelaide to confront Todd over South Australia's and Western Australia's joint decision to charge the full cable rate for forecasts telegraphed from Queensland. Although the meeting between the two men was described as 'cordial' on this occasion,[39] it was clear that Wragge was using the visit to lobby extensively in Adelaide, especially with influential members of the yachting fraternity who contended that without Wragge's storm reports, they would be forced to rely on mere rumour.

A few years earlier, the Wragge lobby had brought pressure to bear on Todd through his immediate superior, the Minister for Education, without overturning his restrictive policy on local forecasts. By August 1895 however, the Queensland meteorologist found an outspoken ally in Ebenezer Ward, a Legislative Councillor, press proprietor and former Todd Minister. His animus against Todd was longstanding. As his superior during the 1870s, Ward acted dictatorially in reducing Todd's budget and depriving him of much-needed staff.[40] In early September 1895 after corresponding with Wragge, Ward, describing himself as a former neighbour of Wragge's, and the recipient of a letter from him dated 17 August 1894, tabled a controversial motion in the Council, requiring that Todd's department publish Wragge's Australasian forecasts as well as its own. It triggered a noisy debate in the Council. On one hand the Colonial Secretary defended the quality of Todd's reports and denounced the impertinence of Wragge as a 'comparative amateur'; on the other, Ward and his supporters asserted that Todd had 'too many duties to perform' and that local mariners relied on Wragge's forecasts.[41] Despite an admission that its acceptance would reflect poorly on the local Observatory and its staff, the controversial motion was carried. Still, Ward was not satisfied. When the Council reconvened in late October, the issue of Todd's fitness to serve as Postmaster General was raised by Ward in the House. Arguably, Ward's new motion was calculated to galvanise long-held resentment on the part of politicians towards Todd, who, as Postmaster General for more than two decades, continued to occupy a position usually reserved for senior members of the Ministry. At this fresh challenge, sanctioned by Wragge, the Council baulked and determined that, irrespective of its previous decision, no such motion would be sanctioned 'out of deference to Sir Charles Todd,' until such time as he chose to vacate the office.[42]

Amid pressure over Wragge's forecasts, Todd refused to be distracted from the larger task of gathering long-range data, with a view to understanding the extremities of the Australian climate. The *Register* put it more bluntly in its 'weather wisdom' editorial, observing that 'skilful and prudent meteorologists may be pardoned for declining to emulate the exploits of weather quacks'.[43] Overlooked in the Legislative Council debate was the important fact that Todd, despite an unusually high workload, had trained several Observatory staff to a high standard of expertise, not only Richard Griffiths but also William Cooke whom he had recruited from St Peter's College and mentored since 1878. Their contribution would continue beyond the boundaries of South Australia and confirm Todd's reputation into the twentieth century. Cooke, who owed his scientific training entirely to Todd after graduating from Adelaide University,[44] credited him with being the first Australian meteorological observer to confirm that weather systems across the continent tracked from west to east rather than the reverse.[45] The implications of this insight were crucial for understanding weather patterns along the Great Australian Bight and the southern part of the continent, exposed as they were to anti-cyclones and pressure systems from the Antarctic Ocean. This situation accounts in part for his reluctance to issue storm forecasts for South Australia, since, unlike Wragge in Queensland, he lacked offshore meteorological stations to provide the necessary warnings of sudden changes in the southern ocean.

The situation was destined to improve when in late 1894, the Western Australian Premier Sir John Forrest took decisive steps under Todd's influence to establish a Perth Observatory. Before his successful entry into politics, Forrest had been Western Australia's Surveyor-General and understood the need for careful astronomical observation as well as mapping of the climate. He farsightedly pushed ahead with the proposal, writing to Todd in December 1894 for advice on the choice of site, equipment and personnel.[46] Forrest's initiative could hardly go unnoticed in South Australia and Todd's reputation, both scientific and diplomatic, rose accordingly. Moreover, Todd's and Forrest's co-operation proved to be more than strategic, connected as their neighbouring colonies now were by the telegraph. It was also a personal one, based on a long-held mutual respect which preceded their attendance and agreement at the 1888 meteorological conference in Melbourne. Forrest first encountered the Overland Telegraph Line in 1874 during his acclaimed exploration of north-west Australia and enjoyed the hospitality afforded by its stations at Todd's request.[47] An optimist like the West Australian Premier, Todd spoke warmly of his host when entertained by him in Perth.[48] Forrest's popularity in turn engendered good will towards Todd during his Perth visit of January 1895, when he was entertained by the West Australian Governor, met his postal counterpart and spoke at a banquet to commemorate Forrest's thirty years of service to the colony. It was a high point of influence for Todd during the turbulent 1890s, one which extended his meteorological influence across southern Australia. For on Todd's commendation, his well trained assistant William Cooke was appointed to head the new Perth Observatory shortly afterwards.

As Cooke explained at the time of his appointment,[49] the potential benefits for South Australia were also considerable, Once a reliable and comprehensive weather network was established in the south and inland of the colony, his Western Australian reports could also be telegraphed to Todd and Griffiths at the Adelaide Observatory. According to his biographer,[50] Cooke was ultimately more successful in his study of tropical cyclones than of Antarctic disturbances. Despite bouts of ill health he set about his task vigorously, inspecting second-class stations and setting the same high standards of observation, as he had done previously in South Australia.

Cooke's training at the Adelaide Observatory had made him sceptical of Wragge's forecasts. Like Todd and Ellery, he was loath at the outset to issue forecasts at all. But public pressure in Perth and on the goldfields was such that he began to issue daily forecasts in February 1896, based on observations taken in Perth and at Cape Leeuwin. In the same month, Cooke issued his first weather map and, by the following year, was operating a meteorological service from the Perth Observatory.[51] Like Todd and Griffiths, Cooke subscribed to the view than an extensive area of low pressure extending from the South Pole was producing upward surges across the southern Australian coastline.[52] Given the west to east movement of southern ocean weather systems, it was not surprising that Cooke's reports were reproduced in South Australia and Victoria. After soaring summer temperatures in 1897, which Todd described as 'the hottest December on record,'[53] Adelaide residents were greatly relieved when their Observatory issued the Perth forecast that a change 'with cool storms [would] reach them by tomorrow'.[54] When the cool New Year change duly arrived as predicted, the *Register* declared Todd 'the most popular man in South Australia'.[55]

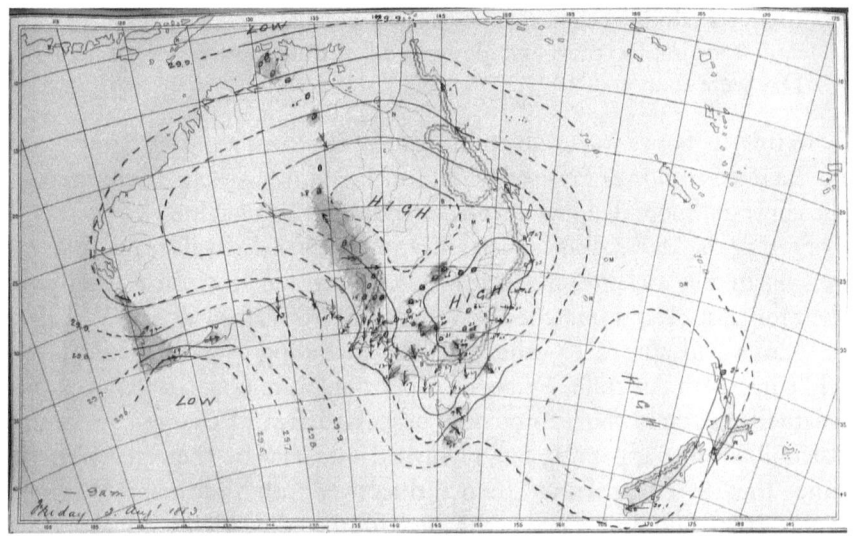

Todd Synoptic Chart showing weather movement WA to SA, 1883

To his credit, Todd maintained not merely a stoical attitude towards the vagaries of weather prediction, but a personal capacity for humour. Lorna Todd provides an amusing glimpse of the 'genial scientist,' when reciting 'one of my father's jokes against himself' on the subject:

> One day when sheltering under a King William Street verandah from a sudden deluge, he [father] saw that the man next to him had an umbrella. 'You're lucky to have that with you' he remarked. 'Oh no' replied the other. 'When the day seems uncertain I always look at the forecast and if Old Man Todd says it will be fine, I take an umbrella!'[56]

This humorous and at times self-deprecating side of Todd's personality was mirrored in the Adelaide press. As a long serving patron of Adelaide clubs including yachting and cricket, he was not infrequently invoked, like some classical deity, when favourable outdoor conditions were required for special events. On one occasion when Todd joined a party on board the *Orlando* at Port Adelaide, the *Register* quipped that he been invited there for his 'primeval jests, though not to bring with him Father Neptune in a towering rage'.[57] The Hunt Club, on one occasion, might bemoan Todd's incapacity to command the weather with the onset of a dust storm, while on another, express its belated gratitude to him for a 'first-class hunting day'.[58] In similar vein, the *Register*, on behalf of the Labor Day committee, reported 'much general anxiety' over Sir Charles Todd's 'ominous weather forecast,' adding that:

> Badly as rain is needed for the general weal, city folk might be pardoned for hoping that it would hold off until the festivities of Labor Day were at an end.⁵⁹

In this, its hopes were to be fulfilled. The *Register*'s reporter, citing Todd on the inexactitude of his profession, concluded that despite his forecast to the contrary, 'more delightful weather could not be imagined'.⁶⁰

During the 1890s, Todd's sociability and humour helped create a literary persona in the Adelaide press, one which, despite ongoing competition over their forecasts, was unmatched by Wragge. By 1897, the row over Wragge's telegrams had spread to other colonies including New South Wales,⁶¹ while in South Australia, Wragge's supporters were now insisting that his weather telegrams should not only be passed free of charge over South Australia's telegraph lines, but published officially by their government. Since the 1894 Legislative Council directive, both Todd's and Wragge's local forecasts now appeared in the press for the edification of the Adelaide public. While complying with its resolution, Todd continued to dispute it, explaining his position to New South Wales Deputy Postmaster General, Stephen Lambton, in the following terms:

> If the forecasts were more accurate than those issued locally, there might be some grounds for the action ... but such I think is not the case.⁶²

That Todd's forecasts were more frequently correct, prompted the *Register* to declare on more than one occasion that 'the local prophet has won the day'.⁶³ On other days, both sets of forecasts were fulfilled.⁶⁴ A comparison of their accuracy, cited in the Melbourne *Argus* of mid-1897, confirmed Todd in his assertion that 'local forecasts nearest the scene should be more reliable than those supplied by a distant bureau,' not only in the case of South Australia, but also for New South Wales and Victoria.⁶⁵ Despite the Wragge controversy, Todd continued to joke with the public about the weather, both at Wragge's and his own expense. Toasting the South Australian cricket team in 1895, he characteristically punned to good effect that:

> The South Australian team has been under a cloud for some time but ... he was going to issue a forecast and if it did not come off, he hoped he would be reduced to rag [*sic*].⁶⁶

The *Chronicle*, commenting on Charles' entrenched habit of word play, confided in the same spirit that he:

> allows himself a little relaxation occasionally ... by perpetuating a mild pun ... When wet weather ensues he likes to be known as the

'raining sovereign' of the weather department.⁶⁷

Even the regional press made mention of Todd's weather puns. At Port Pirie, the local *Recorder*, reporting abrupt changes in weather during December 1899, considered it 'enough to make a mild-mannered individual rise up and slay Sir Charles Todd with one of his own puns'.⁶⁸

Not that competition with Wragge had subsided. Rather the focus of his southern activities had shifted to New South Wales and Victoria. In keeping with the Queensland meteorologist's interests and ambition, he established an observatory on Mt Kosciusko during 1898.⁶⁹ In doing so, he drew criticism from New South Wales observer, Henry Russell, who argued that Wragge's earlier station on Ben Nevis in Scotland had been of little value for forecasting purposes.⁷⁰ Todd was less sceptical, but he shared Russell's concern with Wragge's unprofessional methods, including his recruitment of postal officials in other colonies for the dissemination of his Kosciusko observations. By the turn of the century, meteorologists across the colonies, acting in the co-operative spirit of the 1888 conference resolution, had established joint nation-wide forecasts from which Wragge, who had begun his own *Australasian Weather Almanac* in 1898 remained aloof. But as federation approached and brought with it the likelihood that a central bureau of meteorology would be established in one of the eastern states, Todd joined his colleagues in lobbying against a Commonwealth bureau on the grounds of efficiency, and more especially, one over which Wragge would seek to preside.

Federation was only one challenge facing Todd and his colleagues' weather work. The onset of the Great Drought on the heels of the 1890s depression took a heavy toll on government funding for colonial science. Only Western Australia was exempt. In Victoria, where the longserving Ellery retired in 1895, the Melbourne observatory staff was halved under his replacement, Pietro Baracchi.⁷¹ In New South Wales, Henry Russell, prior to the onset of illness in 1903 and his retirement,⁷² began re-examining cyclical weather patterns and the postulation of eminent British scientist, Sir Norman Lockyer,⁷³ that the earth's weather was influenced by an 11 year sunspot cycle,⁷⁴ In South Australia, Todd had never enjoyed the resources available to his eastern colleagues and though Cooke was now in Western Australia, he continued in collaboration with the reliable Griffiths⁷⁵ to monitor the intensifying drought which was spreading across the entire Australian continent: the 'Great Drought,' as it would later be known.

In such dire circumstances, the good will which Todd had built up with his South Australian public over many years was again put at risk. Keen to dispel the press stereotype of himself as an Olympian scientist 'ensconced in his cool observatory,'[76] Todd, assisted by Griffiths, gave regular briefings to the public and interviews to visiting reporters. As the public mood soured at science's expense, the *Advertiser* came to their defence, denouncing 'the hackneyed jokes which fasten on Sir Charles Todd and his meteorological department as the responsible parties'.[77] Few of those who grumbled at the 'dismal croaking' of their weather prophets[78] knew of Todd's own protracted misadventure on the land. As hard-pressed settlers turned to scripture and prayer for comfort,[79] the *Chronicle* complimented its local 'rainmaker' as 'a most modest and unassuming man,' reminding its readers:

> His weather forecasts are not always right, but so far as reliability can be obtained in this direction, Sir Charles has achieved it.[80]

Wragge's influence did not dissipate under the new Commonwealth in 1901. Despite his reputation for clashing with colleagues in other states, his public advocacy of a centralised weather bureau found a ready reception among politicians. In federal circles, he would continue to be cited as 'the leading Australian authority on meteorology,' based on his writings and regular attendance at international forums.[81] Alert to Wragge's national ambitions, Todd renewed his lobbying against him in mid-1902, confiding to Ellery's successor Pietro Baracchi in Melbourne: 'I am strongly opposed to the establishment of a Central Bureau under any circumstances; but more especially if placed under Mr Wragge'.[82] By the time he reiterated these sentiments to Cooke a few months later,[83] the prospect of a central bureau under Wragge's overweening direction appeared less likely. Across the colonies, cloud seeding experiments using cannon were attempted but failed,[84] nowhere more spectacularly than in rural Queensland, where Wragge's well publicised experiments at outback Charleville proved ineffectual.[85] By July 1902, his Queensland bureau had closed and he was no longer Queensland's official representative in ongoing inter-state deliberations. With Wragge's Queensland situation in doubt, Todd began using his influence in the new federal bureaucracy to undo the public humiliation which Wragge and his local allies had inflicted on him during the 1894 controversy over incoming weather telegrams. During 1902, Todd, who was now federal Deputy Postmaster General for South Australia, was instrumental in overturning the Council's directive at a time when his newly appointed superior, J.G. Drake, was anxious to introduce economies into his sprawling federal department. As part of his drive to reduce burgeoning costs, the flow of inter-state weather telegrams transmitted free of charge was much reduced. On Todd's advice, it was now limited to exchanges between principal meteorological officers,[86] thereby preventing Wragge or his Queensland successors from bypassing Todd or his colleagues, and distributing their reports through other southern channels.

In consequence, Todd was more optimistic by November of that year about the meteorological prospects of the states under the Commonwealth, writing to New Zealand's Postmaster General that: 'we are getting along very well under Federation,' and adding, at a time when the prolonged drought was beginning to break in parts of South Australia, that 'we will certainly be most unpopular if we were to discontinue publishing either the weather reports or the shipping intelligence'.[87] If adverse public opinion during the years of the Great Drought tested Todd's reputation, Wragge's popularity had also been called into question. With his departure from Queensland to New Zealand shortly afterwards, the prospect of another candidate becoming Commonwealth Meteorologist now appeared probable. In the expectation of a national conference to discuss meteorology's future and an impending showdown with Wragge, Todd lobbied hard against his appointment during late 1902, at a time when he still had an ally in New South Wales' Henry Russell. But by 1903, when Russell fell seriously ill, Todd was the only veteran of his generation still in post. As such, he still exercised professional influence in Western Australia but not in the dominant eastern states. After his calls for negotiations to resolve the situation fell on deaf ears, he admitted to Baracchi by the end of that year that 'he had given up all idea of a conference at present'.[88]

Several years elapsed before a Commonwealth meteorological conference took place, during which time Todd's health declined, forcing him to retire from his position as Deputy Postmaster General in the federal bureaucracy. Even so, when the much awaited conference finally convened at Adelaide in May 1905, Todd, now approaching eighty, occupied the chair and demonstrated the same combination of diplomacy and precision which he had exhibited at previous conferences in the 1880s. Nor did he baulk at exposing the constraints of his own situation. The detailed survey of state meteorological departments commissioned for the conference confirmed that the funding of his own Observatory was indeed meagre, with annual salaries amounting to only a third of those paid elsewhere.[89] Todd's fears about starving the observatories were already a reality in his home state. Yet, as he had successfully done previously on the issue of weather telegrams, he sought to turn commonwealth stringency to advantage by arguing that meteorology could be undertaken much more cheaply by the states than by the Commonwealth.[90] Under his guidance, the 1905 conference did not categorically oppose the establishment of a central bureau. Rather it recommended that such a body should engage in 'theoretical and scientific research' concerning 'the dynamics of the atmosphere,' rather than replicate the routine weather work being undertaken by state observatories.[91] In an echo of his earlier statistical contest with Wragge over the value of their respective forecasts, Todd produced data at the conference, which he used to compare their predictions for South Australia over the decade 1892–1902. In so doing he endeavoured to show that his local forecasts had been more accurate than those issued by Wragge interstate. Certainly the figures for his own forecasts, deemed 83% accurate and 17% partly right, compared favourably with those issued by Wragge's bureau at 62% and 38% respectively.[92] But if Todd concluded that 'these figures speak for themselves,' federal politicians would not be so easily swayed. For they continued to pursue their own course on meteorology, indifferent to Todd's arguments or the recommendations of the conference.

When a hastily drafted Meteorological Bill was tabled in the Commonwealth parliament a few months later,[93] the Adelaide conference recommendations were all but ignored. With South Australia and Victoria still unwilling to hand over their meteorological departments to the

Adelaide Conference delegates, May 1905.
L to R, standing: G.F. Dodwell (SA), A.A. Spooner (SA), H.E. Hingsmill (Tas), R.F. Griffiths (SA), S.W. Chettle (SA); seated: P. Barracchi (Vic), Sir Ch. Todd (SA), W.E. Cooke (WA), H.A. Lenihan (NSW)

Commonwealth, federal parliamentarians seized on Baracchi's dissenting report and invoked Wragge's entrenched opinion that meteorology and astronomy should be divorced, leaving the latter activity to the states. Wragge's influence as an unabashed centralist survived him and gave politicians the scientific authority they sought to undermine the Adelaide recommendations and establish a central meteorological bureau along the lines of the United States in Washington.[94] As late as 1906, commonwealth politicians, like their colonial predecessors, were still taking sides in the perennial Todd – Wragge dispute. Yet Todd's remarkable tenure did not go entirely unnoticed in the House of Representatives, where prominent New South Wales parliamentarian, Joseph Cook, deferred to Todd's scientific authority rather to than Wragge's and accused the Ministry of 'not see[ing] fit' to be guided by the advice of the 1905 conference.[95] Sir Langdon Bonython, on behalf of South Australia, directed the attention of members to Todd's telling contrast between Wragge's work and his own.[96] A counter motion to overturn the centralisation of meteorology and the excision of astronomy was lost, albeit not before Bonython paid Todd a ringing tribute. The liberal proprietor of the Adelaide *Advertiser* did not share Todd's political convictions, yet joined with other members in complimenting the now retired fellow South Australian, declaring that:

> There never was in Australia a more efficient public officer. His scientific attainments are recognised throughout the world.[97]

At the close of the interminable 'Wragge affair,' Todd lost his argument with the Commonwealth. Yet, with Wragge out of the race for the commonwealth position, he nevertheless gained the consolation of sending his own experienced meteorological officer, Richard Griffiths, to fill the post of Deputy Commonwealth Meteorologist in Melbourne. Griffiths' subsequent departure from the Adelaide Observatory in January 1908, at a time when the Commonwealth was preparing to exercise its control over the West Terrace grounds and equipment, proved a decisive moment in the careers of both men. Todd farewelled his 'dear old friend' and collaborator of 27 years, presenting him with a 'handsome travel bag' for the occasion. In reply, Griffiths expressed confidence that he would carry his mentor's high standards into the ranks of the commonwealth service. The protracted uncertainty of meteorology under federation had taken its toll on all concerned. As the departing Griffiths ruefully observed, it might be 'the right thing' after all, 'but whether it [had been] carried out in the right manner was another matter altogether'.[98]

13

Deputy Postmaster General: Negotiating the Federal Bureaucracy

With the onset of federation in the late 1890s, Todd's professional career entered a period of protracted uncertainty which continued throughout the last decade of his working life. Amid insinuations of favouritism and renewed calls for civil service rationalisation, his comprehensive departmental report of October 1896 encouraged renewed speculation about possible retirement.[1] As a senior civil servant, Todd could have chosen to retire at sixty, the time of his trip to Europe, or more normally at sixty-five, South Australia's official retirement age, in 1891. Only in exceptional circumstances could its civil servants remain in office for a more extended period.

Salaries and retirement were sensitive issues in the late 1890s, as the South Australian government pressed on with plans to prune the civil service. In 1898, when renewed attempts were being made to lop a further £18,000 from civil servant salaries,[2] Todd again became a potential target. During debate on the Public Service Bill, opposition members took umbrage at the Chief Secretary's assertion that 'at 65 years of age, [officers] in the public service should make way for younger more active [ones],' riposting that 'certain officers who had accumulated information for years... became more valuable as they became older'.[3] In the same vein, the Adelaide *Advertiser* would declare a few years later that:

> The septuagenarians in the service are in some cases the most valuable

officers we have. Sir Charles Todd and Mr W.R. Boothby have such a wealth of knowledge and experience that it would be a public loss if either of them left the public service... both are more active than men ten years younger. An age rule is a poor arbitrary thing at best, and sometimes is absolutely malicious.[4]

Critics within the unions pointed to Todd's unique position as a departmental head earning more than twice that of any of his departmental officers, more than any other Postmaster General in Australia and as much as a Minister of the Crown.[5] Yet, the comprehensive departmental report to parliament in late 1896 confirmed that, in spite of his age, there had been no slackening in the pace or range of Todd's endeavours.

It was still more remarkable that Todd had achieved so much in a decade of colonial depression and austerity. Especially revealing were the comparative staff profiles for 1883 and 1895, buried in the later pages of the 1896 report,[6] showing that many senior positions which had been vacated, had simply not been filled. After the tragic death of his deputy Edward Squire, in 1893, his formal position remained unfilled, leaving Waddy as Departmental Secretary to assume the role in Todd's absence. When overland telegraph veteran, Richard Knuckey retired in 1889,[7] an Inspector of Lines was re-appointed, but solely for telegraphic rather than postal work. The same list reveals that the position of Chief Correspondence Clerk which existed in 1883 had also disappeared by 1895. It was as if the difficult situation confronting Todd in the 1870s, when good junior staff were being removed to other departments without notice, was now reversed. For stringent government economies within posts and telegraphs during the 1890s were throwing more responsibility and work onto his ageing head.

At seventy, Todd had outlived two of his deputies and many other senior officers whose funerals he attended resolutely in the course of that year.[8] Throughout the 1890s, he continued to play an active part on the executive of the Civil Service Association not least on behalf of his long serving post and telegraph workers and their families. Established in 1881, as 'the first public service union in Australia,'[9] the Civil Service Association aimed to promote the interests of public servants and maintain 'esprit de corp'.[10] On the subject of industrial relations, Todd, after returning from England, remained mindful of the 'great and threatening' challenge to capital posed by labour and the unions. While sympathising with the 'poor dock labourers' who had struck in Britain, he considered strikes to be 'bad and ruinous alike to the capitalist and labourer'.[11] Through his work with the Civil Service Association, he sought a middle road when workplace tensions surfaced during the nervous nineties. In his evidence to the Public Service Commission in 1888, Todd stressed the need for a state retirement fund, with 'provision for the widow and family of a superannuated officer'.[12] In 1892, when he was its Vice President, the Association had established a contributory fund and attracted a membership of a thousand.[13] By the nineties, Todd was still serving on the Civil Service Association executive and, as late as 1900, remained its Treasurer, responsible for the provision of sick payments and death allowances to some 760 members.[14] In due course, Todd's leadership role in the South Australian civil service, in times of great uncertainty and union militancy, would earn him the accolade, the 'Good Knight,' and, subsequently, life membership of the Public Service Association.[15]

A distinctive feature of Todd's departmental administration at this difficult time was its capacity to return a profit. Todd took a firm stance against the introduction of penny postage, a popular catch cry with postal reformers, the most prominent of these being the Australian-born Henniker Heaton. By then a British conservative politician, Heaton campaigned for its introduction in Britain. In order to achieve a consistent departmental surplus, Todd continued to resist local pressure to introduce penny postage on the grounds of economy.[16] As Postmaster General, he did not oppose cheaper postal services in principle. Indeed he was prominent in a decision taken by colonial postmasters at Hobart in 1888 to reduce the cost of incoming letters to Australia to 2d.[17] When Heaton began advocating penny postage in British colonies as well as the motherland,[18] Todd maintained a firm and cautious line, arguing in 1890 that 'the adoption of the reduced rate proposed by Mr Henniker Heaton and other advocates would absorb nearly the whole of our present surplus revenue'.[19] Even after the Australasian colonies joined the Universal Postal Union, a European body committed to uniform and cheaper postage rates, Todd and his fellow Postmasters General withheld their full support, pointing out that most of the Australian colonies, including South Australia, were much larger and less centralised than the United Kingdom. If smaller colonies like Victoria and New Zealand could countenance its introduction, it was a different matter for South Australia, Western Australia or Queensland. In his comprehensive departmental review of 1896, Todd went on to identify the main impediment in South Australia as the cost of its inland mail service, amounting to £15,000 in 1895.[20] Because of this stance, he was in a position as late as 1900 to confirm to Thomas Playford, the Agent General, that '[departmental] revenue shows a margin in revenue in excess of expenditure of £51,188'.[21]

Todd, in personal correspondence with Heaton during 1898, estimated the projected losses to the Australasian colonies as a whole, to be in the order of £250,000.[22] Despite their different positions on the eve of federation, there was little animosity in these written exchanges. Instead, Todd sent him a congratulatory letter reiterating his previous estimate of the costs, but qualified this with the proviso that 'this [figure] would not make any allowance for increasing the correspondence' which might result after introduction of the penny concession. Unlike Heaton and local penny postage advocates, Todd believed that colonial ties with the United Kingdom would dwindle after federation and the volume of incoming letters would diminish accordingly. But he was generous enough to add:

> I have watched your movement with great interest for many years. I have no doubt that Penny Postage in the colonies will soon become an accomplished fact and you will have the gratification of knowing that you are the Father of it all.[23]

In a second letter which mingled postal and cable politics, Todd reiterated his in-principle support on the former issue, but speculated: 'how the federal government will be able to look the matter boldly in the face and agree to the temporary loss I do not know'.[24]

Despite the rise of trade unionism during the 1890s and a change in employee-employer relations, there remained a high level of respect in the ranks for Todd's leadership. At the turn of the century, one of his longserving employees Frank Gillen still expressed admiration for Todd's 'splendid administration' of the telegraphs – 'the best in the Australia' – and considered his South Australian department superior to that of Victoria.[25] By the end of the late 19th century, Todd had moved with the times and become closely involved in more recent technological developments such as telephony and wireless. He was no longer simply 'Telegraph Todd' of overland fame. A valuable source of information in these new and related fields was William Preece, engineer-in-chief at the British Post Office. In addition to their shared interest in the effective use of electric lighting for post offices and public buildings, they corresponded regularly on developments in telephony which had grown steadily in South Australia with the recent installation of a new exchange at the Adelaide Post Office, lit by 'incandescent electric lamps' and capable of connecting 1100 subscribers.[26] By mid-1895 a series of smaller exchanges in nearby towns were also linked by trunk line to the Adelaide GPO.[27] Since new phone exchanges were installed in existing post offices, there was often the risk of disturbance to them from the telegraph wires. Preece ascertained that problems of telephone reception usually lay, not with the apparatus itself, but with 'induced currents from other circuits' as well as 'earth returns from electrical lighting mains and tramways'.[28] Despite the fact that his electrical staff at the Adelaide Post Office tested the phone wires on a daily basis to detect faults,[29] the tireless Postmaster General was still grappling with related problems in 1898, including those of 'cross talk' and induced currents to which Preece had alerted him.[30] In a letter of late 1898 to Preece, Todd confirmed his intention to introduce metallic circuits and run wires underground in the major Adelaide streets, with the proviso that 'we can afford it'.[31] For although the phone service was now a paying concern, capital expenditure on lines was heavy, and Todd remained concerned that new telephone services would detract from existing telegraph revenue.

Like Preece, Todd was convinced that, whatever the challenges the phone service was best operated by the Post Office rather than by private interests on the grounds of uniformity. In the same period nevertheless, commercial opportunities beckoned in the new fields of electric lighting and telephony. In Adelaide, one of those who figured prominently in the uptake of new technologies was Todd's own son, Hedley. As Lorna recalled, he was the 'dark horse' of the family, a loyal son who developed a sharp business mind and financial capacity. After honing his business skills with Elders, one of Adelaide's most successful firms, Hedley married Jesse Scott, the third daughter of a well-to-do Adelaide family in 1892,[32] and struck out in partnership with J.K. Samuel.[33] By the mid-1890s, their names were becoming well known in Adelaide as local agents for the London-based Brush Engineering Company and suppliers of incandescent lamps and office telephones to the business community.[34] While Hedley's commercial success paralleled his father's longstanding interest in new technologies, the links between Todd's professional networks and his family were most obvious and sustained in the case of of his son-in-law William Henry Bragg. According to his biographer, Bragg, who lectured at the University of Adelaide was still nervous about his limited knowledge of 'the physics of electricity and magnetism' in 1891,[35] when an advanced course was proposed in electrical engineering. With Todd's encouragement and close support, he took a professional interest in the field, most notably during a visit to England, where at Todd's insistence, Bragg stayed with Preece who introduced him to Marconi, the wireless pioneer. William and Gwendoline then travelled to Cambridge to spend time with Lizzie and with William's former university colleagues.

Todd was helping to lay the basis for Bragg's eminent career in Britain. In early 1893, he and Preece among others, sponsored Bragg's successful nomination as an Associate to the British Institution of Electrical Engineers.³⁶ Charles took pride in his son-in-law's distinguished progress, thanking Preece for his hospitality and professional sponsorship, and confirming that 'the Braggs are full of pleasant reminiscences of England and your kind attention ... They and Maude send their kind regards to you and Miss Mary'.³⁷ It was further evidence of Todd's capacity not only to build lasting professional ties but also of his generosity in sharing social and professional opportunities with those around him. In a subsequent letter, reminiscent of his family friendship with Oppenheimer, Todd passed on to Preece news of Maude's engagement to Reverend Frederick George Masters, an Anglican clergyman and Cambridge MA, whom she had met while in England, at 'our Bishop Dr Harmer's rooms in Corpus Christi College'.³⁸ Charles soon became attached to his future son-in-law, announcing to Preece that 'he [Masters] only arrived in Adelaide a fortnight ago and is now in very nice lodgings. I like him very much and he has made a great impression on the officers of the church and those parishioners with whom he has come into contact'.³⁹ In conversations with Masters, who was interested in science as well as theology, Charles found some of the consolation which he was seeking after Alice's death. Now more prone to introversion, though still cheerful, he wrote philosophically to Sir Fowell Buxton, a former South Australian Governor and family acquaintance:

> One of the great drawbacks in our lives is the constant parting from friends whom we have learnt to love and esteem... Death has been very busy since you left. I have lost many old friends, reminding me that I too am fast getting old.⁴⁰

Among these was the distinguished Surveyor General George Goyder in late 1898. Todd had enjoyed a long and fruitful working relationship with his fellow departmental head since overland telegraph days through their mutual invovlement in the South Australian Institute of Surveyors.⁴¹

After Alice's death, Charles continued to live and work at the Observatory with his two daughters Maude and Lorna 'who take good care of me'.⁴² To his elder son, Dr Charles Todd, visiting Lizzie in Cambridge,⁴³ he passed on thanks for 'all the trouble you have taken with the tablet which you will be glad to know has arrived here'. Subsequently, on the family's behalf, Charles had the commemorative tablet, with Alice's details, mounted on the wall of the Stow Congregational Church where he and Alice had worshipped regularly in Adelaide. Charles, it seemed, could not let her out of his sight confiding to his son:

I have her photo and Lizzie's close to my bed and look at them the last thing at night and the first thing in the morning and often during the night and shall never be the same again.[44]

As ever Todd drew solace in work, 'which distracts my thoughts,' and in close family bonds including his growing number of grandchildren. In weekly correspondence to Lizzie, he thanked her for sending him word of her young family, Charles, Alice and Vaughan, while taking a close and sustained interest in his Adelaide grandchildren: William Lawrence (Willie), ten years old in 1900, and Robert (Bob), then seven, sons of Gwen and Will: as well as in Hedley and Jessie's newborn, Charles Hedley (Tom) Todd.[45]

For Todd, the professional remedy for the loss of Alice lay not only in matters administrative, but in grappling with new technological challenges. At this period, he turned to wireless after repeated difficulties in maintaining underwater cable communication between South Australian lighthouses and the mainland. In the case of the Althorpe lighthouse, located at the western end of Investigator Strait, he had initially laid a 'heavy shore-end cable' to the island for defence purposes during the Russian scare of the mid-1880s.[46] In August 1897, Todd highlighted the intractable problem when he reported to his Minister Cockburn, that despite its 'heavy armour' and cost, the Althorpe cable was 'practically worn out' after ten years, for 'the current was so strong ... the bed so rocky that the cable would not last long'.[47] Austerity played its part; for Todd was concerned that 'any attempt to repair it would be throwing away money' since it might only 'last a few months'. A year later, Todd confirmed to Preece that exposure to heavy seas on the rocky bed had severed the cable a number of times and, in spite of repairs costing £700, it had by that time 'been silent now for many months' and was 'only used for reporting passing vessels'.[48]

Both Preece and Bragg, after his recent visit to England, knew of Marconi's wireless experiments across the Bristol Channel and of the Admiralty's interest in their potential use for offshore signaling.[49] There were, therefore, sound practical reasons for Todd to investigate the local potential of wireless. With encouragement from Cockburn, who knew of the cable problem before being appointed to London, Todd and Bragg found time from their many professional commitments to undertake a series of local wireless experiments. During May and June 1899, they transmitted signals in morse code from a tin shed in the grounds of the Adelaide Observatory to a station at Henley Beach five miles away, where the signals were decoded onto telegraphic tape. Achieving quality reception took some time, but the possibility of solving persistent challenges like the Althorpe lighthouse was eventually confirmed.[50]

These experiments, which preceded similar attempts in other colonies, attracted widespread press attention across Australia, further enhancing Todd's reputation for technological innovation. While acknowledging the contribution of 'my dear old friend Preece' who had supplied apparatus for their experiment, Todd was pleased to have participated in a worthy experiment 'which confirmed that *we will and can* do what others have done [Todd's emphasis]'[51] For even with Preece's apparatus and input, the local trial of Marconi's system still required considerable initiative and improvisation on their part. Bragg, who subsequently delivered a lecture in Adelaide on 'telegraph without wires' was also becoming known to the public,[52] although another decade would elapse before he made the great advances with X-rays, upon which his international reputation would be founded.[53] Galvanised by their success, Todd announced to Cockburn that 'next week or the week after, we hope to be able to make experiments in the Gulf from the Henley Beach station employing the service of the *Governor Musgrave* steamer which will receive and transmit signals at different distances from the land'.[54]

With the abrupt onset of a fresh round of negotiations involving the Eastern Extension Company and the Australian colonies by late 1899, Todd no longer found time to pursue his wireless interests, explaining that 'I only wish I could give more time to this particularly interesting and important matter, but I must do my regular work and so must Bragg'.[55] Like the Marquis of Tweeddale, Pender's successor, who addressed Eastern's shareholders on the subject in 1899,[56] Todd initially considered wireless as still in the experimental stage of development and as posing no immediate challenge to the established cable system, an assertion subsequently challenged by Marconi's successful shortwave broadcast to Canada two years later in 1901. Eastern, in the opinion of its historian Barty-King[57] missed a unique opportunity at that time to co-operate with Marconi. To what extent did Todd grasp the longer-term implications of the new wireless technology in the wake of such advances? With direct knowledge of its potential after his own experiments, he may well have foreseen its future capacity to bypass wires and poles over long-distances and eventually replace his 'great work,' but for the moment, he was more interested in using its potential to resolve specific problems such as the Althorpe island cable presented.

At a time when federation was shaking up his administrative portfolios, the new century brought new professional milestones for Todd. In 1901, he celebrated sixty years in the civil service, forty-six of them in South Australia about which he remained optimistic, declaring to Playford in the previous year that 'there is no better place to live'.⁵⁸ The South Australian press to which he regularly provided copy, continued to extol his efforts as the twentieth century began, declaring him 'a wonderfully useful man' and rehearsing his early epic achievements, especially the construction of the overland line.⁵⁹ As he approached his seventy-fifth year however, Todd was growing more reflective about such acclaim. When asked to provide autobiographical information to a colleague two years later, he enclosed a recent article from the *Register*, with the caveat that 'like all newspaper clippings it is of course far too eulogistic'.⁶⁰

The turning point for post and telegraphs departments throughout Australia came during the federal convention of 1897–98, with a collective decision to vest colonial communications in the hands of the Commonwealth government, a decision contested to the end. South Australia and Western Australia in particular resisted the move on the grounds that centralising post and telegraph services would be detrimental to the more distant colonies.⁶¹ Embedded in South Australia's argument was a real concern that the efficient administration over which Todd continued to preside would suffer at the hands of a Melbourne-based department, a fear which was subsequently upheld by a 1910 Royal Commission.⁶² In opposing centralisation, South Australia's Premier Holder and Forrest in Western Australia, pressed instead for shared responsibility between the Commonwealth and the states, with the intention of restricting commonwealth jurisdiction to international telegraphy and ocean-going mails.⁶³ The defeat of Holder's proposed amendment at the federal convention represented an early setback for state rights and the established alliance between South Australia and Western Australia in matters of telegraphy. Todd watched the federation movement closely, yet ambivalently, in its final phase, unsure as to whether New South Wales would agree to federation unless its influence was paramount.⁶⁴

At federation, there was no doubting Todd's incipient nationalism, grounded in constitutional consensus and imperial loyalty. But it bore little resemblance to the emerging ethos of his telegraph employees up the Line, many of them Irish and irreverent towards British authority figures. Frank Gillen's relationship with South Australia's Governor Kintore was a case in point. As Kintore prepared to depart the colony in 1898, Gillen, formerly postmaster at Alice Springs, sent him a farewell wire expressing the wish 'that his sojourn in South Australia had made him a good home ruler,' a pointed reference to continued agitation for Irish home rule. Gillen later reported that when 'old Charles Todd saw the wire, [he] nearly fainted at what he termed my audacity'.⁶⁵ For Todd, a confidant of Kintore and friend of incoming Governor Hallam Tennyson, later Governor General,[66] Gillen's informal remark smacked of impertinence and was clearly at odds with the etiquette he expected of his employees on such occasions.

Todd, a longstanding royalist with a record of regular attendance at levees for the Queen's birthday and a taste for band music and ceremony, was involved with colonial Boer war activities in a range of capacities.[67] Not only was he patron of the Adelaide nurses' patriotic fund,[68] but as Postmaster General, he assumed professional responsibility for organising the parcel post service to South Australian troops abroad[69] and for the dispatch of telegraph operators to the South African theatre.[70] By February 1900, there were already twenty colonial telegraph operators stationed in South Africa. When a further twenty were requested from the Australian colonies, Todd selected and recommended four South Australians, 'good young men under 25 years' and 'remarkably good operators who shall do credit to South Australia'.[71] When a farewell ceremony was held for their departure at the Post Office in the following month, Todd, at a time of patriotic celebrations throughout the colony, called three cheers for the Queen and the British army.[72] Few of his employees would have been surprised, on the eve of federation, to read the *Register* article of the 7 July 1900, describing him as a 'veteran servant of the Queen' on the occasion of his 74th birthday.[73] For Todd, who liked to be photographed in formal attire with the decorations and honours bestowed on him over the years, remained in the opinion of the same writer 'a man of active temperament, possessing an alert mind – quick to solve a problem, and ever ready to overcome you with a joke'.

The complex work of amalgamating the various Post and Telegraph departments into a single commonwealth unit had already begun in early 1900, when a Public Service Commission held a protracted series of 87 meetings and gathered evidence from 139 witnesses over several months.[74] As the first and largest department to be transferred to the Commonwealth, Post and Telegraphs received priority, in an attempt to establish uniformity between classifications and salaries across the different states. Both Todd and Waddy, in their evidence to the Commission, argued that South Australia should follow the example set by Victoria and New South Wales and 'improve the position of its officers,'[75] in order to guarantee their future status under commonwealth administration. If salaries for some senior South Australian officers did not match those performing equivalent work in other states, they also identified an equally pressing problem among the large proportion of young recruits in the lower grades of the South Australian civil service, most of whom earned a meagre £50 per annum with little prospect of advancement.⁷⁶ Todd, in keeping with his high profile on the Civil Service Association, argued strongly that many officers could be transferred to the fixed list without financial loss to South Australia, since 'some were classified and some were not and it was only justice to put them on the sixth class'.⁷⁷ In arguing for a minimum wage and higher salaries for his women workers, Todd was successful in persuading the Commissioners. On the more urgent question of matching salaries and classification, the South Australian government declined to follow Todd's advice, creating renewed uncertainty among his staff after a decade of retrenchments and pay cuts during the 1890s. Consequently, Todd was forced to call for calm during 1900, as the date of the Commonwealth handover approached.⁷⁸

With his Western Australian counterpart, R.A. Sholl, and Stephen Lambton, a New South Wales postal veteran of fifty years, Todd spent much of his time reviewing existing departmental regulations throughout 1900. In May, aware that such 'a heavy press of work' could not be undertaken by correspondence alone, he wrote to his New South Wales colleague recommending a conference of 'at least 10 days' in Sydney.⁷⁹ A few weeks later, he was again writing to Lambton, registering his personal objection to the proposed title of 'Chief Postmaster' for the state heads, and indicating a preference for 'Deputy Postmaster General' to describe the new positions which he and others would occupy under a Commonwealth Minister.⁸⁰ On Todd's advice, the permanent heads of the various post and telegraph departments convened in Sydney later in the year to complete the daunting task of redrafting a federal Post and Telegraph Act for the first parliament.⁸¹

The tasks facing Todd and his colleagues were indeed overwhelming. Not only were they expected to draft a consolidated Post and Telegraph Act for the new parliament, but also to unify the different regulations of all the colonies on the minutiae of postal, telegraph and telephone services, including the price and printing of commonwealth postage stamps! It must have appeared an impossible task, but with Lambton in the chair, Todd proposed they meet morning and afternoon every day for a month except Sundays in the lead up to the Christmas period.⁸² One example of the many differences between the state departments was the different situation of savings banks which were not yet under the control of Postmasters General in Victoria, Queensland or South Australia. Such anomalies would require fresh legislation in order to impose overarching federal control.⁸³

Despite their uncertain role in the federal department, the assembled Postmasters were aware that they were doing historic work in laying the basis for the first and largest federal department. Although they deferred to the Public Service Commission on the difficult question of staff reclassifications, they made a series of important recommendations, upholding Todd's reservations about the introduction of penny postage, but leaving the incoming federal Minister to decide the issue of ocean mails and the use of special trains between Adelaide and the eastern colonies. Prior to federation, Todd had played an important part in these inter-colonial mail arrangements, and New South Wales Postmaster William Crick still thought them 'an absolute necessity'.[84] In key respects, the development of the overseas mail service before federation paralleled that of the international telegraph; for Adelaide also operated as the 'centre of postal and telegraphic business for the great part of Australia'.[85] Ocean mails for the colonies were landed at nearby Largs Bay and sorted in fast trains to Melbourne, a situation which had conferred unusual importance on Todd and his department as the co-ordinating authority.

On the evening of the final conference day, William Crick on behalf of New South Wales proposed a parting toast to the Permanent Heads, asserting that 'it would be impertinent of any Commonwealth Postmaster General to criticise [their] work'.[86] Todd, replying to Crick, advocated the formation of an advisory board to the Minister, comprising the Deputy Postmasters General, 'so that the interests of any individual state should not be injured'. To which Crick heartily concurred. There were toasts to departed colleagues including Edward Charles Cracknell, Todd's former deputy promoted in New South Wales, but also a measure of collective defiance after their heavy investment in time. Not only did their report to the Minister, yet to be appointed, recommend that his state-based deputies retain significant powers 'much greater than are exercised by the Permanent Heads', Todd was also instrumental in inserting a recommendation that a principal Deputy Postmaster General be appointed from among them, 'charged with the administration, chief control and supervision of the commonwealth service generally'.[87] Along with his fellow Postmasters General, he agreed to monitor and report on projected losses from penny postage on the basis of annual income, explaining to Heaton two years later that 'we felt that it would be injudicious for us to commit or in any way involve the Federal Government at the loss of revenue,' but noting more optimistically that the action of Joseph Ward in New Zealand combined with similar reductions in Victoria, 'will probably bring about the reform you so much desire'.[88]

Though strongly state rights in tone, this recommendation did not represent a power grab on Todd's part or by South Australia. Rather, as he approached 75, Todd harboured the hope that Lambton, the New South Wales representative, would remain in office to 'become chief executive of the federal government' and offset the dominant influence of a new Melbourne-based administration.[89] Lambton however was unenthusiastic about the prospect of a federal department, declaring it 'a great mistake ... to hand over a large body of public servants to the public service board. Nobody could say how much misery it would cause'.[90] Now without Lambton, who had decided to retire, Todd warmed to the initial ministerial appointment of Sir John Forrest, the former West Australian Premier. Forceful and experienced, Forrest was a consistent critic of centralising communications.[91] In the lead up to federation, it became common practice for Forrest, when returning from the eastern colonies, to break his journey back to Perth in Adelaide and visit Todd. Had Forrest accepted the appointment as Commonwealth Postmaster General, Todd may well have retained his former influence as principal Deputy Postmaster General had he chosen to do so. But the death of James Dickson, initially appointed Minister for Defence and Forrest's subsequent decision to quit his portfolio for the more prestigious Defence Department, dealt a blow to Todd's hopes of a smooth transition. Instead Forrest was replaced in early February 1900 by former Queensland Postmaster General and ardent federationist, J.G. Drake,[92] described by one contemporary as 'a plodder'.[93] Under his control, the new department would operate without collectively consulting its deputies. The post and telegraph conferences which had been a feature of pre-federation years, were abruptly discontinued.

As South Australia's confirmed Deputy Postmaster General, Todd figured prominently at the federal handover ceremony held in Adelaide on 1 March 1901, acknowledging that his department had 'closed a book and opened a new one on South Australia's history that day'.[94] Writing to a London acquaintance in the same month, he explained how 'with the title of Deputy Postmaster General I have gone down one step of the ladder but with increased responsibilities'.[95] With Todd reassuring his local workers regarding their future, Drake issued a directive to the Deputy Postmasters General to carry on their departments 'as nearly as possible on existing lines' prior to the commonwealth handover. His tone changed dramatically thereafter with a fresh telegram to his deputies, including Todd, 'requesting them to deal with all minor matters while referring all questions involving important issues to him'.[96] Whether or not this directive was intended as a calculated insult, it marked the beginning of a period of protracted centralisation, under which Todd and his state-based colleagues saw their authority quickly eroded to the point of obscurity.

Contrary to his hopes of preserving relative autonomy under the Commonwealth, the new Postmaster General embarked on a policy of rapid centralisation, driven by the Under Secretaries, with the 'particular desire that the strictest economy be observed in the administration of the several departments'.[97] Control over department expenditure passed to the Commonwealth Treasury, to which the Deputy Postmasters General were required to submit formal requests for staff and facilities as part of Drake's economy drive. When Todd's administration advertised for the construction of the new postal building, he was duly informed that 'all tenders for new buildings needed to be submitted for federal approval'. He was first expected to furnish an estimate from the Public Works Department for 'such repairs as may be considered necessary during the present financial year [and] any future additional repairs,'[98] having regard to the departmental budget, and to proceed only after the Minister of Home Affairs approved payment. A Royal Commission, appointed after Todd's retirement in 1910, would deplore the 'expensive and circumlocutory methods' adopted by the central executive as calculated to 'undermine the Deputy Postmaster General's local authority'.[99] The same Royal Commission identified and rectified some of the worst aspects of the Commonwealth's administration of Posts and Telegraphs over its first decade. Its critical final report concluded that the central executive should have confined itself to 'matters of general policy'. and that 'a great deal of friction between heads of state branches in the central executive' had resulted from its unwillingness to 'draft regulations or consult with the Deputy Postmasters General'.[100] In the interim, Todd and his fellow deputies were left feeling frustrated and humiliated. It was everything he and Lambton had feared about federation. The same report deplored 'the want of definite support of the Deputy Postmasters General by the central executive,' leading it to 'undermine the status of the Deputy Postmaster General with the public and their staffs'.[101] Little wonder that Todd sometimes found his position untenable.

There exists nevertheless some evidence to suggest that Todd, who had worked under difficult South Australian ministers previously, was able to exercise a measure of influence in the much enlarged commonwealth department as opportunities arose. In November 1900, when the federal minister J.G. Drake sent him a proposed new list of standard interstate telegraphic charges. Todd fired back a series of questions, and returned his own amended list, with the summary observation that it would be 'better to adopt sixpence as a minimum rate in each state'.[102] In keeping with a reputation for careful economy, Todd gave cautious advice in the following year concerning the projected losses incurred on liberal new initiatives, such as penny postage and a concession on wordage for telegrams.[103]

It was in the context of this commonwealth austerity that Todd achieved one of his notable successes, designed to blunt the national ambition of his long-standing Queensland rival meteorologist, Clement Wragge. According to Home and Livingston, Todd helped draft new departmental regulations on weather telegrams and harnessed the new austerity to good effect in restricting Wragge's transmission of these messages to other states. Forthwith, the new federal telegraphy regulations limited free departmental telegrams to 'exchanges between principal meteorological offices in different states,'[104] thereby blocking Wragge's willingness to bypass both himself in South Australia and his colleagues in other states. Once Wragge's regular interstate weather reports previously transmitted free by the Queensland government had to be paid for, the financial difficulties which ensued led to the closure of his Queensland meteorological bureau in mid-1902.

At a time when responsibility for meteorology under federation was far from clear, Todd upheld state interests in the face of the proposed centralisation. Writing to William Gray, the New Zealand Postmaster General in December 1902, he observed:

> We are getting along very well under Federation. And I am glad to say there is little or no friction, except with the Public in reference to weather and shipping reports which you will see from the papers Mr Drake wishes to do away with, or to make some changes…We will certainly be more unpopular if we wish to discontinue publishing either the Weather Reports or the Shipping Intelligence … One only has to see the large crowd gathered around our Weather Board at the GPO especially in the Rainfall during a drought such as we have had some years'.[105]

Despite a relatively low profile in posts and telegraphs after federation, Todd acquitted himself better than most of his fellow deputies in other states, many of whom were much less experienced and lacked his knowledge of telegraphy and telephony. In the last phase of his career, when he was increasingly called upon to discipline rather than encourage discontented or unruly employees, Todd made every effort to visit country offices, at a time when federal and state officials were criticised for failing to do so. During the 1870s and 1880s when he was reorganising his growing department, he had resented devoting precious time to country visits and inspections. But in his later years, Lorna who travelled with him on his annual circuit, recalled how:

we would be away for several days at a time ... We were made so welcome everywhere ...

adding mischievously that:

> Like many clever men, he was very simple minded in some ways and I suspected what I early found out to be a fact, that wires were sent ahead of us. 'The Old Man is on the war path,' they said and fatted calves would be prepared at the offices when his arrival was most likely to coincide with lunch-time.[106]

If the amalgamation of postal regulations and departments proved relatively uncomplicated in the wake of the 1901 Sydney conference, the situation with telegraphs and cables remained more fraught and confused. Todd's correspondence on the eve of federation makes it clear he looked to the new Commonwealth as a means of rationalising South Australia's debts on the transcontinental line. If the Overland Telegraph Line was expensive to maintain, South Australians were also becoming impatient with the financial and administrative burdens imposed on them by the Northern Territory over the previous decades. Although discoveries in the MacDonnell Ranges and the prospect of gold and ruby fields near Alice Springs created temporary excitement,[107] these discoveries were never on the scale of the highly lucrative Western Australian goldfields. From the early years of the overland telegraph, Todd had allied himself with the pro-development Territory lobby, which included political allies like Cockburn and Playford. While in England, he had spoken confidently at the Colonial Institute of inland railway development running in tandem with his now famous telegraph line. Colonial proponents nurtured the grand vision of a transcontinental railway line, comparable with the Canadian Pacific in northern America, running from the south to the north of the Australian continent. In evidence to the Northern Territory Royal Commission of 1895, Todd confirmed that he had 'frequently thought' about the construction of a transcontinental railway across the continent and, for reasons of economy, had even begun to shift the Line to align it with the railway, as it crept slowly northwards to Strangways Springs. On the basis of the Overland Telegraph's continued deficits however, Todd saw little chance that a transcontinental railway 'would pay ... from a commercial standpoint'.[108] In its absence, he continued to rely on Afghan camel trains to carry supplies to his telegraph stations in remote South Australia, while horse teams were contracted from Port Darwin for the northern stations. More cautious than his political allies, Todd now saw that the fortune of the overland line would depend in no small measure on the determination of future governments, South Australian and Commonwealth, to proceed on the daunting railway question. Intense intercolonial competition for railway funding from Western Australia and Queensland after federation took priority and threatened to postpone South Australia's and the Territory's dreams still further.

While a consensus prevailed on the transfer of the overland line to the Commonwealth, South Australia's Premier, Charles Kingston, continued to resist pressure from the eastern colonies to join the Pacific cable venture.[109] Todd persisted in arguing as late as 1899 that the duplex line which he was busy installing along the overland route at considerable cost, would, in conjunction with a new duplex Western Australian line, effectively quadruple existing capacity and render new lines to Australia from either the Indian or Pacific oceans unnecessary. If a series of 1898 conferences kept the cable issue alive, 1899 brought with it dramatic new developments which not even Todd could have anticipated. As part of its renewed push before federation, Eastern Extension took the unusual step of laying a new underwater cable from the Cape of Good Hope to Fremantle, despite the refusal by a majority of Australian Premiers to subsidise it. Thereafter, Eastern began to engage with individual Australian colonies in a series of protracted negotiations which by 1902 led to the 'Adelaide Agreement'. The Marquis of Tweeddale, shrewdly enlisted imperial pride at the prospect of an 'all Red Line' encircling the globe and reaped the immediate financial benefits of cable traffic to and from South Africa during the Boer War.[110] Despite colonial reluctance to provide a local subsidy, the commercial advantages were considerable in so far as Eastern no longer needed to negotiate expensive transit fees with intermediate administrations such as Egypt, India or the Far East, as it had previously done with the Port Darwin cable.[111] Moreover, Eastern, in preparation for a Pacific competitor, now offered the colonies substantial rate reductions, falling to as much as fifty percent to 2s 6d per word over the period 1901 to 1906, should existing traffic levels be maintained.[112]

At the outset, Eastern's new Cape Cable proposal disconcerted Todd. Writing to Playford in late 1897 on the subject, he described it as 'quite unnecessary' adding that it 'better not come to South Australia,' for it would deprive the colony of half of its international revenue and only add to its existing financial problems. While questioning its necessity, he subsequently recommended 'that we should support it as better serving our interests,' while pressing on with his own plans to 'erect a second wire to Port Darwin' and 'work duplex on both wires'.[113] As the eastern colonies, unlike

Western Australia, vacillated on the subject, Todd drafted a detailed report for his own government on the implications of Eastern's new proposal.[114] He estimated the loss to South Australia under the new rate would be as much as £11,000, but felt confident that a third of this sum could be absorbed under intercolonial subsidy arrangements which South Australia had put in place. Moreover, Eastern had anticipated Todd's objections and promised to pay South Australia the same terminal rates at Adelaide as it had previously collected at Port Darwin. Todd had been incensed by the volte-face of the Chamberlain government and the prospect of a Pacific competitor 'involving a heavy annual loss for many years'. He was therefore prepared to support Eastern's new offer to prevent, as he put it, the 'company being wholly at the mercy of a federated Australia which might otherwise resort to unfair competition in the event of the Pacific cable proving unremunerative'.[115]

Yet South Australia's concurrence was by no means automatic; for it still wanted the new cable brought to the GPO in Adelaide, and the assurance that 'rates having been once reduced would not again be increased, even though the traffic may fall off'. On such conditions, Todd explained, his government would recognise the Company's rights to establish independent offices in Adelaide, while Todd's own department would make one of its wires to the eastern colonies available for company use 'exclusively for cable traffic'.[116] As previously, South Australia's assent was pivotal to the Eastern's new counter-strategy and regional ambitions. Todd, as the most experienced negotiator in the colonies, had successfully achieved one of his most complex negotiations, albeit at the risk of splitting a newly federating Australia into two separate camps.

With a protracted legal battle looming between the Commonwealth and the Eastern Extension Company, now based in Adelaide as well as in Port Darwin, Todd's position was out of step with the Commonwealth's official support for a Pacific cable. Moreover, under the auspices of the Commonwealth's White Australia policy, the Postmaster General's department was now taking firm measures to dismiss the Chinese workforce upon whom Little and overland telegraph officers had come to rely in the Northern Territory.[117] Isolation and the strategic role of the international telegraph route had previously accorded them special status within the South Australian civil service,[118] a status which was no longer recognised, once the Commonwealth assumed control of both the Line and subsequently of the Northern Territory itself. Afghan carriers who had made a significant contribution as carriers of equipment and supplies to the overland stations also faced the prospect of exclusion once their entry contracts expired. By the early years of the new century, questions were being asked in the South Australian parliament about the treatment of senior overland telegraph officers including J.A.G. Little, the long serving postmaster at Port Darwin, who had been Todd's key organiser and officer in the Northern Territory since the Line's construction. Despite his 47 years with the department, 29 of these spent at Port Darwin, Little's application for promotion was turned down and his salary, unlike Waddy's, was not increased by the South Australian administration in preparation for the federal takeover, a situation which compounded their personal rivalries. Despite a 'please explain' from Melbourne over the retention of his Chinese workers,[119] Little would not yield and threatened to fight the issue by appealing to the Public Service Commission. Todd, who always considered the Line as a national project, can hardly have been impressed by the treatment of one of his most experienced and diligent officers by the Commonwealth.

Todd had already been placed in an invidious position over the long-awaited transfer of Frank Gillen, another overland telegraph veteran, from the country to Adelaide. After long years of service, Gillen, who wanted his young family to receive an education in Adelaide became increasingly disillusioned not only with the Commonwealth government which, after taking control of the overland telegraph, 'pay you as if you had done nothing' but also frustrated with Todd,[120] whom he believed would not accede to his personal request for a transfer to Adelaide.[121] While serving on the overland telegraph, Gillen had engaged in valuable anthropological work with the Arunta around Alice Springs, where he was postmaster and co-authored *The Aboriginal Tribes of Australia*, with noted Melbourne academic and anthropologist, Professor Baldwin Spencer. In letters to Spencer, Gillen described his boss variously as 'a funny old chap' and more harshly as 'a tricky old chap who rather resents my anthro work ... I do not quite trust the old chap's memory'.[122] Within the commonwealth department, uncertainty pervaded the promotion and transfer system, especially since most officers were now fearful of losing their positions.

To his credit, Todd had granted Gillen leave of absence to undertake his fieldwork at Alice Springs and previously offered to transfer him to Port Augusta at the southern end of the Overland Telegraph Line before assigning him a new post at Moonta. Todd's ineffectualness in this instance owed much to the actions of the South Australian classification board which, in mid-1902, deprived many long serving officers of their pay increases and, in Gillen's case, downgraded his position, thereby making it impossible for him to move back to the North Adelaide post office as he hoped.[123] Like other senior staff, Gillen, conscious of the patronage system which formerly prevailed in civil service appointments, felt aggrieved that his years of service had not been rewarded by such a 'powerful friend' as Todd.[124] The reality was that Todd's influence had continued to diminish in federal cable matters. By 1904 when the simmering row between Little and the central Melbourne office flared, Todd no longer held the reins of the South Australian department, leaving unbending commonwealth officials to strip the wayward Darwin postmaster of his remaining travel and leave privileges.[125] Waddy, who would succeed Todd as Deputy Postmaster General, had come up through the ranks of the postal service rather than the telegraph department. As such, he owed little allegiance to Todd's overland telegraph veterans, and may well have resented their longstanding privileges.

For administrative as well as personal reasons, 1904 proved a difficult year for Todd. Speculation over his future resumed with the introduction of a 1903 retirement act stipulating that commonwealth officers over seventy years would now be retained only on a renewable twelve month basis.[126] After protracted ill health lasting many months,[127] he finally asked to be retired from the service by Christmas 1904, with an additional six months leave of absence on full pay until mid-1905. At 78 years – he was due to turn 79 a month after his leave expired – Todd had exceeded the career expectations of most senior commonwealth employees, and fared better than his counterparts in South Australian departments, where retirement at 65 was still the norm. In spite of this, he still held the respect of his local workforce and it became traditional for them to visit him each year on the occasion of his birthday in July.[128]

In January 1905, the Adelaide press was generous in announcing his departure. *The Critic*, speculated that in retirement, the 'Grand Old Man of South Australia' could now devote himself to 'the manufacture of new and more elaborate puns,'[129] but the *Advertiser*, reporting Todd's farewell speech to his staff, captured the poignancy of the moment in noting that:

> It was only when he referred to leaving the chair he occupied for so long that his voice waivered. At the next minute he ventured on a joke remarking that South Australia possessed over 20,000 miles of telegraph wire and was therefore well posted up.[130]

Todd was keen to say farewell to all members of his Adelaide department; but the exacting work of telegraph operators and telephone exchange workers made it difficult for them to discontinue it and attend the ceremony. So he walked the floor of the building thanking them individually for having given him their loyalty and urging them to support his successor as they had done himself. It was now Waddy's turn as acting Deputy Postmaster General to manage South Australia's operations. He would continue to serve in Todd's long shadow; for there were many in South Australia, including country residents, who remembered the efficient department of pre-federation years and called for its restoration.[131]

For the time being, Todd continued to live at the Observatory with his youngest daughter, Lorna, and a nurse to assist him. He still enjoyed his family's company, especially his grandchildren, but regretted the departure of Maude and Frederick Masters to live in Melbourne in October 1904, only a few months before his leave fell due. 'I shall miss them sadly,'[132] he wrote to fellow Melbourne astronomer Robert Ellery. Contemplating his future in October 1904, Todd hoped that the South Australian government, to which he was still attached, would allow him to remain in the Observatory to continue his astronomical work in an honorary capacity. Despite the family pull to Cambridge and Lizzie's family at Cherry Hinton Road, Todd did not wish or intend to leave South Australia to retire to the United Kingdom. His hopes of remaining at the Observatory in retirement were consistent with his previous role there. But the turmoil of federation had not yet run its full course, and even after his retirement from federal service, he would continue to feel its disruptive influence.

14

'An astronomer at heart'[1]: The Final Decades

Todd's high public profile during the 1890s, including his active participation at numerous conferences on behalf of South Australia, often obscures his ongoing work as a trained astronomer and professional observer. In pursuing these tasks, he and his colonial colleagues were aided by the growing popularity of astronomy during the 1870s and 1880s. International interest aroused by the transit of Venus expeditions enabled colonial observatories to secure government support and better equipment, at a time when small refractor telescopes were becoming more available to amateur enthusiasts. Throughout the 1880s, a series of comet sightings and other astronomical events enhanced popular interest and encouraged the formation of colonial scientific societies.[2] At the Adelaide Observatory, Todd moved with the times in helping to establish a local Astronomical Society in late 1891.[3]

One of the attractions of these societies, comprising both professionals and amateurs,[4] lay in the opportunity they provided for members of the public to access professional advice, view equipment at close quarters and consult well stocked libraries such as Todd had accumulated at West Terrace over several decades. It was here that early Astronomical Society meetings were held. After Charles delivered an address on the topic for the evening, Alice provided supper and engaged in the general conversation which ensued. Todd was welcoming of new Society members. At monthly meetings when the weather was clement, he did not hesitate to interrupt proceedings and adjourn to the telescope rooms to observe with other members. This informality, combined with an open approach to visiting groups, constituted a significant departure from Todd's own experience of the Royal Observatory.

Adelaide visiting hours were limited to Friday evenings so that staff could make themselves available for incoming groups. Todd and William Cooke were both on hand in July 1889 when the Adelaide Young Men's Society, in spite of the prevailing cloud, spent one such evening viewing the heavens through a large telescope. Todd, after receiving their vote of thanks, was at pains to point out that the Observatory operated, not only for scientists 'but to enable the public to become better acquainted' with his work.[5] On another occasion, a young men's bible class from the Baptist Church was welcomed by Griffiths, Todd's assistant, under more favourable viewing conditions. Under his supervision, they observed Orion's Belt including 'Sirius, the dog star, the brightest in the heavens'.[6] In so far as he welcomed young religious groups, Todd remained keen to dispel the suspicion of science which lingered among believers during the late nineteenth century. As late as 1899, when Biela's Comet appeared in the southern sky, Todd still felt obliged to scotch an 'absurd rumour of [its] colliding with the earth'.[7]

One of Todd's early contributions to the Astronomical Society as its founding President was a lecture he delivered in 1892 on the 'lives and labours' of two notable British astronomers Sir George Airy and John Couch Adams, previously known to him. The redoubtable Airy, Todd's early employer in mid-century had recently died at ninety in 1892. Adams, who had become Professor of Astronomy at Cambridge University after successfully detecting the planet Neptune, predeceased Airy by two years in 1890. Unlike the powerful Airy, the humble Adams had chosen a quieter career at Cambridge, declining a knighthood and the post of Astronomer Royal.[8] Although his personal associations with both men were implied rather than amplified in his lecture, Todd was undoubtedly a product of Airy's discipline, unlike his brother Henry Todd, who served as Adams' faithful assistant at Cambridge before following him into retirement. In the same address, Todd spoke about Airy's more prestigious career at considerable length, recognising his wide ranging contributions including the production of 'splendid lunar tables,' the development of 'new scientific instruments and a 'vast amount of priceless observations'.[9] In keeping with his role as President, Todd, on this occasion, did not confine himself to British astronomical history, but engaged those present by 'giving valuable hints regarding astronomical observations and recommending such members as had telescopes, especially those with instruments that were equatorially mounted, study certain sections of the sky and make notes of the results'.[10] Todd's support and standing were critical factors in the successful formation of the Astronomical Society. Several other members had played a significant initiating role, among them Clinton Farr, a former student of Todd's son-in-law W.H. Bragg at the University of Adelaide. Before launching his appeal for a society in 1891, Farr first consulted Todd to gain his support.[11] Connections between the Farrs and the Todds spanned several generations. Clinton's father, George Henry, was a well-educated Anglican clergyman who served with distinction as headmaster of St Peter's College before his appointment as Vice Chancellor of the University of Adelaide.[12] For many years Todd served with him on a number of committees, including on the University Council and Library Board. One mark of their long family friendship was the central role played by Archdeacon Farr in presiding at the marriages of several of Charles' and Alice's children. Clinton Farr, destined for a distinguished career, continued his training in the United Kingdom and in Sydney before gaining an academic post in civil engineering in New Zealand.[13]

Edward Sells, one of Farr's friends, also played a substantial role in the Astronomical Society's formation. He was well known to Todd, having worked at the Observatory for a decade after transferring from the Survey Department at age 21. When Sells was compelled by ill health to take leave, Todd sent him overseas to visit and report on two major observatories, Greenwich in southern England and the Cape of Good Hope Observatory in South Africa.[14] Enthusiastic by nature, Sells sought to engage early Astronomical Society members in a search for new and temporary stars of the Milky Way, explaining that 'naked eye observations only are required, but they can be supplemented by observations with field glasses or telescopes by possessors of those instruments'.[15] During the project, Sells asked members to consult the sky 'at least once a week' and compare their observations with those on the charts he provided. Sightings of new stars were to be 'immediately reported to Todd and the Observatory,' and nightly observations undertaken thereafter.[16] Here was scope for both beginners and more advanced members to contribute to the work of the Observatory. But whether the small membership of the Society could sustain the project 'through several years' as Sells hoped, and produce 'a very valuable series of observations' remained to be seen.

Along with Alexander Dobbie's practical demonstrations of his self-made reflecting telescopes,[17] astronomical photographs and reproductions in the form of high-quality lantern slides could now be used with effect at regular monthly meetings. In addition to Sells' paper on his visit to overseas observatories, members came to the Observatory to hear speakers on such wide ranging topics as irradiation and astronomy, comets, the tides, and aspects of stellar photography.[18] Nor was its growing membership confined to senior males from the nautical community. Several young women joined the Society in the mid-1890s, one of whom, Emma Greayer, had been appointed by Todd as an assistant at the Observatory a few years earlier.[19] At this time, women in the United Kingdom were beginning to occupy similar positions within astronomy; but in the Australian scientific community, their involvement was still unusual. A liberal employer of women in his Post and Telegraph department, Todd had previously placed widows in country offices as postmistresses.[20] In a letter to fellow astronomer, Henry Russell, Todd described Greayer enthusiastically as 'a very valuable astronomical assistant' and 'our veritable Caroline Herschel,' an allusion to the famous sister of Sir William Herschel.[21] As elsewhere, the Adelaide Observatory became a closely knit community. For William Cooke, Todd's assistant, had previously married Emma Greayer's sister Jessie in 1887.[22] When Emma married Todd's long serving meteorological officer, Richard Fletcher Griffiths in 1899, Todd commemorated the occasion by presenting the couple with a fine clock and opera glass at the March meeting of the Astronomical Society.[23]

During the 1890s, Emma Greayer's female companion at Society meetings was Todd's own daughter, Maude. Still a single woman at this time, Maude presented several papers to the Society on related topics. Admired by her younger sister Lorna for her 'good brain and good memory' – she had been 'easily top of the class'[24] – Maude, by her early thirties, had developed intellectual tastes, 'read[ing] incessantly – all new books, all the old…she was really very clever'.[25] In her presentation of late 1895, the first to be given by a woman to the Astronomical Society,[26] Maude spoke on the computations of time.[27] Described by the *Register* newspaper as 'an interesting paper,' it outlined attempts by early civilisations to establish systems of time measurement, including the invention of calendars. She went on to favourably compare the timekeeping devices used by the South American Aztecs with historical attempts by Europeans at the same period. Two years later, Maude gave a second presentation on 'The temples of Egypt from an astronomical point of view,' in which she discussed the orientation of temples towards the sun, making the essential point that once Egyptian solar temples were erected, 'they always remain such' for the purpose of astronomical understanding. Attendance, at 13 members, was not so numerous on this occasion, but Charles, despite another pressing engagement, made a special effort to attend.

By the time of Maude's second paper in 1897, the Society's momentum was slowing and membership was static, prompting Todd and the executive to discuss how best to reinvigorate it. Nonetheless, the society's monthly notices, published in the *Register* through the good graces of William Holden, a Society member and retired journalist, continued to be sufficiently well received for the rival *Advertiser* to request including them subsequently on a regular basis.[28] For the purpose of a joint event with the local art and literary societies, conducted in 1893, Todd called on support from Bragg at the university and upon his observatory and post office staff for assistance with displays and equipment.[29] Again in 1895, when the Society became involved in a similar event, Todd and Griffiths provided the displays and lectures, using observatory equipment.[30] By 1896 however, with Farr's departure to New Zealand and the premature death of Edward Sells in the same year, the Society lost two of its most enthusiastic supporters. Todd paid Sells personal tribute at the Society as 'one of our most useful members ... and a most efficient officer at the Observatory,'[31] while Clinton Farr wrote of his departed friend that, 'as an astronomer in the special line of planetary drawings, he was probably without equal in Australia'.[32] Before reading a paper on Jupiter prepared by Sells for the Society before his death, Todd announced that he had sent a copy to the Royal Astronomical Society in London, along with Sell's remarkable collection of 217 drawings of the planet. In the course of his prolonged illness, Sells had been unable to sustain his star project with the Society and it subsequently lapsed.[33] Efforts to increase membership proved elusive, complicated by the Society's financial dependence upon the Royal Society of South Australia, and the latter's inclination to disregard the efforts of amateurs.[34]

Amid his numerous official duties and the regular demand for meteorological reports, Todd nevertheless persisted with large astronomical projects, including extensive observation of the southern stars listed in Weisse's catalogue.[35] Unlike Wragge who disdained the work of observatories, Todd trained his staff meticulously in both astronomy and meteorology. Thus William Cooke whom he employed as a meteorological assistant in the 1870s, had by the 1890s emerged as a highly competent astronomer. Todd's confidence in Cooke by 1895 was such that he recommended him to Western Australia's Premier, John Forrest as:

> a most proficient mathematician; [he] had a most distinguished career at the Adelaide University ... I can write with confidence to recommend him as the very man you want. You certainly could not do better if you went to England.[36]

His faith in Cooke, who had foregone a prestigious Cambridge scholarship to train with him, was well rewarded after his protégé was appointed Western Australian observer, and later Chair in Astronomy at the University of Sydney.[37] Before Cooke left Todd for Perth, their work together had generated a public following in Adelaide, notably in March – April 1892, when they observed a bright new comet during the early hours of the morning on 1 April.[38] After receiving telegraphic information from Henry Russell in Sydney that the comet possessed no fewer than five tails, they continued to observe it and obtained 'a second good set of observations'.[39]

If Cooke during his time at the Adelaide Observatory moved from meteorology to astronomy, Richard Griffiths, Todd's long serving meteorological assistant, had also acquired considerable competence in astronomy. In December 1896, Griffiths presented a paper to the Astronomical Society, alerting members to the reappearance of the famous Leonid meteor showers during mid-November 1899. These periodic 'shooting stars', visible every 33 years,[40] produced thousands of luminous particles when entering the earth's atmosphere at great speed.[41] Although the approaching meteor shower was seen to good advantage in Europe, the same spectacle was not visible in Adelaide, where Griffiths and Todd, observing from 2 am to 4 am on the morning of 15 November 1899, saw only 'a few sporadic meteors'.[42] Whether it involved tracking comets or contributing to the ambitious Carte du Ciel star mapping project, Todd was still motivated by the prospect of ongoing collaboration with other Australian astronomers. But he was now conscious that his generation were approaching the end of their careers and that government funding for astronomy, with the exception of Cooke's new Perth Observatory, was dwindling. As early as 1889, he had voiced frustration with 'hard headed men who have with no sympathy with science' except 'my rain work,'[43] complaining to Russell in 1893 that 'at present everything being so depressed, I have great difficulty in getting any money for observatory work'.[44] Even when extensive projects like Sells' and Cooke's Jupiter observations were undertaken, it was difficult to fund their publication.[45] The appointment of William Cooke to the new Western Australian Observatory in 1895 represented a loss to his own, because the energetic Cooke would not be replaced for some years. Notwithstanding, Todd sent Cooke with a letter of introduction to England in 1896 to inspect the Greenwich Observatory and order instruments and equipment for his own venture,[46] so as to return 'with all the latest improvements and other accessories of a well-appointed observatory'.[47]

At a time when colonial science was entering new territory, funding constraints imposed significant restrictions on Todd's involvement. By the 1890s, seismology was an exciting area of scientific enquiry, promoted by the Australian Academy for the Advancement of Science since its establishment in 1888. Todd sat with fellow colonial astronomers on the AAAS's committee for 'seismological phenomena in Australia'.[48] His interest in seismology predated many of his colleagues, since one of his longstanding roles as Postmaster General was to monitor and identify interference along the extensive overland telegraph network. While colleagues elsewhere had been able to acquire early model seismographs, Todd, for many years, was unable to convince his government to purchase one. This, after no less an authority than Professor Milne, a British authority and the inventor of the seismograph, had written to the South Australian government recommending that suitably equipped seismological stations be established along the Overland Telegraph Line at Adelaide, Alice Springs and Port Darwin.[49] Two months later, a brief but sharp tremor was felt across Adelaide and southern districts on the afternoon of 10 May 1897.[50] Todd reported no damage to the observatory instruments, but apart from understanding the unusual scale of the event, he was unable to provide a scientific analysis. Bragg, on behalf of the AAAS, estimated the earthquake to be of high-intensity, an opinion subsequently confirmed by the Sydney and Melbourne observatories.[51] Todd's difficulty did not go unnoticed in the local press, the *Register* asking at the time why the local observatory still lacked its own seismograph.[52]

Todd continued to enjoy productive relations with young scientists like Cooke in Perth and Bragg in Adelaide, but he did not neglect his longstanding correspondence with his contemporaries, Henry Russell and Robert Ellery. Their exchanges, never solely telegraphic, had steadily strengthened over time through visits, conversations and conferences. Four years after Ellery's retirement from the Melbourne Observatory, Todd warmly recalled their long association of almost half a century:

> How vividly I remember when I had the pleasure of first making your acquaintance over 45 years ago in 1856 at Williamstown...Here we are, the old fellows, having some good work in us still, and the best of friends.[53]

Todd was generous in his professional dealings with Ellery and Russell, writing to congratulate Ellery on his recent appointment as president of the AAAS in 1899.

In the same letter, Todd proceeded at Ellery's request to outline the circumstances of his Adelaide appointment. He dated the history proper of the Adelaide Observatory from 1867, the year in which he had made the controversial boundary determination between South Australia and New South Wales. Prior to this, he explained to Ellery, 'telegraphy occupying my time' and 'having no assistance or instruments, I could do little'. He continued his historical account by referring to the Observatory's instruments and to his transit of Venus observations, referring his correspondent for later developments to his published departmental reports.[54]

Clearly, Todd's heart was still in his astronomical work. Yet increasingly, Australian astronomers were being directed away from group projects to focus on short-term meteorological reporting. So sustained was this pressure that, by 1890, some members of the astronomical community were calling 'enough'. In New South Wales, where Russell was under similar pressure, independent local astronomer John Tebbutt complained about the high proportion of resources being devoted to weather work at the Sydney observatory.[55] By 1900, Russell, on the eve of retirement, had corrected this imbalance. The Victorian situation was little better, leading Ellery to deplore 'the amount of time and money spent on printing volume after volume of base observations'.[56] His successor in 1895, Pietro Baracchi, was equally disdainful of pursuing meteorology at the expense of astronomy.[57] Todd's view of the question was more pragmatic. From the outset, he recognised the importance of meteorology to the future of the Adelaide Observatory and trained his staff accordingly, while retaining a long-standing commitment to astronomy. In 1901, with most staff supporting Griffiths' weather work, he managed to appoint a junior computer, G.F. Dodwell, to assist the Melbourne Observatory with additional observations for the Carte du Ciel project.[58] Over the next decade however, progress remained slow, Dodwell recalled, 'owing to the smallness of the staff and the heavy pressure of meteorology work'.[59]

After enduring repeated provocations from Clement Wragge, Todd and his fellow astronomers came under further strain, as they grappled with the fresh prospect of the Commonwealth divorcing meteorology from astronomy and centralising it in a newly created bureau at the expense of the existing observatories. In anticipation of a national conference to address their future, Todd entered into correspondence with his scientific colleagues, expressing disquiet at the prospect of the Commonwealth 'starving the observatories'. In mid-1902, he warned the aristocratic Baracchi of the risks such a separation might entail, since 'it must be remembered that the Meteorological work is that in which the public take the greatest interest'.[60] Todd, with a better grasp of colonial politics, endeavoured to alert Baracchi to the risk that splitting the two activities 'will very greatly weaken your hand if it were carried out, as I regret you suggest'. Todd's assessment would prove to be prophetic, but went unheeded. In the same month, he confided to Cooke that 'it would be the greatest mistake that could be made to divorce the Meteorology Department from the Observatories,'[61] warning Baracchi again in October that it will take from them 'the most popular portion of their work'.[62] He still hoped a consensus might be reached before any conference took place, but rightly feared that ongoing professional differences would play into the hands of federal politicians.

As the new century dawned, Todd was aware that financial constraints and internal divisions still threatened the scientific community. In Adelaide, where tensions between the Astronomical Society and its parent organisation, the Royal Society of South Australia, reached breaking point in 1901,[63] he had to preside over a difficult disaffiliation, after which both membership and morale declined. Yet the Astronomical Society's second decade was not without genuine high points. At that very moment, it admitted a new member, George Frederick Dodwell to its ranks. Although he was still serving as a junior computer at that time, Dodwell would, in the course of the decade, become a significant force in the Society, delivering a succession of papers on sunspots,[64] cosmical evolution[65] and 'glimpses of starland,' the last of these in 1907 before an audience of 75 visitors in Adelaide's Prince of Wales building.[66] Alexander Dobbie remained a key amateur participant within the Society. A talented instrument maker, he completed the construction of a large equatorially-mounted reflector telescope in 1903.[67] Later that year, Dobbie presented a paper to the Society, showing 'how it was possible for an amateur to make a reflecting telescope at small cost'.[68] Subsequently the Society hosted viewing nights with Mr Dobbie's reflector, subject to the usual caveats of weather.[69]

The revolutionary role of the telescope was also a theme upon which Todd elaborated in his wide-ranging address of September 1903.[70] Entitled *The Earth's Place in the Universe*, it reviewed the contribution of Herschel's powerful telescopes, including subsequent speculation about the possibility of new worlds, in opposition to the more traditional view of a Creator's 'special interest in this world'.[71] Todd had followed this debate since his Cambridge years where science and theology were regular subjects of discussion. At the end of the nineteenth century, these contrary positions were still being hotly debated in the British periodical press, where Herschel's followers contested the more traditional conclusions of William Whewell that the galaxy in which the Earth was located remained at the 'centre of the universe'.[72] Todd, a devout Congregationalist, had been careful to avoid religious topics in his public utterances and writings at a time when society was still polarised between believers and Darwinian sceptics. On this occasion, he came down squarely on the side of Herschel and modern astronomy, declaring it 'very rash and presumptive' to dismiss the possibility that 'some of the star clusters … so abundant in and around the Milky Way were distant spheres, altogether outside our[s]'.[73] Yet while he freely conceded his inability 'to grasp such distances,'[74] Todd's scientific descriptions of celestial phenomena assumed a lyrical quality. When contemplating 'the enormity of space' and 'the vastness of the universe,' he invoked the poetry of Joseph Addison, writing to fellow astronomer Henry Russell of:

> The spacious firmament on high
> And all the blue ethereal Sky
> The spangled heav'ns, a shining frame
> The great original proclaim.[75]

If the printed version of his 1903 address ended on a more conventional note than the spoken version, there is little evidence to suggest that Todd, following Alice's death, abandoned his religious beliefs. Yet neither did he shrink from acknowledging Herschel and the new place of cosmology in astronomy, affirming at the close of his long career, a modern scientific vision which anticipated the future explorations of Edwin Hubble and his great telescope in space.[76]

By 1905, when failing health forced him to relinquish his federal post and telegraph portfolio, Todd was often accompanied in public by Lorna and a nurse. His long tenure at the Observatory continued, and he hoped, despite federal intervention, to remain at West Terrace and continue his observational work. In its nocturnal isolation, he had been able to withdraw from the clamour of the post office and engage in quiet contemplation. Dodwell, his astronomical colleague of later years, confirmed that astronomy provided Todd with 'relaxation from the pressing cares and anxieties of his other official duties' and 'a congenial exercise for his active mental powers'.[77]

Lorna, who lived on site with her father at the family residence, recalled Todd's routine in later years when, at 9 o'clock in the evening:

> Very often our friend the chief clerk George Dodwell, who afterwards succeeded my father as government astronomer, would tap at the door between the dining room and the office and appear just in time for a cup of tea with us.[78]

Even in his final years, Todd proved adept at training staff. By the time he retired, Dodwell was ready to take charge at the Observatory in what were still uncertain times. Lorna shared these evenings with them reluctantly. Now in her late twenties, she was sociable and outgoing by nature. She missed Maude, now married and living in Victoria, and baulked at the quiet routines of the Observatory, punctuated by her father's entrenched habit of wordplay. For he 'always made the same joke' she complained, "I would be odd without my T'.' Only much later did she admit on the subject of her father's pun, that 'it was many years before I realised it had anything to do with spelling!'[79]

If Lorna occasionally cavilled at her dutiful role as Todd's youngest daughter, she was destined in time to become the family's historian. Both she and Dodwell lived well into the twentieth century and subsequently teamed up as late as the 1940s, in a concerted bid to save the West Terrace Observatory from impending demolition, after the site was selected for the construction of the Adelaide Boys' High School. Only a commemorative plaque to the Observatory in the foyer of the new school, would survive in memory of Todd's lasting achievement. When students and officials gathered for the unveiling ceremony in 1959, Lorna, aged 82, recalled her father's last years there. She remembered the evening tea ceremony shared with 'my great friend, Mr George Dodwell,'[80] bound together as they were by that shared memory of intimacy with a long-gone father and colleague. Speaking at the same event, Dodwell described the early Observatory site in detail and his first meeting in 1899 with Todd, then 73, at which he recognised his mentor's 'essential quality [of] genial kindliness'.[81] Nor did he omit to mention Todd's by now forlorn hope that 'the Observatory would last for a very long time'. For he well knew that Todd in his final years had not been spared the uncertainty which dogged astronomy at the Observatory. The persistent tug-of-war between the Commonwealth and the states during the first decade of the twentieth century would leave its mark, not only on Lorna and Dodwell, but on other members of the Todd family as well.

One of Lorna's most difficult tasks, assisted by Hedley's widow, Jessie, was to vacate the Observatory, where she had grown up, and where her father had lived and worked for some 46 years. Initially, for reasons of health, Charles resided on the coast at Grange before securing city premises in Angas Street. With Charles now retired and in uncertain health, family bonds strengthened amid the shock of Hedley's premature death from typhoid fever in August 1907.[82] It was an emotional blow for the family, especially for his surviving brother, Dr Charles Todd who had campaigned to improve the city's water supply ten years earlier.[83] Hedley's son Tom, aged 8, and his wife Jessie survived him. By then, Charles had four other grandchildren, Gwen's two boys and Maude's younger girls, to whom Lorna became a devoted and affectionate aunt. Todd himself, a benign patriarch, encouraged the Bragg boys,[84] Bob for his athletic prowess and Willie for the academic promise which earned him precocious entry to the University of Adelaide at age 15. The latter retained fond memories of the old Observatory, recalling childhood visits to his grandfather and their weekend rounds together to read the instruments.[85] Before his successful matriculation with first-class honours in 1908, he acquired some of his grandfather's and father's mutual interest in seismology, preparing and delivering his first address at age 18 to the local Astronomical Society on the subject of the seismograph in August 1908. According to the meeting report, Willie acquitted himself well 'with comprehensive diagrams' and answered many questions submitted to him by the 12 members and 16 visitors who were present.[86]

Todd's precious time with his growing family proved short. Such was the rising reputation of W.H. Bragg that a university Chair beckoned in the United Kingdom, on the basis of his groundbreaking work in radioactivity and his recent election in March 1907 to the prestigious Royal Society.[87] In the same month, Maude, visiting with her daughters on the occasion of her father's birthday, found both her young sister Lorna 'unwell' and Jessie, who assisted her, suffering from the 'long strain' of Hedley's death and the move from the Observatory to the Grange.[88] Maude confirmed the important family role which Gwen and William Bragg continued to play in Adelaide, noting prematurely in her diary that, like her father, 'Lorna will miss the Braggs a very great deal'.[89] With the city decked in almond blossoms and her daughters dressed in 'red riding hoods,' Maude's visit proved a memorable one, and she took the opportunity to visit her cousin, Fanny and her girls along with many other old friends.[90] On the occasion of his 81st birthday tea, she remembered that 'Father enjoyed himself hugely' and seemed to her 'bright' and 'peaceful' despite persistent health fears about 'the effects of cold on his heart' and 'the choking fits which weaken him'.[91] By this time, her sister Gwen, who was by now nursing a third child, 'Gwendy' as she became, was also pondering the family's future. Determined by nature, Gwendoline had pursued an independent career as an artist in Adelaide, moving comfortably in high social circles with her talented husband. Yet their visits to Lizzie, already in Cambridge, prepared her in some measure for what would follow. She knew that once Willie graduated in late 1908, their lives would change dramatically.

Not that William or Gwen chose to neglect her father in his current situation. Mindful of Todd's generosity and use of his British contacts to assist him professionally, William shared his father-in-law's concern about the fate of the Observatory and began to exert his influence with the University of Adelaide in an attempt to have astronomy incorporated into its research activities. Acting on the suggestion of influential Commonwealth Minister Littleton Groom,[92] Bragg wrote to the Chancellor, Sir Samuel Way with whom Todd was on good terms, in order to canvass such a possibility. For Todd, who had sat on the University Council for many years, some of them with his son-in-law, was regarded in some quarters as enjoying the status of Professor, based on his Cambridge Master of Arts and election to the Royal Society. The close collaboration between himself and Bragg had bred co-operation with the university, including exchanges of equipment and personnel. Nor was it coincidental that Bragg's versatile university colleague, Robert Chapman,[93] began to play a prominent role at the Astronomical Society during Todd's increasing absences.[94]

In his letter to Sir Samuel Way, Bragg made an eloquent case for the inclusion of astronomy in the university curriculum, not merely for the purpose of practical navigation but as a 'valuable moral discipline' with research potential: there being 'many problems of astronomy and solar physics for the solution of which Adelaide presents ideal conditions'.[95] Bragg's biographer, Jenkin, confirms the efforts that he was prepared to make in order to keep astronomy alive in South Australia through a former pupil Geoffrey Duffield in the United Kingdom, who elicited support from prestigious British institutions for his recommendation.[96] After the Chancellor approached both Todd and the state government on the issue, the subject of 'the University making use of the Observatory, with the possible appointment of a Professor of Astronomy'[97] was discussed at the University Council on 29 January 1908. The prospects for astronomy in South Australia were looking brighter; but whether the state government would be prepared to hand over such an expensive facility to the university on these terms was uncertain.

In early February, formal negotiations between the government and a university delegation comprising Way, Bragg and Chapman took place, but did not proceed as well as hoped after the Treasurer A.J. Peake, rejected the Chancellor's suggestion that the West Terrace Parkland might also become a recreation ground for students.[98] Matters were further complicated by the receipt of a letter from William Cooke, Todd's protégé in Perth, arguing that the Observatory be retained by the government and querying university estimates for maintaining the Observatory as too low.⁹⁹ His counter-proposal was more appealing to Peake on financial grounds, and alerted the state government to the potential loss of expensive astronomical equipment which it had funded over four decades. Todd, though retired and spending the summer at Grange, became involved in these high-level discussions. In the same week, he undertook to write to the Treasurer expressing 'very strong support' for the position of the university delegation. Despite his trembling hand, the letter was a model of clarity and persuasion, based on observatory experience of 'nearly 67 years' and 'supervision of the Adelaide Observatory for a little over 50 years'.¹⁰⁰

Todd proceeded to elaborate the functions and benefits of the Observatory for his home state, in the same way as he had previously done for Forrest and the Western Australian government, listing time signals for shipping and commerce, the great cooperative astrographic survey, the tracking of comets and their orbits, lectures and training, and not least, research of the kind which Bragg had already championed in astrophysics. Ever conscious of financial economy, Todd asked, not for a university Chair in Astronomy but for a lectureship 'at or in connection with the University, as urged by the Chancellor'. Along with the Adelaide press,¹⁰¹ he fretted about 'an undermanned observatory' with his replacement not yet in post, and about the deterioration of the expensive but neglected instruments. Treasurer Peake, who represented the government in negotiations with the University, wrote a brief note of thanks to Todd for his 'valuable suggestions,' but the matter dragged on for over a year, pending further state-federal negotiation.

With the South Australian government unwilling to fully fund the University request, Bragg now urged a public subscription in honour of Sir Charles Todd as a means of gaining the necessary funding, estimated to be as much as £3000 per annum.¹⁰² Neither Todd nor Chancellor Way were keen on his suggestion. Aware of the difficult Victorian situation, where his colleague Baracchi had opted for Commonwealth control over astronomy, Todd was by now convinced that there was little hope of generosity from underfunded state governments, confiding his doubts to the Chancellor on the matter of a subscription, that 'the public is more interested in weather forecasts... and know little of the science of astronomy'.¹⁰³ In New South Wales, where Todd's former colleague Henry Russell had served as Vice Chancellor of the University of Sydney, the situation appeared more promising. A few years later, the university there, unlike its Adelaide counterpart, advertised a Chair in Astronomy, funded by the New South Wales government, and subsequently employed William Cooke from Perth. While maintaining a more open position than either Bragg or Cooke on the South Australian situation, Todd continued to canvass university and government co-operation in his home state.

In late 1908, as the Braggs prepared to leave Adelaide and sail for England, the fate of the local observatory was still unresolved. As his family bade farewell to the university and the city, Todd was 'sad to see them go'.[104] He had been similarly agitated in 1887 when his eldest daughter Lizzie, prepared to depart for married life in Cambridge. At his age, there now seemed to be more at stake, since it was unlikely that he would see his daughter Gwendoline, his talented son-in-law or his three grandchildren again. From a professional perspective, however, he had given Bragg an entry to British science, having previously chosen himself to journey to Adelaide for similar reasons. Only after the Braggs reached England in early 1909 did they learn of the fate of the Observatory, after a telegram from the Commonwealth to the South Australian government in April confirmed the appointment of G.F. Dodwell to the Observatory as Todd's state successor.[105] Whatever his disappointment over his subscription proposal to honour his father-in-law, there could be no faulting Bragg's efforts on Todd's behalf, at a period when his own professional activities were propelling him to fame elsewhere.

Dodwell's belated confirmation of appointment by the South Australian government in June 1908 provided the Observatory with the stability which it lacked after Todd's departure in 1906. With the Commonwealth assuming responsibility for meteorology, Todd's successor was able to resume use of the neglected transit circle telescope for star observations, in co-operation with Cooke's Perth Observatory.[106] Todd's twilight years would prove eventful for astronomy. In June 1909, the month of his 83rd birthday, he paid the Observatory a visit to start the much awaited seismograph,[107] an acquisition put to good use five days later to record a major earthquake in the New Hebrides.[108] In late September, when a brilliant aurora australis appeared in the southern skies,[109] Todd, too unwell to observe it on the evening of 26 September, rose at 4 am the next morning to report 'a diffused red light over the greater part of the sky to the south-west'.[110] Two months later on 24 November, when Halley's comet appeared over Adelaide, Todd was one of the few who could recall the silent visitor after its long absence of 75 years.[111]

Along with his abiding enthusiasm for astronomy, Todd maintained a regular social schedule around Adelaide into his eighties, attending cricket games as a long-standing patron of the South Australian club, returning amid 'congratulations on his renewed health and activity' to the Library Board in February 1907[112] and, in the following year, to the University of Adelaide Council.[113] The *Advertiser*, which followed his retirement movements closely, reported only six months before his death that, while 'not in robust physical health ... he is as alert now as he was a decade ago, his sense of humour is as keen as ever [and] his memory is in no way defective'.[114] During the hot summer months, Todd maintained the family's custom of renting a house at Grange or Henley Beach on the coast. In January 1910, he and Lorna decided to take a summer cottage at Semaphore, a location with long-standing personal and professional associations. It was here that Todd spent summer holidays with Alice and their young family in early Adelaide years. Here too, he had erected a time ball in the 1870s to assist incoming shipping. Although it was now partially obscured by new buildings, he still enjoyed the view of shipping in the busy harbour.[115]

There, the end came quite suddenly. On Wednesday 26 January, after his afternoon walk along the esplanade, Todd experienced a blocked vein in the left leg. As acute pain set in that evening, Lorna summoned family members and their doctor to his bedside, where they remained until Friday when he lapsed into unconsciousness and passed away on the afternoon of Saturday 29 January.

News of his death spread rapidly throughout Australia, provoking widespread public mourning. In Adelaide, where the town council adjourned for five minutes to pay its respects, the commonwealth flag was flown at half-mast on the Post Office and at the government offices in King William Street.[116] In Adelaide's churches, the clergy paid high tribute to a 'cultured Christian gentleman'.[117] At the funeral service held on Monday 31 January at the North Road cemetery, the lengthy attendance list read like a 'who's who' of Adelaide. Political representatives both state and federal were present, as were heads of the civil service, representatives of the various professions and some thirty of Todd's departmental veterans who slipped away quietly from their busy offices to remember him.[118]

Across Australia, too, the wires were humming, but without 'Telegraph Todd'. The press, which had followed him throughout his long career, acknowledged the end of an era, while the local *Register* made a point of acknowledging Lorna's 'long years of devotion to Sir Charles in attending upon her father'.[119] Many obituaries would be penned and published to honour his remarkable career, but the last word went to Lorna in later life, when she wrote wistfully that:

> After such an adventurous life and many travels through strange country here, I always feel my father had no fear of his final journey. Rather he looked forward with great interest to his last adventure.[120]

Notes

Introduction

1. K.T. Livingston, T*he Wired Nation Continent*, Melbourne, CUP, 1996, pp. 75–6.
2. *South Australian Register*, 22 August 1870, p. 3.
3. *Empire*, 11 August 1873, p. 2.
4. *Register*, 11 July 1893, p. 6.
5. Todd to R.H. Arnot, 19 September 1902. SASA: GRG 31/1/5.
6. *Register*, 1 February 1905. Press clippings, GSP family papers.
7. London *Times*, Obituary, 1 February 1910. Press clippings, GSP.
8. *Argus*, 15 December 1891, p. 10; *Town and Country Journal*, 12 December 1891, p. 13.
9. Frank Clune, *The Overland Telegraph. An epic feat of endurance and courage*, Sydney, Angus Robertson, 1955, Foreword p. viii, p. 229.
10. Ibid., pp. 225–6.
11. Lorna Todd, 'Telegraph Todd and the Overland Line,' Adelaide *Chronicle*, 4 December 1952, p. 24–31 January 1953, p. 9.
12. G.F. Dodwell, 'Plea made for Adelaide Observatory,' *Advertiser*, 8 January 1952, p. 2; Astronomical Society of South Australia, Manuscript of a recording made during the unveiling of a bronze plaque at the Adelaide Boys High School, 25 September 1959.
13. Lorna Todd, 'Courage triumphs over all setbacks,' *Chronicle*, 18 December 1952, p. 11.
14. Lorna Todd, 'Telegraph Todd's Alice,' *Chronicle*, 15 October 1953, p. 15 and 12 November 1953, p. 12; 'Observatory life was secure,' *Chronicle*, 24 December 1952, p. 9.
15. Australia Post, *The Overland Telegraph Line*, pamphlet 1972. Reproduced by Telecom 1979.
16. Institute of Engineers Australia, *Centenary of the Adelaide–Darwin overland telegraph line. Papers presented to the symposium*, Sydney, Australian Post Office, 1972.
17. G.W. Symes, Sir Charles Todd entry, *ADB*, vol. 6, MUP, 1976.
18. G.W. Symes and Brian J. Ward, 'Charles Todd and the Overland Telegraph,' *Proceedings of the Royal Geographical Society of Australasia*, vol. 81, 1980–81, p. 71.

19. Peter Taylor, *An End to Silence. The building of the overland telegraph line from Adelaide to Darwin*, Sydney, Methuen, 1980.
20. Alice Thomson, *The Singing Line*, London, Random House, 1999, Acknowledgements, p. 281.
21. W.H. Bragg, 'Sir Charles Todd KCMG. 1826–1910,' *Proceedings of the Royal Society of London*, 1911, p. 4.
22. Taylor, *An End to Silence*, 1980, p. 39.
23. Thomson, *The Singing Line*, 1999, p. 65.
24. Bragg, 'Sir Charles Todd KCMG. 1826–1910,' 1911, p. 4.
25. Ann Moyal, *Clear Across Australia. A history of telecommunications*, Melbourne, Nelson, 1984, p. 42.
26. Ibid., p. 43.
27. Ibid., p. 54.
28. 'A tradition of innovation,' *Australian*, 13 May 1997, p. 6.
29. Donald Lamberton, 'The subversive and the manager: organising knowledge in a hard place,' The 2000 Charles Todd oration, *Telecommunications Journal of Australia*, vol. 51, no. 1, Autumn 2001, p. 68.
30. Telecom Australia, *Telecommunication Museum, Adelaide, a brief guide to historical records*, 1980 (pamphlet SLSA); Margaret Bevan, Singing Strings exhibition (pamphlet, Adelaide, n.d.).
31. Livingston, *The Wired Nation Continent*, 1996.
32. K.T. Livingston, 'Todd, Sir Charles' entry, *Oxford Dictionary of National Biography* online, Oxford University Press, 2004–2010.
33. John Nethercote, 'Anonymous in Life, Anonymous in Death. Memoirs and biographies of administrators,' in Tracey Arklay et al, *Australian Political Lives. Chronicling political careers and administrative histories*, Canberra Australian National University 2006, p. 87.
34. Jan Sheldrick, *Nature's Line. George Goyder. Surveyor, environmentalist, visionary*, Adelaide, Wakefield Press, 2013, pp. 6–8; John Jenkin, *William and Lawrence Bragg. Father and Son*, Oxford, Oxford University Press, 2008, pp. 68, 132.
35. Peter Putnis, 'The early years of international telegraphy in Australia: a critical assessment,' *Media International Australia*, no 129, November 2008, pp. 140–8; Edgar Harcourt, *Taming the Tyrant*, Sydney, Allen and Unwin, 1987.
36. Kevin Livingston, 'Charles Todd. Powerful communication technocrat in colonial and federating Australia,' *Australian Journal of Communication*, vol. 24, no. 3, 1997, pp. 1–10.
37. Symes and Ward, 'Charles Todd and the Overland Telegraph,' 1980–81, p. 72.
38. P.G. Edwards, 'Charles Todd in the Adelaide Observatory,' *Proceedings of the Astronomical Society of Australia*, vol. 10, no. 4, 1993, p. 350.
39. Wayne Orchiston, 'Amateurs in the Antipodes,' *Monthly Notices of the Astronomical Society of Australia*, vol. 65, nos. 11–12, December 2006, p. 201.
40. Orchiston, 'Amateur – Professional collaboration in Australian science. The earliest astronomical groups and societies,' *Historical Records of Australian*

Science, vol. 12, no. 2, December 1998, p. 167.
41. Raymond Haynes et al, *Explorers of the Southern Sky. A history of Australian Astronomy*, Cambridge, CUP, 1996, pp. 81–4.
42. Jenkin, *William and Lawrence Bragg*, pp. 56, 68.
43. Ibid., pp. 79–80, 153–5, 191; see also G.M. Caroe, *William Henry Bragg 1862–1942. Man and Scientist*, Cambridge, CUP, 1978, pp. 32–4.
44. R.W. Home and K.T. Livingston, 'Science and technology in the story of Australian federation: the case of meteorology 1876–1908,' *Historical Records of Australian Science*, vol. 10, no. 2, December 1994, p. 122.
45. David Day, *The Weather Watchers. 100 years of the Bureau of Meteorology*, Carlton, MUP, 2007, pp. 56–7; Commonwealth Parliament. *Debates*. Meteorological Bill, pp. 2137–40.
46. Denis Cryle, 'From data to news: weather reporting, telegraphy and the press in colonial Australia,' *Media International Australia*, no. 159, November 2015, pp. 93–102.
47. Mac Benoy, 'The birth of the familiar everyday map,' *The Globe Journal of the Australian and New Zealand Map Inc*, no. 67, 2011, pp. 9–22.
48. Tony Rogers, *Weather and the Science of Settlement*, Adelaide, Australia Meteorological Association, 2011, chs. 5 and 8.
49. Neville Nicholls, 'Climatic outlooks: from revolutionary sites to orthodoxy,' in Tim Sherratt et al., *A change in the weather. Climate and culture in Australia*, Canberra, National Museum of Australia, 2008, pp. 19, 21, 26–7.
50. *Sir Charles Todd Symposium*, Adelaide, Australian Meteorological Association, 17 August 2012.

Chapter 1

1. Todd to R.H. Arnot, 3 February 1904, SASA, GRG 31/1/5.
2. Errol Morgan, Todd family tree, unpublished monograph, pp. 3, 9, GSP.
3. Newspaper clipping, 18 October 1841 in Airy Papers, Meteorological observations and papers, 1837–48. RG0 6/699, CUA.
4. *Britannia* newspaper clipping, n.d., Airy Papers, Meteorological observations and papers, 1837–48, p. 693.
5. Griffith Todd c.1801 entry, Geraldine Charles, Family Tree, June 2013. Frank Carr Papers, NMM Archives.
6. Lorna Todd to Guy Fisher, typescript, n.d. Symes Papers, RGSSA, file 35.
7. Charles Todd, birth certificate 7 July 1826, Lower Street Islington online at http://www.bmdregisters.co.uk/ accessed 26 June 2012.
8. K.S. Binnie, *The story of the Roan schools, 1643 to 1956*, London, Berryman and Sons, 1956.
9. St Mary's Greenwich, Parish Letter, April 1896 in William Ellis, Notebook. CUP, RGO 54/2.
10. H.D.T. Turner, *The Royal Hospital School Greenwich*, London, Chichester Phillimore, 1980, p. 9.

11. J.W. Kirby, *History of the Roan School and its founder*, London, Blackheath Press, 1929, pp. 99–100.
12. Binnie, *The story of the Roan schools, 1643 to 1956*, p. 17.
13. Howson, *A history of mathematics education in England*, p. 105.
14. Lorna Todd to Guy Fisher, typescript.
15. Griffith Todd (1799–1878) entry, Morgan, Todd family tree, p. 3.
16. George Todd (1760–1825) entry, Morgan, Todd family tree, p. 1.
17. Howson, *A history of mathematics education in England*, p. 99.
18. Edwin Dunkin, *A far-off vision. A Cornishman at Greenwich Observatory*, Cornwall, Royal Institute of Cornwall, 1999, p. 72.
19. Cited in David Allen Grier, *When computers were human*, Princeton and Oxford, Princeton University Press, 2005, p. 52.
20. M.T. Bruck and S Grew, 'A family of astronomers – the Breens of Armagh,' *Irish Astronomical Journal*, vol. 26, no. 2, 1999, p. 123.
21. Reductions of the observation of the planets, Airy Papers. CUA, RG0127/13/1, 2a and 2b.
22. *Advertiser*, 26 November 1906, p. 7.
23. Todd to Airy, 11 May 1854. CUA, RGO 6/3.
24. Edwin Dunkin, Obituary, *MNRAS*, 1898–99, vol. 59, p. 222.
25. *Register*, 2 December 1891, p. 6.
26. *Advertiser*, 6 December 1901. Overland Telegraph news cuttings, SLSA.
27. *Report of the Astronomer Royal to the Board of Visitors*, 1842, p. 4.
28. *Report of the Astronomer Royal*, 1843, p. 6.
29. *Advertiser*, 23 June 1909, p. 6.
30. *Report of the Astronomer Royal*, 1847, p. 7.
31. James Glaisher (1809–1903), biographical entry, Dewhirst files D258. IoA, Cambridge.
32. Dunkin, *A far-off vision*, p. 74.
33. Ibid., p. 5.
34. Ibid., p. 4.
35. Bruck and Grew, 'A family of astronomers – the Breens of Armagh,' pp. 121–8.
36. Ibid., p. 122.
37. Ibid., p. 126.
38. *Pigot's Directory of Kent for 1839*, p. 2.
39. Alan Chapman, *The Victorian amateur astronomer. Independent astronomical research in Britain 1820–1920*, Chichester, Wiley and Sons, 1998, p. 174.
40. Chapman, *The Victorian amateur astronomer*, p. 171.
41. *South Australian Register*, 23 September 1882, p. 6.
42. Dina L. Moche, *Astronomy. A self teaching guide*, New Jersey Wiley and Sons, 2009, p. 293.
43. G.W. Symes, Sir Charles Todd biographical entry notes. ADB archives,

Australian National University.
44. John Jenkin, *William and Lawrence Bragg, father and son*, 2008, p. 225.
45. *Register*, 8 February 1865, p. 3.
46. David Bebbington, 'Gospel and culture in Victorian nonconformity' in Jane Shaw and Alan Kreider, *Culture and the nonconformist tradition*, Cardiff University of Cardiff Press, p. 58; Gerald Parsons, 'From dissenters to free churchmen: the transitions of the Victorian Nonconformity,' in Gerald Parsons, *Religion in Victorian Britain*, Manchester, Manchester University Press, 1988, vol. 1, pp. 71, 77.
47. David Ramzan, *Greenwich Centre of the World*, Gloucestershire, The History Press, 2009, pp. 28–9.
48. Todd to William Gray, n.d. 1899. SASA, GRG 31/1/4.
49. Griffith George Todd to his parents, 1 April 18, Carr Papers. CARGEN/12, NMM archives.
50. G.G. Todd entry, British Library India office. Asia, Pacific and Africa collection, IOR/L/MAR 18/7.
51. Errol Morgan, Todd Family chart, pp. 1–2. Communication to the author, 24 April 2008.
52. Charles Todd to his family on the barque *Irene*, 28 October 1855. Livingston Papers.
53. *Report of the Astronomer Royal*, 1845, *Astronomische Nachrichten*, no. 547, p. 292.
54. *Report of the Astronomer Royal*, 1845, p. 293.
55. Dunkin, *A far-off vision*, pp. 90–1.
56. G.F. Dodwell, 'Sir Charles Todd government astronomer 1856–1906. An appreciation,' Press clippings on the death of Sir Charles Todd. CUA, RG07 /248.
57. *Report of the Astronomer Royal*, 1844, p. 3.
58. *Report of the Astronomer Royal*, 1847, p. 9.
59. James Glaisher, Testimonial for Edwin Dunkin, 1844 in Airy Papers. CUA, RG0 6/1.
60. Frank Carr to Gwendolen Caroe, 10 October 1979, Carr Papers. Todd/003, box 1, September–October 1979, NMM archives.
61. *Advertiser*, 27 September 1909, p. 7.
62. Charles Todd to the *Register*, 30 March 1860, p. 3; Chapman, *The Victorian amateur astronomer*, p. 40.
63. Tom Standage, *The Neptune File*, London, Penguin Books, 2000, pp. 78–9.
64. Standage, *The Neptune File*, pp. 153–4.
65. *The Times*, 10 September 1846, p. 8.
66. James Challis, *Astronomical Observations made at the University of Cambridge*, VXVI I, 1846–48, Preface.
67. Glaisher to Professor James Challis, 3 January 1848, Charles Todd file, p. 3. IoA, Cambridge.
68. Charles Todd, Testimonial. Quoted in Symes, Life of Sir Charles Todd, vol. 1, p. 7.

Chapter 2

1. G.W. Symes, Life of Sir Charles Todd, vol. 1, p. 7 (MSS, Symes Papers RGSSA).
2. George Airy, *Royal Observatory Report*, 1846, pp. 1–2.
3. Rex Sly, *Soil in their souls: a history of Fenland farming*, Gloucestershire, The History Press, 2010, p. 13.
4. Stephanie Boyd, *The Story of Cambridge*, Cambridge, CUP, 2012, p. 70.
5. Robert Willis and John Willis Clark, *The Architectural History of the University of Cambridge*, Cambridge, CUP, p. 198.
6. Todd to Airy, 11 May 1854. CUA, RGO 6/3.
7. David Dewhirst, Institute of Astronomy newsletter, December 2001. DWD files 214, IoA.
8. *Cambridge Independent Press*, 11 March 1848, p. 3.
9. James Challis, *Report of the Observatory Syndicate*, 1849, p. 1.
10. Charles Todd to James Glaisher, 22 February 1848 in Airy Papers, Meteorological observations and papers 1837–48. RG0 6/699, CUA.
11. *Cambridge Chronicle* clipping, 23 November 1848 in Meteorological observations and papers 1837–48.
12. *Cambridge Independent Press*, 8 April 1848, p. 3.
13. Challis, *Report of the Observatory Syndicate*, 1851, p. 2.
14. Charles Astor Bristed, *An American in Victorian Cambridge*, Exeter, University of Exeter Press, 2008, p. 291.
15. Lorna Todd to Guy Fisher, 1952. Symes Papers, File 35 RGSSA.
16. Edith Carr, 'Alice Bell of Cambridge and Alice Springs,' *Cambridgeshire, Huntington and Peterborough Life*, July 1972–June 1973, p. 43.
17. Cambridge Corporation Rentals, 1847. Cambridgeshire Collection, Cambridge Public Library.
18. *St Andrews Church Book*, Baptist Historical Society, Tyndale Press, 1991, p. 174.
19. Census of 1841, Edward and Charlotte Bell and family, Cambridge.
20. Silhouette of the family of Edward Bell, corn and seed merchant of Cambridge, Christmas 1842. GSP.
21. Bell family births and deaths, Carr genealogy box 1. Carr Papers, NMM 25.
22. William Ranger, *Report to the General Board of Health*, London, W. Clowes and Sons, 1849, pp. 6–7.
23. M.E. Bury, and J.D. Pickles (eds.), *Romilly's Cambridge Diary 1848–1864*, Cambridge, CUP, 2000, pp. 18, 47, 186, 191.
24. Ibid., entry of 20 June 1854, p. 210.
25. Airy to Challis, 30 June 1846. Quoted in Bruck and Grew, 'A family of astronomers – the Breens of Armagh,' p. 124.
26. Challis, *Astronomical Observations*, vol. vxvii (1846–48), 1854, Preface.
27. Challis, *Report of the Observatory Syndicate*, 1848, p. 2.
28. Frank Carr to David Dewhirst, 8 July 1983, p. 3. DWD 251:9, IoA.

29. Challis, *Report of the Observatory Syndicate*, 1847, p. 2.
30. John Couch Adams entry, D. Todd and J.A. Angelo, *A to Z of scientists in space and astronomy*, New York, VB Textbooks, 2009, p. 2.
31. *Cambridge Chronicle*, 1 April 1848, p. 3.
32. Institute of Astronomy, *The Northumberland Equatorial 1838*, University of Cambridge, p. 2.
33. George Airy, Correspondence with the Duke of Northumberland. CUA RG0 6/157.
34. Carr to Dewhirst, 8 July 1983, p. 3.
35. M.E. Bury, and J.D. Pickles (eds.), *Romily's Cambridge Diary 1842–47*, entry of 23 July 1847, Cambridge, CUP, 1994, p. 215.
36. Harvey W. Beecher 'Voluntary Science in 19th-century Cambridge University to the 1850s,' *British Journal for the History of Science*, 1986, vol. 19, no. 1, p. 69.
37. Bury, and Pickles, *Romilly's Cambridge Diary 1848–1864*, entry of 29 September 1849, p. 37.
38. Enid Porter (ed.), *Victorian Cambridge. Josiah Chater's Diaries 1844–1884*, London, Phillimore, 1975, pp. 14–15.
39. Alan Chapman, *The Victorian Amateur Astronomer*, 1998, p. 40.
40. Challis, *Astronomical Observations*, vol. vxviii (1849–1851), Preface.
41. Richard Todd, Autobiography (1831–1912), Book 1, p. 5. Typescript, GSP.
42. Adrian family heritage, Cambridge.
43. Carr, 'Alice Bell of Cambridge and Alice Springs,' p. 3.
44. *Cambridge Independent Press*, 23 February 1850, p. 3; *Morning Post*, 26 May 1853, p. 6.
45. Bell family births and deaths. Carr Papers, NMM Archives.
46. Todd heritage item, History Trust of South Australia.
47. Census of 1851, Edward and Charlotte Bell and family, Cambridge.
48. Lorna Todd, 'Telegraph Todd and the overland telegraph line,' no. 2, *Chronicle*, 4 December 1952, p. 24.
49. Bruck and Grew, 'A family of astronomers – the Breens of Armagh,' p. 125.
50. *St Andrews Street Baptist Church, 250th anniversary*, Cambridge, 1971, p. 28.
51. Ibid., p. 30.
52. Challis, *Report of the Observatory Syndicate*, 1851, p. 1.
53. Charles Todd, Notes on the comet of February 1880, *Transactions of the Philosophical Society of Adelaide*, Adelaide, p. 6.
54. Bruck and Grew, 'A family of astronomers – the Breens of Armagh,' p. 125.
55. Challis, *Report of the Observatory Syndicate*, 1854, p. 2.
56. R.F. Griffiths, 'Astronomical photography,' *ASSA Minutes*, 14 August 1894, vol. 1, p. 42.
57. Todd Obituary Notice, *MNRAS*, 1911, p. 272.
58. Challis, *Report of the Observatory Syndicate*, 1853, p. 2.

59. Wilfred Airy, *Autobiography of Sir George Biddle Airy*, Cambridge, CUP, 1896, p. 215.
60. Airy to Challis, 2 September 1852. Airy papers, CUA, RGO 6/633.
61. Challis to Airy, 4 May 1853.
62. K.G. Beauchamp, *Exhibiting Electricity*, London, The Institution of Electrical Engineers, 1997, pp. 80–3, accessed online 6 April 2016.
63. Airy to Challis, 5 May 1853.
64. Alan Chapman, *Edward Dunkin, A Far-Off Vision*, 1999, Preface, p. 5
65. Challis to the London *Times*, 21 May 1853, p. 7.
66. Airy to Challis, 18 May 1853.
67. Airy to Challis, 20 May 1853.
68. Airy to Todd, 10 April 1854. Papers on government superintendence, CUA, RG0 6/3.
69. Challis to Airy, 12 April 1854.
70. *Report of the Observatory Syndicate*,1855, p. 3.
71. James Breen to Todd, n d, 1855. Cited in G.W. Symes, The Life of Sir Charles Todd, vol. 1, pp. 8–9.
72. Airy to Todd, 13 April 1854.
73. Airy to Todd, 17 April 1854.

Chapter 3

1. Wilfred Airy, *Autobiography of Sir George Biddell Airy*, Cambridge, CUP, 1896, p. 205.
2. Derek Howse, *Greenwich Time and the Longitude*, Philip Wilson, NMM, 1997, p. 97.
3. John A. Chaldecott, 'Platinum and the Greenwich system of time signals in Britain,' *Platinum Metals Review*, 1986, vol. 30, no. 1, p. 34.
4. Ellis Papers. CUA RGO 54/2.
5. Todd to Airy, 8 July 1854 (Airy Papers, CUA, RGO 6/611).
6. Chaldecott, 'Platinum and the Greenwich system of time signals in Britain,' pp. 29–30.
7. Airy to Preece, 7 November 1854; Preece to Todd, 8 November 1854.
8. Latimer Clark Obituary, *MNRAS*, 1898–99, p. 243; Todd to Latimer Clark, 11 July 1874. SASA, GRG154/24.
9. Preece to Airy, 8 November 1854.
10. Airy to Todd, 27 November 1854.
11. Latimer Clark to Airy, 13 March 1855.
12. Howse, *Greenwich Time and the Longitude*, pp. 100–1.
13. Todd to Airy, 1 February 1855 and 3 February 1855.
14. Chaldecott, p. 31.
15. Charles V. Walker, *Electric Telegraph Manipulation*, London, George Knight

and Sons, 1850, accessed online 19 May 2016.
16. Walker to Airy, 26 March 1853.
17. Airy, Address to the British Horological Institute, 1865. Cited in Howse, p. 102.
18. T.P. Schaffner, *The Telegraph Manual*, New York, Broadway, D. Van Nostrand, 1867, p. 235, accessed online 19 May 2016.
19. Howse, p. 102.
20. Todd to Airy, 9 December 1854.
21. Todd to Airy, 31 January 1855.
22. Airy to Todd, 2 February 1855.
23. Airy to Merivale, Papers on telegraphic communication 1851–55. Airy Papers, RG0 6/627.
24. Airy to Merivale, November 1854.
25. Henderson to Airy, 8 January 1855.
26. Airy to Peel, 30 January 1855.
27. Todd to Airy, 1 February 1855.
28. James Glaisher, Meteorological paper, 1858. Cited in Dewhirst biographical file 258. Cambridge, IoA.
29. *Report of Astronomer Royal*, 1855, p. 99.
30. Todd to Airy, 5 February 1855.
31. Ibid.
32. Airy to the Secretary of the Colonial Office, 10 February 1855. South Australia, Duplicate Dispatches, SASA, GRG 2/1 v 15.
33. Todd to Airy, 8 February 1855. Airy Papers, RG0 6/627.
34. Ibid.
35. G.W. Symes, Life of Sir Charles Todd, MSS, vol. 1, p. 32.
36. Alice Thomson, *The Singing Line*, London Random House, 1999, p. 11.
37. *Advertiser*, 26 November 1906, p. 7.
38. Todd to Merivale, 6 March 1855.
39. Todd to Charles Sturt, 3 March 1855.
40. Sturt to Todd, 14 March 1855.
41. Airy to Todd, 23 April 1855.
42. Todd to Edward Barnet, 26 March 1855.
43. Ibid.
44. James Breen to Todd, 16 March 1855. SASA, GRG154/24.
45. *Cambridge Independent Press*, 7 April 1855, p. 8.
46. Bruck and Grew, 'A family of astronomers – the Breens of Armagh,' p. 125.
47. Lorna Todd, 'Telegraph Todd and the overland telegraph line,' *Chronicle*, 4 December 1952, p. 24.
48. G.F. Dodwell, 'Sir Charles Todd' Obituary, 1910. Newspaper clippings, NLA.

49. Lorna Todd, 'Telegraph Todd and the overland telegraph line,' p. 24.
50. Charles Todd to his father, mother, brothers and sisters, 28 October 1855. Sir Charles Todd family correspondence, SLSA, PRG 630/29.

Chapter 4

1. *South Australian Register,* 13 March 1856, p. 2.
2. Douglas Pike, *Paradise of Dissent. South Australia 1829–1857*, MUP, 1957, p. 456; Lorna Todd, 'Telegraph Todd's Alice,' *Chronicle*, 15 October 1953, p. 15.
3. *Register*, 24 January 1896, p. 6
4. Symes and Ward, 'Charles Todd and the Overland Telegraph,' 1980, p. 59.
5. C.C. Manhood, 'MacDonnell, Sir Richard Graves '(1814–81),' *ADB*, MUP, 1974, vol. 5.
6. Colonial Secretary to Superintendent of Electric Telegraphs, 19 January 1856, Miscellaneous Todd Papers. SASA, GRG154/24.
7. Report on Public Works, 11 August 1857, p. 3 in *SAPP* 1857–58, vol. 2, no. 102; Charles Todd, 'Telegraphic Enterprise in Australasia,' *Proceedings of the Royal Colonial Institute*, vol. 17, 1885–6, p. 146.
8. Todd, 'Telegraphic Enterprise in Australasia,' p. 147.
9. G.H. Mann, Memoirs, p. 86. SLV, MS 9288.
10. G.W. Symes, The Life of Sir Charles Todd, MSS, vol. 1, p. 51.
11. Jean Gittins, 'McGowan, Samuel Walker (1829–1887), *ADB*, MUP, 1974, vol. 5, pp. 156–7.
12. Todd to MacDonnell, 22 September 1857 in House of Commons, *Parliamentary Papers*, vol. 40. Enclosure 2, no. 33 p. 262. Accessed online 6 September 2016.
13. Symes, The Life of Sir Charles Todd, MSS, vol. 1, p. 77.
14. Todd to MacDonnell, 25 July 1856 (Todd Papers, SASA, GRG 154/24).
15. Cracknell to Todd, 14 August 1856.
16. Todd to MacDonnell, 25 July 1856.
17. Charles Todd to the Colonial Secretary, 'The Adelaide and Melbourne Electric Telegraph,' 17 October 1856, *South Australian Government Gazette*, 23 October 1856.
18. Todd to the Colonial Secretary, 'The Adelaide and Melbourne Electric Telegraph'.
19. McGowan to Todd, 21 October 1856. SASA, GRG154/24.
20. Janis Sheldrick, *Nature's Line. George Goyder*, South Australia, Wakefield Press, 2013, p. 311.
21. Report on Public Works, 8 August 1857 p. 3 in *SAPP* 1857–58, no. 102, vol. 2.
22. Report on Public Works, 24 July 1858 p. 6 in *SAPP* 1858, no. 22, vol. 1.
23. Todd, Telegraphic Enterprise in Australasia, p. 148.
24. *Register*, 24 June 1858, p. 2.
25. Report on Public Works 1858, p. 10 in *SAPP* 1858, no. 23, vol. 1,
26. Symes, The Life of Sir Charles Todd, MSS, vol. 1, p. 73.

27. Gisborne to Stanley, 29 May 1858. SASA GRG 2/32.
28. Charles Todd, 'Projected line of telegraph between India and Australia,' 2 December 1858, Enclosure in Governor's Dispatch 276. Australian Joint Copying project CO13/97.
29. MacDonnell to the Secretary of State, 8 December 1858. SASA, Governor's Dispatches 276.
30. MacDonnell to the Duke of Newcastle 10 October 1859 in *SAPP* 1861, no. 47.
31. Moyal, *Clear Across Australia*, p. 38; W.L. Manser, 'the Overland Telegraph: whose idea?' Supplement to the *South Australian Education Gazette*, April 1966, pp. 1–2.
32. Todd, Overland Telegraph Address, 1873; Report on departments, 1886, p. 153.
33. Symes, The Life of Sir Charles Todd, MSS, vol. 1, p. 190.
34. Charles Todd, 'Overland Telegraph Address,' 1873.
35. Charles Todd, Report on the Europe and Australian Telegraph, 18 July 1858 in *SAPP* 1859 vol. 2 no. 127.
36. Todd, Report on the Europe and Australian Telegraph, 18 July 1859 in *Sydney Morning Herald*, 3 August 1859, p. 5.
37. Ibid.
38. Ibid.
39. *Register*, 9 April 1858, p. 2.
40. Alice Todd to Sarah Squires, c.1857. NMM 25, CARGEN 1/009.
41. Symes, The Life of Sir Charles Todd, MSS, vol. 1, p. 63.
42. Alice Todd to Sarah Squires, c.1857. Carr Papers, Todd box 1, NMM.
43. Derek Whitlock, *Adelaide. From Colony to Jubilee. A Sense of Difference*, Adelaide, Savvas Publishing, 1995, pp. 196–7.
44. Whitlock, Adelaide. *From Colony to Jubilee*, pp. 194–5.
45. Brian L Jones, 'Stow Thomas Quinton (1801–1862), *ADB*, MUP, vol. 2, 1967, pp. 491–2.
46. Report on Public Works 1857, p. 8 in *SAPP* 1858, no. 22.
47. Report on Public Works 1861, p. 16 in *SAPP* 1861, vol. 1, no. 25.
48. Todd to Ellery, 2 October 1899. SASA GRG 31/1/4.
49. Michael Cannon, *Melbourne after the Gold Rush*, Melbourne, Lock Haven books, 1993, p. 380.
50. David Walker and Jurgen Tampke (eds.), *From Berlin to the Burdekin. The German contribution to the development of Australian science, exploration and the arts*, Sydney, UNSW Press, 2003, p. 52.
51. Georg Neumayer, Results of the Magnetical, Nautical and Meteorological *Observations made at the Flagstaff Observatory Melbourne*, Melbourne, 1864.
52. Neumayer to Todd, 26 February 1864. SASA GRG154/24.
53. Charles Todd, Speech and official opening of the inter-colonial telegraph line. Cited in Symes, MSS, vol. 1, p. 75.
54. *South Australian Advertiser*, 14 October 1858. Press clippings, Livingston Papers.

55. *Advertiser*, 11 July 1860; 10 November 1858; 8 January 1861.
56. Report on Public Works, 1861, p. 16 in *SAPP* 1862, vol. 1, no. 25.
57. Todd to Airy, 5 April 1858. Airy papers, NLA mfm G27594.
58. Todd to Airy, 26 April 1860.
59. Airy to Todd, 23 May 1861.
60. Todd to Airy, 26 November 1861.
61. Report on Public Works, 1861, p. 17.
62. *Advertiser* clipping, 11 November 1861. Livingston Papers.
63. *Advertiser*, 29 June 1860, p. 2.
64. Whitlock, *Adelaide. From Colony to Jubilee*, p. 184.
65. Gene Vecchio, 'The Adelaide Observatory and 140 years of weather observations at West Terrace,' Bureau of Meteorology Adelaide, 2004, accessed 19 March 2009.
66. *Register*, 27 October 1862, p. 1.
67. Todd to McGowan, 6 August 1866 (Todd Letterbook, SASA).
68. L.G. Todd, Family History, Typescript, pp. 35. Symes Papers, File 35, RGSSA.
69. Todd to Airy, 26 November 1861.
70. Report on Public Works, 1861, p. 16, in *SAPP* 1862, vol. 1, no. 25.
71. *Register*, 28 January 1863, p. 3.
72. Report on Public Works 1862, Appendix p. vi, in *SAPP* 1863, vol. 1, no. 19.
73. Todd to Oppenheimer, 29 November 1866. SASA, GRG154/26.
74. Sheldrick, *Nature's Line*, 2013, pp. 196–9.
75. Todd to McGowan? 8 June 1869.
76. Charles Todd, Annual Report, *SAPP* 1869–70, vol. 3, no. 118, p. 5.
77. Charles Todd, 'Report on the Anglo Australian Telegraph,' 28 July 1869, p. 5, *SAPP* 1869–70, no. 41A.
78. Edgar Harcourt, *Taming the Tyrant*, Sydney, Allen and Unwin, 1987, pp. 24–5.
79. Dwayne R. Winseck and Robert M Pike, *Communication and Empire*, Durham and London, Duke University Press, 2007, pp. 35–8.
80. Todd to Osborn, 16 August 1869; Todd to Osborn, 30 March 1870. SASA 154/26.
81. H.D.T. Strangways to H.W. Varley, 7 February 1908. Melbourne, Telecom Historical Collection, OTL file.
82. P.A. Howell, 'Constitutional and political development 1857–1890,' in Dean Jaensch (ed.), *The Flinders History of South Australia*, Adelaide, Wakefield Press, 1986, pp. 135, 152.
83. Todd to Strangways, 4 December 1873. Private Letterbook 1873–77, Todd Papers, SLSA.
84. Charles Todd, Report to the Treasurer, 18 April 1870 in *Register*, 25 April 1870, p. 5.
85. Harcourt, *Taming the Tyrant*, pp. 50–1.

86. *SAPD*, 'Port Augusta to Port Darwin Telegraph Bill', 10 June 1870, pp. 189–90.
87. Harcourt, *Taming the Tyrant*, p. 55.
88. *SAPD*, 10 June 1870, p. 189.
89. Ibid., p. 192.
90. Blyth to Dutton 20 June 1870; Dutton to the South Australian Treasurer, 11 August 1870 in *SAPP* 1870–71, vol. 3, no. 131, pp. 1, 3.
91. Agent General Dutton to the Governor of South Australia, 4 September 1870 in *SAPP* 1870–71, vol. 3, no. 131, p. 5.

Chapter 5

1. Todd, Address, 1873, p. 7.
2. Moyal, *Clear Across Australia*, p. 43.
3. William Townsend MLA November 1869. Quoted in G.W. Symes, The Life of Sir Charles Todd, vol. 2, p. 197 (MSS, Symes Papers, RGSSA).
4. Symes and Ward, 'Charles Todd and the Overland Telegraph,' 1980 p. 65.
5. Todd to John Ross, 7 July 1870 in Todd, *Report*, 1884, p. 142.
6. Charles Todd, Instructions to Overseers, Adelaide, 30 September 1870, no. 27. Telecom Archives, Sydney.
7. Colin Harris, 'Oases in the desert': the mound springs of northern South Australia,' *Proceedings of the Royal Geographical Society of Australia*. South Australian branch, vol. 81, 1980–81, p. 26.
8. Harris, 'Oases in the desert,' p. 35.
9. Powell, *Far Country: a short history of the Northern Territory*, Melbourne, MUP, 1996, pp. 77–8.
10. Todd, Instructions to Overseers, nos. 39–44.
11. Alfred Giles, *Exploration in the seventies and the construction of the Overland Telegraph Line*, Adelaide, Thomas, 1926, p. 14.
12. *South Australian Register*, 22 August 1870, p. 3.
13. Giles, *Exploration in the seventies*, p. 9.
14. Ibid., Introduction.
15. Moyal, *Clear Across Australia*, p. 44.
16. Ibid., p. 45.
17. Michael Cigler, *The Afghans in Australia*, Melbourne, AE Press, 1986, p. 108.
18. Charles Todd, Overland Telegraph Line Diary, 3 November 1870. SASA, GRG 154/14 /2.
19. *South Australian Advertiser*, 4 November 1870, p. 2 and 9 November 1870, p. 4.
20. Todd, Overland Telegraph Line Diary, 2 November 1870. SASA, GRG 154/14 /1.
21. Todd, Address, 1873, p. 7.
22. Ibid., p. 13.
23. Todd, Overland Telegraph Line Diary, 12 October 1870.

24. Elliott Whitfield Mills, *Experiences of the Darwin survey and overland telegraph parties and the discovery of the Alice Spring* by William Whitfield Mills, Adelaide, EW Mills, 1993, p. 22.
25. Todd to Mills, 25 November 1870 in Mills, p. 24.
26. Todd, *Report on departments*,1884, p. 143.
27. Todd, Instructions to Overseers, no. 56.
28. Todd, Instructions to Overseers, Instructions for constructing the line, nos. 54–71.
29. Todd, Address,1873, p. 7.
30. *Advertiser*, Supplement, 31 January 1871, p. 4.
31. Todd to C.H. Babbage, 16 March 1871. SASA 350, p. 262. Quoted in Symes and Ward, 'Charles Todd and the Overland Telegraph,' p. 66.
32. Mills, Report to Todd, 12 December 1872. Quoted in Mills, *Experiences of the Darwin survey and overland telegraph parties*, p. 30.
33. Quoted in Mills, *Experiences of the Darwin survey*, p. 31.
34. Mills, *Experiences of the Darwin survey*, p. 35.
35. Agreement between the British Australian Telegraph and the government of South Australia, 29 August 1871, article 12. OTC, Sydney Archives, S2322, BAT file.
36. Ray Langford, *Singing Strings. A history of the Cardwell to Normanton telegraph line. Far north Queensland*, Atherton, Undaval, 2008, pp. 25–6.
37. Superintendent of Telegraphs, *Annual Report*, Brisbane, Government Printer, 1871.
38. Todd, 'Port Augusta and Port Darwin Telegraph,' *SAPP* 1871, vol. 2 no. 25, p. 2.
39. Langford, *Singing Strings*, pp. 25–6.
40. Todd, Address,1873, p. 11.
41. Todd, Report on Departments,1884, p. 143.
42. R.C. Patterson to Charles Todd, 25 September 1871 in *SAPP* no 83, 'Reports on Overland Telegraph Construction,'1872, vol. 2. p. 68.
43. Alan Powell, *Far Country*, p. 74.
44. J.A.G. Little, Journal, 29 September 1871. SLSA, PRG 329.
45. G.G. Todd entry, List of Pilots in the East India service 1796–1860, British Library, Asia Pacific and African Collections. IOR/L/MAR/8/7.
46. Griffith George Todd to Charles Todd junior, 20 October 1871. SLSA A1159.
47. Little, Journal, 8 October 1871.
48. Little, Journal, 10 November 1871.
49. Patterson to Todd, 24 October 1871, *SAPP* 1872, vol. 2, no. 83.
50. Charles to Alice, 20 March 1872
51. Charles to Alice, 6 October 1872
52. Patterson to Todd, 24 October 1871.
53. Patterson to Todd, 10 November 1871.
54. Ibid.

55. Patterson to Todd, 3 November 1871.
56. Patterson to Todd, 7 November 1871.
57. Patterson to Todd, 3 November 1871.
58. Little, Journal, 9 November 1871.
59. Patterson to Todd, 3 November 1871.
60. Todd, Address, 1873, p. 9.
61. Ibid., p. 10.
62. Charles to Alice, 1 February 1872.
63. Robert Charles Patterson, Diary, 14 February 1872. SLSA D8107.
64. Charles to Alice, 6 October 1872.
65. Lamberton, 'The subversive and the manager: organizing knowledge in a hard place,' p. 68.
66. Todd, Address, 1873, p. 10.
67. Ibid., p. 10.
68. Charles to Alice, 1 February 1872.
69. J A.G. Little, Journal, 8 February 1872.
70. R.C. Patterson memorandum, 3 June 1874 in *SAPP* 1875, no. 100, p. 13.
71. Little, Journal, 27 January 1872
72. Charles to Alice, 2 March 1872.
73. Charles to Alice, 1 February 1872.
74. Charles to Alice, 2 March 1872.
75. Todd, Address, 1873, p. 10.
76. Ibid., p. 11.
77. Margaret Goyder Kerr, *The surveyors. The story of the founding of Darwin*, Adelaide, Rigby, 1971, pp. 137–41.
78. Charles to Alice, 12 May 1872.
79. Ibid.
80. Charles to Alice, 2 March 1872.
81. Ibid.
82. Ibid.
83. Ibid.
84. Charles to Alice, 1 February 1872.
85. Charles to Alice, 2 March 1872.
86. Ibid.
87. Ibid.
88. Ibid.
89. Ibid.
90. Taylor, *An End to Silence*, p. 133.
91. Lizzie Todd to Charles, 23 May 1872.

92. Alice to Charles, 9 July 1872.
93. Charles to Alice, 3 April 1872.
94. Little, Journal, 31 March and 1 April 1872.
95. Charles to Alice, 3 April 1872.
96. Little, Journal, 1, 18 and 21 April 1872.
97. Charles to Alice, 12 May 1872.
98. Patterson to Todd, 29 April 1872. Quoted in G.W. Symes, The Life of Sir Charles Todd, MSS, vol. 2, p. 321.
99. Charles to Alice, 3 April 1872.
100. Giles, *Exploration in the seventies*, p. 134.
101. Ibid., p. 156.
102. Patterson, Diary, 17 July 1872.
103. Lizzie Todd to Charles Todd, 29 May 1872.
104. Ibid.
105. *Advertiser*, 19 April 1871, p. 2.
106. Frank Carr family tree. Supplied by Geraldine Charles, NMM, Greenwich. Carr genealogy, CARGEN/005, NMM 25.
107. Lorna Todd, 'Telegraph Todd's Alice,' *Chronicle*, 15 October 1953, p. 15.
108. Lorna Todd, 'Family life in Adelaide in the Victorian era,' *Chronicle*, 22 October 1953, p. 14.
109. Alice to Charles, 19 September 1872 and 24 September 1872.
110. Charles to Charlie and Hedley, 20 March 1872.
111. Charles Todd, Private Letterbook 1873–77. PRG 630/14.
112. Alice to Charles, 11 August 1872.
113. Alice to Charles, 9 July 1872.
114. John McDouall Stuart, *Exploration across the continent of Australia with charts 1861–62*, entry of 14 September 1862, Adelaide, Friends of the SLSA, 1996, p. 74.
115. Alice Blackwell and Rupert Lockwood, *Alice on the Line*, Adelaide, Rigby, 1965, p. 55.
116. Richard Knuckey, *Report on pastoral country about Barrow Creek telegraph station*, Northern Territory, Adelaide, Frierson, 1882.
117. Blackwell and Lockwood, *Alice on the Line*, p. 7.
118. Alan Powell, *Far Country*, 1996, p. 116.
119. South Australian Police Records. SASA 261/1874. Cited in G.H. Pitt, Notes on steps taken to capture the Natives concerned in the attack on Barrow Creek Telegraph Station, Research Note no. 174, SLSA, p. 1.
120. Pitt, Notes on steps taken to capture the Natives, p. 2.
121. Charles Todd, Report on Departments, 1885, p. 150.
122. *Advertiser*, 28 February 1874, editorial, p. 2.
123. Todd to Airy, n.d. 1876, Letterbook 1875–80. SASA 154/26/2.
124. Taylor, *An End to Silence*, p. 184.

125. Todd to the Chief Secretary, 22 August 1872. Quoted in the *Advertiser*, 23 August 1872, p. 2.
126. Alice to Charles, 29 August 1872.
127. Alice to Charles, 5 September 1872.
128. *Register*, 16 November 1872, p. 11.
129. Alan Powell, *Far Country*, 1996, p. 107.
130. Alice to Charles, 9 September 1872.
131. Alice to Charles, 17 October 1872.
132. Alice to Charles, 11 August 1872.
133. Alice to Charles, 19 September 1872.
134. Ibid.
135. Alice to Charles, 23 October 1872.
136. Alice to Charles, 24 September 1872.
137. Alice to Charles, 19 September 1872.
138. Ibid.
139. *Advertiser*, 30 October 1872, p. 2.
140. Alice to Charles, 23 October 1872.
141. Ibid.
142. *Register* 11 July 1893, p. 6.
143. Todd to Harry Squires, 30 January 1873, Private Letterbook (1873–77).
144. *Advertiser*, 20 January 1873, p. 5S.
145. *Sydney Morning Herald*, 16 November 1872, p. 2.
146. *Brisbane Courier*, 22 November 1872, p. 3.
147. *Brisbane Telegraph*, 8 November 1872. Cited in Charles Todd, 'Stability of the Adelaide to Port Darwin Telegraph', *SAPP*, 1873, vol. 3, no. 28, p. 2.
148. Alice to Charles, 17 October 1872.
149. Todd to the Chief Secretary, 2 December 1872, *SAPP* 1873, vol. 3, no. 28, p. 1.
150. Todd, 'Construction and completion of the Adelaide and Port Darwin Telegraph', *SAPP*, 1873, vol. 2 no. 29, p. 4.
151. R.C. Patterson, Memorandum to the Chief Secretary, 3 June 1874, *SAPP*, 1874, vol. 3, no. 180, p. 3.
152. Todd to the Chief Secretary, 30 July 1874.
153. Patterson to the Chief Secretary, 3 June 1874.
154. *Register*, 3 April 1873, p. 1.
155. Todd, 'The Overland Telegraph,' Address, 28 July 1873, p. 14. Livingston Papers.
156. Todd, Address, 1873, p. 1.
157. Todd to F.C. Dutton, 31 January 1873, Private Letterbook (1873–77).
158. *Empire*, 11 August 1873, p. 2.
159. Australasian Sketcher, 12 July 1873, p. 72; *Sydney Mail*, 14 July 1873,

Supplement; *Illustrated London News*, 22 February 1873, pp. 1–2.

Chapter 6

1. J.W. Lewis, Minutes of evidence on mail contracts, 22 November 1869, *SAPP*, 1869–70, no. 159, vol. 3, pp. 8–9.
2. Ibid.
3. Anthony Trollope, *Australia and New Zealand*, 2nd ed., London, Dawsons, 1968, p. 639.
4. *South Australian Register*, 17 June 1871, p. 1S.
5. Todd, 'Report on the Post Office, Telegraph and Observatory Departments', *SAPP*, 1884, no. 19, vol. 4, p. 45.
6. Report of Commission into the organisation and working of the Post Office Department, *SAPP*, 1875, no. 20, vol. 2, p. iv.
7. Report of Post Office Commission, Minutes of Evidence, *SAPP*, 1875, no. 20, vol. 2, p. 8.
8. Minutes of Evidence, *SAPP*, 1875, no. 20, vol. 2, p. 82.
9. Ibid., p. 82.
10. *Clarence and Richmond Examiner*, 26 May 1874, p. 3.
11. Letter from Postmaster General on commission's report. Charles Todd to the Honorary Secretary, 28 December 1874, *SAPP*, 1875, no. 20A, vol. 2, p. 12.
12. *Register*, 8 May 1874, p. 7.
13. *South Australian Chronicle*, Assembly report of 6 May in 9 May 1874, p. 5
14. *Register*, 20 May 1874, p. 6S. Cited in *Clarence and Richmond Examiner*, 26 May 1874, p. 3.
15. Minutes of Evidence, p. 81.
16. *Border Watch*, 2 May 1874, p. 2
17. Ibid., p. 2
18. Todd to the Chamber of Commerce, 8 January 1875 in *Register*, 28 January 1875, p. 5.
19. 'The Post Office Robbery,' *SAPD*, 4 November 1874, p. 2214.
20. *Register*, 13 May 1874, p. 5.
21. *Sydney Morning Herald*, 23 July 1874, p. 5.
22. *Advertiser*, 21 June 1875, p. 12.
23. Report of Post Office Commission p. 1.
24. Charles Todd, 7 September 1874. Minutes of Evidence to the Commission, pp. 8–9.
25. Todd to the Honorary Secretary, 28 December 1874, p. 9.
26. Todd to Turner, 28 July 1874. SASA GRG154/24.
27. Ibid.
28. Ibid.
29. Todd, 7 September 1874. Minutes of Evidence, p. 9.

30. Todd to the Chief Secretary,15 August 1874, in Letter from Postmaster General on commission's report, p. 7.
31. Todd, 20 November 1874. Minutes of Evidence, p. 67.
32. Ibid., p. 69.
33. Ibid., p. 68.
34. Ibid.
35. Todd to the Honorary Secretary, 28 December 1874, p. 9.
36. Todd, Note of 1874 to the Chief Secretary, Private Letterbook 1873–77. PRG 630/14, SLSA.
37. Edward Squire, Obituary, *Advertiser*, 9 October 1893, p. 6.
38. Todd, 'Report on Departments', 1884, pp. 38–41.
39. *Register*, 28 January 1875, p. 5; *Advertiser*, 20 January 1876, p. 5; *Register*, 26 October 1876, p. 5.
40. Todd, 4 September 1874. Minutes of Evidence, p. 9.
41. Todd, 7 September 1874. Minutes of Evidence, p. 10.
42. Todd, Confidential letter to the Treasurer, 8 July 1874, Private Letterbook 1873–77.
43. Todd, 4 September 1874. Minutes of Evidence, p. 9.
44. Todd to the Chief Secretary,15 August 1874 in Letter from Postmaster General on commission's report, p. 10.
45. Personal letter to Sir Henry Ayers, 10 September 1877. SASA, GRG 154/26/2.
46. Todd to the Honorary Secretary, 28 December 1874, p. 4.
47. Ibid., p. 5.
48. Todd, 20 November 1874. Minutes of Evidence, p. 69; *Advertiser*, 21 June 1875, p. 12.
49. Personal letter to Sir Henry Ayers, 10 September 1877.
50. Todd, Report on Departments, 1884, p. 45.
51. *Register*, 9 January 1883, p. 6.
52. Todd, Report on the Post Office, p. 45.
53. Todd to the Honorary Secretary, 28 December 1874, p. 1.
54. Suggestions from Heads of Department. Civil Amendment Bill, 13 October 1881 *SAPP*, 1881, vol. 4, p. 144.
55. Todd to the Honorary Secretary, 28 December 1874, p. 10.
56. Ibid., p. 7.
57. Report to the Minister of Agriculture and Education, 6 June 1877. SASA, GRG 154/26/2.
58. Todd, 4 September 1874. Minutes of Evidence, pp. 1–2.
59. Todd to the Honorary Secretary, 28 December 1874, p. 9; Todd, 4 and 7 September 1874. Minutes of Evidence, pp. 4 and 11.
60. 'Humours of an Astronomer,' *Tid Bits*, 26 March 1910, p. 32.
61. *Advertiser*, 20 October 1880, p. 6.

Chapter 7

1. *South Australian Advertiser*, 12 December 1871. Livingston Papers, astronomy folder, newspaper clippings.
2. Ellery to the Adelaide Philosophical Society, 22 April 1871 in *South Australian Register*, 2 June 1871, p. 5. Livingston Papers, newspaper clippings.
3. *Advertiser*, 12 December 1871. Livingston Papers.
4. Wayne Orchistan, 'The role of the large refracting telescope in Australian amateur astronomy,' Australian *Journal of Astronomy*, vol. 7, no. 3, November 1997, p. 106.
5. Todd to Airy, 2 January 1874. Airy Papers NLA, microfilm G 27594.
6. Todd to Airy, undated 1873, Airy Papers.
7. Robert Jenkins, 'Sir Charles Todd's work in astronomy,' *Sir Charles Todd symposium*, Adelaide August 2012, p. 4.
8. P.G. Edwards, 'Charles Todd and the Adelaide Observatory,' *Proceedings of the Astronomical Society of Australia*, vol. 10, no. 4, 1993, p. 351.
9. Physics Stack Exchange. Question and Answer, 2 June 2012., online at htpp//www.physics.stackexchange.com 2 June 2012.
10. Jeff Foust, Review of Nick Lomb's *Transit of Venus*, 2012, *The Space Review*, http//www.thespace review.com, accessed 6 June 2012.
11. Fundamentals of mapping, 25 February 2015 at http//www.icsm.gov.
12. Robert Ellery, cited in the *Advertiser*, 19 May 1874. Livingston Papers.
13. Nick Lomb, *The Transit of Venus. 1631 to the present*, Sydney, NewSouth Publishing, 2011.
14. *Advertiser* clipping, 19 May 1874.
15. Dutton to Airy, 28 October 1873, 1 and 17 November 1873. NLA, Airy Papers.
16. Airy to Todd, 11 March 1874. Airy Papers.
17. Dutton to Airy, 17 November 1873. Airy Papers.
18. Dutton to Cooke, 6 August 1874.
19. Dutton to Airy, 11 July and 15 July 1874.
20. Cooke to Airy, 18 August 1874.
21. Todd to Dutton, 18 August 1874.
22. Todd to Dutton, 7 September 1874.
23. Todd to Oppenheimer, 9 October 1874. SASA GRG 154/26/2.
24. Todd to Airy, 6 November 1875.
25. Todd to Dutton, 5 December 1874.
26. B.A.J. Clark and Wayne Orchistan, 'The Melbourne Observatory Dallmeyer photoheliograph and the 1874 transit of Venus,' *Journal of Astronomical History and Heritage*, vol. 7 no. 1, June 2004, p. 44.
27. Charles Todd, *Observations of the Transit of Venus, 8–9 December*, Adelaide, 1874, p. 93.
28. Todd, *Observations of the Transit of Venus*, p. 94.

29. Ibid.
30. Ibid., p. 95.
31. Todd to Dutton, 14 Jan 1875. SASA, GRG 154/26/2; Todd to Ellery, 1 July 1873. Private Letterbook, SLSA, PRG 630/14.
32. Todd to Ellery, 8 February 1875. SASA, GRG 154/26/2.
33. Todd to Dunkin, 18 May 1876. SASA, GRG 154/26/2.
34. Todd to Airy, November 1875. SASA, GRG 154/26/2.
35. Sydney Observatory, *Report 1874–75*, Sydney, Government Printer, vol. 1, p. 1.
36. Sydney Observatory, Self-guided tour. Viewing the transit of Venus 2012, online at www.sydneyobservatory.com.au/transit-of-venus/ accessed 6 June 2012.
37. Melbourne Observatory, *Annual Report*, Melbourne, Government Printer, 1875, p. 8.
38. Todd to Ellery, 17 June 1875. SASA, GRG 154/26/2.
39. Ibid.
40. John Jenkin, William and Lawrence Bragg, 2008, p. 82.
41. Todd to Airy, 18 May 1876. SASA, GRG 154/26/2.
42. Todd to Ellery, 17 June 1875.
43. Edward Dunkin, *The Midnight Sky*, London, The Religious Tract Society, 1879. p. 211.
44. Edward Dunkin, Obituary of Sir George Biddell Airy, *The Observatory*, no 185, 1892, p. 74, accessed online 1 October 2015.
45. Todd to Airy, 6 November 1875. Airy Papers (mfm 627595, NLA).
46. Todd to Airy, 6 November 1875. SASA, GRG 154/26/2.
47. Airy to Todd, 2 January 1874. Airy Papers.
48. G.F. Dodwell, explanatory note, in Edward Sells and W.E. Cooke, *Physical observations of Jupiter during the years 1884–1893*, Adelaide government printer, 1913.
49. *Advertiser* clipping, 2 July 1877. Airy Papers.
50. Todd to Airy, 27 February 1877 and 6 May 1878, *MNRAS*, vol. 39, pp. 19–21.
51. Todd, Notes on the Transit of Mercury, 7 May 1878. SASA GR G31/1/1.
52. Dunkin, *The Midnight Sky*, p. 231.
53. Wilfred Airy, *Autobiography of Sir George Biddell Airy*, CUP, 1896, p. 317.
54. *MNRAS*, vol. 35, 1874–75, pp. 309–10
55. Edwards, 'Charles Todd and the Adelaide Observatory,' p. 351.
56. Dunkin, *The Midnight Sky*, p. 231.
57. Wayne Orchistan, and Alex Buchanan, '"The Grange,' Tasmania: survival of a unique suite of 1874 transit of Venus relics,' *Journal of Astronomical History and Heritage*, vol. 7 no. 1, June 2004, p. 37.
58. Airy Papers, Correspondence, 1880–1888 on 1882 Transit. NLA, Mfm G 27611.
59. Airy, *Autobiography of Sir George Biddell Airy*, p. 325.

60. G.F. Dodwell, *Observatory report*, Adelaide government printer, 1910, p. 27.
61. George Airy, 'Transit of Venus 1882', *MNRAS*, vol. 40, 1879–1880, p. 382.
62. Todd to Airy, 11 July 1877. SASA, GRG 154/26/2.
63. Ibid.
64. Todd to Airy, 29 July 1867. Airy Papers.
65. Edwards, 'Charles Todd and the Adelaide Observatory,' p. 351.
66. John Porter and Andrew Jones, 'Sir Charles Todd's work in surveying,' *Sir Charles Todd symposium*, Adelaide August 2012, summary, p. 2.
67. Airy, *Autobiography*, p. 346.
68. Papers of G.T. Tupman. RGO Archives, CUA.
69. J. Dreyer and H. Turner, *History of the Royal Astronomical Society, 1820–1920*, p. 163 at http://books.google.com.au/ 4 November 2015.
70. Todd to Stone, 24 November 1882. SASA GRG 31/1/3.
71. Ibid.
72. Todd to Ellery, 23 November 1882.
73. Todd to Stone, 24 November 1882.
74. Ibid.
75. Todd to Dunkin 25 November 1882.
76. Todd to Stone, 24 November 1882.
77. Todd to Dunkin, 25 November 1882.
78. Correspondence with Airy and Simms, October-December 1880. SASA, GRG 154/24.
79. *Advertiser*, 15 November 1881, p. 1.
80. Jenkins, 'Sir Charles Todd's work in astronomy,' p. 5.
81. Charles Todd, Report on Departments, 1884, no. 19, vol. 4, p. 201.
82. Todd to Stone, 16 December 1882.
83. Todd, Report on Departments, 1884, no. 19, vol. 4, pp. 202, 201.
84. Todd to Stone, 31 July 1884.
85. Edwards, 'Charles Todd and the Adelaide Observatory,' pp. 351–2.
86. Todd to Stone, 31 July 1884.
87. Todd to Stone, 5 July 1883.
88. Todd to Ellery, 2 October 1899. SASA GRG 31/1/4.

Chapter 8

1. Astronomy and meteorology post 1877, typescript, p. 10, Livingston Papers. Sydney, OTC archive, S26/5.
2. Ibid., p. 10.
3. Ibid., p. 1.
4. Charles Todd, *Meteorological Observations for the year 1879*, *SAPP*, 1881, vol. 3, no. 31, p. 2.

5. Mac Benoy, 'The birth of a familiar everyday map,' *The Globe. Journal of the Australian and New Zealand Map Inc*, no 67, 2011, pp. 9–22.
6. Charles Todd, Report on departments, *SAPP*, 1896, no. 128, vol. 3. p. 29.
7. Benoy, 'The birth of a familiar everyday map,' p. 11.
8. Charles Todd, 'Report on departments', *SAPP*, 1884, no 19, vol. 4, Appendix L, Interruptions on the Port Darwin telegraph line, 1872–1883.
9. Todd to Oppenheimer, 23 February 1878. Todd Letterbook (SASA, GRG 154/26).
10. Todd to Oppenheimer, 6 May 1880.
11. Kirsty Douglas, *'Under Sunny Skies:' understanding weather in colonial Australia, 1860–1901*, Australian Government Bureau of Meteorology, *Metarch Papers*, no. 17, May 2007, pp. 1, 3.
12. Charles Todd, *Meteorological observations for the year 1879*, *SAPP*, 1881, vol. 3, no. 31.
13. Tim Sherratt, Tom Griffiths and Libby Robin (eds.), *A Change in the Weather: climate and culture in Australia*, Canberra, National Museum, 2005, p. 58.
14. Charles Todd, *Meteorological observations for the year 1874*. NAA, Adelaide, AP 810.
15. Todd, *Meteorological observations for the year 1875*, Adelaide, 1876.
16. Charles Todd, Report on the Adelaide Observatory, *SAPP*, no. 146, 1875, p. 1
17. *Sydney Morning Herald*, 4 April 1876, p. 4.
18. *South Australian Register*, 20 August 1877, editorial, p. 5.
19. Georg Neumayer, *Results of the Magnetical, Nautical and Meteorological Observations made at the Flagstaff Observatory, Melbourne*, Melbourne, 1864.
20. John W. Zillman, 'Meteorology in colonial Australia: the link with Astronomy,' Melbourne, Astronomical Society of Victoria, November 2013, pp. 10, 15.
21. Home and Livingston, 'Science and technology in the story of federation: the case of meteorology, 1876–1908', December 1994, pp. 111–12; David Day, *The Weather Watchers. One hundred years of the Bureau of Meteorology*, Carlton, MUP, 2007, pp. 115–16.
22. *Minutes of the intercolonial meteorological conference*, Melbourne, 1881, p. 11.
23. Ibid., pp. 8–9.
24. Ibid., p. 19.
25. *South Australian Advertiser*, 19 April 1871, p. 2.
26. Charles Willoughby Davies, Diary, transcribed by L. Fredericks, 2010, p. 1, SLSA, D7380 L.
27. Charles Todd, Letter of 1 January 1881, in *Advertiser*, 20 January 1881, p. 6; Todd to the Adelaide Chamber of Commerce, *Advertiser*, 28 April 1881, p. 6.
28. Norman A. Richardson, *The pioneers of the northwest of South Australia, 1856–1914*, Adelaide, Library Board of South Australia, 1969, p. 23.
29. South Australia. Blue Book for 1876, in *SAPP*, 1877, vol. 1, p. 52.
30. *SAPD*, 29 November 1872, pp. 2835–37.

31. *Register*, 30 January 1875, p. 6.
32. Todd to Danagan, 29 January 1876 in Private Letterbook 1873–77. Todd Papers SLSA, PRG 630/14.
33. South Australia. Blue Book, 18 February 1875.
34. Alice to Charles, 1 February 1872. PRG 630/2/25, SASA.
35. Todd to Danagan, 29 January 1876.
36. Todd to Oppenheimer, 7 June 1882. SASA, GRG 31/1/3.
37. Dirk Van Dissel, The Adelaide gentry 1885–1915, A study of a colonial upper class, Master of Arts thesis, University of Melbourne, 1973, p. 23.
38. *Register*, 9 August 1877, p. 5.
39. L.G. Todd, Family History, typescript, p. 5. Symes Papers, folder 35, RGSSA.
40. Hedley Todd, Obituary, *Adelaide Observer*, 10 August 1907, p. 40.
41. *Register*, Obituary, 20 February 1888, p. 2S.
42. *Observer*, Obituary, 18 February 1888, p. 6.
43. Charles Willoughby Davies, Diary, p. 138.
44. Ibid., p. 139.
45. Symes G W, Davies Todd Davies typescript. Adrian Family Papers, Cambridge.
46. Todd to Blyth, July 1877. Letterbook, SASA, GRG 31/1/3.
47. Todd to Oppenheimer, 28 December 1881. Letterbook, SASA, GRG31/1/3.
48. Charles Edward Todd Obituary, *Advertiser*, 25 May 1917. Cambridge, IoA, DWD files 251:9.
49. Todd to Oppenheimer, 7 June 1883.
50. Don Garden, *Droughts, Floods and Cyclones. El Ninos that shaped our colonial past*, Melbourne, Australian Scholarly Publishing, 2009, p. 146.
51. Todd to Oppenheimer, 16 June 1882.
52. Symes, Davies Todd Davies typescript. Adrian Family Papers, Cambridge.
53. Todd to Oppenheimer, 31 July 1884.
54. *Advertiser*, 11 September 1884, p. 3.
55. G.W. Symes, Papers on Charles Todd and the Overland Telegraph Line, File 31/1, Davies, Todd, Davies. MS, RGSSA.
56. Richardson, *The pioneers of the northwest of South Australia*, p. 23.
57. Symes, Davies Todd Davies typescript.
58. Alice Thomson, *The Singing Line*, London, Chatto and Windus, 1994, p. 265
59. *Advertiser*, 15 October 1894, p. 4.
60. Todd to Preece, 13 October 1898. Letterbook SASA, GRG 31/4.
61. Symes, Davies Todd Davies typescript.
62. See William McMinn, Contract Assign to transfer money to Henry Scott, 27 August 1880, item 169, Registrar's department correspondence (1872–1923), University of Adelaide Archives.
63. Symes, Davies Todd Davies typescript.

64. Lorna Todd, Telegraph Todd's Alice series No. 2 'Family Life in Adelaide during the Victorian period,' *Chronicle*, 22 October 1953, p. 14.
65. Symes, Davies Todd Davies typescript.
66. Frank Carr, Family tree. Carr Papers, NMM archives, Greenwich.
67. Garden, *Droughts, Floods and Cyclones*, p. 237.
68. South Australia. Blue Book for 1889 in *SAPP*, 1889, vol. 3, no. 31. Annual rainfall by place.
69. Alice Thomson, *The Singing Line*, p. 264.
70. Richardson, *The pioneers of the northwest*, p. 24.
71. Evidence of William Sells, Vermin Proof Fencing Commission, *SAPP*, 1893, no. 59, p. xviii.
72. Van Dissel, The Adelaide gentry 1885–1915, p. 25.
73. Todd, 'Remarks on the weather during January 1884,' Observatory Letterbook, vol. 1, 1877–1905, p. 166. SASA, GRG 31/1/1.
74. Todd, Observatory Letterbook, vol. 1, July 1884, p. 263.
75. Todd, 'Remarks on the weather during July 1884'.
76. Todd to Preece, 18 March 1889. Letterbook, SASA, GRG31/1/3.
77. *Argus*, 28 December 1888, p. 4.
78. Garden, *Droughts, Floods and Cyclones*, p. 147.
79. Day, *The Weather Watchers*, pp. 17–18.
80. *Register*, 3 October 1889, p. 7.
81. Todd to Russell, 17 July 1889. SASA, GRG 31/1/3.
82. *Argus*, 3 October 1889, p. 8.
83. *Register*, 3 October 1889, p. 7.
84. Ibid.
85. Garden, *Droughts, Floods and Cyclones*, p. 148.
86. *Argus*, 28 December 1888, p. 4.
87. Neville Nicholls, 'Climatic outlooks: from revolutionary science to orthodoxy,' in Tim Sherratt et al (eds.), *A Change in the Weather*, 2005, p. 19.
88. *Advertiser*, 17 November 1892 in Meteorology file: newspaper clippings. NAA, Adelaide.
89. Katharine Anderson, *Predicting the Weather. Victorians and the science of meteorology*, Chicago, Chicago University Press, 2005, pp. 276–7.

Chapter 9

1. Charles Todd, Report on departments, *SAPP*, 1884, no. 19, vol. 4, p. 8.
2. Todd, Report on departments, 1884, p. 202.
3. *South Australian Advertiser*, 22 April 1885, p. 6.
4. *Advertiser*, 22 April 1885, p. 6.
5. Todd to Joseph Oppenheimer, 29 November 1866. SASA, GRG154/24/1.
6. Todd to Oppenheimer, 21 April 1883. SASA, GRG31/1/3.

7. Todd to Harry Squires, 30 January 1873. Private Letterbook 1873–77, SLSA, PRG 630/14.
8. Todd to Francis Dutton, 31 January 1873, Private Letterbook.
9. Todd to Dutton, 14 January 1875.
10. Ibid.
11. Todd to E.J. Stone, 31 July 1884. SASA, GRG 31/1/3.
12. *Advertiser*, 8 July 1868, p. 2.
13. Bell family tree, Carr genealogy. CARGEN /005, National Maritime Museum.
14. Charles to Reverend Symes, 18 April 1877. Private Letterbook.
15. Lorna Todd, Family History, April 1955, p. 5
16. Lorna Todd, Family History, p. 8.
17. *Advertiser*, 22 April 1885, p. 6.
18. *Advertiser*, 1 June 1886, p. 7.
19. Todd, Letter to the London *Times*, 25 September 1885. Cited in *Advertiser*, 29 October 1885, p. 5.
20. *Register*, 16 September 1885, p. 5.
21. *Register*, 1 August 1885, p. 7.
22. *Register*, 1 June 1886, p. 7.
23. Todd to Preece, 22 October 1886. SASA, GRG 31/1/3; John Jenkin, *William and Lawrence Bragg*, 2008, p. 129.
24. Edward Cecil Baker, *Sir William Preece FRS*, London, Hutchinson, 1976, pp. 51–5.
25. Todd to Preece, 26 January 1887, SASA, GRG 31/1/3 and 13 October 1896, SASA GRG 31/1/4; Jenkin, William and Lawrence Bragg, 2008, p. 164.
26. Charles Todd to his family, 18 July 1855. Livingston Papers.
27. Henry Todd to James Challis, 11 January 1859. Carr Papers, NMM, NMM 25.
28. Henry Todd to Challis, 21 February 1860.
29. Todd family, Census of 1881. Public Record Office, RG 11/1670.
30. *Register*, 1 August 1885, p. 7.
31. Ibid.
32. John Burnett, 'Airy, Christie and 1881,' *Journal of the British Astronomical Association*, vol. 1, no. 92, p. 11.
33. Airy Papers, NLA, mfm G27594.
34. Todd to Colonel Glover, 18 M. SASA, GRG154/26.
35. Todd to John Pender, 28 January 1887. SASA, GRG 31/1/3.
36. Kevin Livingston, *The Wired Nation Continent*, 1996, p. 100.
37. Todd to Pender, 29 December 1877, SASA, GRG 154/26; Todd to James Anderson, 30 January 1873, Private Letterbook, SLSA; Todd to Col Glover, 18 April 1876, SASA GRG 154/26.
38. Todd, *Report on Departments*, 1884, p. 53.

39. Todd to the London *Times*, 25 September 1885. Cited in *Advertiser*, 29 October 1885, p. 5.
40. Livingston, *The Wired Nation Continent*, p. 113.
41. *Australian Town and Country Journal*, 7 November 1885, p. 19.
42. Ibid.
43. Charles Todd, Diary 1885–86, 19 and 20 September 1885. Todd Papers, SLSA, PRG 630/6.
44. *Town and Country Journal*, 7 November 1885, p. 19.
45. Todd, Diary, 22 September 1885, SLSA, PRG 630/6.
46. Diary, 23 September 1885.
47. Diary, 25 September 1885.
48. Diary, 30 September 1885.
49. Diary, 18 October 1885.
50. Todd to Oppenheimer, 1 February 1887.
51. Alice to Charles, 24 January 1886. SLSA, PRG 630/2/17.
52. *Argus*, 5 July 1884, p. 6.
53. Heritage Advisory Council to the Minister for the Environment and Heritage, *Statement of heritage value. Fergusson River overland telegraph line pylons and Oppenheimer telegraph poles*, June 2011.
54. *Argus*, 31 July 1861, p. 6.
55. Jenkin, *William and Lawrence Bragg*, pp. 63–4.
56. Ibid., p. 62.
57. F.V. Squires, Leeches and Breaches, family typescript, p. 3.
58. Todd to Oppenheimer, 1 February 1887. SASA GRG 31/1/3.
59. Diary, 7, 9 and 10 November 1885.
60. Diary, 30 November 1885.
61. Diary, 11 December 1885.
62. P.G. Edwards, 'Charles Todd and the Adelaide Observatory,' *Proceedings of the Astronomical Society of Australia*, vol. 10, no. 4, 1993, p. 352.
63. Alice to Charles, 24 February 1886. Todd family letters, PRG 630/2/17.
64. Alice to Charles, 24 February 1886.
65. Diary, 6 January 1886.
66. Diary, 5 January 1886.
67. Squires, Leeches and Breaches, p. 55.
68. Todd to Municipal Corporation of Cambridge, 22 December 1886. Cambridgeshire Archives, CB/2/CL/19/6/317.
69. Errol Morgan, Todd family tree, pp. 12–13.
70. Frank Carr to Gwendolen Caroe, 10 October 1979. Todd 003 box 1 September–October 1979, NMM.
71. Morgan, Todd family tree, p. 12.

72. Ibid., pp. 9–10.
73. Diary, 25 January 1886.
74. Charles Todd to his family, 28 October 1855. Todd family letters, PRG 630/2/29.
75. Diary, 31 January 1886.
76. Queensland Agent General, James Garrick to Colonial Secretary Thomas McIlwraith, 31 December 1885 in Queensland Parliament, *Votes and Proceedings*, 1886, vol. 1, p. 731.
77. Charles Todd, 'Telegraphic enterprise in Australasia,' *Proceedings of the Royal Colonial Institute*, vol. 17, 1885–86, p. 144.
78. Todd, 'Telegraphic enterprise in Australasia,' pp. 146, 152.
79. Ibid., p. 155.
80. Ibid., p. 154.
81. Ibid., p. 162.
82. Livingston, *The Wired Nation Continent*, p. 117.
83. Todd, 'Telegraphic enterprise,' p. 179.
84. Diary, 10 March 1886.
85. *Cambridge Chronicle*, 12 March 1886. Overland Telegraph news cuttings book, SLSA.
86. Diary, 10–11, 14 and 22 March 1886.
87. Charles Todd, Report on departments, *SAPP* no. 128, 1896 vol. 3, p. 208.
88. Symes Papers, RGSSA F34; Charles Todd, membership record, 10 December 1873, Society of Telegraph Engineers archive. Stephen Gillam-Smith to the author, 31 January 2013.
89. Symes Papers, F34
90. Bragg Papers, Special Collections, University of Adelaide. MSS 0144, folder 00406.
91. Todd to Henry Russell, 17 July 1889. SASA, GRG 31/1/3.
92. *MNRAS*, vol. 29, no 3, 1868, pp. 4–5, 11.
93. Wayne Orchistan, November 1997 article; 'Observations of the Great Southern Comet,' *MNRAS*, 1880, vol. 40, pp. 298–9.
94. Orchistan, 'The tyranny of distance and antipodean cometary astronomy,' *Australian Journal of Astronomy*, vol. 7, pp. 115–26; *Register*, 23 September 1882, p. 6.
95. Todd, Diary, 10 March 1886.
96. Diary, 14 March 1886.
97. Diary, 4 April 1886.
98. Diary, 7 April 1886.
99. Squires, Leeches and Breaches, p. 4.
100. Diary, 9 April 1886.
101. Diary, 11 April 1886.

102. Diary, 17 and 20 April 1886.
103. Diary, 20 April 1886.
104. J.A. Froude, *Oceana*, CUP, 1886.
105. Diary, 21 April 1886.
106. Diary, 24 April 1886.
107. Diary, 27 April 1896.
108. Jenkin, *William and Lawrence Bragg*, p. 85.
109. Diary, 15 and 18 May 1886.
110. *Advertiser*, 23 December 1886, p. 6.
111. Symes papers, F34.
112. Lorna Todd, Family History, transcript, April 1955, p. 8.
113. Todd to Preece, 26 January 1887. SASA, GRG 31/1/3.
114. Todd to Oppenheimer, 1 February 1887. SASA, GRG 31/1/3.
115. Lorna Todd, family history, p. 9. Symes Papers, RGSSA.
116. Alice to Maude, fragment 1891. PRG 630/2/19.
117. *Register*, 3 May 1897, p. 4.

Chapter 10

1. *Town and Country Journal*, 29 August 1885, p. 41.
2. K.T. Livingston, *The Wired Nation Continent*, 1996, pp. 122–3.
3. Charles Todd, 'Telegraphic enterprise in Australasia,' pp. 178–9.
4. Adelaide to Port Darwin telegraph line, Paper no 13, Post and Telegraph conference, Sydney, 1888 in *Reports of Postal and Telegraph conferences, 1883–1896*, NLA.
5. Todd, 'Telegraphic enterprise in Australasia,' pp. 166–7.
6. The Australasian cable question, paper no. 5, Post and Telegraph conference, Sydney, 1888.
7. Ibid.
8. *West Australian*, 12 February 1898, p. 4.
9. *Chronicle*, 16 September 1897, p. 21.
10. James Anderson to Thomas Mallard Reade, 25 April 1883. Thomas Mallard Reade, Correspondence. Latrobe Collection M832, State Library of Victoria.
11. *Argus,* 10 July 1888 p. 8.
12. Ibid.
13. *Argus*, 29 October 1888, p. 9.
14. F.P. O'Grady, 'The overland telegraph line technology of the 1870s,' in *Papers presented to a symposium for the Centenary of the Adelaide–Darwin overland telegraph line*, Sydney Australian Post Office, August 1972, pp. 19–30.
15. Engineers Australia. Western Australian division, *Broome to Java submarine telegraph cable*, 2006, p. 3.
16. Quoted in Post and Telegraph conference, Adelaide, 1890, p. 64.

17. Kevin T Livingston, 'Charles Todd: powerful communication technocrat in colonial and federating Australia,' *Australian Journal of Communication*, vol. 24, no. 3, 1997, p. 2.
18. *South Australian Register*, 17 January 1894, p. 4.
19. Livingston, *The Wired Nation Continent*, p. 130.
20. *Register*, 7 December 1891, p. 6.
21. *Argus*, 5 June 1893, p. 6.
22. *Register*, 11 July 1893, p. 6.
23. Richard Refhauge, 'Kintore, ninth earl of (1852–1930),' *ADB*, vol. 5, MUP, 1974, accessed online 29 May 2014.
24. Jenkin, *William and Lawrence Bragg*, 2008, pp. 122–32.
25. Lorna Todd, 'Fancy dress ball a thrill for Adelaide children,' *Chronicle*, 5 December 1953, p. 12.
26. *Register*, 11 August 1893, p. 6
27. Lorna Todd, 'How Sir Charles Todd was made a knight,' *Chronicle*, 12 November 1953, p. 14.
28. John Playford, 'Kingston, Charles Cameron' (1850–1908), *ADB*, vol. 9, MUP, 1983, accessed online 15 May 2014.
29. Public Salaries Bill, *SAPD*, 17 August 1893.
30. Playford, 'Kingston, Charles Cameron' (1850–1908).
31. Ibid.
32. 'Humours of an astronomer,' *Tit Bits*, 26 March 1910, p. 32.
33. Public Salaries Bill, *SAPD*, p. 1495.
34. Ibid., p. 2147.
35. *Advertiser*, 9 October 1893, p. 6.
36. Charles Todd, Report on departments, *SAPP*, no. 128, 1896, vol. 3, pp. 84–5.
37. *Advertiser*, 11 August 1893. p. 4, editorial.
38. *Advertiser*, 22 September 1894, p. 6
39. Simon Potter, *News and the British World. The emergence of an imperial press system*, Oxford, Oxford University Press, 2000, pp. 56, 58.
40. *Register*, 3 November 1893, p. 6
41. Todd to Pender, 4 October 1894. SASA, GRG 31/1/4.
42. Michael Bassett, 'Joseph Ward' entry, *Dictionary of New Zealand Biography*, 1993, vol. 2, accessed online 29 May 2014.
43. Post and Telegraph conference, 1891. Hour zone time, pp. 25–7.
44. Post and Telegraph conference, 1893. Pacific cable, p. 23.
45. *Brisbane Courier*, 13 March 1893, p. 5
46. *Register*, 8 March 1894, p. 4 editorial.
47. *Register*, 17 January 1894, p. 4.
48. Todd to Ward, 15 November 1901. SASA, GRG 31/1/5.

49. *Sydney Morning Herald*, 16 January 1893, p. 5.
50. Livingston, *The Wired Nation Continent*, p. 145.
51. Post and Telegraph conference, 1893, p. 23.
52. Todd, Report on departments, 1896, p. 6.
53. Todd to Sholl, 30 July 1895. SASA, GRG 31/1.
54. *Hobart Mercury*, 19 April 1895, p. 4.
55. John Forrest, *Exploration in Australia*, London, Sampson Low, 1875, pp. 256–9.
56. Knuckey to the *Coolgardie Courier*, February 1895. Quoted in *Western Mail*, 2 February 1895, p. 15.
57. *Perth Daily News*, 4 April 1895, p. 2.
58. *West Australian*, 23 February 1894, p. 4; *Inquirer and Commercial News*, 23 March 1894, p. 18.
59. *Western Mail*, 17 January 1896, pp. 6, 7.
60. *Sydney Morning Herald*, 17 January 1896, p. 5.
61. *West Australian*, 2 January 1895 p. 5: *Register*, 21 January 1895, p. 5.
62. *Argus,* 23 January 1895, p. 5.
63. *Register,* 25 January 1895, p. 5.
64. Post and Telegraph conference,1896, p. 11.
65. Todd, Report on departments, 1896, p. 8.
66. Post and Telegraph conference,1896, p. 8.
67. George Johnson, *The All Red Line. The annals and aims of the Pacific cable project*, Ottawa, James Hope and Sons,1903, p. 224.
68. Johnson, *The All Red Line*, pp. 225, 226.
69. *Advertiser*,12 January 1897, p. 4.
70. Hugh Barty-King, *Girdle round the Earth. The story of Cable and Wireless and its predecessors*, London Heinemann, 1979, p. 1.
71. Dwayne Winseck and Douglas Pike, *Communication and Empire*, Durham and London, Duke University Press, 2007, pp. 179–80.
72. Todd to Cockburn, 8 June 1899. SASA, GRG 31/1/4.
73. *Register*, 3 March 1898 p. 4 editorial.
74. *Hobart Mercury*, 5 April 1898, p. 3.
75. *Register*, 3 March 1898, p. 4.
76. Livingston, *The Wired Nation Continent*, p. 171.
77. Todd to Cockburn, 8 June 1899. SASA, GRG 31/1/4.
78. Todd to Hesse, 16 November 1899. SASA, GRG 31/1/4.
79. Todd to Heaton 21 November 1899. SASA, GRG 31/1/4.
80. *Brisbane Courier*, 22 November 1900, p. 6.
81. House of Commons,12 August 1901. Quoted in Barty-King, *Girdle round the Earth*, p. 307.
82. *Register*,15 September 1899, p. 4.

Chapter 11

1. *St James Gazette*, 9 December 1891 in Livingston Papers, OTC newspaper collection: Sir Charles Todd; *South Australian Register*, 2 December 1893, p. 6; *Argus*, 12 December 1891, p. 13.
2. Mac Benoy, 'Todd's work in meteorology,' *Proceedings of Sir Charles Todd Symposium*, Adelaide, 17 August 2012.
3. Gilbert E Satterthwaite, The history of the Airy transit circle at the Royal Observatory Greenwich, University of London, Master of Science dissertation, September 1995. Greenwich, NMM.
4. Ian R. Bartsky, 'The adoption of standard time,' *Society for the History of Technology*, 1989, pp. 25–56.
5. Marjorie Ferguson, *Public Communication. The new imperatives: future directions for media research*, London, Sage, 1990, p. 154.
6. Douglas Bateson, Leslie Abell and Roger Kimms, 'Time balls at Greenwich and Adelaide – a direct personal connection,' *Antiquarian Horology*, vol. 35, part 3, September 2014, pp. 567–8.
7. Roger Kinns and Leslie Abell, 'The contribution of Maudslay, Sons and Field to the development of time balls in Australia,' *International Journal for the History of Engineering and Technology*, vol. 79, no 1, January 2009, pp. 59–90.
8. Todd to Airy 6 November 1875 in Airy papers. NLA MS27595.
9. *Register*, 27 November 1875, p. 4.
10. Denis Cryle, 'From outback icon to imperial time lord: 'reinventing' Sir Charles Todd (1910–2010), *Journal of Australian Studies*, vol. 35, no 1, March 2011, pp. 65–82.
11. Graeme Davison, *The Unforgiving Minute. How Australia learned to tell the time*, Melbourne, Oxford University Press, 1993, p. 56; Peter Putnis, 'News, time and imagined community in Colonial Australia,' *Media History*, vol. 16, no. 2, May 2010, pp. 153–70.
12. *Argus*, Standard Time Bill, 17 January 1895, p. 7. Livingston Papers, OTC newspaper collection.
13. J.P. Thomson, 'Universal time measurement,' *Proceedings and Transactions of the Queensland branch of the Royal Geographical Society of Australasia*, 1891–92, vol. 7, pt. 1, pp. 30–50. Livingston Papers.
14. 'Royal Observatory Greenwich,' Greenwich, NMM, 2012, p. 52.
15. Ian R. Bartsky, *One Time Fits All: the campaign for global uniformity*, Stanford, Stanford University Press, 2007.
16. Postal and Telegraph conference, 1891 pp. 21–3, in *Reports of Postal and Telegraph Conferences, 1883–1896*, Melbourne, Government Printer, 1897.
17. Ibid., p. 12.
18. *Register*, 7 November 1892. Sir Charles Todd newspaper clippings, Overseas Telecommunications Commission.
19. George Symes, Todd entry, *Dictionary of National Biography*, vol. 6, Melbourne, MUP.

20. *Register* clipping, 7 November 1892.
21. *Age* clipping, 5 November 1892. Todd file, OTC.
22. J.P. Thomson, 'Universal time measurement', p. 39.
23. Davison, *The Unforgiving Minute*, p. 72.
24. Postal and Telegraph conference, 1893, p. 26.
25. *West Australian*, 28 August 1893, p. 4.
26. Postal and Telegraph conference, 1893, p. 26.
27. Hour Zone Time, *Queensland Votes and Proceedings*, 1893, vol. 1, p. 26.
28. Resolution Two of the Washington conference. William Christie, Papers on Universal Time, CUA RGO 7/146.
29. Resolutions Four to Six. Christie Papers.
30. Bartsky, 'The adoption of standard time,' pp. 49–54. Christie Papers.
31. H.C. Russell to William Christie, 1 February 1895. Christie Papers.
32. *Advertiser*, 25 November 1893, p. 5.
33. *West Australian*, 28 August 1893, editorial p. 4.
34. Clark Blaise, *Time Lord. Sir Sandford Fleming and the creation of standard time*, London, Phoenix, 2001.
35. K.T. Livingston, *The Wired Nation Continent*. 1996, pp. 141–2.
36. Sandford Fleming to Christie, 30 December 1893. Christie Papers.
37. *Advertiser*, 20 January 1894, editorial p. 4.
38. Quoted in *Advertiser*, 20 January 1894, p. 4.
39. Grimwade MP. Quoted in the *Argus*, 17 January 1895, p. 7.
40. Sir Thomas McIlwraith to the Premiers of the Australian colonies, 19 August 1893 in *QV&P*, 1894, vol. 1, Appendix 1, p. xliii.
41. Davison, *The Unforgiving Minute*, p. 73.
42. McIlwraith to the Premiers of the Australian colonies, 19 August 1893 in *QV&P*, 1894, vol. 1, p. xliv.
43. Referendum by Sir Charles Todd PMG relative to the hour zone system, 10 November 1893 in *QV&P*, 1894, vol. 1, Appendix 2, p. xlv.
44. Postal and Telegraph conference, 1894, p. 26.
45. Davison, *The Unforgiving Minute*, p. 71.
46. *Advertiser*, 31 January 1895 editorial, p. 4.
47. H.C. Russell to William Christie, 1 February 1895. Christie Papers.
48. *Sydney Telegraph* clipping, 31 January 1895. Christie Papers.
49. Todd to Christie 7 August 1895. Christie Papers.
50. Hon G.M. McGregor, *SAPD*, 1898–99, p. 84.
51. D.J. Wharton to Christie 24 December 1896; London *The Times* clipping, 9 January 1897. Christie Papers.
52. Chief Secretary, 3 August 1898, *SAPD* 1898–99, p. 80.
53. *SAPD*, 1898–99, p. 80.

54. Ibid., p. 85.
55. Ibid., p. 97.
56. A.R. Addison, *Advertiser* parliamentary report, August 1898. Cited in Brian Waters, *A reference history of the Astronomical Society of South Australia*, vol. 1 (1891–1901), p. 86. Livingston Papers.
57. Death certificate of Alice Todd, 9 August 1898. Adelaide, Births, Deaths and Marriages registration office.
58. Alice to Maude, December 1897 in Todd family correspondence. SLSA PRG 630.
59. Lorna Todd, 'Telegraph Todd's Alice,' no. 5, *Chronicle*, November 1953.
60. *Register*, 22 December 1896, Hospital enquiry submission p. 9.
61. Lorna Todd, 'Telegraph Todd's Alice'.
62. Maude Masters, Memoirs, GSP.
63. Lorna Todd, 'Telegraph Todd's Alice'.
64. *Chronicle*, 8 May 1897, p. 5.
65. *Register*, 10 August 1898, p. 4.
66. Alice Thomson, *The Singing Line*, 1999, pp. 196–7.
67. Jenkin, *William and Lawrence Bragg*, 2008, p. 165.
68. Adelaide *Observer*, 13 August 1898, p. 29.
69. *Register*, 10 August 1898, p. 4.
70. *Register*, 25 August 1898. Cited in D. Waters, *A reference history of the Astronomical Society of South Australia*, vol. 1, 1980, p. 88.
71. Waters, 1980, p. 93.
72. *Advertiser*, 15 November 1897, p. 4.
73. Waters, Minutes of 25 August 1898, p. 89.
74. *Advertiser*, 2 September 1898, editorial, p. 4.
75. *SAPD*, 1898–99, p. 164.
76. Waters, Discussion. The Standard Time Bill, p. 93.
77. *Advertiser*, 1 November 1898, p. 4.
78. *Advertiser*, 1 November 1898, clipping. Christie Papers.
79. *Advertiser*, 2 September 1898. Christie Papers.
80. *Advertiser*, 1 November 1898, p. 4.

Chapter 12

1. Gennaro Vecchio, 'The Adelaide Observatory and 140 years of weather observations at West Terrace,' Australian government Bureau of Meteorology, South Australian regional office, 13 November 2004 at http://www.bom.gov.au/accessed 19 March 2009.
2. Peter Adamson, *Clement Lindsay Wragge (1852–1922) FRGS, FRMS, meteorologist, astronomer, ethnologist and collector*, Walkerville, South Australia, The Author, 2002, p. 20.

3. Clement Wragge, *Experiences of a meteorologist in South Australia*, Warradale, Pioneer Books, 1980, p. 21.
4. *South Australian Advertiser*, 15 May 1886, p. 7.
5. Day, *The Weather Watchers. 100 years of the Bureau of Meteorology*, 2007, p. 19.
6. Charles Todd, Report on departments, 1896, p. 207.
7. *South Australian Register*, 25 September 1888, pp. 4–5.
8. Clement Wragge, Letter to the *Launceston Examiner*, 17 April 1897, p. 7.
9. *Sydney Morning Herald*, 24 October 1888, p. 7.
10. Clement Wragge, Queensland post and telegraph department. *Meteorological branch report*, Brisbane James Beal printer, 1888, p. 7.
11. Letter to the *Launceston Examiner*, 17 April 1897, p. 7.
12. Katharine Anderson, *Predicting the Weather. Victorians and the science of meteorology*, Chicago, Chicago University Press, 2005, p. 130.
13. Ibid., p. 40.
14. *Register*, 8 January 1887, p. 4.
15. *Argus*, 28 December 1888, p. 4.
16. Todd to Robert Ellery, 17 July 1889. SASA, GRG 31/1/3.
17. Todd to Henry Russell, 17 July 1889. SASA, GRG 31/1/3.
18. *Register*, 25 September 1888, pp. 4, 5.
19. Wragge, Letter to A Le Rey Boucaut, 13 February 1891, in Livingston Papers, newspaper clippings: meteorology, *Advertiser*, 25 February 1891. Adelaide, NAA.
20. Letter to the *Advertiser*, January 1891. Newspaper clipping, NAA.
21. 'Weather Forecasts and Mr Wragge,' 1891. Newspaper clipping, NAA.
22. 'Mr Wragge and Weather Forecasts,' *Advertiser*, 25 February 1891. NAA.
23. Jenkin, *William and Lawrence Bragg*, 2008, p. 122.
24. Ibid., pp. 79–80.
25. W.H. Bragg to Gwendoline Todd, 28–30 August 1888. Quoted in John Jenkin, *The Bragg family in Adelaide: a pictorial celebration*, Adelaide University of Adelaide foundation in conjunction with the Latrobe University, 1986, p. 69.
26. R.W. Home 'Australian science and its public,' in F.B. Smith and S.L. Goldberg (eds.), *Shaping spirits*. Australian Cultural History no 7, 1988, p. 96.
27. Roy McLeod, *Archibald Liversidge FRS: Imperial science under the Southern Cross*, Sydney, Royal Society of New South Wales in Sydney University Press, 2009, pp. 256–8.
28. Charles Todd, *Meteorological Work in Australia. A review, 1826–1910*, Adelaide, 1894.
29. Clement Wragge, Reply to Charles Todd, 1893. Newspaper clippings, NAA.
30. Charles Todd, *Meteorological Work in Australia*, p. 22.
31. Todd, *Meteorological Work in Australia*, pp. 2–3.
32. Ibid., pp. 6, 24.

33. Todd to Governor James Fergusson, July 1874. SLSA, Private Letterbook 1873–77, PRG 630/14.
34. *Register*, 1 February 1894, p. 6.
35. Ibid.
36. *Register*, 16 February 1894, p. 7.
37. Letter to the *Register*, 1 February 1894. Newspaper clipping, NAA.
38. *Register*, 2 June 1894, p. 4.
39. *Register*, 17 July 1894, p. 7.
40. Todd, personal letter to Sir Henry Ayers, 10 September 1877. SASA, GRG 154/26/2.
41. South Australia. Legislative Council, Meteorological forecasts, 5 September 1894. AP236/6 no 2, Cuttings Book, Adelaide, NAA.
42. Legislative Council, 24 October 1894 in *Advertiser,* 25 October, p. 6.
43. *Register*, 2 June 1894, p. 4.
44. Day, *The Weather Watchers*, p. 31.
45. Ibid., pp. 21–2.
46. Todd to Sir John Forrest, undated 1895. SASA, GRG 31/1/4.
47. John Forrest, *Exploration in Australia*, London, Sampson, Low, Marston, Low and Searle, 1875, pp. 258–9.
48. *West Australian*, 8 January 1895, p. 4.
49. Day, *The Weather Watchers*, p. 31.
50. D. Hutchinson, 'William Ernest Cooke, astronomer 1863–1947,' *Historical Records of Australian Science*, vol. 5 no. 2, 1980, p. 63.
51. Day, *The Weather Watchers*, p. 22.
52. Hutchinson, 'William Ernest Cooke,' p. 63.
53. *Advertiser*, 29 December 1897, p. 4.
54. *Daily News*, 29 December 1897, p. 4.
55. *Register*, 1 January 1898, p. 4.
56. Lorna Todd, 'Humanity a big element in Todd's make up,' *Chronicle*, 1 January 1953, p. 9.
57. *Register*, 20 April 1895, p. 4.
58. *Register*, 9 October 1893, p. 7.
59. *Register*, 2 September 1896, p. 5.
60. Ibid.
61. Todd to Stephen Lambton, 2 December 1897. SASA, GRG 31/1/4.
62. Todd to Lambton, 2 December 1897.
63. *Register*, 9 March 1898, p. 4.
64. *Register*, 28 September 1899, p. 4.
65. 'Weather prophecies,' *Argus*, 5 June 1897. NAA.
66. *Advertiser*, 3 April 1895, p. 6.

67. *Chronicle*, 1 October 1898, p. 10.
68. *Port Pirie Recorder*, 30 December 1899, p. 3.
69. *Brisbane Courier*, 17 March 1898. Newspaper clipping, NAA.
70. Day, *The Weather Watchers*, p. 28.
71. Ibid., p. 23.
72. Raymond Haynes et al, *Explorers of the southern sky. A history of Australian astronomy*, Melbourne, CUP, 1996, p. 64.
73. *Chronicle*, 26 April 1902, p. 33.
74. *Register*, 29 January 1902, p. 4.
75. *Register*, 30 October 1902, p. 5.
76. *Advertiser,* 9 March 1901, p. 10.
77. Ibid.
78. *Register*, 18 January 1901, p. 4.
79. *Advertiser*, 28 October 1902, p. 5.
80. *Chronicle*,18 March 1899, p. 23.
81. Rod Home and Kevin Livingston, 'Science and technology in the story of federation,' 1994, p. 121.
82. Todd to Baracchi, 12 June 1902. SASA, GRG 31/1/5.
83. Todd to Cooke, 2 October 1902. SASA, GRG 31/1/5.
84. *Register*, 29 October 1896, p. 7.
85. Home and Livingston, 'Science and technology in the story of federation,' p. 121.
86. Ibid.
87. Todd to William Gray, 12 November 1902. SASA, GRG 31/1/5.
88. Todd to Baracchi, 23 December 1903. SASA, GRG 31/1/5.
89. Report of interstate astronomical and meteorological conference, May 1905, *SAPP*, 1905, vol. 2 no. 25, p. 5.
90. Todd to Hallam Tennyson, 14 June 1905. SASA, GRG 31/1/5.
91. Report of interstate astronomical and meteorological conference, pp. 8–9.
92. Ibid., p. 8.
93. *Commonwealth Parliamentary Debates*. Meteorological Bill, 12 July–9 August 1906, vol. 32, pp. 2136ff.
94. Day, *The Weather Watchers*, p. 53.
95. *Debates*,1906, vol. 32, p. 2174.
96. Ibid., p. 2159.
97. Ibid., p. 2177.
98. *Advertiser*, 3 January 1908, p. 6.

Chapter 13

1. Charles Todd, Report on departments, *SAPP*, no. 128, vol. 3, 1896.

2. Public Salaries Bill, *SAPD*, August–October 1893, pp. 987ff.
3. Public Salaries Bill, *SAPD*, December 1898, p. 447.
4. *Advertiser*, 24 June 1902, p. 6.
5. *Chronicle*, 1 December 1906, p. 41.
6. Todd, Report on departments, 1896, pp. 84–5.
7. Ibid., p. 84.
8. *Advertiser*, 20 August 1896, p. 4; *Advertiser*, 24 September 1896, p. 5.
9. Ian Radbone and Jane Robbins, 'The History of the South Australian Public Service' in Jaensch *The Flinders History*, 1986, p. 456.
10. *Advertiser*, 30 May 1908, p. 14.
11. Todd to Mrs Sampson, 5 January 1890. SASA, GRG 31/1/4.
12. *Advertiser*, 22 February 1893, p. 7.
13. *Advertiser*, 30 April 1892, p. 7.
14. *Register*, 25 April 1900, p. 6.
15. *Advertiser*, 7 April p. 6 and 1 May 1909, p. 9.
16. Charles Todd, Report on departments, 1884, p. 68.
17. Post and Telegraph conference, Hobart, 1893, p. 5.
18. Livingston, *The Wired Nation Continent*, 1996, p. 122.
19. *Register*, 3 May 1890, p. 6.
20. Todd, Report, 1896, p. 4.
21. Todd to Playford n.d. 1900. SASA, GRG 31/1/4.
22. Todd to Heaton, 23 March 1899. SASA, GRG 31/1/4.
23. Ibid.
24. Todd to Heaton, 21 November 1899.
25. Frank Gillen to Baldwin Spencer, 13 May 1898, in John Mulvaney, Howard Morphy and Alison Petch, *My Dear Spencer. The letters of F.J. Gillen to Baldwin Spencer*, Melbourne Highland House, 1997, p. 38.
26. Todd, Report, 1896, p. 77.
27. Ibid., p. 74.
28. Edward Cecil Baker, *Sir William Preece FRS*, London, Hutchinson, 1976, p. 256.
29. Todd, Report, 1896, pp. 83–85.
30. Baker, *Sir William Preece FRS*, p. 198.
31. Todd to Preece, 2 November 1898. Bragg Papers, MSS0144, series 5, F00409, SASA GRG 31/1/4.
32. *Register*, 19 August 1892, p. 4.
33. *Register*, 29 December 1896, p. 2.
34. *Register*, 6 May 1893, p. 2.
35. Jenkin, *William and Lawrence Bragg*, 2008, p. 130.
36. Ibid., p. 131.
37. Todd to William Preece 10 August 1899. Bragg Papers, series 5, F00409,

SASA, GRG 31/1/4.
38. Todd to Preece, 15 March 1900. Bragg Papers, SASA, GRG 31/1/4.
39. Ibid.
40. Todd to Sir Fowell Buxton, 15 March 1899. Bragg Papers, SASA, GRG 31/1/4.
41. Todd to William Henry Bragg, 10 November 1898. Bragg Papers, SASA, GRG 31/1/4.
42. Todd to Preece, 15 March 1900.
43. Todd to Charles E. Todd, 14 December 1899. SASA, GRG 31/1/4.
44. Ibid.
45. Jenkin, *William and Lawrence Bragg*, p. 227; Errol Morgan, Todd family tree, pp. 21, 33 (GSP).
46. Todd to Preece, 2 November 1898.
47. Todd to the Minister of Education and Agriculture, 27 August 1897, Federal Post Office correspondence, Adelaide, NAA. AP236/6, vol. 1, 1896–1903, pp. 70–1.
48. Todd to Preece, 2 November 1898.
49. Baker, *Sir William Preece FRS*, p. 275.
50. *Register*, 12 August 1899, p. 4; Todd to Cockburn 13 July 1899. Bragg Papers, SASA, GRG 31/1/4.
51. Todd to Stevens, 30 June 1899. Bragg Papers, SASA, GRG 31/1/4.
52. *Register*, 28 September 1899, p. 4.
53. Jenkin, *William and Lawrence Bragg*, pp. 260ff.
54. Todd to Cockburn, 13 July 1899.
55. Todd to Stevens, 30 June 1899.
56. *Sydney Morning Herald*, 24 July 1899, p. 3.
57. Hugh Barty-King, *Girdle round the Earth. The story of cable and wireless and its predecessors*, London, Heinemann,1979, pp. 130–1.
58. Todd to Playford, n.d. 1900.
59. *Southern Argus*, 12 July 1906, p. 3.
60. Todd to R.H. Arnot, 2 February 1902. SASA, GRG 31/1/5.
61. Livingston, *The Wired Nation Continent*, pp. 161–6.
62. Royal Commission on postal services. *Commonwealth Parliamentary Papers*, 1910, vol. 4, pp. 34–40.
63. Livingston, *The Wired Nation Continent*, p. 163.
64. Todd to Sir Fowell Buxton, 15 March 1899.
65. Frank Gillen to Baldwin Spencer, 2 February 1895.
66. Roma D Hodgkinson, 'Hallam Tennyson,' *ADB* entry, vol. 12, 1990.
67. *Advertiser*, 21 April 1900, p. 6.
68. *Advertiser*, 17 February 1900, p. 10.

69. *Chronicle*, 8 March 1900, p. 7.
70. *Chronicle*, 24 February 1900, p. 12.
71. *Register*, 5 February 1900, p. 4.
72. *Advertiser*, 3 March 1900, p. 6.
73. *Register*, 7 July 1900, p. 5.
74. Minutes of Public Service Commission, *SAPP*, vol. 2, p. xxxvii.
75. Public Service Commission, p. xliv.
76. Ibid.
77. Ibid.
78. *Register*, 1 March 1901. Cited in Livingston, p. 183.
79. Todd to Lambton, 8 May 1900. SASA, GRG 31/1/4.
80. Todd to Lambton, 31 May 1900.
81. Livingston, *The Wired Nation Continent*, p. 185.
82. Report of the Post and Telegraph conference, Sydney, Nov.–Dec. 1900, *SAPP* 1901, no. 25, vol. 2, p. 18.
83. Post and Telegraph conference, Sydney, Report of the Permanent Heads, p. 4.
84. Report of the Permanent Heads, pp. 17–18.
85. Livingston, *The Wired Nation Continent*, p. 131.
86. Post and Telegraph conference, Sydney, 'After dinner speeches' typescript.
87. Report of the Permanent Heads, p. 5.
88. Todd to Heaton, 2 January 1901. SASA, GRG 31/1/4.
89. Todd to Lambton, 31 May 1900.
90. Post and Telegraph conference, Sydney, 'After dinner speeches'.
91. Livingston, 1996, p. 181.
92. Conference meetings of Heads 1900 and 1901, Post Office Register, Special Subjects, vol. 1, 1896–1903, p. 381. NAA, AP236/6.
93. H.B. Gibbney, 'James G Drake' entry, *ADB*, vol. 8, 1891–1939, p. 338.
94. *Advertiser* clipping, March 1901, Post Office Register, Special Subjects, p. 383.
95. Todd to T.E. Wickstoed, 13 March 1901. SASA, GRG 31/1/4.
96. Livingston, *The Wired Nation Continent*, p. 184.
97. Federal Postmaster General to Deputy Postmasters General, 1 March 1901. Post Office Register, Special Subjects, vol. 1, p. 381.
98. Federal Postmaster General to Deputy Postmasters General, 20 August 1898. Post Office Register, Special Subjects, vol. 1, p. 262.
99. Royal Commission on postal services, p. 17.
100. Ibid., pp. 10,11,13.
101. Ibid., pp. 14–15.
102. Federal Postmaster General to Todd, Telegraph Rates, 18 November 1901; Todd to the Postmaster General, November 1901. Post Office Register, Special Subjects, vol. 3, 1903–1913, pp. 21–2.

103. Deputy Postmasters General to Federal Postmaster General, 21 February 1904. Post Office Register, Special Subjects, vol. 3, 1903–4, p. 72.
104. Home and Livingston, 'Science and technology in the story of federation,' 1994, p. 121.
105. Todd to William Gray, GPO Wellington 12 December 1902. SASA, GRG 31/1/5.
106. Lorna Todd, 'Humanity big element in Todd's make up,' *Chronicle*, 1 January 1953, p. 9.
107. *Report of the Northern Territory Commission*, Adelaide, Government Printer, 1896, p. xxxiv.
108. Charles Todd, Evidence of 19 March 1895 to the Northern Territory Commission, *SAPP*, no. 19, 1895, vol. 2, pp. 88–9.
109. Premiers Conference, Melbourne, 7–10 March 1898, Post Office Register, Special Subjects, vol. 1, 1896–1903, p. 92. NAA, AP236/6.
110. *Advertiser*, 21 April 1900, p. 6; Barty-King, *Girdle around the Earth*, pp. 142–3.
111. Half yearly meeting, Eastern Telegraph Company, *Sydney Morning Herald*, 24 September 1899, p. 3
112. *Register*, 15 September 1899, p. 4.
113. Todd to Playford, 23 November 1897. Bragg Papers, SASA, GRG 31/1/4.
114. Report by the Postmaster General on the cable question, 3 August 1899, *SAPP*, 1899, no. 65.
115. Report by the Postmaster General on the cable question, pp. 2, 5.
116. Todd to H.W. McPherson (EETC), 20 November 1899 Post Office Register, Special Subjects, vol. 1, 1896–1903, Enclosure for Premiers' Conference, Melbourne, 7–10 March 1898, pp. 92ff. AA, AP236/6.
117. Federal Post Office, Outward Register vol. 24, 4 December 1901 and 21 October 1902. NAA, AP236/1.
118. William Sowden, *The Northern Territory as it is. The narrative of the South Australian parliamentary party trip*, Adelaide, Thomas,1892, p. 13.
119. Federal Post Office, Outward Register vol. 25, 21 October 1902. NAA, AP236/1.
120. Baldwin Spencer to FT Gillen, 28 April 1904, *My Dear Spencer,* pp. 479–80.
121. Gillen to Spencer, 23 December 1898, pp. 247–8, 16; 21 September 1900, p. 290.
122. Gillen to Spencer, 30 July 1902, p. 383 and 18 June 1904, p. 459.
123. Gillen to Spencer, October 1903, p. 474, fn. 66.
124. Gillen to Spencer, 31 May 1903, p. 453.
125. Acting DPMG to Sec PMG, 28 February and 21 March 1905, Post Office Register. Special subjects, vol. 3, 1901–1913, p. 143. NAA, AP236/6.
126. *Commonwealth Government Gazette*. Post Office Retirement Act, 1903–4. G.W. Symes, 'Sir Charles Todd' full entry, *ADB* files, ANU.
127. Todd to Hallam Tennyson, 14 June 1905. SASA, GRG 31/1/5.

128. *Register*, 7 July 1906, p. 7.
129. *Critic*, 18 January 1905. OTL news cuttings book SLSA, p. 161.
130. *Advertiser*, 30 January. OTL news cuttings book SLSA, p. 161.
131. *Advertiser*, 18 August 1908, p. 9.
132. Todd to Hallam Tennyson, 14 June 1905.

Chapter 14

1. G.F. Dodwell, 'Government Astronomer 1856–1906. An appreciation,' William Henry Christie Papers, Personal Obituaries. Death of Sir Charles Todd, newspaper clipping, *Chronicle*, 12 February 1910. NLA microfilm 627615.
2. Wayne Orchiston, 'Tebbutt vs Russell: passion, power and politics in nineteenth-century Australian astronomy' *Proceedings of the International Astronomical Union conference*, Kyoto. August 1997, p. 174
3. Brian Waters, *A reference history of the Astronomical Society of South Australia*, vol. 1, 1891–1901, Adelaide, The Author, 1980, pp. 6–7
4. Wayne Orchiston, 'Amateur – professional collaboration in Australian science: the earliest astronomical groups and societies,' *Historical Records of Australian Science* vol. 12 no. 2, December 1998, p. 166.
5. *South Australian Register*, 8 July 1889, p. 5.
6. *Register*, 13 March 1893, p. 7.
7. *Register*, 11 November 1899, p. 6.
8. Todd, 'The 'lives and labours' of two notable British astronomers,' in Waters, *A reference history of the Astronomical Society*, vol. 1, 14 June 1892, pp. 12–13.
9. Waters, vol. 1, 14 June 1892, p. 13.
10. Ibid.
11. Waters, vol. 1, December 1891, p. 6.
12. Jenkin, *William and Lawrence Bragg*, p. 226.
13. Ibid., p. 138.
14. Obituary, *Chronicle*, 1 August 1896, p. 9.
15. Edward Sells to the Society, 28 June 1893 in Waters, vol. 1, pp. 68–9.
16. Waters, vol. 1, pp. 68–9.
17. Wayne Orchiston,'The role of the amateur in popularizing astronomy: an Australian case study,' in *Journal of Astronomy*, vol. 7, July 1997, p. 40.
18. Waters, First annual report, in vol. 1, 12 September 1893, p. 24.
19. Charles Todd, Report on departments, 1896, p. 114.
20. Lorna Todd, 'Telegraph Todd and the overland line', no. 5, *Chronicle*, 1 January 1953.
21. Todd to Russell, 29 March 1899. SASA, GRG 31/1/4, p. 345.
22. Cooke biographical entry, in Waters, vol. 1, p. 34.
23. Waters, vol. 1, 28 March 1899, p. 102.
24. Lorna Todd, Family History, Typescript, April 1955, p. 4. Symes papers, folder

35, RGSSA.
25. Ibid., p. 14.
26. Waters, vol. 1, 12 November 1895, p. 58.
27. *Register*, 13 November 1895, p. 7.
28. Brian Waters, *A reference history of the Astronomical Society of South Australia*, 15 August 1905, vol. 2, 1902–1911, Adelaide, The Author, 1981, p. 197.
29. Waters, vol. 1, 14 November 1893, p. 39.
30. Waters, vol. 1, 22–23 November 1895. p. 59.
31. Waters, vol. 1, 11 August 1896, p. 62.
32. C. Farr to the Secretary for the Astronomical Society, August 1896 in Waters, vol. 1, p. 62.
33. Waters, vol. 1, 23 April 1894, p. 72.
34. Reverend Father Bustelli, Address to the Society, 4 September 1963, in Waters, vol. 1, 15 August 1899, pp. 142–4.
35. Edwards, 'Charles Todd and the Adelaide Observatory,' *Astronomical Society of Australia*, 1993, p. 352.
36. Todd to Forrest, undated 1895. SASA, GRG 3/1/4.
37. D. Hutchinson, 'William Ernest Cooke, Astronomer 1863–1947,' *Historical Records of Australian Science*, vol. 5 no 23, 1980, p. 71.
38. *Register*, 2 April 1892.
39. *Register*, 1 April 1892, p. 6.
40. Griffiths in Waters, vol. 1, 15 August 1899, p. 104.
41. Edward Dunkin, *The Midnight Sky*, London, The Religious Tract Society, 1879. p. 299.
42. *Advertiser*, 16 November 1899, p. 4.
43. Todd to Russell, 17 July 1889. SASA, GRG 31/1/3.
44. Todd to Russell, 3 December 1893. SASA, GRG 31/1/4.
45. G.F. Dodwell, explanatory note in Edward Sells & W.E. Cooke, *Physical observations of Jupiter during the years 1884–1893*, Adelaide, Government Printer, 1913.
46. Todd to Dunkin FRS, 23 June 1896. GRG 31/1/4.
47. Waters, vol. 1, Address by William Cooke, 23 April 1901, p. 129.
48. Jenkin, *William and Lawrence Bragg*, 2008, p. 247.
49. *Register*, 4 March 1897, p. 7.
50. *Advertiser*, 14 May 1897, p. 6.
51. *Register*, 12 May 1897, p. 5.
52. Ibid.
53. Todd to Ellery, 2 October 1899. SASA, GRG 31/1/4.
54. Charles Todd, Report on departments,1884, pp. 194–202; Report on departments, 1896, pp. 113–16.
55. Ragbir Bhathal, *Australian astronomer John Tebbutt*, Sydney Kangaroo Press, 1993, p. 29.

56. Ellery to Tebbutt in Bhathal, *Australian astronomer John Tebbutt*, p. 30.
57. Day, *The Weather Watchers*. 2007, p. 23.
58. Haynes, Malin and McGee, *Explorers of the Southern Sky*, 1996, p. 62.
59. G.F. Dodwell, *Observatory report*, Adelaide government printer, 1910, p. 17.
60. Todd to Baracchi, 12 June 1902. SASA, GRG 31/1/5.
61. Todd to Cooke, 12 June 1902.
62. Todd to Baracchi, 24 October 1902.
63. Wayne Orchiston, 'Amateur – professional collaboration in Australian science,' 1998, pp. 167–8.
64. Waters, vol. 2, 11 July 1905, p. 196.
65. Waters, vol. 2, 12 June 1906, p. 207.
66. Waters, vol. 2, 21 May 1907, p. 217.
67. Wayne Orchiston, 'The role of the amateur in popularising astronomy,' p. 40.
68. Waters, vol. 2, 14 July 1903, p. 173.
69. Waters, vol. 2, 17 September and 15 October 1904, p. 180.
70. Waters, vol. 2, 15 September 1903, pp. 174–5.
71. Charles Todd, *The earth's place in the universe. Are there more worlds than one?*, Adelaide, Thomas, 1903, p. 5.
72. Todd, *The earth's place in the universe*, pp. 2, 11.
73. Waters, vol. 2, 15 September 1903, p. 175.
74. Todd, *The earth's place in the universe*, p. 10.
75. Todd to Henry Russell, 3 December 1898. SASA, GRG31/1/4.
76. Robert Jenkins, 'Sir Charles Todd's work in astronomy,' *Sir Charles Todd symposium*, Adelaide August 2012, pp. 5–6.
77. Dodwell, 'Government astronomer 1856–1906. An appreciation,' in William Christie Papers, Press clippings on Charles Todd. NLA, microfilm RG07.
78. Lorna Todd, 'Observatory life was secure,' *Chronicle*, 1 January 1953, p. 9.
79. Lorna Todd, Adelaide Boys High School address transcript, Astronomical Society of South Australia, 1959, p. 7.
80. Ibid., p. 7.
81. Lorna Todd address, p. 10.
82. *Observer*, 10 August 1907, p. 40.
83. Charles E. Todd, Cutting Book 1894–1900, newspaper clippings of 1897–98. SLSA, PRG 164.
84. Jenkin, *William and Lawrence Bragg*, p. 232.
85. W.L. Bragg, Autobiographical Notes. Cited in Jenkin, *William and Lawrence Bragg*, pp. 139–40.
86. Waters vol. 2, 11 August 1908, p. 24.
87. Jenkin, *William and Lawrence Bragg*, pp. 221–2.
88. Maude Masters, Diary, March 1907, pp. 4–5. GSP.

89. Ibid., p. 7.
90. Maude, Diary pp. 7–9. 11.
91. Ibid., p. 6.
92. *Commonwealth Parliamentary Debates*, Meteorological Bill, vol. 32 1906, p. 2138.
93. Jenkin, *William and Lawrence Bragg*, pp. 92–3.
94. Waters, vol. 2, 1907, p. 216.
95. W.H. Bragg to Sir Samuel Way, 29 January 1908 in Bragg Papers. MS 0144, File 00222, University of Adelaide.
96. Jenkin, *William and Lawrence Bragg*, pp. 286–7.
97. *Advertiser*, 29 January 1910, p. 10.
98. Jenkin, *William and Lawrence Bragg*, p. 285.
99. Cooke to the Treasurer, 4 February 1908. Todd Papers, Adrian family collection.
100. Todd to A.J. Peake, 8 February 1908 in Bragg Papers, University of Adelaide, File 00222, G.W. Symes to Mrs Caroe, 3 October 1978.
101. *Advertiser*, 15 April 1908, p. 6; *Chronicle*, 18 April 1908, p. 35.
102. T.R. Lyle to Bragg, 9 February 1908. Todd Papers, Adrian Collection, Cambridge.
103. Todd to the Chancellor, 27 June 1909. Adrian Collection.
104. Jenkin, *William and Lawrence Bragg*, p. 297.
105. Prime Minister Alfred Deakin to the Premier of South Australia, 29 April 1909. Adrian Collection.
106. G.F. Dodwell, *Observatory report*, Adelaide, Government Printer, 1910, p. 17.
107. Waters, vol. 2, 22 June 1909, p. 250; *Advertiser*, 23 June 1909, p. 6.
108. Dodwell, *Observatory report*, 1910, p. 17.
109. Waters, vol. 2, 25–26 September 1909, p. 254.
110. Quoted in *Advertiser*, 27 September 1909, pp. 7–8.
111. Waters, vol. 2, 14 June 1910, p. 261.
112. *Register*, 16 February 1907, p. 7
113. *Advertiser*, 28 January 1908, p. 10.
114. *Advertiser*, 27 September 1909, pp. 7, 8.
115. Dodwell, *Observatory report*, 1910, p. 13.
116. *Register*, 31 January 1910, p. 7.
117. Ibid., p. 7.
118. *Register*, 1 February 1910 p. 8.
119. Ibid., p. 10.
120. Lorna Todd, 'Observatory life was secure,' *Chronicle*, 1 January 1953, p. 9.

Select Bibliography

Archives

Cambridge University Archives
Airy Papers
Papers of William Ellis
Papers of William Christie

National Archives of Australia (Adelaide)
Postmaster General's Department. South Australia: correspondence and special subjects relating to postal services 1887–1913

South Australian State Archives
Miscellaneous Papers of Charles Todd 1852–83
Overland Telegraph line diaries and notebooks
Todd letter books
Observatory letter books

Manuscripts

United Kingdom
Adrian family Papers
David Dewhirst, Biographical files, Institute of Astronomy, Cambridge
Gillam-Smith family Papers

South Australia
Bragg Papers, University of Adelaide
Symes Papers, Charles Todd and the Overland Telegraph Line, RGSSA
Papers of Sir Charles Todd, SLSA

Government Reports and Parliamentary Papers

Cambridge Observatory, *Reports of the Observatory Syndicate*, Cambridge University, 1844–55

Challis, James, *Astronomical Observations made at the University of Cambridge*, vol. VXVI I, 1846–48 and vol. VXVIII, 1849–51

Dodwell, G.F., *Observatory Report*, Adelaide, Government Printer, 1910

Report of Commission into the organisation and working of the Post Office Department, *SAPP*, 1875, no. 20, vol. 2

Reports of Postal and Telegraph conferences, 1883–96, Melbourne, Government Printer (NLA)

Royal Observatory, *Reports of the Astronomer Royal to the Board of Visitors*, Greenwich, 1842–55

Todd, Charles, Report on the Post Office, Telegraph and Observatory departments of South Australia, *SAPP*, 1884, no. 19, vol. 4

Todd, Charles, 'Telegraphic enterprise in Australasia', *Proceedings of the Royal Colonial Institute*, vol. 17, 1885–86, pp. 144–79

Todd, Charles, *Meteorological Work in Australia. A review, 1826–1910*, Adelaide, 1894

Todd, Charles, Report on the Post Office, Telegraph and Observatory departments of South Australia, *SAPP,* 1896, no. 128, vol. 3

Waters, Brian,*A reference history of the Astronomical Society of South Australia*, vol. 1 (1891–1901), 1980 and vol. 2 (1902–1911), 1981

Newspapers and Press Clippings

Online Newspapers

British News Archive 1845–55

Times Digital Archive 1848–55

Trove National Database: South Australian and inter-colonial titles 1855–1910

Print Records

Australian Dictionary of Biography, Sir Charles Todd full entry, ANU

Charles Todd biographical cuttings, NLA

Sir Charles Todd Overland Telegraph newspaper cuttings, SLSA

Todd Obituaries in Gillam-Smith and Christie Papers

Lorna Todd newspaper series on Charles and Alice Todd, 1952, 1953, 1961

Books

Airy, Wilfred, *Autobiography of Sir George Biddell Airy*, Cambridge, CUP, 1896

Baker, Edward Cecil, *Sir William Preece FRS*, London, Hutchinson, 1976

Bartsky, Ian R., *One Time Fits All: the campaign for global uniformity*, Stanford, Stanford University Press, 2007

Chapman, Alan, *The Victorian Amateur Astronomer*, Chichester, Praxis Publishing, 1998

Clune, Frank, *The Overland Telegraph. An epic feat of endurance and courage*, Sydney, Angus Robertson, 1955

Day, David, *The Weather Watchers. One hundred years of the Bureau of Meteorology*, Carlton, MUP, 2007

Dunkin, Edwin, *A far-off vision. A Cornishman at Greenwich Observatory*, Cornwall, Royal Institute of Cornwall, 1999

Harcourt, Edgar, *Taming the Tyrant*, Sydney, Allen and Unwin, 1987

Jenkin, John, *William and Lawrence Bragg, father and son*, Oxford, Oxford University Press, 2008

Livingston, K.T., *The Wired Nation Continent*, Melbourne, CUP, 1996

Moyal, Ann, *Clear Across Australia. A history of telecommunications*, Melbourne, Nelson, 1984

Sheldrick, Jan, *Nature's Line. George Goyder. Surveyor, environmentalist, visionary*, Adelaide, Wakefield Press, 2013

Sir Charles Todd Symposium, Adelaide, Australian Meteorological Association, 17 August 2012

Taylor, Peter, *An End to Silence. The building of the overland telegraph line from Adelaide to Darwin*, Sydney, Methuen, 1980

Thomson, Alice, *The Singing Line*, London, Random House, 1999

Journals and Periodicals

Bateson, Douglas; Abell, Leslie and Kimms, Roger, 'Time balls at Greenwich and Adelaide – a direct personal connection', *Antiquarian Horology*, vol. 35, part 3, September 2014, pp. 964–72.

Benoy, Mac, 'The birth of the familiar everyday map', *The Globe Journal of the Australian and New Zealand Map Inc*, no. 67, 2011, pp. 9–22

Bragg, W.H., 'Sir Charles Todd KCMG, 1826–1910', *Proceedings of the Royal Society of London*, 1911, 4

Chaldecott, John A., 'Platinum and the Greenwich system of time signals in Britain', *Platinum Metals Review*, 1986, vol. 30, No. 1, pp. 29–37

Edwards, P.G., 'Charles Todd and the Adelaide Observatory', *Proceedings of the Astronomical Society of Australia*, vol. 10, no. 4, 1993, pp. 349–54

Home, R.W. and Livingston, K.T., 'Science and technology in the story of Australian federation: the case of meteorology 1876–1908', *Historical Records of Australian Science*, vol. 10, no. 2 December 1994, pp. 109–27

Lamberton, Donald 'The subversive and the manager: organising knowledge in a hard place', The 2000 Charles Todd oration, *Telecommunications Journal of Australia*, vol. 51, no. 1, Autumn 2001, pp. 65–72

Livingston, Kevin, 'Charles Todd. Powerful communication technocrat in colonial and federating Australia', *Australian Journal of Communication*, vol. 24, no. 3, 1997, pp. 1–10

Orchiston, Wayne, 'Amateur – Professional collaboration in Australian science. The earliest astronomical groups and societies', *Historical Records of Australian Science*, vol. 12, no. 2, December 1998, pp. 163–81

Symes, G.W. and Ward, Brian J., 'Charles Todd and the Overland Telegraph', *Proceedings of the Royal Geographical Society of Australasia*, vol. 81, 1980–81, pp. 59–73

Index

Page references in **_bold italic_** relate to illustration.

Aborigines 85, 88, 95–6
Adelaide Chamber of Commerce 106, 198
Adelaide Observatory 68–9, 219, 228, 243–4, 250, 255–7
Adelaide University 163
Airy, George 16, **_17_**, 19–20, 27, 69, 116–7, 122–5, 151, 244; see also Astronomer Royal
Adams, John Couch 27, 35, 157, 244
Afghan cameleers 80, 237, 239–40
Alice Springs 82, 95
Althorpe cable 228
Anderson, James 152, 159
Astronomer Royal 123, 124–5, 194
Astronomical Society of South Australia 201–2, 243–7, 251
astronomy 8, 40, 68; see also Adelaide Observatory, Astronomer Royal, Cambridge Observatory, comets, Royal Observatory, transit of Venus
Australasian Association for the Advancement of Science 210, 249
Ayers, Henry 89, 99

Babbage, Benjamin 64, 78, 127
Baracchi, Pietro 217, **_220_**, 250–1
Barrow Creek station 95
Bell, Alice Gillam 2, 32, 38–9, 50–1; see also Todd, Alice
Bell, Charlotte (née Clark) 33, 93–4, 137
Bell, Charlotte Diana (daughter) 38–9
Bell, Edward (son) 137
Bell family 32–4, 38–9
Benoy, Mac 10
Boer War 231, 238
Bonython, Sir Langdon 221
boundary question 125–6, 129
Bragg, Bob **_165_**
Bragg, Gwendoline (née Todd) **_165_**, 200, 210, 254, 257
Bragg, Lawrence **_165_**, 254
Bragg, William Henry 9, 155, **_165_**, 174–5, 210, 226–7, 228–9, 249, 255, 256–7
Breen, Hugh (senior) 20, 21
Breen, James 21, 28, 34, 39–40, 43–4, 52
British Association for the Advancement of Science 28, 210
British Australian Telegraph

Company 71–2, 82–3; *see also* Eastern Extension Telegraph Company
Buxton, Governor Fowell 227

Cambridge 29–30, 34, 242
Cambridge Observatory 28–32, 35–8, 40–4
Cambridge University 28, 160
Cape Cable 238–9
Carrington, Richard 37
Challis, James 32, 35, 43
Chapman, Robert 255
Chettle, S.W. **220**
Christie, William 151, 193, 195, 197, 198, 203
Civil Service Association 223–4
Clark, Latimer 46–7
Cockburn, Joseph 177, 182–3, 197, 228
comets 22, 40, 68, 244
Commonwealth Bureau of Meteorology 219, 220–1, 250–1
Commonwealth Postmaster General's Department *see* Postmaster General's Department
conferences
  post and telegraph 152, 172–3, 178–9, 185, 191, 192, 193, 195–6, 197, 232
  meteorological 34, 205, 208, 219–20, 221
Cooke, William 130, 204, 213, 214, **220**, 247–9, 253, 256
Cracknell, Edward Charles 51, 54, 60, 62, 152–3, 179
Crick, William 233
Cunningham, W.J. 79, 137

Davies, Dr Charles 138

Davies, Charles Willoughby 93, 135, 138, 142
Davies, Frances 142; *see* Todd, Frances
Deal 48, 49
Dobbie, Alexander 245, 251
Dodwell, G.F. **220**, 250, 251, 252–3, 257
Drake, J.G. 218, 234
drought 142–4, 217–18
Dunkin, Edwin 21, 25, 42–3, 122, 127
Dutton, Francis 74, 99, 102, 116–7

Eastern Extension Telegraph Company 7, 149, 152, 156, 159, 169–70, 172, 177, 183, 186, 229, 238–9
electric telegraph; *see* telegraph
Electric Telegraph Company (UK) 41–2, 45, 46–7
Ellery, Robert 67, 114, 120–1, 194, 208, 217, 249, 250
Ellis, William 46

Farr, Clinton 245
Farr, Reverend George Henry 245
Fergusson, Governor James 92, 93, 98
Fleming, Sir Sandford 177, 191, 194–5
Forrest, Sir John 180–1, 184, 205, 213–4, 234

Giles, Alfred 80
Gillen, Frank 225, 230–1, 240–1
Gisborne, Lionel 63, 65
Glaisher, James 20–1, 26, 28, 31
Government House (SA) 66, 174, 199

Goyder, G.W. 76–7, 86, 116, 192, 227
Greayer, Emma 246
Gregory, A.C. 192–3
Greenwich 15, 16, 22, 23, 158; *see also* Royal Observatory
Greenwich Mean Time 188, 192, 193
Griffiths, Richard Fletcher 201, 204, *220*, 221, 246, 248

Hart, John 73, 74, 83–4
Heaton, Henniker 169, 178–9, 185, 186, 224–5, 233
Henderson, J.C. 49
Hingsmill, H.E. *220*
Holdfast Bay yacht club 209
Hurst, Henry 104, 112

Irene 53, 54–5, 70
Islington 16

Jenkin, John 9, 255
Jupiter, satellites of 123

Khedive 148
Kingston, Charles 175–6
Kintore, Earl of (Governor) 174, 175–6, 230
Knuckey, Richard 90–1, 102, 181, 223
Kraajen, C.W.I. 86

Lake Alexandrina 63
Lamb, Horace 155
Lambton, Stephen 232, 234
Legislative Council (SA) 199, 212
Lenihan, H.A. *220*
Lewis, James 103, 108–9
Little, J.A.G. 84, 87, *90*, 127, 171–2, 240

Livingston, Kevin 7, 152, 173
longitude 41–2, 125

MacDonnell, Governor Richard 57, *58*, 60, 63–4
MacGeorge, James 57, 58
McGowan, Samuel 59, 62, 65
McIlwraith, Sir Thomas 196–7
McMinn, William 82, 83
Mattawarrungala station 93, 135, 140, 142
Masters, Reverend Frederick George 227, 242
meridians; *see* longitude
Mercury 123
Meteorological Society of Australasia 205
meteorology 10, 27–8, 132–3, 142–4, 211, 215; *see also* Commonwealth Bureau of Meteorology
Minister for Education and Culture 173, 177, 182, 209
Mills, William Whitfield 81, 82
Mitchell, A.J. *90*
Moonarie station 139–40, 142
Moyal, Ann 6

Nautical Almanac 25, 198, 201, 202
newspapers 31, 60, 68–9, 89, 100, 102, 106, 134, 137, 143–4, 182, 202–3, 206, 215, 230, 241
Neptune 26–7
Neumayer, Georg 67–8, 134
Nonconformity 15, 18, 22–3, 66–7, 94
Northern Territory 87–92, 130, 237

Omeo 86, 87, 101
Oppenheimer, Joseph 59, 60, 132,

139, 146, 155–6
Osborn, Captain Sherard 72
Overland Telegraph Line 2–4, 70–1, 96–7, 127, 132, 170–2, 182, 185, 237–9; rivalry with Queensland 72–4, 83, 159–60; *see also* telegraph

Pacific Cable 177, 178, 185
Patterson, Robert C. 83–5, 86–7, *90*, 92, 100–1
Peake, A.J. 255, 256
Pender, John 99, 149, 150, 152, 158, 169, 172, 181; *see also* British Australian Telegraph Company, Eastern Extension Telegraph Company
Playford, Thomas 177, 183
Post Office (Adelaide) 102, 109, 149, 154, 189, 190; Commission of Inquiry into 106–7, 108–9, 113
Postmaster General's Department 219, 230, 231–5

Preece, William 46, 150, 160, 184, 225, 226–7, 228, 229
Proctor, Richard 120
Public Service Commission 231

religion; *see* Nonconformity, science
Ringwood, Alexander 117–8, 119, 130
Roan School 17, 18
Roper River 87–92
Royal Observatory 16, 25, 42, 121, 188–9
Royal Society of London 149, 160–1, 174, 255
Russell, Henry Chamberlain 120–1,

134, 197, 208, 210, 217, 219, 250, 256

science and religion 33–4, 39, 45–6, 251–2; *see also* astronomy, meteorology, seismology
Scott, Henry 140–1
seismology 249, 254
Sells, Edward 245, 247
Semaphore 188, 258
Sholl, R.A. 180, 232
South East Railway Company 47
Spooner, A.A. *220*
Squire, Edward 110
Squires, Charles 157, 161–2
Squires, Elizabeth 164, *165*, 227–8; *see also* Todd, (Charlotte) Elizabeth
Squires, William Bell 93
standard time 189, 190–203; legislation 197, 198–203
Stirling, Dr Edward 138–9, 174
Stone, Edward 126, 163, 223
Stow, Reverend Thomas 67
Stow Congregational Church 67, 227
Strangways, Henry Bull Templar 72–3
Stuart, John McDouall 64, 70, 78, 79, 95, 96
Sturt, Charles 51
Symes, George W. 4, 64, 141

telegraph 29, 41, 57, 59–61, 63, 71, 158, 172, 180–1, 206–7, 218–9, 236, 238; *see also* Overland Telegraph Line, Pacific Cable
telescopes 35–7, 40, 116–9, 127–8
Thomson, Alice 5
Threlfall, Richard 163

time 188, 190; *see also* Greenwich Mean Time, standard time
time ball 188; *see also* Deal
time zones 192
Todd, Alice 3, 4, 52, *54*, 66, 70, 89, *90*, 93, 94, 97–8, 147–8, 156, *165*, 199–201, 227–8; *see also* Bell, Alice Gillam
Todd, Charles *90*, *165*, *220*
   civil servant 2, 5, 8, 136, 145–6, 173, 176, 218, 219, 222, 241
   Companion of St Michael and St George 99, *100*
   election to Royal Society 160–1
   knighthood 2, 174
   scientific training 8–10, 19, 26, 27, 30–2, 38, 43, 46
   sheep farming 135, 137, 139, 140, 141–2
   'Telegraph' Todd 1, 53
   wedding to Alice 52–3
Todd, Charles Edward (son) 65, 138–9, 141, 156, *165*, 174, 227
Todd, (Charlotte) Elizabeth (daughter) 56, 148, 153, 157, 161–2, 163; *see also* Squires, Elizabeth
Todd, Elizabeth (sister) 157
Todd, Elsie (*née* Backhouse) *165*
Todd, Frances (Fanny) 70, 93, *136*; *see also* Davies, Frances
Todd, Griffith (father) 15–6, 18
Todd, Griffith George (brother) 24
Todd, Griffith George (nephew) 84, 91
Todd, Gwendoline *see* Bragg, Gwendoline
Todd, Hedley 70, 137–8, *165*, 253
Todd, Henry 21, 24, 48, 150–1, 160, 244

Todd, Jessie *165*, 226, 253
Todd, Lorna 3, 136, 141, 164, *165*, 175, 199–201, 236–7, 253, 254, 258
Todd, Mary (mother) 16
Todd, Mary (sister) 157
Todd, Maude 137, 164, *165*, 227, 246, 254
Todd, Richard 37–8
transit of Venus 115–6, 118–9, 122, 123–4, 126–8
Tupman, Colonel George 126, 127

Valetta 162

Waddy, R.W.M. 223, 240, 241, 242
Walker, Charles Vincent 47–8, 50
Ward, Ebenezer 74, 212
Ward, Joseph 179–80
Way, Sir Samuel 255, 256
weather
   forecasts 209, 211, 214, 216, 220, 236
   maps *131*, *215*
   records 130, 132
   reports 131, 133, 207, 211, 216
   see also drought, meteorology
West Parklands (Adelaide) 69–70
wireless experiments 228
Wragge, Clement 204, 205, *206*, 206–9, 211–13, 216–19, 221, 236

About the Author

Denis Cryle has published widely in the fields of Australian colonial history and biography, as well as on Commonwealth communications, telegraphy and the newspaper press. His books and edited collections include: *Murdoch's Flagship* (2008), *Consent and Consensus* (2005), *Disreputable Profession* (1997) and *The Petrie Family* (1992). He is an Emeritus Professor at Central Queensland University.

www.ingramcontent.com/pod-product-compliance
Lightning Source LLC
Chambersburg PA
CBHW051209300426
44116CB00006B/484